Communication
and Aging

LEA's COMMUNICATION SERIES
Jennings Bryant/Dolf Zillmann, General Editors

Selected titles in the Applied Communication Subseries
(*Teresa L. Thompson, Advisory Editor*) include:

Beck/Ragan/du Pre • *Partnership for Health: Building Relationships Between Women and Health Caregivers*

Braithwaite/Thompson • *Handbook of Communication and People with Disabilities: Research and Application*

Nussbaum/Coupland • *Handbook of Communication and Aging Research*

Ray/Donohew • *Communication and Health: Systems and Applications*

Socha/Diggs • *Communication, Race, and Family: Exploring Communication in Black, White, and Biracial Families*

Williams/Nussbaum • *Intergenerational Communication Across the Lifespan*

For a complete list of other titles in LEA's Communication Series, please contact Lawrence Erlbaum Associates, Publishers.

Communication and Aging

2ⁿᵈ Edition

Jon F. Nussbaum
Pennsylvania State University

Loretta L. Pecchioni
Louisiana State University

James D. Robinson
University of Dayton

Teresa L. Thompson
University of Dayton

 LAWRENCE ERLBAUM ASSOCIATES, PUBLISHERS
2000   Mahwah, New Jersey   London

An instructor's manual for this text is available to all adopt-
ers. To obtain a copy, please contact the publishers at
1-800-926-6579 or www.erlbaum.com

Lawrence Erlbaum Associates, Inc., Publishers
10 Industrial Avenue
Mahwah, NJ 07430

Cover design by Kathryn Houghtaling Lacey

Library of Congress Cataloging-in-Publication Data

Communication and aging / Jon F. Nussbaum ... [et al.].
—2nd ed.
p. cm.
Includes bibliographical references and index.
ISBN 0-8058-3331-5 (alk. Paper)
ISBN 0-8058-3332-3 (pbk. : alk. paper)
1. Aged—Communication—United States. 2. Interpersonal communication. 3. Aging—Psychological aspects. 4. Old age—Social
aspects—United States. I. Nussbaum, Jon F. II. Series.
HQ1064.U5 C5364 2000
305.26—dc21   99-045143
                                                             CIP

Books published by Lawrence Erlbaum Associates are printed on acid-
free paper, and their bindings are chosen for strength and durability.

Printed in the United States of America
10 9 8 7 6 5 4 3 2 1

This book is dedicated to our parents:

Richard and Mary Nussbaum
Joseph and Loretta Pecchioni
Karl and Jo Ann Robinson
Jean and Jerry Thompson

Contents in Brief

Contents

Chapter 13   Death and Dying   292

Chapter 14   Successful Aging   328

Preface

As the twenty-first century dawns, for the first time in human history, there are more individuals over the age of 65 than under the age of 18. On a global scale, human life expectancies continue to increase. For whatever reasons—advances in medicine, nutrition, technology, evolution, and so forth—humans are living longer and healthier lives. As a result, policymakers and scholars are increasingly aware of the serious implications of this aging society and its possible effects on each individual. Not only "the experts," however, are concerned with the aging process. Each person is likely to know a number of individuals over the age of 65. It is hoped that each person will experience many years of healthy old age him- or herself. This book takes a communication perspective as it examines the aging process and the ability of individuals to successfully adapt to aging.

We view aging not only as a physiological or psychological process, but also a social process. The vehicle through which aging as a social process occurs is communication. We bring an expertise in relational communication to the continually increasing knowledge-base of gerontology. Although we are not suggesting that other, nonrelational considerations are of no consequence in the aging process, we focus on the consequences such processes have for human relationships and the ability to age successfully. As an example, hearing loss, in and of itself, is not a relational concept. Such a physiological loss, however, does directly impact an individual's relationships with others and his or her quality of life.

In understanding the process of aging, individuals must understand the dynamics and consequences of social relationships of the elderly. These social relationships develop across the life span. The authors of this book emphasize a life-span approach toward understanding the social interaction that occurs during later life. One cannot truly explain or understand the communicative behavior of elderly people without first realizing that the social behavior of elderly people is well couched within a long history of previous relationships. We believe that the communicative relationships of elderly people are of vital importance and that those relationships should be maintained throughout life.

For a host of social, cultural, economic, psychological, and physiological reasons, elderly people are forced to adapt to what can be a cruel and unforgiving environment. By understanding how elderly people adapt to significant changes in their environment, one can gain great insight into both the process of communication and the process of aging. On a more pragmatic level, an improved understanding of the communicative behavior of elderly people can result in significant improvements in their life satisfaction and life quality.

Our purpose in writing this book is to help people understand how important their communicative relationships are and how important they remain across the life span. It seems doubtful that the significance of an individual's relationships diminishes as that person ages. It is apparent, however, that some difficulties surrounding the creation and maintenance of such relationships increase with age. These difficulties, for the most part, are not insurmountable and can often be remedied with some understanding of the interconnected processes of communication and aging. We hope this book helps raise people's awareness of the barriers facing elderly people in conversation and the importance such conversations play in elderly people's lives.

The book is organized into 14 chapters. Each chapter is written so that the reader is presented with an exhaustive review of the pertinent and recent literature from the social sciences. Readers familiar with the first edition will find that the organization remains essentially the same, with the research updated since that edition. As in the first edition, when the literature is empirically based, the communicative ramifications are then discussed.

Chapter 1 introduces the study of communication and aging with special emphasis given to the pragmatic and theoretical reasons for studying the older population. In addition, the chapter lays the foundation for the rest of the book by providing an overview of the life-span perspective and those theories of successful aging that stress the importance of social interaction. Each of the remaining chapters concentrates on one major area in the communicative lives of older people.

Chapter 2 concentrates on attitudes and ageism. The stereotyping of older people and the ageist beliefs of Western society are discussed. Ageist beliefs are known to affect the social lives of elderly people and the chapter outlines these effects, focusing particularly on recent research conducted by communication scholars that verifies the communicative effects and relational implications of these ageist attitudes.

Chapter 3 highlights the theoretical and practical implications of relational communication. The purpose of the chapter is to identify the significant concepts within the relational perspective and discuss issues that influence all types of social relationships of elderly people. Therefore, the importance for elderly people of reminiscence, sexual activity, communicative competence, interactional control, confirming messages, and loneliness are discussed.

The discussion of the mass media and aging has been divided into two chapters, 4 and 5, in this edition. Chapter 4 describes the media use patterns of elderly people. A new section in this edition discusses computer use by elderly people. Chapter 5 provides an overview of historical and contemporary theories of media influence, the reasons elderly people use the media, and how elderly people are portrayed in the various media. In addition, the relationships between media use and the interpersonal relationships of elderly people are discussed.

Chapter 6 discusses work, leisure, and retirement. Both the leisure world and the work world are inherently social. With the advent of retirement and the changing nature of leisure for elderly people, the social interactions within the contexts of leisure and work must also change. This chapter discusses the communicative implications of the leisure and work environments of elderly people and the transition to a social world of retirement.

Chapters 7, 8, 9, and 10 concentrate on the unique communicative functions of relationships between older individuals and their family and friends. Chapters 7 and 8 focus on the marital relationship and related lifestyles (e.g., divorce and widowhood). Chapter 9 examines other familial relationships: the adult child–elderly parent relationship, the grandparent–grandchild relationship, and the sibling relationship. Chapter 10 discusses the nature and importance of friend relationships in later life.

Chapters 11, 12, and 13 concentrate upon the communicative ramifications of health and death for older people. These chapters cover the important areas of the changing physiological and cognitive abilities of elderly people (Chapter 11), physician–patient interaction and the effects of relocation (Chapter 12), and coping with death, and the communication of and with dying people (Chapter 13). Again, the topics in these three chapters have great relational significance and represent contexts in which communication and communicative relationships are particularly important, but sometimes difficult.

Chapter 14 of the book is entitled "Successful Aging." Within this chapter, we highlight the many social correlates of successful adaptation to the aging process that have been demonstrated empirically. This research clearly demonstrates the importance of communicative relationships throughout the life span. Those relationships are of particular importance to elderly people.

Some of the gaps in knowledge noted by those who used the first edition of this book continue into this edition. These gaps continue because the empirical knowledge required to fill these gaps still does not exist. While researchers know a great deal about aging and the important role that communication plays in that process, a great deal still remains to be learned. We hope that this book will help to inspire others to address these gaps, so that the next edition is a more complete reflection of the experiences of the intertwined processes of communication and aging.

An instructor's manual is available for this text. It includes chapter outlines, activities for the classroom and student research, and objective and short-answer questions.

There are several people we would like to thank for their help with this book. First, we would like to thank Louise Waller and Gerry Phillips for initiating the first edition of this book. In addition, we would like to thank the people at Lawrence Erlbaum Associates for making a new home for this book, especially Linda Bathgate for her confidence and support as the second edition was prepared. We would like to thank many others at Erlbaum, including Mary Price and Mike Reynolds, for their assistance in bringing the book to print. We thank Jon Croghan for assisting the second author in checking information for this edition. Finally, Loretta Pecchioni would like to thank Scott Arnett and Teresa Thompson would like to thank the Cusellas—Lou, Tony, and Alyse—for their patience and support as we worked on this project.

—Jon F. Nussbaum
—Loretta L. Pecchioni
—James D. Robinson
—Teresa L. Thompson

CHAPTER 1

Communication and Aging: Pragmatic and Theoretical Considerations

*T*he aging process has both fascinated and frightened human beings since the beginning of time. Only within the last several decades, however, have social scientists, including a growing number of communication scholars, systematically attempted to document, understand, and explain the dynamic changes in behavior that occur as an individual ages. This book approaches the aging process from a communication perspective. The purpose of this book is to shed new light on the ever-increasing amount of information concerning individuals of ages 65 and over that constantly flows from the social sciences.

In this chapter, we will briefly explain what is meant by a communication perspective and how this perspective is a particularly interesting and useful way of viewing the behavior of elderly individuals. In addition, we will highlight the importance of a *life-span view* as a means of organizing and understanding human communication. Finally, we will conclude with a brief discussion of the most popular theories of successful aging, which have at their core the successful maintenance of an individual's communicative world.

COMMUNICATION WITHIN AN AGING SOCIETY

Every author who writes for the field of communication must at some point attempt to define communication. Hundreds of authors have offered definitions using concepts such as intentionality, shared meanings, feedback loops, and symbol systems. The problem with the great majority of these definitions is the state of confusion they create. In some ways we knew more about communication before we attempted to articulate a precise definition of communication.

For the purpose of this book, therefore, we will simply state that *communication* entails an individual emitting cues in the presence of another individual and the meaning that those cues produce (Wilmot, 1980). This view equates communication with behavior and stresses the pragmatic, functional nature of that behavior. The communication (behavior) that takes place between two or more individuals defines their *relationship*. It is at this level, the *relational* level, that this book is written. Gregory Bateson, a noted anthropologist, and his followers (many of whom, like William Wilmot, Edna Rogers, and B. Aubrey Fisher, are communication scholars) have written extensively on the relational nature of communication and the benefits of describing human behavior from this perspective. For us, the elderly individual is not seen as a personality inventory or an entity fulfilling a prescribed role, but as an *active participant in a system of relationships, who is constantly adapting and attempting to maintain relational equilibrium.* We believe the ability to lead a long, satisfying life is dependent to a great extent on each individual's relational system and how that system is maintained.

Before analyzing the factors that impact the communicative world of the elderly individual, we briefly discuss the reasons for studying communication and aging. We begin with the demography of aging.

The United States is becoming an increasingly mature country. The Administration on Aging (1998) published information, based on data from the U.S. Bureau of the Census, that in 1997 people 65 years old or older numbered 34.1 million or 12.7% of the U.S. population. Since 1900, the percentage of

Americans over the age of 65 has tripled, while the number of these individuals has grown by a factor of 11. By the time the youngest members of the baby-boom generation reach 65 (in the year 2030), depending on how the estimate is conducted, between 58 and 78 million Americans, representing 19 to 21% of the total population, will be over 65. The present older population is, of course, also getting older. The fastest growing segment of the population is the oldest-old, those individuals 85 years old and older. This group increased by 274% between 1960 and 1994. For whatever reason, be it advances in medical technology, improved social programs for elderly people, or some evolutionary advance in the adaptational mechanism of the human species, we are all living longer. This longevity affects every facet of our lives, from marital relationships to marketing strategies to architectural design. For no other reason than their sheer numbers, older people in this society are gaining attention.

Coupled with the increasing population of elderly individuals are the special needs, based in part on physiological imperatives, that make this subsegment of the population qualitatively different from other subsegments of American society. As individuals pass the age of 65, they must constantly adapt to changes in their lives that are often beyond their control. Elderly individuals experience physical declines in capabilities, ranging from slowed reaction time (Stern, Oster, & Newport, 1980) to reduced problem-solving ability (Giambra & Arenberg, 1980). At this same time, elderly individuals must cope with their feelings of being near death (Kubler-Ross, 1975) or the notion that they are entering the final stage of life (Erikson, 1963). The ability to cope and to successfully adapt to these life changes may be dependent on the communicative skills of the elderly individual as they are used to produce a stable relational network. These relational networks help determine the satisfactory or unsatisfactory nature of later life.

Therefore, in addition to the demographic imperative for studying older adults, there are a variety of theoretical and practical reasons for studying communication and aging. Significant developmental changes occur in older adults, which affect communicative processes, which in turn directly affect older people. As Nussbaum, Hummert, Williams, and Harwood (1996) note " ... these changes significantly alter the very nature of social life for members of this group" (p. 2). On the theoretical level, communication scholars have not accounted for these developmental life-span changes in "mainstream" communication theories.

For example, theories of relational development and maintenance do not account for the increasing experience and, it is hoped, knowledge from managing relationships that occurs throughout an individual's life span. This lack of attention to the life span limits the generalizability of any such theory.

On the pragmatic level, older adults use a variety of communicative strategies in order to maintain their sense of identity and place in the larger world. One of the compelling pragmatic reasons for studying communication and aging is the unique function that communication plays within the older population. The communicative behavior of older people serves several critical helping functions (Troll, 1980). First, communication defines the changing power relationships between the elderly person and both family and friends that occur as the individual ages. As an elderly individual retires or in some way becomes more dependent upon family members and friends, this loss of independence is accompanied by a loss of power in these relationships. This power loss is not only reflected but created within these relationships by communication. Neugarten and Gutmann (1968) demonstrated that with increasing age elderly men become less competitive and less dominant, whereas elderly women tend to become more dominant and more competitive. These behavioral changes have profound effects not only on their marital relationships but also on their relationships with their children, grandchildren, and friends. The fuel for these relational changes is the communication that transpires within the relationships.

Communication serves a second important pragmatic function as the one mechanism that can aid in the replacement of lost mobility; such a replacement is necessary to ensure an individual's active participation in family affairs, religious activities, and community events. Through the relational network of family and friends, an older person continues to share information about the larger world. If an elderly individual cannot physically place himself or herself at a community function, the individual will lose touch—unless friends or family members serve as messengers or information sources.

A third important pragmatic function of communication within the aging society is the simple awareness of needs. Cicirelli (1981) discovered that adult children who interact more frequently with their elderly parents not only were more informed about the needs and desires of their parents, but also were regarded as being more likely to help their parents. Cicirelli (1981) suggests that adult children be encouraged to communicate frequently with their parents so as to be better able to understand and to fulfill the special needs of their elderly parents.

In addition, the elderly are of interest to communication scholars because they have participated in more and longer-lasting relationships. They have had to adapt to more communicative situations than any other group of individuals. The elderly have a wealth of communicative information to impart, and all we have to do to benefit from their experience is to simply listen!

LIFE-SPAN DEVELOPMENTAL COMMUNICATION

The field of communication has only recently begun to examine the developmental nature of the communicative act, as evidenced by Nussbaum (1989) and Coupland and Nussbaum (1993). Other social sciences have placed a major emphasis on human development for much longer, as evidenced by the work of Reese and Overton (1970), Baltes, Reese, and Nesselroade (1977), and Lerner and Ryff (1978). One trend in the fields of psychology and sociology is to focus on development throughout an individual's life span (Santrock, 1983), and a major goal of this book is to suggest that *communication* is a developmental phenomenon with important implications throughout life.

The major theme of a developmental approach to the study of human behavior is *change.* "The life-span developmental approach emphasizes the lifelong nature of development and asserts that our understanding of any point in the life-span is enhanced by taking into account the individual's past history and perhaps his or her future expectations" (Huyck & Hoyer, 1982, p. 2). Life-span developmentalists do not postulate any specific theory of change. Instead, they tend to be pluralistic, accepting several worldviews as useful explanations of human development. A central concept within life-span development is *process.* Just discovering change is not enough. One must strive to understand and explain the process of that change.

A popular misconception about the *process of change,* which has existed since Piaget and Erikson first posited stages in their theories of development, has been that the postulation of stages is a necessity for the understanding of change. Actually, stages only serve as a tool to aid our understanding of human development. It would be limiting to think that human communicative behavior must pass through predetermined stages.

Because life-span development is a relatively new way of viewing human behavior, many interesting debates can be found in the social scientific literature. Readers interested in a more exhaustive discussion of the theoretical underpinnings of life-span development should see Baltes, Reese, and Lipsett's (1980) thorough overview.

The study of human behavior across the life span has led to new research methods consistent with an emphasis on the process of change. The most common research methods in life-span development are the *cross-sectional method*, the *longitudinal method*, and various *sequential methods*. Of these, the most frequently used method is the cross-sectional method, which involves gathering information from individuals of different ages at one point in time. The researcher can then compare, for example, the behavior of married individuals at age 25 with the behavior of married individuals at age 65. The major disadvantage of this method is the confounding of *cohort* influences within the design. This is to say that individuals born in 1934 may have had different life experiences than individuals born in 1974, and these different experiences may have nothing to do with age variation. Their marital relationships, for example, may be different because of their life experiences rather than their different ages.

A researcher using the longitudinal method gathers information from the same individuals at several times. This is the ideal method for studying developmental change. The researcher can compare each individual at 25 years old, 30 years old, 35 years old, and so forth, noting trends as the individual ages. This method, however, does have several nagging problems, such as the selective attrition of both subjects and researchers, repeated testing with the same test, and enormous costs. Schaie (1983) summarizes the major longitudinal studies to that date from throughout the world and offers the reader an excellent description of the longitudinal method.

The many problems associated with the previous methods led researchers to the various sequential-method data-collection strategies. Cross-sequential strategies combine longitudinal with cross-sectional methods to eliminate or at least control many confounding problems. In cross-sequential studies, individuals from several age categories are studied over a relatively short period of time. Baltes, et al. (1977) provide a very readable explanation of sequential methods.

The methods employed by life-span developmental researchers are only one of the several pragmatic conventions used to better understand life-span behaviors. An additional convention with widespread acceptance is to divide the life-span into 10 life phases: preconception, prenatal, infancy, early childhood, late childhood, adolescence, early adulthood, middle adulthood, old age, and death (Reese, 1978). This book concentrates upon the old-age phase of the life span. But one must keep in mind the *developmental* nature of communication. The relationships about which we write and those factors that affect the relational world of older people have a developmental history that enables us to more fully describe, explain, and understand communication and aging.

THEORIES OF SUCCESSFUL AGING

Human beings share at least one fact with simple, single-celled organisms—the process of aging. The physiology of all living beings determines their structures and functions to a great degree. The causes of aging have been the subject of many decades of research by numerous biologists. Biological aging is a constant, and, although it is a fascinating process, we, as social scientists, are much more concerned with how human beings cope with and adapt to aging than we are with the actual physiology of aging. *We believe that at the core of any successful attempt to adapt to biological aging is communication.* Because humans predict, understand, and control their environments to a great degree symbolically, such a conclusion seems warranted. Many social scientists share this belief and have constructed numerous theories of successful aging. Of these, the following six theories will be discussed: disengagement theory, activity theory, continuity theory, socioemotional selectivity theory, selective optimization with compensation model, and social-environmental theory.

Disengagement Theory

Cumming, Dean, Newell, and McCaffrey (1960) first advanced the disengagement theory of aging as a functional approach to social interaction. Disengagement refers to a mutual withdrawal by elderly people from society and a withdrawal by society from elderly people. This withdrawal is thought to be universal as well as inevitable. Disengagement theorists conceive of the "golden years" as a graceful withdrawal from society (Gubrium, 1973). Gubrium outlines these defining characteristics of disengagement theory:

1. *Mutuality:* Persons do not act or construct as much as they carry out a normatively defined mutual disengagement.
2. *Insuitability:* The system's needs are dealt with rather than personal needs and interests, with systematic needs inevitably being fulfilled.
3. *Universality:* All social systems, if they are to maintain equilibrium, must necessarily operate so as to disengage from the elderly, disengagement being a functional prerequisite to social stability (pp. 20–21).

According to this perspective, the elderly individual who accepts and is even desirous of the withdrawal process will successfully adapt to aging. The elderly individual who does not engage in the withdrawal process will not be fulfilling his or her destiny or the functional needs of the society and will have a hard time adapting to old age.

The communication implications of disengagement theory are profound. Havighurst, Neugarten, and Tobin (1968) and Nussbaum (1981) suggest that this withdrawal is characterized by both a quantitative and qualitative change in the relational system of elderly individuals. Research suggests that the elderly do have fewer interactions as they age, but are still able to maintain high morale during this process (Havighurst et al., 1968; Lowenthal & Boler, 1965; Maddox & Eisdorfer, 1962; Tallmer & Kutner, 1969). There is little evidence, however, to suggest *how* relationships change in a qualitative way. Does relational closeness decrease with age? Within which relationships does the decline occur?

In addition, because of the societal withdrawal from elderly people, the *function* of each relationship will be altered. For instance, relationships will not serve to expand the knowledge of elderly people, but, more likely, will serve to aid elderly people in maintaining basic needs. This becomes clear when one considers how society handles the special needs and interactional restrictions on elderly people. One example of these imposed social restrictions is nursing homes that are seemingly constructed to protect the active community from elderly people.

In short, if the disengagement theory of aging is correct, communication should change in the following ways for an elderly individual to successfully adapt to later life: (a) the elderly individual should enter into fewer relationships with increasing age, (b) the closeness of the elderly individual's relationships should lessen with increasing age, and (c) the lessening of the quantitative and qualitative aspects of the relational network of the elderly individual should be apparent within the communicative acts of the individual. For instance, conversation will be more oriented to securing personal needs or health concerns and less oriented toward community events or "others."

Activity Theory

A second theoretical approach toward successful aging predates disengagement theory and is more a collection of research findings than a formally accepted theory. Within activity theory," successful aging is linked to an active social life. Burgess (1954), Lebo (1953), and Reichard, Livson, and Peterson (1962) found a direct relationship between high levels of activity and high morale. In addition, Tobin and Neugarten (1961); Adams (1969); Bley, Goodman, Dye, and Haiel (1972); Lemon, Bengtson, and Peterson (1972); Cutler (1973); Larson (1978); and Nussbaum (1983a, 1983b) reported a positive relationship between life satisfaction in an elderly individual and high levels of social interaction.

The communication implications for activity theory are quite different than those for disengagement theory. Activity theory suggests that communication should be maintained at an active level throughout the aging process. Although retirement and widowhood will occur, these events do not necessitate that an aging individual withdraw from social interaction, nor should these events be construed as a sign to withdraw. The quantity of interaction should not decline if the individual wishes to successfully adapt to the aging process. In addition, Lowenthal and Haven (1968) and Nussbaum (1985) report that the maintenance of stable, close relationships is an important predictor of life satisfaction in the elderly. Thus, the quality of an individual's relational world should remain stable throughout the course of life.

If activity theory is correct, communication should transpire in the following ways for an elderly individual to successfully adapt to later life: (a) an elderly individual should enter into frequent interactions, (b) the relationships entered into should retain a high level of closeness throughout the aging process, and (c) the level and type of activity within the relational network should be apparent within the communicative acts of the elderly individual. For instance, conversation within interaction should reflect an interest in community events and other topics that are oriented toward others.

Continuity Theory

Neugarten, Havighurst, and Tobin (1968) postulated that successful aging is dependent on each individual's personality. The individual's personality is the pivotal link between communication and successful aging. According to Neugarten et al. (1968), the aging individual "continued to exercise choice and to select from the environment in accordance with his (*sic*) own long-established needs. He (*sic*) aged according to a pattern that has long history and that maintains itself, with adaptation, to the end of life" (pp. 176–177). One would expect each individual to continue those communicative behaviors that have served him or her well throughout life. If the individual was socially active, then this activity would be expected to continue throughout life. If the individual was withdrawn, then one could expect disengagement in later life. In either case, one's ability to successfully adapt to old age is dependent upon the individual's ability to maintain consistency.

The continuity theory of successful aging helps to explain some of the contradictory evidence that supports both disengagement theory and activity theory. Certain personality types can disengage with comfort and remain satisfied with life. Certain other personality types remain active and satisfied with life. A problem occurs when, for one reason or another, continuity cannot be maintained.

The communication implications of continuity theory are straightforward. One must first describe each individual's personality and link communication to that personality. Then, for an individual to achieve successful adaptation to old age, these communicative behaviors must be maintained throughout life. This theory of successful aging is a pure life-span theory because one must chart the individual's pattern of behavior throughout his or her life to have an indication of consistency.

Socioemotional Selectivity Theory

Carstensen (1991, 1992) proposed the socioemotional selectivity theory as another integrative view of aging addressing the contradictory findings of disengagement theory and activity theory. According to this theory, aging individuals reduce their number of overall interactional partners, but maintain those relationships that provide the most satisfaction. By narrowing their social networks, older individuals devote more of their emotional resources to fewer but closer relationships.

Socioemotional selectivity theory is basically a social exchange theory. Social interaction entails certain costs (e.g., time, energy, and negative emotion) and rewards (e.g., information, practical assistance, maintenance of self-identity). The relative importance of these costs and rewards varies across an individual's life span. Early in life, new contacts are likely to provide new information. As an individual ages, however, the chances of a new individual providing novel information diminishes. Contact with strangers and acquaintances may become costly in terms of energy expenditure and negative risk potential. Contact with long-time friends and family, however, may be particularly rewarding because of the benefits to positive self-esteem and practical assistance. As Carstensen (1992) states, the reduction in rates of interaction in old age are "the result of lifelong selection processes by which people strategically and adaptively cultivate their social networks to maximize social and emotional gains and minimize social and emotional risks" (p. 331). Socioemotional selectively theory, therefore, takes a life-span approach to the accumulation of rewarding relationships and the discarding of dissatisfying relationships.

Although the overall size of social networks diminishes with age, the number of emotionally close relationships does not distinguish age groups. In addition, personality factors, such as extroversion and openness to experience, are not related to the average emotional closeness of social partners in an older individual's network, but family status is (Lang, Staudinger, & Carstensen, 1998). This suggests that contextual factors play a larger role in emotional closeness than do personal factors.

The communication implications for socioemotional selectivity theory are significant because relational closeness is achieved through communication. As individuals age, they develop more successful strategies for optimizing the rewards from their close personal relationships, while minimizing the costs. Conversely, older individuals also develop strategies for minimizing costly interactions with relatively unknown others.

If socioemotional selectivity theory is correct, communication should transpire in the following ways for an elderly individual to successfully adapt to later life: (a) an elderly individual should enter into frequent interaction with those to whom he or she feels particularly close and avoid interaction with those who are strangers or acquaintances; (b) the relationships that are maintained should retain a high level of closeness throughout the aging process; and, (c) the level of activity within the quantitative and qualitative aspects of the relational network should be apparent within the communicative acts of the elderly individual. For instance, conversation within inter-action with a valued, close individual should reflect an interest in community events and other topics that are oriented toward others. Conversely, conversation within interaction with less close individuals should be more oriented to securing personal needs or health concerns and less oriented toward community events or others.

Selective Optimization with Compensation Model

Baltes and Baltes (1990), summarizing a vast body of research, suggested a series of strategies for successful aging in which they viewed aging as a life-long adaptive *process,* an ongoing dynamic of selective optimization with compensation. In their view, "old age, if approached properly, harbors many opportu-nities for positive change and productive functioning" (Baltes & Baltes, 1990, p. 2). Their model, which they described as prototheoretical, is based on a framework of propositions re-garding human aging from a psychological point of view. These propositions are:

1. There are major differences among normal, optimal, and sick (pathological) aging.
2. There is much heterogeneity (variability) in aging.
3. There is much latent reserve (ability that has previ-ously been untapped but that may be called upon when needed).
4. There is an aging loss near the limits of reserve; that is, with age we begin to lose some of our reserve ca-pacities, but this loss is at the extreme end of the pro-cess.
5. Knowledge-based pragmatics and technology can offset age-related decline in cognitive mechanics.
6. With aging, the balance between gains and losses be-comes less positive.
7. The self remains resilient in old age.

For the purpose of examining communication and aging, the most important propositions point out the tremendous vari-ability in the aging process, the amount of latent reserve each individual has available in the face of cognitive declines, the importance of pragmatic knowledge as a powerful compensation for physiological decline, and the adaptation of the individual's sense of self throughout the aging process.

Successful aging within the selective optimization with compensation model, then, entails an adaptive interplay of gains and losses. The three elements of this model are selection, optimization, and compensation. As an individual ages, increasing restrictions are imposed by physical and cognitive limitations. Individuals select or specialize their efforts into areas of high priority. Although the individual may not perform as well in all aspects of life as he or she once did, this does not preclude the individual from setting new priorities or goals in life.

The successfully aging individual continues to engage in behaviors that enrich and augment his or her physical and mental reserves. This optimization process allows individuals to continue to maximize their chosen life courses.

As restrictions in range and potential increase, the individual may compensate for these restrictions through psychological and technological strategies. Psychological strategies may include external memory aids such as adopting new mnemonic devices, while technological strategies may include using a hearing aid.

The three elements of this model interplay with one another to produce a dynamic process, so that an individual may suffer from a reduction in general capacity and losses in specific functions, but, through the process of selection, optimization, and compensation, create a transformed and effective life. Of course, this process of adaptation is never complete.

The implications for communication are derived from the nature of the adaptive processes through which the individual passes and the reactions of those around him or her. When an individual suffers from some diminution in abilities, the people involved with that individual can either support continued independence or reinforce a dependent set of behaviors. For example, Baltes and Wahl (1987) pointed out that staff in a nursing home reacted to dependent behaviors of residents but ignored independent behaviors, further reinforcing the dependent behaviors.

If the selective optimization with compensation model is correct, then communication for an elderly individual should transpire so that the individual maintains as many options as possible in selecting and optimizing the conditions of his or her life. Compensation should be used to maximize an individual's ability to continue controlling his or her life. The quantity and quality of interaction should focus on maintaining a positive self-identity by allowing the individual to retain control over his or her environment as much as possible.

Social-Environmental Theory

Hendricks and Hendricks (1986) describe social-environmental theory as emphasizing "the functional context surrounding the daily lives of the elderly" (p. 3). This context or environment is both social and individual (Gubrium, 1973). While social scientists such as Lawton (1983, 1985), Skinner and Vaughan (1985), and Nussbaum (1981) concentrate on the impact the environment has on social interaction, Gubrium (1973), Marshall (1986), and others stress the importance of individual realities interpreted from environmental cues. In either case, the environment is said to mediate, structure, and even dictate the communication within its context.

Social-environmental theorists are very concerned with the pragmatic, functional impact of the environment on communication for elderly individuals. For instance, the architectural design of a nursing home can "control" the interaction within the building. If the nursing home is designed with a central nursing station and has residential wings extending from the center, it is very unlikely that individuals who are placed in separate wings will enter into a relationship. Proximity is a primary factor for selecting an individual for interaction, and the architecture often dictates who will be close both physically and relationally.

It is also important to view environments as *more* than just physical structures. Other individuals are important elements of an elderly individual's environment. Factors such as age segregation in a neighborhood or a retirement community can be important determinants of an elderly individual's social world (Nussbaum, 1981). In addition, psychological constructs such as attitudes and values are important parts of an environment that can shape communication within a given context. Therefore, within the social-environmental view, communicative behaviors reflect a complex interplay of the individual's unique combination of personal and sociodemographic characteristics, life experiences, and the constraints or opportunities of the external social environment.

Social-environmental theory incorporates the key aspects of successful aging from disengagement theory, activity theory, and continuity theory into one theory of larger scope. Aspects of socioemotional selectivity theory and the selective optimization with compensation model are also present. Successful aging is seen as a function of factors external to the individual in combination with internal factors. Consequently, the study of the relational world of elderly people and how their environment changes across their life spans is viewed not only as being appropriate but also as being essential to understanding successful adaptation to aging.

Each of the six theories discussed, disengagement theory, activity theory, continuity theory, socioemotional selectivity theory, the selective optimization with compensation model, and social-environmental theory, have strengths and weaknesses. It is not the purpose of this book to argue the correctness of any one theory of successful aging over any other theory. It is, however, the opinion of the authors that the most useful way to approach communication and aging is to incorporate the functional pragmatic perspective of social-environmental theory into descriptions of the aging process. Communication within this perspective is both directly influenced by environmental factors and serves specific functions for the inhabitants of the environment.

One important environmental factor that overlays the aging process is culture. Cultural and social norms define the roles that elderly people fill and influence attitudes towards aging (Holmes & Holmes, 1995). Different cultures view aging differently and this impacts the relational world of the elderly. Holmes and Holmes (1995) point out that some cultures revere their ancestors. In these cultures, elderly people are viewed as "almost ancestors." Other cultures fear death. In these cultures, elderly people are viewed as "already dead" or "nearly dead." It is not difficult to imagine that interaction with elderly people will be quite different in these cultures. In addition, a country may have many co-cultures; the United States is particularly noted for this (Al-Deen, 1997). Because we are concerned with the experience of aging as an individual lives his or her life within a family, community, and society, co-cultural variation should not be ignored in trying to understand that experience (Hill, Long, & Cupach, 1997). *Our task, then, is to describe and understand the environment of elderly people and how the environment affects their relational world, which, in turn, affects their ability to successfully adapt to the aging process.*

SUMMARY

This chapter introduces several key ideas concerning communication and aging. First, the study of communication is seen as including all the behaviors of an individual in the presence of at least one other individual and the *meanings* derived from those behaviors. Second, elderly individuals are active participants in a system of relationships throughout their life span that can aid or hinder their ability to successfully adapt to the aging process. The communication that transpires within the relational network of an elderly individual fulfills many functions. Several of these functions are especially important for individuals beyond their 65th birthday. Third, to truly understand communication and aging, one must understand that communication is a life-span phenomenon. Finally, of the six major theories of successful aging presented, the social-environmental theory is viewed by the authors of this book as being the most useful way to describe and understand communication and aging.

The remaining chapters of this book are devoted to topics that impact the relational world of elderly individuals. We begin with the study of attitudes and how the ageist society in which we live affects communication. The chapters that follow consider work and retirement, leisure activities, the media, the family, friendship, health, and death and dying. The concluding chapter deals with successful aging.

■ REFERENCES

Adams, D. (1969). Analysis of a life satisfaction index. *Journal of Gerontology, 24,* 470–474.

Administration on Aging. (1998). *Profile of Older Americans 1998* [On-line]. Available: *http://www.aoa.dhhs.gov/aoa/stats/profile*

Al-Deen, H. S. N. (1997). Preface. In H. S. N. Al-Deen (Ed.), *Cross-cultural communication and aging in the United States* (pp. xi–xiii). Mahwah, NJ: Lawrence Erlbaum Associates.

Baltes, M. M., & Wahl, H. -W. (1987). Dependency in aging. In L. L. Carstensen & B. A. Edelstein (Eds.), *Handbook of clinical gerontology* (pp. 204–221). New York: Pergamon.

Baltes, P. B., & Baltes, M. M. (1990). Psychological perspectives on successful aging: The model of selective optimization with compensation. In P. B. Baltes & M. M. Baltes (Eds.), *Successful aging: Perspectives from the behavioral sciences* (pp. 1–34). Cambridge, England: Cambridge University Press.

Baltes, P. B., Reese, H. W., & Lipsett, L. P. (1980). Life-span developmental psychology. *Annual Review of Psychology, 31,* 65–110.

Baltes, P. B., Reese, H. W., & Nesselroade, J. P. (1977). *Life-span developmental psychology: Introduction to research methods.* Monterey, CA: Brooks/Cole.

Bley, N. B., Goodman, M., Dye, D., & Haiel, B. (1972). Characteristics of aged participants in age segregated leisure programs. *Gerontologist, 12,* 368–370.

Burgess, E. W. (1954). Social relations, activities, and personal adjustment. *American Journal of Sociology, 59,* 352–360.

Carstensen, L. L. (1991). Socioemotional activity theory: Social activity in life-span context. *Annual Review of Gerontology and Geriatrics, 11,* 195–217.

Carstensen, L. L. (1992). Social and emotional patterns in adulthood: Support for socioemotional selectivity theory. *Psychology and Aging, 3,* 331–338.

Cicirelli, V. G. (1981). *Helping elderly parents: The role of adult children.* Boston: Auburn House.

Coupland, N., & Nussbaum, J. F. (Eds.). (1993). *Discourse and lifespan identity.* Newbury Park, CA: Sage.

Cumming, E., Dean, L., Newell, D., & McCaffrey, I. (1960). Disengagement tentative theory of aging. *Sociometry, 23,* 23–35.

Cutler, N. (1973). Age variations in the dimensionality of life satisfaction. *Journal of Gerontology, 28,* 96–100.

Erikson, E. H. (1963). *Childhood and society.* New York: Norton.

Giambra, L. M., & Arenberg, D. (1980). Problem solving, concept learning, and aging. In L. W. Poon (Ed.), *Aging in the 1980's: Psychological issues* (pp. 253–259). Washington, DC: American Psychological Association.

Gubrium, J. F. (1973). *The myth of the golden years: A socio-environmental theory of aging.* Springfield, IL: Charles C Thomas.

Havighurst, R. I., Neugarten, B. L., & Tobin, S. C. (1968). Disengagement and patterns of aging. In B. L. Neugarten (Ed.), *Middle age and aging* (pp. 161–172). Chicago: University of Chicago Press.

Hendricks, J., & Hendricks, C. D. (1986). *Aging in mass society: Myths and realities* (3rd ed.). Boston: Little, Brown.

Hill, L. B., Long, L. W., & Cupach, W. R. (1997). Aging and the elders from a cross-cultural communication perspective. In Al-Deen, H. S. N. (Ed.), *Cross-cultural communication and aging in the United States* (pp. 5–22). Mahwah, NJ: Lawrence Erlbaum Associates.

Holmes, E. R., & Holmes, L. D. (1995). *Other cultures, elder years* (2nd ed.). Thousand Oaks, CA: Sage.

Huyck, M. H., & Hoyer, W. J. (1982). *Adult development and aging.* Belmont, CA: Wadsworth.

Kubler-Ross, E. (1975). *Death and final stage of growth.* Englewood Cliffs, NJ: Prentice-Hall.

Lang, F. R., Staudinger, U. M., & Carstensen, L. L. (1998). Perspectives on socioemotional selectivity in late life: How personality and social context do (and do not) make a difference. *The Journals of Gerontology, Series B, 53,* P21–P30.

Larson, R. (1978). Thirty years of research on the subjective well-being of older Americans. *Journal of Gerontology, 33,* 109–124.

Lawton, M. P. (1983). Environmental and other determinants of well-being in older people. *The Gerontologist, 23,* 249–357.

Lawton, M. P. (1985). Housing and living environments of older people. In R. H. Binstock & E. Shanas (Eds.), *Handbook of aging and the social sciences* (pp. 450–478). New York: Van Nostrand Reinhold.

Lebo, D. (1953). Some factors said to make for happiness in old age. *Journal of Clinical Psychology, 9,* 384–390.

Lemon, B. W., Bengtson, V. L., & Peterson, J. A., (1972). An exploration of the activity theory of aging: Activity types and life satisfaction among in-movers to a retirement community. *Journal of Gerontology, 27,* 511–523.

Lerner, R. M., & Ryff, C. D. (1978). Implementation of the life-span view of human development: The sample case of attachment. In P. Baltes (Ed.), *Life-span development and behavior,* (Vol. 1, pp. 2–44). New York: Academic Press.

Lowenthal, N. F., & Boler, D. (1965). Voluntary and involuntary social withdrawal. *Journal of Gerontology, 20,* 363–371.

Lowenthal, N. F., & Haven, L. (1968). Interaction and adaptation: Intimacy as a critical behavior. *American Sociological Review, 33,* 20–30.

Maddox, G., & Eisdorfer, C. (1962). Some correlates of activity and morale among the elderly. *Social Forces, 40,* 254–260.

Marshall, V. W. (1986). *Later life: The social psychology of aging.* Beverly Hills, CA: Sage.

Neugarten, B. L., & Gutmann, P. L. (1968). Age-sex roles and personality in middle age: A thematic apperception study. In B. L. Neugarten (Ed.), *Middle age and aging* (pp. 58–71). Chicago: University of Chicago Press.

Neugarten, B. L., Havighurst, R. J., & Tobin, S. S. (1968). Personality and patterns of aging. In B. L. Neugarten (Ed.), *Middle age and aging* (pp. 173–177). Chicago: University of Chicago Press.

Nussbaum, J. F. (1981). *Interactional patterns of elderly individuals: Implications for successful adaptation to life.* Unpublished doctoral dissertation, Purdue University, West Lafayette, IN.

Nussbaum, J. F. (1983a). Perceptions of communication content and life satisfaction among the elderly. *Communication Quarterly, 31,* 313–319.

Nussbaum, J. F. (1983b). Relational closeness of elderly interaction: Implications for life satisfaction. *Western Journal of Speech Communication, 47,* 229–243.

Nussbaum, J. F. (1985). Successful aging: A communicative model. *Communication Quarterly, 33,* 262–269.

Nussbaum, J. F. (Ed.). (1989). *Life-span communication: Normative processes.* Hillsdale, NJ: Lawrence Erlbaum Associates.

Nussbaum, J. F., Hummert, M. L., Williams, A., & Harwood, J. (1996). Communication and older adults. In B. Burleson (Ed.), *Communication yearbook 19* (pp. 1–47). Thousand Oaks, CA: Sage.

Reese, H. W. (1978). *Phases of development across life–span.* Lecture given to graduate seminar in advanced developmental psychology, West Virginia University, Morgantown, WV.

Reese, H. W., & Overton, W. F. (1970). Models of development and theories of development. In L. R. Goulet & P. B. Baltes (Eds.), *Life-span development psychology: Research and theory* (pp. 115–145). New York: Academic Press.

Reichard, S., Livson, F., & Peterson, P. G. (1962). *Aging and personality.* New York: Wiley.

Santrock, J. W. (1983). *Life-span development.* Dubuque, IA: Brown.

Schaie, K. W. (1983). *Longitudinal studies of adult psychological development.* New York: Guilford.

Skinner, B. F., & Vaughan, M. (1985). *Enjoy old age.* New York: Warner Books.

Stern, J. A., Oster, P. J., & Newport, K. (1980). Reaction time measures, hemispheric specialization, and age. In L. W. Poon (Ed.), *Aging in the 1980's: Psychological issues* (pp. 309–326). Washington, DC: American Psychological Association.

Tallmer, M., & Kutner, B. (1969). Disengagement and the stresses of aging. *Journal of Gerontology, 24,* 70–75.

Tobin, S. S., & Neugarten, B. L. (1961). Life satisfaction and social interaction in aging. *Journal of Gerontology, 16,* 344–346.

Troll, L. E. (1980). Interpersonal relations: Introduction. In L. W. Poon (Ed.), *Aging in the 1980's: Psychological issues* (pp. 435–440). Washington, DC: American Psychological Association.

Wilmot, W. W. (1980). *Dyadic communication* (2nd ed.). Reading, MA: Addison-Wesley.

CHAPTER 2

Attitudes and Ageism

O ne of the most actively researched areas of communication and aging during the past decade examines attitudes toward aging and the consequences these
attitudes have for interaction. Attitudes toward aging and elderly people influence how we interact with older individuals
and how we interpret the aging process itself. The attitudes we
hold, however, do not necessarily reflect the reality of other
people's lives. Although most older individuals are healthy and
active, widely held negative attitudes towards aging, as we discuss in this chapter, influence our perception of elderly people
and the ways in which we choose to interact with them.

Before we can fully discuss the implications of attitudes toward the aging process, we must first define what is meant by
an attitude and why attitudes toward the aging process are important. Atchley (1980) offered a very simple definition of an *attitude*. He wrote that "attitudes are likes and dislikes. They may
develop out of purely personal preferences, but they are often
logical extensions of beliefs and values" (Atchley, 1980, p. 256).
Attitudes are complex and can be distinguished from beliefs
and values because they have an affective component as well as
a behavioral and a cognitive component. This simply means
that attitudes represent positive or negative feelings, which are

thought out to some degree and reflect an intention to act on feelings (Bennett & Eckman, 1973).

It is important to note that attitudes are not arbitrary thought processes or feelings. In order to manage the tremendous amount of information that humans receive at any given moment, humans tend to create categories or schema for interpreting people, things, and situations. For each category, humans develop a set of beliefs, values, and attitudes. When people meet, for example, an older person, they access their knowledge about the category "older person" in order to determine how to interact with that person. Attitudes, therefore, influence behavior. The attitudes a person holds regarding any particular category often reflect the social, political, and economic world in which he or she lives.

Attitudes are important for those who study and write about communication and aging for three major reasons. First, attitudes felt toward elderly people may influence all aspects of their relational world. If young people feel that old age is a time of decreased health and productivity, this feeling could influence their likelihood of entering into and maintaining a relationship with an elderly individual. Second, attitudes may influence the way an aging individual behaves when that person becomes elderly. If individuals feel that old age is a time of bad health and dependency, they may begin to act in ways that fulfill those expectations once they consider themselves old; they will act as if they are unhealthy and dependent. Finally, Palmore (1982) writes that "many, if not most, of the 'problems of aging' stem from or are exacerbated by prejudice and discrimination against the aged" (p. 333). If this is true, it is vital that we study attitudes so that we can better understand the problems of old age.

ATTITUDES TOWARD THE AGING PROCESS

Philip Slater (1964) suggests that our ideas and attitudes about the aging process stem from two contradictory traditions of thought. The classical Greek view of aging is very negative. The ancient Greeks stressed the great fortune of youth and the great misfortune of the old. Within the classical Greek view, once a person has passed his or her youthful years, it is better to die than to suffer the indignities of old age. The Middle Eastern view of aging, on the other hand, is very positive. "Age brings status and prestige to a man not only in his family but also in his community, where it almost automatically confers political influence" (Slater, 1964, p. 229). This disparity between the opposing traditions is best seen in the reasons given for the death of a young person. The Middle Eastern view is that the wicked die young. Old age is a blessing, and, therefore, if a person dies young, that individual is not blessed. The ancient Greeks believed that an individual who dies young is loved by the gods. A person who lives into old age is being punished by the gods.

The differing nature of the attitudes toward old age in ancient Greek culture and Middle Eastern culture has a modern-day parallel. Attitudes toward aging in primarily agricultural societies and in primarily industrial societies have been found to be quite different. Although the research is sometimes quite sketchy, it does appear that "attitudes were more positive in stable agricultural societies, and that there has generally been a decline in positive attitudes toward the aged with industrialization" (Palmore, 1982, p. 335). Sociologists explain this difference in attitudes toward older people in terms of productive roles. In an industrialized society, the most productive roles are filled by young people, whereas in an agricultural society older people, with their knowledge of farming and access to wealth through ownership of the land, can be productive for many more years.

The social scientific research that reports on aspects of attitudes toward the aging process is quite extensive. Since the pioneering work of Dinkel (1944), which first suggested a difference between the way young adults view elderly people and the way elderly people view themselves, well over 200 empirical studies have appeared in scholarly journals. The vast majority of these articles associate negative attitudes with the aging process. This should not be surprising, considering that the United States is a culture that is derived primarily from ancient Greek tradition and that has developed into a highly industrialized society. Nevertheless, the literature is far from exclusively negative, as some studies point to the emergence of more positive attitudes toward aging since the early 1980s.

It is well beyond the scope of this chapter to review and discuss the implications of each study written over the last 60 years that has investigated attitudes and aging. Several excellent reviews documenting major research trends exist in the gerontological and communication literature (e.g., Bennett & Eckman, 1973; Botwinick, 1984; Hummert, Shaner, & Garstka, 1995;

Kastenbaum, 1964; Palmore, 1982). Palmore (1982) summarized the major conclusions of this body of research as follows:

1.   Relative to ratings of other age categories, ratings of old age tend to be more negative.
2.   Most people have mixed feelings about various aspects of old age and tend to rate old age positively on some dimensions and negatively on others. *←deep cultural belief systems*
3.   There are more stereotypes associated with old age than with younger ages.
4.   Many negative stereotypes are held by a majority of people.
5.   Knowledge about aging can be improved and misconceptions can be reduced by training in gerontology, but attitudes are more resistant to change (pp. 340–341).

Recent research shows that this summary of attitudes towards aging continues to be an accurate reflection of Western attitudes. Hummert's (Hummert, 1994; Hummert, Shaner, & Garstka, 1995) work focused on identifying the stereotypes that individuals hold toward the elderly across the life span. Hummert, Garstka, Shaner, and Strahm (1994) report that across the life span, the most commonly held negative stereotypes of the elderly are *severely impaired, despondent, shrew/curmudgeon,* and *recluse.* The most commonly held positive stereotypes are *golden ager, perfect grandparent,* and *John Wayne conservative.* While individuals have both negative and positive stereotypes of elderly people, the complexity of these stereotypes increases with age. Older individuals have more variation in their attitudes than do middle-aged individuals, who in turn have more variation in their attitudes than do younger individuals.

Because individuals have both positive and negative stereotypes about aging, Hummert (1994) asked the question, What activates a given stereotype? She proposed a model that attempts to answer this question. Several elements of the model interact in order to activate a given stereotype. These elements are the context, characteristics of the perceiver, and characteristics of the elderly individual.

Context plays a role in activating either positive or negative stereotypes by making positive or negative aspects of aging salient in the encounter. For example, meeting an older person in a nursing home would make the negative aspects of aging more salient while meeting that same older person on a cruise ship would make the positive aspects of aging more salient.

Characteristics of the perceiver influence whether positive or negative stereotypes are activated. Because people tend to have more complex stereotypes toward aging as they themselves age, the age of the perceiver influences which stereotypes are available to be activated. In addition, an individual's cognitive complexity and quality of prior contact with elderly people influence the schema he or she has available to be activated. Individuals with higher cognitive complexity have a larger array of traits within stereotypes from which to select. Individuals who have had more positive experiences with the elderly are more likely to anticipate a repeat of those experiences (Fox & Giles, 1993).

Characteristics of the elderly individual will influence which stereotypes are activated by reinforcing or altering the perceptions of the perceiver. If the older person exhibits traits that are related to negative stereotypes, these are the stereotypes that will be activated. Conversely, if the older person exhibits traits associated with positive stereotypes, these will be activated.

The model proposed by Hummert (1994) is additive. Therefore, the more elements that support the activation of positive stereotypes, the more likely that those stereotypes will be activated. For example, a cognitively complex middle-aged person encountering a healthy older person on a cruise would most likely have positive stereotypes activated. Conversely, a younger adult who has not experienced positive interactions with older individuals meeting a frail older person in a nursing home would most likely have negative stereotypes activated.

As mentioned previously, the negative attitudes toward the aging process found in the majority of social scientific research should be no surprise. The United States is a youth-oriented society that during the last several decades seems to have focused on the power of youth. The decade of the 1980s, however, was seen by some as a turning point in the negativism felt toward the aging process (Austin, 1985; Tibbitts, 1979). Researchers have begun to ask if attitudes toward the elderly are becoming more positive.

Several critical events took place during the 1980s that may signal a move away from pervasively negative attitudes about aging. The citizens of the United States elected in 1980 and then reelected in 1984 a senior citizen as president. This senior citizen president recorded the highest approval rating received by any president in the history of the republic. In the 1990s a relatively young president was elected in the United States, but he was the first member of the Baby Boom generation to attain this high office. As the Baby Boomers begin to turn 50, they are also beginning to contemplate their own retirement and the passing of their parents. Their own attitudes towards aging must inevitably change. A second event in the 1980s that signaled changing attitudes toward elderly people was the movement to eliminate mandatory retirement. Perhaps 65 years of age is a bit too young to be considered unproductive. This may be reflected in the use of subcategories for elderly people, such as "young-old" and "old-old." More recently, the United Nations designated 1999 as the International Year of Older Persons, acknowledging the fact that in the year 2000, older people will outnumber children for the first time in human history. A series of events was designed to highlight the challenges and opportunities of a rapidly aging global population. Finally, the media are beginning to realize that elderly people actually do exist in our world. Two later chapters in this volume are devoted to the mass media and elderly people, concentrating on such topics as the portrayal of elderly people in the media and the elderly audience as a market.

These events have led researchers to compare attitudes toward aging held in the 1950s and 1960s to attitudes held in the 1980s. David Austin (1985) supplied evidence that suggests that attitudes toward aging have improved significantly since the early 1970s. Although Austin did not concur with Schonfield (1982) that negative attitudes toward aging are a "social myth" perpetuated by gerontologists, Austin did provide some much needed good news. Individuals are beginning to realize that aging does not necessarily signal a time of total decline and that rewards can come with advancing age. Hummert's (1994) work supports this more complex view of both positive and negative aspects of aging.

It should be noted that, while a majority of the research on intergenerational communication has focused on the negative aspects of these interactions, some scholars are focusing on the more positive aspects of these interactions. Al-Deen (1997a) pointed out that the members of most minority co-cultures in the United States report satisfaction with their intergenerational communication. While these co-cultures use different communicative strategies, they all find ways to maintain cross-generational continuity and interdependence (see Al-Deen, 1997b; Kalbfleisch & Anderson, 1997; Kimoto, 1997). Kimoto (1997) argued that scholars need to examine how these co-cultures manage to successfully negotiate their intergenerational relationships. This is definitely an area that deserves more attention.

AGEISM

Attitudes, positive or negative, are an unavoidable aspect of human life. The difficulty with attitudes, however, is that they can lead to the stereotyping of one segment of society, which then manifests itself in discriminatory practices against that part of society. Differing attitudes toward men and women in this society have led to sexist stereotyping, which may be partially responsible for everything from pay inequities to violent crimes against women. Differing attitudes toward individuals based upon their skin color have created a racist society, with Americans of European descent reaping rich rewards while Americans of African and First Nations descent have suffered innumerable atrocities. Differing attitudes felt toward individuals who have lived for over a half a century lead to a "discrimination based on age; especially the discrimination against middle-aged and elderly people" (Morris, 1979, p. 24). Robert Butler (1969) coined the term *ageism* to connote wholesale discrimination against all elderly individuals.

One does not need to look far to find evidence of ageism in our society. "Age discrimination occurs when human beings are avoided or excluded in everyday activities because they are the 'wrong age'" (Atchley, 1980, p. 261). From institutions of higher learning, which are geared almost exclusively to those in their twenties or thirties, to your local newspaper, which is printed so that aging eyes cannot read its content, ageism is rampant in today's world. One of the worst forms of ageism occurs in the workplace. For many of us, our jobs define a large part of our self-image. In this youth-oriented society many of the best jobs are off-limits for anyone over 60 years old. Job discrimination forces older workers out of their present jobs and makes it nearly impossible for them to find new employment. Difficulties associated with maintaining or finding new employment have become more prevalent with the massive downsizing of American corporations in the 1980s and 1990s. Older workers are likely to be offered early retirement, which neither meets their financial needs nor their needs for active involvement in larger society.

Nuessel (1982) reported some fascinating evidence concerning the language of ageism. For instance, what term or word is an acceptable designation for the group of individuals 65 years old and over? Should we use the term "senior citizen" or "mature American" or "golden ager" or "old man" or "old woman"? Nuessel prefers the term "elderly" because it is neutral and omits any suggestion of stereotypes. It is the suggestion that discrimination based on age is in our language that concerns many gerontologists. "Ageist terms are derogatory and demeaning because they depict the elderly as possessing largely undesirable traits and characteristics" (Nuessel, 1982, p. 273). Terms such as "bag," "coot," "goat," "granny," "old maid," "hag," "witch," and "senior citizen" are part of a list of ageist terms compiled by Nuessel. One measure of the overall negativity with which a group is held can be the sheer number of pejorative terms for that group. Each of these terms dehumanizes elderly people and serves to reinforce existing myths and stereotypes. The Sapir-Whorf hypothesis (Kay & Kempton, 1984; Sapir, 1951), now commonly accepted by communication scholars and linguists, argues that language creates our perceptions of reality. If we do not have a term for something, we are unlikely to see the phenomenon. The words that we have for something create the perceptions that we have of that entity. Thus, the words that we have for elderly people create our views of elderly people as "old bags" or "coots."

A common example of ageist language noticed by the authors of this book are the names given to nursing homes. A large phone directory of the state of Oklahoma lists Bethany Village, Fairview Manor, Golden Acres, Lackey Manor, and Windsor Gardens as full-care nursing facilities. Such pleasant names. Although it is not uncommon for any housing development to have an idyllic name, these names become particularly astonishing when considered in conjunction with most people's attitudes about life in a nursing home. Most people think that older individuals go into nursing homes to die, but nothing bad could ever happen in a community named "Golden Acres"! It should be pointed out that stereotyping includes not only negative stereotypes, but any preconception that is unidimensional and limiting. Even pleasant-sounding names can fit the criteria of stereotypical names.

RELATIONAL IMPLICATIONS OF ATTITUDES AND AGEISM

So far, a case has been presented that negative attitudes toward the aging process and ageism exist. The question still remains, however, whether these negative attitudes, which can produce ageist language, can also lead to discriminatory behavior in an elderly individual's relational world. Are ageist attitudes likely to influence interactions between young and elderly people or to somehow change the way elderly people interact among themselves (Kastenbaum & Durkee, 1964)? Research over the last decade, much of it conducted by communication scholars, shows that attitudes towards aging and elderly people have profound consequences for intergenerational interaction and the relationships of elderly individuals.

In an early research project, Levin and Levin (1981) addressed the question of whether young adults (male undergraduate students) were willing to interact with an "old person." They found that students were just as willing to attend a formal talk with a 25-year-old lecturer, a 50-year-old lecturer, and a 75-year-old lecturer. However, subjects were far less willing to attend an informal discussion and coffee hour with a 75-year-old lecturer than with either a 50-year-old or a 25-year-old lecturer. Additional analysis of the data indicated the relationship income level plays in willingness to interact with an "old person." The students became interested in attending the discussion and coffee hour with a 75-year-old lecturer when that person's level of income increased.

Much of the recent research conducted by communication scholars has been framed within Communication Accommodation Theory (Coupland, Coupland, Giles, & Henwood, 1988; Giles, Coupland, & Coupland, 1991; Ryan, Giles, Bartolucci, & Henwood, 1986). Communication Accommodation Theory (CAT) is an extension of Social Identity Theory, which claims that individuals define their social identity through the groups to which they belong. Individuals compare their own group's status in society to that of other groups, finding ways to bolster their self-esteem by identifying the positive aspects of their own group. When an individual meets another person, he or she identifies whether the other person is a member of the same group (in-group) or another group (out-group). If the other person is a member of a desirable out-group (i.e., of a more powerful social status), an individual is more likely to attempt to converge (i.e., become more like) the other person in speech style. If the other person is a member of a less desirable out-group, the individual is more likely to diverge (i.e., become less like) from the other person.

Communication Accommodation Theory has been applied to aging by identifying that one categorization made by individuals is whether or not the other person is an age peer or a member of a different age group. Individuals who are identified as members of the "old age" group, because of negative stereotypes of aging, are placed in an undesirable position in the interaction, and find that others diverge from them.

This process of using age as a group identifier has been most succinctly summarized by the Communication Predicament of Aging (CPA) model (Harwood, Giles, Fox, Ryan, & Williams, 1993; Ryan, et al., 1986). The CPA model proposes a spiraling effect of aging-related expectations, conversational experiences, and future expectations for interaction. Age-related cues (e.g., wrinkles and gray hair) activate expectations about the older person's communicative capabilities in interaction. Older individuals are believed to have more difficulty with both receptive (e.g., hearing, keeping track of what has been said, and asking for repetition) and expressive (e.g., talking too much, losing track of what is being said, and difficulty identifying words) communicative skills (Ryan, Kwong See, Meneer, & Trovato, 1994). These expectations lead the younger person to modify his or her speech in order to accommodate these presumed difficulties. As a result, the older person is constrained by these modifications, reinforcing expectations that older persons do indeed have difficulties in conversation. The younger person's assumptions that older people have difficulty conversing is reinforced, which increases their expectations of difficult interactions in the future, resulting in a generalized reluctance to enter into conversations with older individuals. The older person assumes that his or her communicative competence is indeed waning and, thus, experiences a reduction is self-esteem and may even begin to take on "elderly" behaviors, developing an "old" identity.

Research in this area reveals a variety of problems during intergenerational interactions, including both over- and underaccommodation. When a younger person encounters an older person and assumes that the older person has typical "elderly" problems in interaction (e.g., difficulty hearing, poor memory, and slow processing), the younger person may modify his or her speech, albeit with good intentions. The younger person may speak more loudly and slowly, use simpler sentences, and limit the topics of conversation. These speech modifications may also include a change in vocal register and the use of terms such as "dearie" or "good girl." This overaccommodation on the part of the younger person is seen as patronizing by most older individuals (Giles, Fox, & Smith, 1993; Harwood, et al., 1993; Ryan, Bourhis, & Knops, 1991). These patronizing messages implicitly question the competence of the older person.

The older person may begin to believe that his or her competence is impaired and will display these characteristics, termed "instant aging" (Giles, Fox, Harwood, & Williams, 1994). One can see how a spiraling effect can result. The young person expects the older person to act "elderly" and treats the older person likewise. The older person is constrained by the younger person's behavior and begins to act in ways supporting the negative stereotype. Both individuals expect their next encounter to be more fraught with difficulty, reinforcing negative expectations for future interaction.

Of course, older individuals can also patronize younger individuals, which is equally displeasing to the recipient. When young people report on the dissatisfying aspects of interaction with the elderly, one of the most common themes is being patronized through disapproval and overparenting (Giles & Williams, 1994). While neither party appreciates being patronized, they may both patronize their communicative partners, which leads to a competitive and dissatisfying cycle (Giles, et al., 1994).

Not only are intergenerational interactions hampered by overaccommodation in the form of patronization, but they are also hampered by underaccommodation. One of the most frequently reported forms of underaccommodation is painful self-disclosures. Uncertainty reduction theory (URT) suggests that when strangers meet, they will attempt to gather information from each other in order to reduce their uncertainty. One of the primary tenets of URT is that individuals will not reveal negative information too early in their relationship. Contrary to this prediction, older individuals in interactions with younger individuals often reveal very painful events from their lives (e.g., family bereavements and ongoing medical problems), even to complete strangers (Coupland & Coupland, 1990; Coupland, Coupland, & Giles, 1991). Sharing this difficult information is seen as underaccommodative on the part of the older person because the conversational topic is not attuned to the partner. These revelations leave the younger partner in an accommodative dilemma. One choice available to the younger person in these situations is to switch topics and discourage such further revelations, which appears to be either aggressive or dismissive. A second choice is to signal interest and involvement, encouraging further painful disclosures. The consequences of such an interaction may well lead the younger person to avoid contact not only with this particular older individual but with all older people. This further reduces the interactive world of older individuals.

There are several important implications from these lines of research. First, as the social distance between individuals decreases, young people may be less likely to enter into interaction with the elderly. In Levin and Levin's (1981) study, the discussion and coffee hour is a more intimate environment leading to closer interaction, as compared to the environment of a formal talk. This finding is similar to previous research done by Golde and Kagan (1959) and Long, Ziller, and Thompson (1966), who reported that young people were less willing to become close friends with an elderly individual than with someone younger.

A second important implication involves the greater importance of level of income over age when young people are asked about their willingness to interact with an "old person." Levin and Levin (1981) concluded that "wealth can overcome the social stigma of old age; willingness to associate with a wealthy person may not be affected by that person's age" (p. 214). It is a common myth in this society that old age equals poverty. Perhaps, in this society, which worships wealth above all else, the halo of being wealthy overshadows the stigma of being old and, therefore, poor. Indeed, money equals power.

Levin and Levin (1981) attributed the unwillingness to interact with elderly individuals to the negative attitudes we hold toward the aging process. They concluded that "the aged are a minority group against whom prejudice and discrimination have been directed" (p. 215). Certainly, the other studies reviewed in this section support this conclusion. Negative attitudes do affect the relational world of elderly people by decreasing the satisfaction derived from intergenerational encounters and reducing the number of encounters that occur.

Another way that the negative attitudes toward elderly people are manifested is in conversation. All messages contain both content and relational information. This relational dimension of the message not only serves to define the relationship between communicants, but also provides contextual information necessary to interpret the content of a message. While the content of patronizing speech may not always be negative in and of itself, the relational message that an individual is frail and incompetent has a tremendous impact on both parties.

Tuckman and Lorge (1953) and others suggested that a commonly held attitude is that elderly people are "failing in mental power." Studies in the developmental psychology literature suggest that such perceptions of cognitive inability are related to the intentional modification of message content (Blount,

1972; Broen, 1972; Cross, 1975; Shatz & Gelman, 1973; Snow, 1977) and the style in which a message is presented (Nussbaum, Robinson, & Grew, 1985). That is to say, it appears that when people have the attitude that the receiver of a message is cognitively simple, the message and the way the message is presented becomes simpler. Messages presented in a style that some authors suggest resembles "baby-talk without the nurturant dimension" (cf. Tamir, 1982) could result in decreased feelings of self-esteem and efficacy. Certainly such a conversation would be viewed as less than satisfying for both interactants, and it would also appear to have negative consequences for the elderly individual. The Communication Predicament of Aging model captures this process of a spiraling negative effect (Harwood, et al., 1993; Ryan, et al., 1986).

Additional evidence supporting the idea that ageism and negative attitudes affect the relational world of elderly people is provided by Nussbaum (1981) and Nuessel (1982). They pointed out that U.S. society often segregates elderly people into urban ghettos, so-called retirement communities, and into nursing homes, separated from the mainstream of daily activity. The labels given these environments make them sound utopian. In reality, "this misuse of language facilitates the segregation of the elderly ... where their isolation from our daily existence occurs without guilt or remorse" (Nuessel, 1982, p. 274).

Throughout this chapter on attitudes toward aging and the elderly, it has been demonstrated that people have, in general, negative stereotypical attitudes about elderly people. Individuals of all ages have been shown to hold attitudes that are inaccurate. For example, it is commonly thought that most elderly people are institutionalized in nursing homes or that many elderly individuals are senile. In actuality, only about 4 percent of elderly people are in nursing homes at any one time (Administration on Aging, 1998). Estimates of individuals suffering from severe dementia increase with age, ranging from less than 1% of the 60- to 70-year-old population to around 16% for those 85 and older (Gatz, Kasl-Godley, & Karel, 1996). Gatz et al. (1996) reported that if milder forms of dementia are included, the numbers for these same ages are about 1% and 24%. Other mental disorders, such as depression, anxiety disorders, and schizophrenia are less prevalent in the elderly population than in young adulthood and middle-age, affecting less than 5% of those 65 and older. These disorders generally reflect a lifelong history of problems and are not late-onset disorders (Gatz et al., 1996).

There are obviously many reasons why such attitudes exist. Even though many of these attitudes are not accurate reflections of reality, the reality that these attitudes exist must be confronted. Such attitudes exist because many people do not spend a significant amount of time with elderly people. In addition, healthy, vigorous elderly people are viewed as being younger than they are. In the same vein, younger unhealthy adults may be seen as being older than they actually are. The shifting of perceived age reinforces the notion that elderly people are unhealthy. Unrealistic mass media portrayals can also contribute to stereotypical attitudes. Finally, unpleasant personal experiences with elderly family members can play a role in the development of these negative attitudes.

It is one thing to observe that negative attitudes toward aging and elderly people exist, but it is quite another to suggest that such attitudes actually impact the lives of elderly people. Most research into attitudes toward the elderly has concentrated on describing common attitudes, the identification of other concerns that are related to these ageist attitudes, or both. In an excellent program of experimental research, however, Langer found that such attitudes do indeed decrease the quality of life for elderly people. Langer and Abelson (1974) found that, when people are assigned stereotypic labels (e.g., a mental patient), evaluations of that person's behavior are significantly altered by the label. In this study, the people watching a videotape of a "mental patient's" behavior described the "patient's" behavior as pathological. When the same tape was shown to a different audience, and the "patient" was described as a "job applicant," the person's behavior was described as well-adjusted.

Although this research did not deal with stereotyped behavior of elderly people, it does offer strong support for the idea that attitudes toward any group of people that are based on stereotypes are potentially devastating. Imagine how much the perceptual process must be disrupted for a "well-adjusted" individual to be considered "pathological."

Unfortunately, the effects of such attitudes based on stereotypes impact more than perceptions of behavior. Continuing this line of research, Langer and Benevento (1978) found that such labels help define the relationship between people during conversation and that these labels affect task performance. In this case, people were asked to perform a simple task and the results were recorded. These same people were then labeled as an "assistant" or a "boss" and were asked to repeat the task. It is interesting and significant to note that those people labeled "assistant" performed the task less successfully than those people labeled as "boss." In addition, those people labeled "assistants" performed the task about half as well as they had before they were stigmatized. The impact of such labeling makes it easier to understand how certain interaction styles might result in "instant aging" (Giles & Coupland, 1991).

Using this research as a model for investigating the impact on elderly people of being labeled in a negative stereotypical fashion, Langer (1983) reported that adults over the age of 25 are much more likely to evaluate an elderly individual as being senile than they are to evaluate a younger adult as being senile. In addition, the same behaviors exhibited by a young and old model are not evaluated similarly. When an older adult forgets something, the behavior is evaluated much more negatively than when a younger adult forgets something. It seems from the data reported by Langer (1983) that elderly people evaluate other older adults more positively than do younger adults. However, those same older adults rate the negative features of aging (e.g., forgetfulness, sickness, mental incompetence, and physical incapacity) more negatively than do younger adults.

Research into the effects of ageist labeling in a health care setting will be more fully discussed in chapter 12, but suffice it to say that physicians and health care professionals hold quite negative attitudes toward elderly patients (cf. Miller, Lowenstein, & Winston, 1976). The data suggest that the health care of elderly people suffers from such stereotyping, and in many ways the factors contributing to the creation and maintenance of such attitudes are prevalent in the health care community.

In addition to negative labeling impacting the quality of health care that the elderly individual receives, such attitudes also impact interpersonal interaction. Langer (1983) points out that these attitudes result in less positive evaluations of the self by elderly people. Such attitudes inhibit their performance on tasks and decrease their perceptions of environmental control. Although Langer (1983) pointed out that on an individual level some changes can be made, social change on a much larger scale is necessary to improve the quality of life for elderly people. These attitudes, then, must not be viewed as something that is inconvenient or inconsiderate, but rather as something that significantly affects the quality of life for elderly people. Such negative attitudes work as a self-fulfilling prophecy.

Perhaps even more important is whether negative attitudes toward the aging process and the ageist society that these attitudes produce hamper in any way the ability of the elderly to successfully deal with growing older. If younger individuals do not wish to become part of the relational world of elderly people, who suffers? It can be argued that, in the short run, elderly people suffer. They lose contact with the changing world, begin to stagnate, eventually believe they are useless, and simply die. In the long run, however, it is youth who will suffer, for one day, they too will face the "shame" of being old. Additionally, the richness and diversity of life experiences are diminished for all.

SUMMARY

Attitudes are likes and dislikes, which often lead to prejudice and discrimination. Most of the literature over the past 60 years examines the existence of widespread negative attitudes toward the aging process. Although more recent investigations support the contention that attitudes toward the aging process are becoming more positive, these attitudes are still predominantly negative. These attitudes have led to an ageist society. This ageism can be found in the everyday language we use to refer to elderly people. Of more importance, however, is the effect that negative attitudes have on the relational world of elderly people. Studies have shown, for instance, that young people are sometimes unwilling to interact with elderly individuals. The result of these negative attitudes and ageism is the creation and maintenance of a minority group of elderly people against whom prejudice and discrimination are directed.

■ REFERENCES

Administration on Aging. (1998). *Profile of Older Americans 1998* [On-line]. Available: *http://www.aoa.dhhs.gov/aoa/stats*

Al-Deen, H. S. N. (1997a). Introduction. In H. S. N. Al-Deen (Ed.), *Cross-cultural communication and aging in the United States* (p. 65). Mahwah, NJ: Lawrence Erlbaum Associates.

Al-Deen, H. S. N. (1997b). Trends in cross-generational communication among Arab Americans. In H. S. N. Al-Deen (Ed.), *Cross-cultural communication and aging in the United States* (pp. 83–96). Mahwah, NJ: Lawrence Erlbaum Associates.

Atchley, R. C. (1980). *The social forces in later life.* Belmont, CA: Wadsworth.

Austin, D. R. (1985). Attitudes toward old age: A hierarchical study. *The Gerontologist, 45,* 431–434.

Bennett, R., & Eckman, J. (1973). Attitudes toward aging. In C. Eisdorfer & P. Lawton (Eds.), *The psychology of adult development and aging* (pp. 575–597). Washington, DC: The American Psychological Association.

Blount, B. G. (1972). Parental speech and language acquisition: Some Luo and Samoan examples. *Anthropological Linguistics, 14,* 119–130.

Botwinick, J. (1984). *Aging and behavior* (3rd. ed.). New York: Springer.

Broen, P. A. (1972). The verbal environment of the language-hearing child. *American Speech and Hearing Association Monograph, 17.*

Butler, R. (1969). Ageism: Another form of bigotry. *The Gerontologist, 9,* 243–246.

Coupland, N., & Coupland, J. (1990). Language and later life. In H. Giles & W. P. Robinson (Eds.) *The handbook of language and social psychology* (pp. 451–470). Chichester, England: Wiley.

Coupland, N., Coupland, J., & Giles, H. (1991). *Language, society and the elderly.* Oxford, England: Basil Blackwell.

Coupland, N., Coupland, J., Giles, H., & Henwood, K. (1988). Accommodating the elderly: Invoking and extending a theory. *Language in Society, 17,* 1–41.

Cross, T. G. (1975). Some relations between mothers and linguistic level in accelerated children. *Papers and Reports on Child Language Development, 10,* 117–135.

Dinkel, R. (1944). Attitudes of children toward supporting aged parents. *American Sociological Review, 9,* 370–379.

Fox, S., & Giles, H. (1993). Accommodating intergenerational contact: A critique and theoretical model. *Journal of Aging Studies, 7,* 423–451.

Gatz, M., Kasl-Godley, J. E., & Karel, M. J. (1996). Aging and mental disorders. In J. E. Birren & K. W. Schaie (Eds.), *Handbook of psychology and aging* (4th ed., pp. 365–382). San Diego, CA: Academic Press

Giles, H., Coupland, J., & Coupland, N. (Eds.). (1991). *Contexts of accommodation: Developments in applied sociolinguistics.* Cambridge, England: Cambridge University Press.

Giles, H., & Coupland, N. (1991). Language attitudes: Discursive, contextual and gerontological considerations. In A. G. Reynolds (Ed.), *Bilingualism, multiculturalism, and second language learning.* Hillsdale, NJ: Lawrence Erlbaum Associates.

Giles, H., Fox, S., Harwood, J., & Williams, A. (1994). Talking age and aging talk: Communicating through the life-span. In M. L. Hummert, J. M. Wiemann, & J. F. Nussbaum (Eds.), *Interpersonal communication in older adulthood: Interdisciplinary theory and research* (pp. 130–161). Newbury Park, CA: Sage.

Giles, H., Fox, S., & Smith, E. (1993). Patronizing the elderly: Intergenerational evaluations. *Research on Language and Social Interaction, 26,* 129–149.

Giles, H., & Williams, A. (1994). Patronizing the young: Forms and evaluations. *International Journal of Aging and Human Development, 39,* 33–53.

Golde, P., & Kagan, N. E. (1959). A sentence completion procedure for assessing attitudes toward old people. *Journal of Gerontology, 14,* 355–363.

Harwood, J., Giles, H., Fox, S. Ryan, E. B., & Williams, A. (1993). Patronizing young and elderly adults: Response strategies in a community setting. *Journal of Applied Communication Research, 21,* 211–226.

Hummert, M. L. (1994). Stereotypes of the elderly and patronizing speech. In M. L. Hummert, J. M. Wiemann, & J. F. Nussbaum (Eds.), *Interpersonal communication in older adulthood: Interdisciplinary theory and research* (pp. 162–184). Newbury Park, CA: Sage.

Hummert, M. L., Garstka, T., A., Shaner, J. L., & Strahm, S. (1994). Stereotypes of the elderly held by young, middle-aged and elderly adults. *Journal of Gerontology: Psychological Sciences, 49,* 240–249.

Hummert, M. L., Shaner, J. L., & Garstka, T. A. (1995). Cognitive processes affecting communication with older adults: The case for stereotypes, attitudes, and beliefs about communication. In J. F. Nussbaum & J. Coupland (Eds.), *Handbook of communication and aging research* (pp. 105–131). Mahwah, NJ: Lawrence Erlbaum Associates.

Kalbfleisch, P. J., & Anderson, A. (1997). Mentoring across generations: Culture, family, and mentoring relationships. In H. S. N. Al-Deen (Ed.), *Cross-cultural communication and aging in the United States* (pp. 97–118). Mahwah, NJ: Lawrence Erlbaum Associates.

Kastenbaum, R. (1964). *New thoughts on old age.* New York: Springer.

Kastenbaum, R., & Durkee, N. (1964). Young people view old age. In R. Kastenbaum (Ed.), *New thoughts on old age* (pp. 237–249). New York: Springer.

Kay, P., & Kempton, W. (1984). What is the Sapir-Whorf hypothesis? *American Anthropologist, 86,* 65–79.

Kimoto, D. M. (1997). Pidgin to da max: A bridge toward satisfying cross-generational communication among the Hawaiians. In H. S. N. Al-Deen (Ed.), *Cross-cultural communication and aging in the United States* (pp. 67–81). Mahwah, NJ: Lawrence Erlbaum Associates.

Langer, E. (1983). *The psychology of control.* Beverly Hills, CA: Sage.

Langer, E., & Abelson, R. (1974). A patient by any other name ... : Clinician group differences in labeling bias. *Journal of Consulting and Clinical Psychology, 42,* 4–9.

Langer, E., & Benevento, A. (1978). Self-induced dependence. *Journal of Personality and Social Psychology, 36,* 886–893.

Levin, J., & Levin, W. C. (1981). Willingness to interact with an old person. *Research on Aging, 3,* 211–217.

Long, B. H., Ziller, R. C., & Thompson, E. E. (1966). A comparison of prejudices: The effects upon friendship ratings of chronic illness, old age, education and race. *Journal of Social Psychology, 70,* 101–109.

Miller, D., Lowenstein, R., & Winston, R. (1976). Physicians' attitudes toward the ill, aged, and nursing homes. *Journal of American Geriatric Society, 24,* 498–505.

Morris, W. (Ed.). (1979). *The American heritage dictionary of the English language.* Boston: Houghton Mifflin.

Nuessel, F. H. (1982). The language of ageism. *The Gerontologist, 22,* 273–276.

Nussbaum, J. F. (1981). *Interactional patterns of elderly individuals: Implications for successful adaptation to aging.* Unpublished doctoral dissertation, Purdue University, West Lafayette, IN.

Nussbaum, J., Robinson, J., & Grew, D. (1985). Communicative behavior of the long-term health care employee: Implications for the elderly resident. *Communication Research Reports, 2,* 16–22.

Palmore, E. B. (1982). Attitudes toward the aged: What we know and need to know. *Research on Aging, 4,* 333–348.

Ryan, E. B., & Bourhis, R. Y., & Knops, U. (1991). Evaluative perceptions of patronizing speech addressed to elders. *Psychology and Aging, 6,* 442–450.

Ryan, E. B., Giles, H., Bartolucci, G., & Henwood, K. (1986). Psycholinguistic and social psychological components of communication by and with the elderly. *Language and Communication, 6*, 1–24.

Ryan, E. B., Kwong See, S., Meneer, W. B., & Trovato, D. (1994). Age-based perceptions of language performance among younger and older adults. *Communication Research, 19*, 311–331.

Sapir, E. (1951). The status of linguistics as a science. In D. Mandelbaum (Ed.), *Selected writings of Edward Sapir* (p. 160). Berkeley, CA: University of California Press.

Schonfield, D. (1982). Who is stereotyping whom and why? *The Gerontologist, 22*, 267–272.

Shatz, M., & Gelman, R. (1973). The development of communication skills: Modifications in the speech of young children as a function of listener. *Monographs of the Society for Research on Child Development, 38* (5, Serial No.152).

Slater, P. E. (1964). Cross-cultural views of the aged. In R. Kastenbaum (Ed.), *New thoughts on old age* (pp. 229–236). New York: Springer.

Snow, C. E. (1977). Mother's speech research: From input to interaction. In C. Snow & C. Ferguson (Eds.), *Talking to children* (pp. 31–49). New York: Cambridge University Press.

Tamir, L. (1982). *Communication and the aging process: Interaction through the life cycle.* New York: Pergamon.

Tibbitts, C. (1979). Can we invalidate negative stereotypes in aging? *The Gerontologist, 19*, 10–20.

Tuckman, F., & Lorge, I. (1953). Attitudes toward old people. *Journal of Social Psychology, 37*, 249–260.

CHAPTER 3

Relational Considerations

T he relational implications of communication as people age are discussed in subsequent chapters. There are some communicative issues, however, that do not fit neatly into any of the traditional headings and that, although important, have not yet been the subject of much research. These include issues such as reminiscence, the communication of intimacy, communicative competence, interactional control, confirmation versus disconfirmation, and helping and loneliness. These issues have implications for all kinds of relationships—marriage, family, friendship, and others—but are not unique to any. This chapter focuses on these issues, which we call relational considerations. Consistent with a communication perspective, these issues all focus on the *dyad* as the unit of analysis, not the individual. An individual can talk to himself or herself, but an individual cannot communicate alone. A person can only *participate* in communication with another person.

REMINISCENCE

We begin this discussion by focusing on reminiscence—a topic that has been the subject of more research among the elderly than all the other topics discussed in this chapter combined. Although reminiscence per se is primarily a communicative activity, it has been a favorite subject of research by gerontologists coming from a number of different fields—psychology, sociology, and social work, among others.

Reminiscence typically refers to the act of recalling events that happened long ago. Such recall can, of course, occur simply in one's mind, or it can occur in writing or in conversation with others. Our primary concern here is reminiscence as a communicative activity, occurring in conversation with others.

Interest in the social sciences in this activity stems originally from the work of Butler, who first described the importance of the life review. Butler (1968) argued that the life review was not necessarily the same as reminiscence because one can review one's life by oneself. Some work, discussed in what follows, indicates that life review done in solitude can be depressing. Such a depressing effect is less likely when reminiscing with others.

The act of reminiscence can take several forms. Lo Gerfo (1980) described three types of reminiscence: informative, evaluative, and obsessive. Informative reminiscence "involves recollection for the pleasure of reliving and retelling ... [and] can be used to revive interest, self-esteem, and personal relationships" (p. 39). Evaluative reminiscence is more similar to Butler's life review; the range of memories recalled is broader, and, Lo Gerfo suggested, it is more helpful when this kind of reminiscence is shared with others. Obsessive reminiscence, however, results from guilt, stress, or grief.

Historical Overview

Reminiscence has, since ancient times, been associated with old age (Kaminsky, 1984b). It has been argued that attitudes toward reminiscence are indicative of attitudes toward elderly people. In earlier times, elderly people occupied positions of power and dignity because their memories provided the transmission of culture. With the onset of printing, memory became less important because it was seen as being unreliable. Kaminsky (1984b) argued that this is an important factor leading to the devaluation of elderly people.

Attitudes toward reminiscence (and toward elderly people) have typically been rather negative in dominant Western cultures (Moody, 1984). Even the attitudes of professionals working with elderly people—social workers, psychiatrists, psychologists, and counselors—have been negative (Moody, 1984).

Reminiscence is seen as a tiresome self-indulgence. The attitudes of professionals have begun to change since Butler's work on the life review, however; they now acknowledge many of the positive effects of reminiscence.

Pervasiveness of Reminiscence

Tamir (1979) argued that reminiscing dominates the conversation of elderly people. It is associated with the kinds of recall patterns that are observed in older people. Belsky (1984), however, cited other research that indicated that older people do not think about the past an inordinate amount of the time. Findings on this topic seem to depend on how the variable is measured.

Topics of Reminiscence

The topics of reminiscences were studied by Unruh (1983). He found that reminiscences are unpredictable and spontaneous—they are situationally controlled. Those who are more alone now recall past social involvements more. The focus of recollection is usually the family, although the work environment also comes up frequently. Research by Riegel (1972) demonstrated that elderly people recall more about their distant past, whereas younger people think more about the recent past, the present, and the future. Revere and Tobin (1980) concluded that elderly people are more involved in the past than are younger people, and that elderly people have a tendency to mythologize figures from their past.

Reasons for Reminiscing

There are many reasons for reminiscing. Reminiscence can be viewed as a coping mechanism, as art, or as identity management, as well as serving several other functions. Butler (1974; 1980) argued that reminiscence or the life review is a coping mechanism that usually focuses on unresolved conflicts and fears. It apparently helps one cope with the fear of death, with grief and depression, and with a loss of self-identity and self-esteem (McMahon & Rhudick, 1964). Kaminsky (1984b), however, cited instances in which reminiscence is associated with the denial of aging. Portnoy (1997) argued that reminiscence is useful as a coping strategy because individuals can recall times in the past when they have successfully adapted to changes. Sharing successful past coping not only leads to the reinforcement of ego integrity, but can stimulate the recaller to apply these strategies to the present as well.

Researchers also discussed the importance of reminiscing in literature and the arts (Kaminsky, 1984a; Moody, 1984), citing such examples as the writings of Mark Twain, Homer, and Virgil. Without reminiscences our culture would be much poorer.

Unruh (1983) found that recollections usually reveal identity in some way—the recallers try to recreate their identity because it is no longer immediately apparent in old age. Less-elderly people focus on the recent past; very old people focus on the distant past. Older elderly individuals have to reach further back in memory to find times during which they were valued.

As mentioned earlier, the life review is used to help one prepare for oncoming death (Butler, 1968). It also has other uses, however. Reminiscence helps one defend one's self-esteem and beliefs (Priefer & Gambert, 1984; Tamir, 1979), feel loved (Becker, Blumfield, & Gordon, 1984), gain self-awareness and self-understanding (Kiernat, 1983; Tamir, 1979), disengage from society (Kaminsky, 1984b), adapt to stress (Priefer & Gambert, 1984), and see one's part in the larger historical and cultural context (Kaminsky, 1984b).

Research generally indicates that reminiscing does, in fact, accomplish many of the purposes just mentioned. The therapeutic value of reminiscing has been well documented (Baum, 1980; Belsky, 1984; Perrotta & Meacham, 1981; Sable, 1984). Butler (1968) argued that the life review leads to candor, serenity, and wisdom. Other research indicated that reminiscing leads to the establishment of group cohesiveness (Lesser, Lazarus, Frankel, & Harasy, 1981), intimacy (Gardella, 1985), feelings of self-worth (Baker, 1985; Perschbacher, 1984), and life satisfaction (Haight & Bahr, 1984). There is also empirical support for Butler's claim that life review decreases one's denial of death (Georgemiller & Maloney, 1984).

Buchanan and Middleton (Buchanan & Middleton, 1990, 1993; Middleton, Buchanan, & Suurmond, 1991), working with reminiscence groups of elderly people in the United Kingdom, report that older people accomplish several important interactional tasks. Through reminiscence, they can maintain and reestablish their individual and social identities. Reminiscing allows them to account for diminishing abilities related with aging. By sharing their experiences out loud, individuals deal with dislocation and loss. In addition, Buchanan and Middleton (1993) argued that what the elders are accomplishing through reminiscence is not just a phase of life or mere adaptation to the aging process, but social action through which participants define for themselves and those around them what "reminiscence" and "old age" represent.

In medicine, Harris and Harris (1980) concluded that oral history techniques enable the physician to gather more insightful information about patients. In addition, Bramwell (1984) advocated life-review techniques for nurses. She found that they are not only helpful in diagnosis, but also serve as a "vehicle for expansion of consciousness and thus promotion of health" (p. 37) in patients.

Reminiscence can also have broader effects, as is indicated by Perschbacher's (1984) finding that encouraging elderly people to reminisce in an educational setting with children leads to more community understanding. And many have pointed out that reminiscing provides a historical contribution (Becker, Blumfied, & Gordon, 1984) and facilitates the handing down of culture (Kaminsky, 1984c).

It appears, then, that reminiscence is an activity with generally positive effects that should be encouraged rather than discouraged. Belsky (1984) reminded researchers that reminiscence can be brought about by asking questions of elderly people. In order to be successful, of course, one must also listen to the answers to these questions.

Negative Consequences of Reminiscing

Not all of the consequences of reminiscing are positive. Some authors argued that the negative consequences of reminiscence can include depression, guilt, and a sense of inner panic (Tamir, 1979). Evidence seems to indicate that these negative effects are most likely if reminiscing is done in solitude (Butler, 1968).

One study found that unsuccessful reminiscence may be associated with unsuccessful and pathological mourning—an inability to deal with loss and grief (Evans, Millicovsky, & Tennison, 1984). For some people, the uncovering of certain memories may be painful or difficult, and may require the assistance of a therapist (Priefer & Gambert, 1984). Sherman (1985) suggested a phenomenological approach to reminiscence to overcome these problems. His approach emphasizes experiencing memories beyond the range of simple recall of external details, particularly recalling the feelings and meanings for the person. He argues that this allows people to review their lives without becoming overwhelmed by feelings of anxiety or depression. Brink (1985), however, found no impact of reminiscing on depression.

The life review, then, can serve some useful functions if approached with care. One study even indicated that reminiscing in a group can facilitate the development of intimacy. Because intimate relationships are an important part of all of our lives, we turn now to this topic.

COMMUNICATION OF INTIMACY

The notion of intimacy is frequently linked to sexual relationships, but actual intimacy, of course, is not limited to relationships involving sex. Traupmann, Eckels, and Hatfield (1982) articulated the multidimensional nature of intimacy, especially for older women. Intimacy includes mutual trust, support, understanding, and the sharing of confidences. Traupmann and his colleagues found that satisfaction with an intimate relationship is related to life satisfaction and psychological well-being and that contentment with an intimate relationship is associated with companionate love, passionate love, and sexual satisfaction. In a related study, Lowenthal and Haven (1968) found that one intimate stable relationship is more closely associated with high morale than are overall high levels of social interaction.

Intimacy is essential for self-esteem and emotional health (Genevay, 1986). Intimacy seems to be rare for elderly people, however. Consistent with the relational perspective we advocate in this book, Genevay argued that reminiscing with another person can bring about intimacy. More specifically, confronting the past, speaking the unspeakable, acknowledging difficulty, and talking about death can lead to the development of an intimate relationship. Discussing such intimate issues leads to relationships between people because relationships are created through communication.

Sexuality in Intimate Relationships

Although sexuality is only one dimension of intimacy, it is a dimension that is problematic for many elderly individuals. Sexual intercourse per se is, of course, only one part of sexuality. Dailey (1981) suggested that sexuality includes sensuality, intimacy, identity, reproduction, and sexualization (the use of sexuality to influence the behavior or attitudes of others). Dailey also pointed out the importance of fantasy and memories to sex, and mentions "skin hunger" or the desire for physical contact as a part of sensuality.

There are many myths about sex and elderly people (Dailey, 1981). These myths, and the distortions associated with them, are brought about by a lack of communication about sex and elderly people in U.S. society (Dailey, 1981). When Americans do talk about sex and elderly people, it is usually to joke about the topic—the "laughter curtain" (Dailey, 1981, p. 313). This laughter curtain occurs even in interaction between elderly people and health care providers, and it results in the questions that are asked by elderly people going unanswered. Sometimes this can exacerbate sexual problems.

Jokes about sex and elderly people are based on many stereotypes. There are stereotypes about asexual and about hypersexual elderly people (e.g., the "dirty old man"). The release in 1998 of the potency drug Viagra provided comedians new fodder for jokes about this issue. Belsky (1984) pointed out, however, that *any* stereotype is limiting. Generally, there is a taboo against sex in old age—not just against discussing it, but against engaging in it (Pfeiffer, 1977). There are still feelings that sex is for procreation, something that is not relevant to most older individuals. Negative social attitudes toward sexuality in elderly people lead to problems like premature impotence, frustration, self-deprecation, and loneliness (Sviland, 1981). Further, loneliness and feelings of being unattractive are likely to bring about depression. Sviland (1981) added that adult children and nursing homes are frequently the worst offenders—they discourage healthy sexuality in elderly people.

Researchers have observed some changes in these attitudes, however. Arluke, Levin, and Suchwalko (1984), for instance, examined advice books for elderly people and found more encouragement for sexual activity than had been discovered in the past. These books still provided little support for remarriage and dating, however, and one must wonder about the options left for sexual fulfillment if remarriage and dating are ruled out.

Sexual Behavior of Elderly People

When discussing sexual behavior in elderly people, it is important to distinguish between the genders. Men and women respond differently to sexuality during the aging process. First of all, Belsky (1984) points out that women are seen as less sexually attractive with increasing age, whereas men become more sexually attractive with age (until retirement). This is because a man's sexual attractiveness is based in part on his position in society, his status. With retirement, however, much of this status is lost.

Sexual drives or interest are also different for older men as compared with older women. Overall, sexual interest declines somewhat with increasing age (Newman & Nichols, 1970), although interest still exists and shows continuity. Those with the strongest interest when they were younger also report the strongest interest when they are older. Continuity is greater for women than it is for men (Garza & Dressel, 1983). Generally, sexual interest is higher in older men than it is in older women (Verwoerdt, Pfeiffer, & Wang, 1970). Sexual activity, however, declines more rapidly than does sexual interest (Huyck, 1994). There is also some guilt caused by sexual feelings in older people (Newman & Nichols, 1970).

Nonetheless, sexual activity does occur in relationships involving elderly people (Ludeman, 1981). Masters and Johnson's (1968) studies on sexuality included fairly small samples of elderly people, but they indicated that sexual activity frequently continues into the 70s. With occasional exceptions, there is little sexual activity over the age of 75 (Newman & Nichols, 1970). The Duke University studies indicated that one half of elderly women remain sexually active through their 60s and one half of married men remain active through their mid-70s (Palmore, 1981). Women appear to end sexual activity at a younger age than do men because they typically marry older men and stop engaging in sex when their husbands do (Pfeiffer, 1977).

Physiological arousal changes somewhat with increasing age, although older people still become aroused and enjoy sex. Masters and Johnson (1968) reported that older men are slower to be aroused, to develop erections, to effect intromission, and to ejaculate. This could, of course, have some positive consequences for their sexual partners because older women, while a little slower to become aroused than younger women, are not slower to orgasm. There are some physiological changes accompanying menopause that may affect sexual enjoyment in women, including hormonal and steroid changes. Psychological changes, however, are usually greater than the physiological ones. For some women, the inability to become pregnant leads to cessation of sexual activity, but for others it leads to a feeling of relief and increased sexual interest and activity—almost a second honeymoon. Masters and Johnson pointed out that if a woman has had a bad sex life all along, it will likely get worse with menopause. This, of course, is consistent with continuity theory. Regular sexual activity seems to lead to more "young-like" responses (Belsky, 1984).

Although the frequency of sexual activity declines with age, enjoyment of sex does not (Dailey, 1981). Some of the reasons for decreased sexual responsiveness in men have been delineated by Masters and Johnson (1968):

1. Monotony in the sexual relationship.
2. Preoccupation with career or economic pursuits.
3. Mental or physical fatigue.
4. Overindulgence in food or drink.
5. Physical or mental infirmities in the man or in his spouse.
6. Fear of inability to perform.

Generally, Masters and Johnson argue that the environmental impacts are much greater than are the physiological effects of aging. Sviland (1981) concurs, emphasizing that worries over sexual failure frequently lead to secondary impotence in older men.

Several other variables can also influence sexual activity in older individuals. One of these is religious devoutness, which is inversely related to sexual frequency (Garza & Dressel, 1983). Religious devoutness can even mitigate the relationship that otherwise exists between marital status and sexual activity. In one study, 7% of people 60 to 90 years old who were widowed, single, or divorced were sexually active, while 54% of the married respondents were still sexually active (Newman & Nichols, 1970). Other research, however, is not completely consistent with these findings. Pfeiffer (1977) found large differences between married and single women in sexual activity, but no significant differences between married and single men. Verwoerdt, et al. (1970) also reported that marital status had little effect on sexual activity or interest in men. Unmarried men seem to find sex anyway, but unmarried women do not. Note, however, that these data are over 30 years old; current social conditions may yield different findings.

Another important factor influencing sexual activity is health (Newman & Nichols, 1970). This is particularly true in the case of men, who may suffer from erectile dysfunction due to hypertension, diabetes, spinal cord injury, or prostate surgery (Federal Drug Administration, 1999). The drug Viagra (sildenafil) was released to address problems related to erectile dysfunction (Federal Drug Administration, 1999). The severity and importance of this problem might be indicated by the fact that over 6 million prescriptions were written, many of which were to older men, for Viagra in 1998 alone. Illness-related barriers to sexual activity may to some extent be overcome through these types of medications. Belsky (1984) cited research indicating, however, that medication, including frequently prescribed medications used to treat hypertension and diabetes, can affect sexual activity, as can feeling sick or fear of heart attacks. She also noted that there are few documented cases of heart attack and death actually occurring during sex. Apparently, the fear of heart attack during sex is more of a problem than is the reality, however, reports of a few men suffering fatal heart attacks while taking Viagra has led the Federal Drug Administration (FDA) (1999) to modify prescription standards warning against prescribing this drug for men who have cardiovascular disease. Although health-related problems may lead to a decrease in sexual activity, subjective ratings of illness correlate more highly with sexual interest and activity than do objective ratings (Belsky, 1984). The importance of sexual activity for elderly people is reflected in the Duke University studies, which indicate that good health can be a *consequence* of sexual relations as well as a cause (Palmore, 1981).

One additional variable was mentioned by researchers as a factor that can influence sexual activity: privacy. Sex requires some privacy, and privacy may be denied many older people—especially those living in nursing homes or with children (Pfeiffer, 1977).

As has been implicit in parts of this discussion, much of the responsibility for sexual activity rests with men. Research indicates that both men and women report that the man is usually responsible for either continuing or ending sex in a relationship (Pfeiffer, Verwoerdt, & Wang, 1970).

Consequences of Sexual Activity

The Duke University studies indicated higher life satisfaction as a result of sexual activity in both men and women (Palmore, 1981). Marital happiness, however, does not really seem to be dependent on sexual activity. Apparently, in marital relationships without sexual activity, there is the compensation of more emotional intimacy, as expressed by sitting and lying close to-gether, touching, holding hands, confiding, and a lot of giving and taking (Garza & Dressel, 1983). Garza and Dressel also cited data indicating that the severity of marital problems is closely related to the severity of sexual problems, but this is less so in el-derly people.

Some research has linked depression to lack of sexual expres-sion (Sviland, 1981). Weiner and White (1982) agreed, and they argued that depression represents a loss of self, whereas sexual expression represents an affirmation of self.

From another perspective, it might be argued that too much emphasis on sexual activity for elderly people could lead to de-pression if the activity is not forthcoming. For many older women this is a strong possibility, if for no other reason than the shortage of partners. Thomas (1982) suggests that it might be more profitable if one uses as an analogy for sexual activity in elderly people the idea that it is "popcorn," instead of an "es-sential vitamin." There may be some merit in this more light-hearted view of sex.

Unfortunately, no research has examined how, or even if, older couples discuss declining sexual activity (Mares & Fitzpatrick, 1995). This lack of research extends to whether or how discussions about changing interest and activity affect overall marital satisfaction. One can only speculate that couples who have openly discussed their sexual expression of intimacy in younger years will continue to do so in their older years.

Homosexuality

A discussion of sexuality in any age group would be incomplete without some mention of homosexuality. There are just as many older gay men and lesbians as there are younger gay men and lesbians, even though the current cohort of older people is less open about their homosexuality (Huyck, 1994). In fact, many older lesbians were previously in a heterosexual relationship and entered into homosexual relationships after fulfilling soci-etal expectations to get married and have children (Huyck, 1994). About half of older gay men and three-fourths of older lesbians consider themselves to be in a relationship (Peplau & Cochran, 1990).

Older homosexual couples report levels of relational satis-faction and love comparable to those of heterosexual couples (Peplau & Cochran, 1990). However, homosexual couples also report little legal and social support for their relationships and varying levels of familial support (Dynes, 1990; Peplau & Cochran, 1990). In addition, they struggle with special problems arising in later life related to difficulties with inheritance, being open with health care providers, and receiving support for bereavement when a partner is lost (Kimmel, 1990).

Lipman (1986) wrote that homosexuality is not just a sexual orientation, but a life style. And he stated that gender is a more important determinant of behavior than is sexual orientation. For instance, lesbians typically emphasize love and relationships, whereas gay men do not. There is generally more role flexibility in homosexual relationships than in heterosexual relationships. Homosexual relationships involving older people are characterized by achieving security, a more future-oriented perspective of the relationship, reaffirming the partnership, and remembering. Generally, older gay men are more content with life than are younger gay men. Friendships can be more important than familial relationships, especially if the gay man has not "come out" or if he receives negative reactions from his family. Gay men and lesbians tend to have more friends than do heterosexual people. Their closest friends are other homosexual people. Older gay men and lesbians in long-term relationships are happier and better adjusted than are those who are not in these relationships.

Sexuality, then, is a part of intimacy for older people, homosexual or heterosexual, just as it is for younger people. But it is not the only aspect of intimate relationships. One determinant of relationship intimacy development is communicative ability—the topic to which we now turn.

COMMUNICATIVE COMPETENCE

In most ways, of course, the communication of older people is the same as the communication of younger people. However, there are a few ways in which the communication of older people is unique, and these characteristics may affect intergenerational interaction.

For instance, there is evidence that elderly people are a bit more cautious in their communication than are younger people (Botwinick, 1973). Older people desire greater certainty, and they are more reluctant to suggest courses of action. They are more likely than younger people to say "I don't know" or to express no opinion about issues.

Elderly people may also take longer to react during conversation (Ryan, Kwong See, Meneer, & Trovato, 1994; Tamir, 1979). Information processing changes somewhat with age, which may affect communication. One study found that sentence-comprehension abilities decrease throughout the life span (Feier & Gerstman, 1980). Elderly people not only make more mistakes in sentence comprehension, but the mistakes are of a more serious nature. Tamir (1979) also points out that elderly people may have difficulty asking appropriate or strategic questions, or synthesizing information. When elderly people do express opinions, their verbalizations tend to be more dogmatic and idiosyncratic, and somewhat less sensitive. But longitudinal studies do not show increasing rigidity with age, as is commonly believed.

Tamir argued that some of these changes may be a result of elderly people having less need for verbal skills because their world has become so restricted. They no longer find themselves in situations where adaptation is important because they are more likely to be interacting with the same people day after day.

Welford (1983) concurred with this idea. Welford also, however, argued that there are some factors that make social skills even more important for elderly people than for younger people. These include dependency upon others and reduced mobility, which means they must leave the initiation of contacts to others. People are not likely to visit those who are unattractive in conversation. Physiological factors, such as loss of hearing or memory loss, can make communication more difficult and create more of a need for compensatory social skills. And living in close proximity to others, which occurs in many residential facilities or when older people are living with adult offspring, leads to a need for effective interaction.

Much of Ryan's (Harwood, Giles, Fox, Ryan, & Williams, 1993; Ryan, Giles, Bartolucci, & Henwood, 1986; Ryan, et al., 1994) work (as discussed in chap. 2) focused on the expectations that people of all ages have for older individuals' abilities in interaction. She reported a mixed bag of expectations—from problems with hearing and memory to telling more interesting stories and being more sincere. When individuals, old and young alike, bring certain expectations to their interactions, these expectations can influence not only the content of the interaction, but even whether an interaction will take place.

Communication skills, then, appear to be important for elderly people on many levels. Welford (1983) provided some suggestions to professionals for social skills training for elderly people. Zaks and Labouvie-Vief (1980) actually tested a method of training elderly people in perspective taking and communication skills. They found significant improvement as a result of their training program. A related study found that training can also improve empathic abilities in elderly people (Isquick, 1981).

One study of communicative behavior in elderly people examined such things as greeting behavior (Marn & Bennett, 1972); this study found that appropriateness of greeting behavior is an indication of social adjustment in a nursing home. In another nursing home study, Schroeder (1986) concluded that complaining by elderly residents is both expected and acceptable; indeed, it is seen as a positive sign by the nursing home staff.

Finally, two studies focused on the relationship between communication and life satisfaction. Nussbaum (1983a, 1983b) found a relationship between the network of closeness of communication in elderly people and reported life satisfaction. These close relationships allow for more self-disclosure. Consistent with this, he concluded that conversational content co-varies with life satisfaction. Elderly individuals who report high levels of satisfaction, happiness, and zest for life report discussing world and national events, topics that show less preoccupation with self, whereas those with low levels of these characteristics do not report discussing these topics. Those living in their own home or in retirement villages discuss these topics, as well as community affairs, more than do those in nursing homes. Communication, then, not only creates relationships, it also affects our feelings about life.

INTERACTIONAL CONTROL

One of the ways in which communication creates relationships is through *interactional control patterns*. The notion of interactional control comes primarily from a perspective labeled the *pragmatic view of human communication*, articulated most directly by Watzlawick, Beavin, and Jackson (1967). This view involves discerning the effect of communicative behaviors on further communicative behaviors, rather than looking at intent or other cognitive, or in-the-head, variables. It argues that control is exercised in all interactions—not control over people, per se, but control over the interaction and the relationship. Messages can be looked at as either exerting control over the direction of a conversation (*one-up* messages) or allowing the other person to control the direction of the conversation (*one-down* messages). Messages that neither take nor explicitly give up control are referred to as *one-across* messages (Rogers & Farace, 1975).

Interactional patterns can be described by comparing two sequential messages. A set of paired messages is called an *interact*. For instance,

JOHN: I think I'd like to go to the movies tonight.
MARY: Sounds good to me.

In this interact, John's statement is a one-up message because he is taking control of the direction of the conversation. Mary's statement is a one-down message because she is allowing John to take control. A conversation like this, composed of a one-up and a one-down statement, is called a *complementary* interact. An interact that is composed of two similar statements (both one-up, both one-down, or both one-across) is called a *symmetrical* interact. Here is an example of a symmetrical interact:

JOHN: I think I'd like to go to the movies tonight.
MARY: I'm tired of going to the movies. Let's go out to dinner instead.

In this case, both John and Mary are trying to take control of the interaction (two one-up statements). An interact is also symmetrical if neither participant is willing to take control.

JOHN: I don't know what to do tonight. What do you want to do?
MARY: I don't know. What do you want to do?

This is symmetrical, because it contains two one-down statements.

A *parallel* (or transitioning or neutralized) interact occurs when a one-across statement is coupled with either a one-up or one-down statement; for instance,

JOHN: I think I'd like to go to a movie tonight.
MARY: Hmm.

Whereas John's statement is one-up, Mary's is one-across—it neither gives nor takes control.

A parallel interact, then, is composed of a one-across message and either a one-up or a one-down message. A complementary interact is made up of a one-up and a one-down message. And a symmetrical interact includes two similar statements, either two one-up, two one-down, or two one-across messages.

The notion of interactional control becomes relevant to elderly people when we observe that elderly people are frequently allowed little interactional control (Tamir, 1979). As Tamir points out, decreasing power or control is a major issue for elderly people (Rosow, 1974; Sussman 1976). The prerogative for initiating interaction, a basic one-up maneuver, usually depends upon the younger person in the interaction. Hampe and Bievins (1975) demonstrated that frequent visits from children are not comforting if the parent feels that he or she does not have any control over the initiation of the visit. And several studies concluded that older people find it difficult to change interaction patterns when they want to initiate new relationships or renegotiate older ones (Britton & Britton, 1972; Chown, 1977; Fitzgerald, 1978). The research cited earlier (Botwinick, 1973) indicating cautiousness in the communication of the elderly is an additional indication of one-down or one-across communication.

Further research indicated that elderly people often become deferential (take the one-down position) for fear that the other person will stop initiating contact (Bengtson & Cutler, 1976). Bennett and Eckman (1973) found that elderly people are easily persuaded, especially if they have little contact with others; agreement, of course, is a one-down behavior.

Interaction patterns can be changed, of course, by any one person changing his or her behavior. If one stops making a lot of one-up statements during interaction with elderly partners, one will no longer be in the one-up position so consistently. One can encourage elderly people to take one-up positions by asking them for their opinions about things (a one-down behavior). In this way, control is shared more equally—a more satisfying and stimulating conversational exchange usually results.

CONFIRMATION VERSUS DISCONFIRMATION

Another important communication concept that has implications for communication with elderly people is confirmation versus disconfirmation (Buber, 1957; Laing, 1961). *Confirming* statements are those that acknowledge and validate the other

person and his or her experience of reality (feelings, perceptions, etc.). For instance, if Mary says, "I don't feel well," and
John responds with, "Oh, that's too bad," John is acknowledging Mary and her perception of how she feels (her reality).
Disconfirming statements do not provide this acknowledgment
and validation. The most complete form of disconfirmation
would be completely ignoring someone. Many philosophers
have speculated that the worst hell a human being can experience would be to be put down somewhere on the planet and to
be ignored by everyone. Although this rarely happens, most
people have experienced being in a group and saying something, only to have it ignored by everyone. It is a rather disconcerting experience. If Mary says, "I don't feel well," and John
ignores her, he has disconfirmed her.

There are also more subtle types of disconfirmation. One of
these has been labeled *imperviousness* (Laing, 1961). This occurs
when John communicates to Mary that he knows how she is
feeling or what she has experienced better than she does. If
Mary says, "I don't feel well," and John says, "Oh, yes you
do—you feel just fine," Mary will feel disconfirmed by John's
imperviousness.

Disconfirmation can also occur through disqualification
(Bavelas, 1983; Bavelas & Chovil, 1986), most frequently in the
form of tangential remarks. A tangential remark is just barely
related to the previous remark. If Mary says, "I don't feel well,"
and John responds with, "I'm feeling pretty good today," John's
remark is just barely related to Mary's. John is addressing the issue of feelings, but he is certainly not addressing the feelings
that Mary was expressing.

Disconfirmation is not only disconcerting, but it can make
people begin to doubt their sense of self. If people continually
receive impervious messages, they may begin to doubt the accuracy of their self-perceptions and feelings. This weakens their
sense of self—their self-concept. If they continually receive tangential messages or if they are frequently ignored, they will
likely begin doubting their importance to other people—their
self-esteem will be weakened.

Unfortunately, disconfirmation is exactly what happens to
many older people. Although there has been little research focusing specifically on disconfirmation toward elderly people,
researchers do know that younger people frequently try to
avoid interaction with elderly people (unless the older person
is wealthy), a form of ignoring (Levin & Levin, 1981). Elderly
people themselves express a preference for interaction with

people of many different ages, not just other elderly people (Daum, 1982).

Further, Tamir (1979) concluded that "the older adult finds his (*sic*) identity difficult to maintain, for the image that he (*sic*) holds of himself (*sic*) is not the image that others perceive" (p. 143)—a feeling of disconfirmation. Talking to older adults as if they were children (Ferguson, 1977) is also disconfirming. Remember the discussion in chapter 2, which addressed baby talk directed towards older individuals and other forms of patronizing speech—which can be quite disconfirming.

Disconfirmation, however, is not just a problem of communication of younger people toward older people. In many cases, the behavior of elderly people can be disconfirming to those who are younger. We touch on this issue in chapter 2. One example of older-to-younger disconfirmation is forgetting. Although the research on memory in older adults is not completely consistent in terms of the types of information that is recalled or forgotten, researchers do know that elderly memory is not as consistent as is memory in younger people (Belsky, 1984; Walsh, 1975). When an older person forgets something that he or she has been told by a younger person, or forgets who the younger person is, the younger person is likely to feel disconfirmed.

Extreme examples of forgetfulness and disconfirming behavior, of course, are likely to be found in individuals with Alzheimer's disease and other forms of senility. The following stages of Alzheimer's disease (Semlak, 1986) demonstrate the progression of this behavior.

Stage 1: Normal aging, no subjective or objective changes in intellectual functioning.

Stage 2: Normal older forgetfulness, not remembering names or where things have been put; does not impair functioning.

Stage 3: Early confusion, begins to interfere with work and social interactions; at this stage the family begins to blame the individual for mistakes and accuses him or her of carelessness.

Stage 4: Late confusion, loses the ability to handle such routine activities as marketing or managing finances; communication becomes very difficult; the individual withdraws from conversations if feels lost.

Stage 5: Early dementia, cannot recall one's address, the year, or major information about one's life; behavior is erratic; friends stop interacting with the individual.

Stage 6: Middle dementia, requires assistance with basic behaviors, such as bathing and toileting; may not recall spouse.

Stage 7: Late dementia, loses ability to speak and walk; communication becomes nonexistent.

As the disease progresses, disconfirming behaviors mount. Along with all of the other changes in the individual, communication, when it does occur, is becoming less and less fulfilling. These disconfirming behaviors no doubt make a very difficult situation even worse.

HELPING AND LONELINESS

A chapter on the relational considerations of elderly people would not be complete without a discussion of helping and loneliness. While these two issues may not seem to be highly related, research by Chappell (1983) and others has indicated that social support is a key determinant of life satisfaction and an independent lifestyle.

Only about 4% of elderly people are institutionalized at any given time (U.S. Census Bureau, 1996); therefore, most older adults are living in the community, and research suggests they do so without an inordinate amount of assistance (Chappell & Havens, 1985). Informal help from neighbors and family members, however, is common and is often needed even when formal care is being provided.

Research into the social support system of elderly people suggests that most people feel that elderly people should receive assistance from the family and, if necessary, from formal agencies (Rosow, 1967). Not surprisingly, elderly people receive most help from their children living nearby. This type of support is discussed in more detail in chapter 9.

Research by Goodman (1984) and others suggested that neighbors also provide some assistance for elderly people. Goodman found three types of neighborhood helpers and described them as high helpers, mutual helpers, and neighborhood isolates. *High helpers* are those people who provide a great deal of very professional assistance and receive little or no help in return. *Mutual helpers* are those people who provide some assistance to others and also accept some help when they need it. The *neighborhood isolates* receive their help from people living outside their own neighborhood.

The neighborhood isolates identified by Goodman are probably similar to the group selected for Anderson's (1984) study of loneliness. After identifying individuals who were lonely, Anderson developed an intervention program to get them involved in activities. One group became involved in a protest against the local bus company, while others engaged in letter-writing campaigns of various sorts. The majority of the participants reported less loneliness as a result of this involvement. This, no doubt, is a technique that could be implemented on a broader scale.

The notions of helping and loneliness are both related to another issue of increasing importance in the social gerontology literature, social support. Chappell (1983) reviewed this research and concluded that support is provided by both family and peers, but that experts in the area tend to place too much emphasis on the family as informal support and not enough emphasis on peers. Her conclusions appear to coincide with some of the other research, cited previously.

Mullins and Mushel (1992) studied the effect of emotional closeness on loneliness among older persons. They found that loneliness was not related to closeness (or the lack thereof) in relationships with a spouse and children, but was related to having friends, even if the friendships were not of a particularly close nature. Social isolation from friends may influence loneliness more than the family network.

SUMMARY

The issues discussed in this chapter have all focused on concerns that involve both elderly individuals and their interactional partners. The research in these areas seems to indicate that reminiscence is an important and profitable communicative activity and that sexual intimacy is alive and well in most older relationships, if not quite as frequent as it used to be. Research also shows that interactional control and disconfirmation are important issues when studying communication and aging. These areas should all be the focus of additional research, as should helping and loneliness—two key issues concerning elderly people that have yet to receive enough attention by researchers.

■ REFERENCES

Anderson, L. (1984). Intervention against loneliness in a group of elderly women: A process of evaluation. *Human Relations, 37*, 295–310.

Arluke, A., Levin, J., & Suchwalko, J. (1984). Sexuality and romance in advice books for the elderly. *The Gerontologist, 24*, 415–419.

Baker, N. J. (1985). Reminiscing in group therapy for self-worth. *Journal of Gerontology, 11*, 21–24.

Baum, W. (1980). Therapeutic value of oral history. *International Journal of Aging and Human Development, 12*, 49–52.

Bavelas, J. B. (1983). Situations that lead to disqualification. *Human Communication Research, 9*, 130–145.

Bavelas, J. B., & Chovil, N. (1986). How people disqualify: Experimental studies of spontaneous written disqualification. *Communication Monographs, 53*, 70–74.

Becker, D. G., Blumfield, S., & Gordon, N. (1984). Voices from the eighties and beyond: Reminiscences of nursing home residents. *Journal of Gerontological Social Work, 8*, 83–100.

Belsky, J. (1984). *The psychology of aging: Theory, research and practice.* Monterey, CA: Brooks/Cole.

Bengtson, V. L., & Cutler, N. E. (1976). Generations and intergenerational relations. In R. H. Binstock, & E. Shanas (Eds.), *Handbook of aging and the social sciences* (pp. 130–159). New York: Van Nostrand Reinhold.

Bennett, R., & Eckman, J. (1973). Attitudes toward aging: A critical examination of recent literature and implications for future research. In C. Eisdorfer & M. P. Lawton (Eds.), *The psychology of adult development and aging* (pp. 575–597). Washington, DC: American Psychological Association.

Botwinick, J. (1973). *Aging and behavior: A comprehensive integration of research findings.* New York: Springer.

Bramwell, L. (1984). Use of the life history in pattern identification and health promotion. *Advances in Nursing Science, 7*, 37–44.

Brink, T. L. (1985). Geriatric depression scale reliability: Order, examiner and reminiscence effects. *Clinical Gerontologist, 3*, 57–60.

Britton, J. H., & Britton, J. O. (1972). *Personality changes in aging.* New York: Springer.

Buber, M. (1957). Distance and relation. *Psychiatry, 20*, 94–104.

Buchanan, K., & Middleton, D. J. (1990, July). *Reminiscence: Discourse analysis in socio-historical studies of collective remembering.* Paper presented at the Second International Congress on Activity Theory, Lahti, Finland.

Buchanan, K., & Middleton, D. J. (1993). Discursively formulating the significance of reminiscence in later life. In N. Coupland & J. F. Nussbaum (Eds.), *Discourse and lifespan identity* (pp. 55–80). Newbury Park, CA: Sage.

Butler, R. N. (1968). The life review: An interpretation of reminiscence in the aged. In B. Neugarten (Ed.), *Middle age and aging* (pp.486–496). Chicago: University of Chicago Press.

Butler, R. N. (1974). Successful aging and the role of the life review. *Journal of the American Geriatrics Society, 22*, 529–535.

Butler, R. N. (1980). The life review: An unrecognized bonanza. *International Journal of Aging and Human Development, 12,* 35–38.

Chappell, N. L. (1983). Informal support networks among the elderly. *Research on Aging, 5,* 77–99.

Chappell, N. L., & Havens, B. (1985). Who helps the elderly person: A discussion of informal and formal care. In W. A. Peterson & J. Quadagno (Eds.), *Social bonds in later life* (pp. 211–228). Beverly Hills, CA: Sage.

Chown, S. M. (1977). Morale, careers, and personal potentials. In J. E. Birren & K. W. Schaie (Eds.), *Handbook of the psychology of aging* (pp. 672–691). New York: Van Nostrand Reinhold.

Dailey, D. M. (1981). Sexual expression and aging. In F. J. Berghorn & D. E. Schafer (Eds.), *The dynamics of aging* (pp. 311–330). Boulder, CO: Westview Press.

Daum, M. (1982). Preferences for age-mixed social interaction. In B. L. Neugarten (Ed.), *Age or need? Public policies for older people* (pp. 247–262). Beverly Hills, CA: Sage.

Dynes, W. R. (Ed.). (1990). *Encyclopedia of homosexuality.* New York: Garland.

Evans, D. L., Millicovsky, L., & Tennison, C. R. (1984). Aging, reminiscence and mourning. *Psychiatric Forum, 12,* 19–32.

Federal Drug Administration. (1999). Viagra (sildenafil) prescription reports [On-line]. Available: *http://www.fda.gov*

Feier, C. D., & Gerstman, L. J. (1980). Sentence comprehension abilities throughout the adult life span. *Journal of Gerontology, 35,* 722–728.

Ferguson, C. (1977). Baby talk as a simplified register. In C. Snow & C. Ferguson (Eds.), *Talking to children* (219-235). New York: Cambridge University Press.

Fitzgerald, J. M. (1978). Actual and perceived sex and generational differences in interpersonal style: Structural and quantitative issues. *Journal of Gerontology, 33,* 394–401.

Gardella, L. G. (1985). The neighborhood group: A reminiscence group for the disoriented old. *Social Work with Groups, 8,* 43–52.

Garza, J. M., & Dressel, P. L. (1983). Sexuality and later-life marriages. In T. H. Brubaker (Ed.), *Family relationships in later life* (pp. 91–108). Beverly Hills, CA: Sage.

Genevay, B. (1986). Intimacy as we age. *Generations, 10 (4),* 12–15.

Georgemiller, R., & Maloney, H. (1984). Group life review and denial of death. *Clinical Gerontologist, 2* (4), 37–49.

Goodman, C. C. (1984). Natural helping among older adults. *The Gerontologist, 24,* 138–143.

Haight, R. K., & Bahr, R. T. (1984). The therapeutic role of the life review in the elderly. *Academic Psychology Bulletin, 6,* 287–299.

Hampe, G. D., & Bievins, A. L., Jr., (1975). Primary group interaction of residents in a retirement hotel. *International Journal of Aging and Human Development, 6* (4), 309–320.

Harris, R., & Harris, S. (1980). Therapeutic uses of oral history techniques in medicine. *International Journal of Aging and Human Development, 12,* 27–39.

Harwood, J., Giles, H., Fox, S., Ryan, E. B., & Williams, A. (1993). Patronizing young and elderly adults: Response strategies in a community setting. *Journal of Applied Communication Research, 21,* 211–226.

Huyck, M. H. (1994). Marriage and close relationships of the marital kind. In R. Blieszner & V. H. Bedford (Eds.), *Aging and the family: Theory and research* (pp. 181–200). Westport, CN: Praeger.

Isquick, M. F. (1981). Training older people in empathy: Effects of empathy, attitudes, and self-exploration. *International Journal of Aging and Human Development, 13,* 1–14.

Kaminsky, M. (1984a). The arts and social work: Writing and reminiscing in old age: Voices from within the process. *Journal of Gerontological Social Work, 8,* 225–246.

Kaminsky, M. (1984b). The uses of reminiscence: A discussion of the formative literature. *Journal of Gerontological Social Work, 7,* 137–156.

Kaminsky, M. (1984c). Transfiguring life: Images of continuity hidden among the fragments. *Journal of Gerontological Social Work, 7,* 3–18.

Kiernat, J. M. (1983). Retrospection as a life span concept. *Physical and Occupational Therapy in Geriatrics, 3*(2), 35–48.

Kimmel, D. (1990). *Adulthood and aging: An interdisciplinary, developmental view.* New York: Wiley.

Laing, R. D. (1961). *Self and others.* London, England: Tavistock.

Lesser, J., Lazarus, L. W., Frankel, R., & Harasy, S. (1981). Reminiscence group therapy with psychotic geriatric patients. *The Gerontologist, 21,* 291–296.

Levin, J., & Levin, W. C. (1981). Willingness to interact with an old person. *Research on Aging, 3,* 211–217.

Lipman, A. (1986). Homosexual relationships. *Generations, 10* (4), 51–54.

Lo Gerfo, M. (1980). Three ways of reminiscence in theory and practice. *International Journal of Aging and Human Development, 12,* 39–48.

Lowenthal, M. F., & Haven. L. (1968). Interaction and adaptation: Intimacy as a critical behavior. *American Sociological Review, 33,* 20–30.

Ludeman, K. (1981). The sexuality of the older person: Review of the literature. *The Gerontologist, 21,* 203–208.

Mares, M-L., & Fitzpatrick, M. A. (1995). The aging couple. In J. F. Nussbaum & J. Coupland (Eds.), *The handbook of communication and aging research* (pp. 185–205). Mahwah, NJ: Lawrence Erlbaum Associates.

Marn, S. C., & Bennett, R. (1972). Greeting behavior and social adjustment in aged residents of a nursing home. In D. P. Kent, R. Kastenbaum, & S. Sherwood (Eds.), *Research planning and action for the elderly* (pp. 201–209). New York: Behavioral.

Masters, W. H., & Johnson, V. E. (1968). Human sexual response: The aging female and the aging male. In B. L. Neugarten (Ed.), *Middle age and aging* (pp. 209–279). Chicago: University of Chicago Press.

McMahon, A. W., & Rhudick, P. J. (1964). Reminiscing: Adaptational significance in the aged. *Archives of General Psychiatry, 10,* 292–298.

Middleton, D. J., Buchanan, K., & Suurmond, Jr. (1991, June). *Communities of memory: Issues of "re-membering" and belonging in reminiscence work with the elderly.* Paper presented at the annual conference of the British Psychological Society's Psychologists' Special Interest Group in the Elderly, Grey College, Durham University.

Moody, H. R. (1984). Reminiscence and the recovery of the public world. *Journal of Gerontological Social Work, 7,* 157–166.

Mullins, L. C., & Mushel, M. (1992). The existence and emotional closeness of relationships with children, friends, and spouses: The effect on loneliness among older persons. *Research on Aging, 14,* 448–470.

Newman, G., & Nichols, C. R. (1970). Sexual activities and attitudes in older persons. In E. B. Palmore (Ed.), *Normal aging* (pp. 277–281). Durham, NC: Duke University Press.

Nussbaum, J. F. (1983a). Perceptions of communication content and life satisfaction among the elderly. *Communication Quarterly, 31,* 313–319.

Nussbaum, J. F. (1983b). Relational closeness of elderly interaction: Implications for life satisfaction. *Western Journal of Speech Communication, 47,* 229–243.

Palmore, E. (1981). *Social patterns in normal aging: Findings from the Duke longitudinal study.* Durham, NC: Duke University Press.

Peplau, L. A., & Cochran, S. D. (1990). A relationship perspective on homosexuality. In D. P. McWhirter, S. Sanders, & J. Reinisch (Eds.), *Homosexuality/heterosexuality: Concepts of sexual orientation* (pp. 321–349). New York: Oxford University Press.

Perrotta, P., & Meacham, J. A. (1981). Can a reminiscing intervention alter depression and self-esteem? *International Journal of Aging and Human Development, 14,* 23–30.

Perschbacher, R. (1984). An application of reminiscence in an activity setting. *The Gerontologist, 24,* 343–345.

Pfeiffer, E. (1977). Sexual behavior in old age. In E. W. Busse & E. Pfeiffer (Eds.), *Behavior and adaptation in late life* (pp. 130–141). Boston: Little, Brown.

Pfeiffer, E., Verwoerdt, A., & Wang, H. S. (1970). Sexual behavior in aged men and women. In E. B. Palmore (Ed.), *Normal aging* (pp. 299–303). Durham, NC: Duke University Press.

Portnoy, E. J. (1997). Older women as cultural figures of aging. In H. S. N. Al-Deen (Ed.), *Cross-cultural communication and aging in the United States* (pp. 23–41). Mahwah, NJ: Lawrence Erlbaum Associates.

Priefer, B. A., & Gambert, S. R. (1984). Reminiscence and life review in the elderly. *Psychiatric Medicine, 2,* 91–100.

Revere, V., & Tobin, S. S. (1980). Myth and reality: The older person's relationship to his past. *International Journal of Aging and Human Development, 12,* 15–26.

Riegel, K. F. (1972). Time and change in the development of the individual and society. In H. W. Reese (Ed.), *Advances in child development and behavior* (Vol. 7, pp. 81–113). New York: Academic Press.

Rogers, L. E., & Farace, R. V. (1975). Analysis of relational communication in dyads: New measurement procedures. *Human Communication Research, 1,* 222–239.

Rosow, I. (1967). *Social integration of the aged.* New York: Free Press.

Rosow, I. (1974). *Socialization to old age.* Berkeley, CA: University of California Press.

Ryan, E. B., Giles, H., Bartolucci, G., & Henwood, K. (1986). Psycholinguistic and social psychological components of communication by and with the elderly. *Language and Communication, 6,* 1–24.

Ryan, E. B., Kwong See, S., Meneer, W. B., & Trovato, D. (1994). Age-based perceptions of language performance among younger and older adults. In M. L. Hummert, J. M. Wiemann, & J. F. Nussbaum (Eds.), *Interpersonal communication in older adulthood: Interdisciplinary theory and research* (pp. 15–39). Thousand Oaks, CA: Sage.

Sable, L. M. (1984). Life review therapy: An occupational therapy treatment technique with geriatric clients. *Physical and Occupational Therapy, 3*(4), 49–54.

Schroeder, A. B. (1986, November), *An analysis of the interaction patterns of the elderly: The deterioration of relationships.* Paper presented at the Annual Convention of the Speech Communication Association, Chicago.

Semlak, W. (1986, November). *Communication and Alzheimer's disease.* Paper presented at the Annual Convention of the Speech Communication Association, Chicago.

Sherman, E. (1985). A phenomenological approach to reminiscence and life review. *Clinical Gerontologist, 3*(4), 3–16.

Sussman, M. B. (1976). The family life of old people. In R. H. Binstock & E. Shanas (Eds.), *Handbook of aging and the social sciences.* New York: Van Nostrand Reinhold.

Sviland, M. P. (1981). Sexuality and intimacy in later life. In R. Kastenbaum (Ed.), *Old age on the new scene.* New York: Springer.

Tamir, L. M. (1979). *Communication and the aging process: Interaction throughout the life cycle.* New York: Pergamon.

Thomas, L. E. (1982). Sexuality and aging: Essential vitamin or popcorn? *The Gerontologist, 22,* 240–243.

Traupmann, J., Eckels, E., & Hatfield, E. (1982). Intimacy in older women's lives. *The Gerontologist, 22,* 493–498.

Unruh, D. R. (1983). *Invisible lives: Social worlds of the aged.* Beverly Hills, CA: Sage.

U.S. Census Bureau. (1996). *65+ in the United States.* (U.S. Census Bureau, Current Populations Reports, Special Studies, P23–190). Washington, DC: U. S. Government Printing Office.

Verwoerdt, A., Pfeiffer, E., & Wang, H. S. (1970). Sexual behavior in senescence. In E. B. Palmore (Ed.), *Normal aging* (pp. 282–298). Durham, NC: Duke University Press.

Walsh, D. A. (1975). Age differences in learning and memory. In D. S. Woodruff & J. E. Birren (Eds.), *Aging: Scientific perspectives and social issues* (pp. 125–151). New York: Van Nostrand.

Watzlawick, P., Beavin, J., & Jackson, D. D. (1967). *The pragmatics of human communication.* New York: Norton.

Weiner, M., & White, M. (1982). Depression as the search for the lost self. *Psychotherapy: Theory, Research and Practice, 19,* 493.

Welford, A. T. (1983). Social skill and aging: Principles and problems. *International Journal of Aging and Human Development, 17,* 1–5.

Zaks, P. M., & Labouvie-Vief, G. (1980). Spatial perspective taking and referential communication skills in the elderly: A training study. *Journal of Gerontology, 35,* 217–224.

CHAPTER 4

Mass Media Use and Aging

P eople of all ages spend a great deal of time with the mass media. Spring (1993) estimates that elderly people spend as much as 40% of their leisure time watching television, listening to the radio, reading, going to the movies, and listening to music. While any behavior that consumes so much time should be of interest to social scientists, media use is of particular importance because it affects other leisure activities (Robinson, 1972, 1981), impacts interpersonal interaction (Bleise, 1982; Faber, Brown, & McLeod, 1979; Katz, Gurevitch, & Haas, 1973; Lull, 1980), affects our mental and physical health (Berkman & Syme, 1979), and can influence perceptions of aging and elderly people (Davis, 1984; Gerbner, Gross, Signorelli, & Morgan, 1980).

All too frequently, however, the role that the mass media play in the lives of elderly people has been ignored. Communication scholars are starting to find evidence that the mass media are being used in a variety of ways. The mass media allow elderly people to keep up with the ever-changing world around them, provide topics of conversation, and can be used as a surrogate for interpersonal relationships in some cases. The media also provide their audience with normative and comparative reference points for self-evaluation. Audience members can compare themselves to characters on television just as they can compare themselves to other people in an effort to evaluate their opinions and abilities. Finally, the media provide elderly people with opportunities for entertainment and a way to pass the time. The reduction in mobility that is associated with growing old may result in a decrease in social and entertainment opportunities. In such situations, the media can be used to fulfill the needs of some elderly adults.

This chapter is divided into five sections. The first section outlines the television-use patterns of elderly people and their content preferences. The second section discusses the radio-use habits of elderly people. The third section focuses on the reading habits of elderly people, including books, magazines, and newspapers. Section four discusses movie attendance, film genre preferences, and VCR use of elderly people. The final section examines the personal computer use of older adults.

TELEVISION VIEWING

It has been said that more homes in the United States have television sets than have running water or indoor plumbing. Roughly 97% of all homes in the United States have at least one television set and about 85% of all homes have a color TV set (Faminghetti, 1998). About 73% of all homes have two or more sets, and 38% have three or more working TV sets (Faminghetti, 1998). Only 1% of homes report having a single black-and-white TV set as their sole source of television programming (Faminghetti, 1998). Approximately 97% of all homes in the United States have access to cable (Robinson, 1993; Simmons Market Research Bureau, 1996) and just under 67% of those homes subscribed to at least a basic cable package in 1997 (Brunner, 1998). About one third of those homes also subscribed to at least one premium cable channel (Brunner, 1998).

A typical home has the TV set running about 7 hours and 17 minutes per day (Faminghetti, 1998). Estimates of how much time adults 18 years of age and older actually spend watching television vary depending on how TV consumption is conceptualized and measured. Faminghetti (1998) reported that in 1996 the average adult spent between 3 and 6 hours per day watching television, depending on age and gender. In an effort to further clarify this issue we examined the interviews of

32,380 adults conducted between 1975 and 1994 (National Opinion Research Center, 1997). The results of these interviews clearly demonstrate that adults (people 18 years of age and older) have watched about 3 hours of television per day for the past 20 years, though the amount of time spent watching does vary by age and gender.

The amount of time adults spend viewing television increases with age (Bogart, 1972; Bower, 1973; Chaffee & Wilson, 1975; Harris & Associates, Inc., 1975; Hoar, 1961; National Opinion Research, 1997; Steiner, 1963; Simmons Market Research Bureau, 1991, 1996; Time Buying Services, 1986, 1989). In fact, elderly people spend more time per day watching television than any other age cohort, including children (Simmons Market Research Bureau, 1991, 1996); this trend has held true for the past 20 years (National Opinion Research Center, 1997).

Estimates of how much time adults spend watching television vary, but suffice it to say that elderly people spend between 3.5 and 6 hours a day watching television. Since 1975, the average adult 65 and older has spent over 3.5 hours a day watching television (National Opinion Research Center, 1997). Other age cohorts (25–54 and 55–64) spent less than 3 hours per day watching television over this same 20-year period (National Opinion Research Center, 1997).

Using data from A. C. Nielsen, Faminghetti (1998) reported that men 55 and older spend nearly 5.5 hours per day watching television and women in the same age group watch nearly 6 hours per day. Men 55 and older spend nearly 90 minutes more each day watching television than men 25 to 54 years of age and nearly 2.5 hours more per day than men 18 to 24 years of age. Similarly, women 55 and older watch slightly more than 90 minutes of television than women 25 to 54 years of age and nearly 4 hours per week more than men of the same age. The General Social Survey data (National Opinion Research Center, 1997) also supported the claim that differences in television viewing exist among elderly men and women. Elderly women watch about 30 more minutes of television per day than their male counterparts (National Opinion Research Center, 1997).

Television viewing continues to be the most frequently reported daily activity for elderly Americans (DeGrazia, 1961; Schramm, 1969; Spring, 1993; Time Buying Services, 1986). Spring (1993) estimated that elderly people spend as much as 40% of their leisure time with the mass media and more than 30% watching television. Davis and Kubey (1982) and Kubey (1980) suggested that retired elderly adults and widowed elderly adults spend even more of their day watching television than their still partnered or working counterparts. This may help explain the gender differences, in that women are more likely to be widowed and remain unmarried than are men.

While television viewing increases with age, it is generally accepted that elderly people watch more television because they have the time and the opportunity. As Bower (1985) pointed out "A person's age, sex, race, education, income make little difference—everyone views television about the same amount except when prevented from doing so by external factors, like work" (pp. 40–41). Thus it is not surprising, given the increase in leisure time that accompanies retirement and the ready availability of television, that elderly people watch more than younger adults. This is particularly salient, however, because television viewing tends to reduce the time spent reading, listening to the radio, and attending movies (Robinson, 1972, 1981).

While elderly people spend more time watching television than any other age cohort, they are somewhat less likely to subscribe to cable television than are their younger adult counterparts (Simmons Market Research Bureau, 1996). In 1997, approximately 67.4% of the homes in the United States subscribed to cable television (Kagan, 1998). In the case of adults 65 and older, only 62% were cable TV subscribers, whereas in all other age cohorts at least 67% subscribed to cable (Simmons Market Research Bureau, 1996). Some elderly individuals undoubtedly live in areas without cable television; others are on limited incomes and cannot afford cable. Still others simply choose not to have cable television in their homes. Whatever the reason, cable television use among elderly people is significantly lower than in other age cohorts, although such use is still high.

TV Content Preferences

Knowing that the elderly spend more of their leisure time watching television than doing any other single activity, it seems reasonable to ask: What do elderly people like to watch on television? Research suggests elderly people enjoy television programs that are predominantly information oriented, such as the news, documentaries, and public affairs programming (Bower, 1973; Davis, 1971; Davis & Westbrook, 1985; Goodman, 1990; Korzenny & Neuendorf, 1980; Meyersohn, 1961; Phillips & Sternthal, 1977; Simmons Market Research Bureau, 1991, 1996; Steiner, 1963; Wenner, 1976). Not surprisingly, elderly people also report enjoying other types of informational programming, such as travelogues and game shows (Bower, 1973; Danowski, 1975; Davis, 1971). Consistent with this premium-on-informational-programming hypothesis, Atkin and LaRose (1991) reported that even though elderly people are less likely than other adults to be cable television subscribers, when they do have cable television, retired elderly adults in particular watch more community access programming than all other age cohorts except the 25 to 34 age group and that they are generally more satisfied with such programming than are the other age cohorts (Atkin & LaRose, 1991).

In addition, elderly people constitute the single largest group of television news viewers (Davis & Westbrook, 1985). Data from Simmons Market Research Bureau (1991) comparing the news-viewing patterns of adults 65 and older with those of other adults indicates that elderly people are more likely to watch prime-time network news programs than adults 18 to 34. When the differences between adults 55 to 64 and 65 and older are compared, the percentage of news viewers in the 65 and older cohort is higher than in the 55 to 63 cohort, but the difference is not significant; just over 62% of the 65 and over age cohort, 51.2% of the 55 to 64 cohort, and 35% of the 18 to 34 cohort watch the prime-time network news on a regular basis. Similarly, elderly adults are more likely to watch the local news than are adults 18 to 54. Just under 73% of elderly adults watch the local evening news, whereas only 50% of the 18 to 34 audience and 62% of the 55 to 64 audience typically watch the local evening news (Simmons Market Research Bureau, 1991).

The data provided by Simmons Market Research Bureau (1996) indicated that these trends have not changed. When examining show-type preferences of the various age cohorts, it is clear that elderly people prefer the genre "prime-time documentary news" and watch this at a higher rate than do other age cohorts; nearly 53% of adults 65 and over watch prime-time documentary news programming, while just under 24% of those 18 to 24 typically watch such programming.

Goodman (1990) also found that elderly men and women report news and public affairs programming to be their favorite. Elderly men, however, report sporting events to be their second-favorite type of programming, whereas elderly women prefer educational programming. Elderly men report their third favorite type of programming to be educational, whereas elderly women rank dramas as their third-favorite program type and sporting events as their least favorite type of programming.

Mundorf and Brownell (1990) also examined the TV show preferences of elderly people. They asked elderly adults to rank their favorite shows, identify their motivations for viewing, and to name their favorite TV characters. Not surprisingly, the self-reported program preferences are generally consistent with the viewing patterns reported by Goodman (1990). When asked why they watch TV, however, elderly people, like the younger viewers surveyed, report that their primary motivation for watching TV was entertainment. Almost 70% of college-age and elderly adults watch TV to be entertained. The second most common motivation for most viewers was the desire to be informed, but this motivation was dwarfed by the desire to be entertained.

Previous research also suggested that elderly people enjoy travelogues, game shows (Bower, 1973; Danowski, 1975; Davis, 1971), and soap operas (Barton, 1977). The 1990 viewing-patterns data (Simmons Market Research Bureau, 1991) indicated that elderly people do watch these types of programs at a rate slightly higher than other age cohorts, but the differences are not statistically significant.

As for soap operas, Mundorf and Brownell (1990) reported that almost 91% of the college-age and 60% of the elderly women report watching soaps. Over 50% of the college-age men also report watching soaps on a regular or occasional basis, but only 18.8% of the elderly men watch soaps. It will be interesting to see if those college-age men continue watching soaps throughout their life span.

Previous research has suggested that elderly people enjoy programs that include older characters and actors (Harris & Associates, 1975; Harwood, 1997; Meyersohn, 1961; Parker, Berry & Smythe, 1955). Mundorf and Brownell (1990) asked elderly and college-age viewers to list their favorite characters and found, generally, that older adults do prefer elderly characters and programs that contain elderly characters. College-age adults generally prefer programs featuring younger stars. More recently, Harwood (1997) conducted an experiment to test whether TV viewers prefer shows with characters close to their own age. The results suggest that elderly people, like the other age cohorts examined, do prefer programs that feature characters similar to their own age. This conclusion is further substantiated by the 1990 television viewing patterns (Simmons Market Research Bureau, 1991). The data indicated that this pattern appears to have continued. For example, *Golden Girls* and *Murder, She Wrote*, were the two most often-watched fictional TV programs for the elderly audience. While these two programs were also quite popular with other age cohorts, the popularity was much higher for the older age groups.

Burnett (1991) examined the media use of elderly people and found that there are significant differences in program preferences attributable to gender and income. Specifically, he reports that affluent elderly men prefer shows like *Family Ties* and shows on PBS, premium cable, and CNN, whereas less affluent elderly men watch more prime time-movies, *Monday Night Football*, late-night reruns, and religious programs. Much like their male counterparts, affluent elderly women watch shows such as the *Cosby Show* and shows on PBS, premium cable, and CNN, whereas less affluent elderly women prefer to watch prime-time movies, late-night reruns, religious programs, and soap operas.

RADIO LISTENING

In 1990, nearly 99% of all U.S. homes had at least one radio and the average home contained 5.6 (*Universal Almanac*, 1991). This figure does not include the 200 million radios in cars, trucks, and vans or the radios being played in the workplace. Because over 40% of all radio listening occurs outside the home (Beville, 1985) and radio use often occurs simultaneously with other activities (e.g., driving and working) the importance of these additional radios cannot be ignored.

In 1995 over 85% of adults 18 years old and older listened to the radio at least once during a typical week (National Opinion Research Center, 1997; Simmons Market Research Bureau, 1996). While estimates vary, adults 18 years old and older listen to the radio just under 4 hours per day (National Opinion Research Center, 1997; Time Buying Services, 1986, 1989). During the years 1978, 1982, and 1983, men listened to radio programming an average of 3.68 hours per day and women listened 3.99 hours per day (National Opinion Research Center, 1997).

Adults report using the radio to listen to the news, weather, and early warnings of emergencies at least as often as they listen to music (Zorn, 1987). When listening to radio news, listeners pay particular attention to weather information, local and regional news, and school closings (Zorn, 1987). In addition, in recent years talk radio and sports programming have become increasingly popular radio fare.

Generally speaking, radio use decreases across the life span (Chaffee & Wilson, 1975; National Opinion Research Center, 1997; Simmons Market Research Bureau, 1991, 1996; Time Buying Services 1986, 1989). In 1995, 77.2% of all adults (18 years old and older) listened to the radio at least once during a typical week (National Opinion Research Center, 1997). Only 58.4% of adults 65 years of age and older, however, listened to the radio during a typical week (National Opinion Research Center, 1997). In contrast, over 85% of adults 18 to 24 years old, 82.5% of adults 25 to 54, and 66.8% of the adults 55 to 64 listened to the radio at least once per week (National Opinion Research Center, 1997). Adults between the ages of 18 and 24 listen to the radio the most (about 4.2 hours per day) and adults 71 years old and older listen to the radio the least (about 2.7 hours per day).

It is interesting to note that, while radio use declines across the life span, there is an increase in use between the years of 65 and 70. Older adults in this age cohort listen to the radio about 3.6 hours per day—the most of any age cohort except adults 18 to 24 (National Opinion Research Center, 1997).

There is a precipitous drop in radio use after the age of 70, however. Keep in mind that those elderly individuals who do listen to the radio listen a great deal. Although the data are dated the 1963 study by Beyer and Woods (as cited in Atkin, 1976) found that less than 17% of elderly people surveyed reported listening to the radio on a daily basis, but those who did reported listening about 14 hours a day. Also keep in mind that women of all age cohorts listen to the radio 15 to 30 minutes per day more than their male counterparts (National Opinion Research Center, 1997).

Early radio studies by Lazarsfeld and Kendall in 1948 and Whan in 1957 (as cited in Atkin, 1976) reported that elderly people did not enjoy popular music as much as younger audience members. More recently, Bower (1973) found a higher than average listening rate for light music by elderly people, suggesting perhaps that elderly people do listen to music on the radio but not to currently popular music. With the increases in the number of older listeners, radio stations have begun programming more Big Band music from the 1940s and 1950s (Davis & Davis, 1985). While FM radio programming is preferred by younger audiences, AM programming with its heavy emphasis on talk, news, and public affairs is favored by elderly listeners (Davis & Davis, 1985; Phillips & Sternthal, 1977; Schiffman, 1971; Schreiber & Boyd, 1980). As Davis & Davis (1985) point out, radio programming changed dramatically in the 1980s and is now much more in tune with the needs of elderly people. Some of these format changes seem to be an attempt to woo elderly listeners.

When elderly people listen to the radio, they prefer country music, talk radio, adult contemporary music, news, and nostalgia programming (Simmons Market Research Bureau, 1991). Comparing the radio use of the three age cohorts shows that people 65 years old and older are no more likely to listen to talk and news programming than are the 55 to 64 cohort, but both of these groups are more likely to listen to talk and news than are the 18 to 34 age group, which are much more likely to listen to music.

Burnett (1991) found that differences in radio listening by the elderly population correlate to income. Specifically, he found that affluent elderly men and women prefer easy listening music, while less affluent men like to listen to country and western music, religious and gospel music, and sports. The less affluent elderly women enjoy the same music as their male counterparts, but do not listen to sports on the radio.

READING

In general, the amount of time spent reading decreases with age (Gordon, Gaitz, & Scott, 1976; Harris & Associates, 1975; McEnvoy & Vincent, 1980). Excluding television viewing and socializing, however, adults spend more time reading than they spend participating in any other single leisure activity (Spring, 1993). On a weekly basis, adults spend about 2.5 hours reading books, magazines, and newspapers (Spring, 1993). Although 2.5 hours per week may not seem like a lot of time, keep in mind that adults spend only about 3 hours a week socializing (Spring, 1993).

In 1997, half of the adults in the United States bought at least one book (Dortch, 1998). These figures are somewhat misleading because only about 50% of all Americans can be described as literate and consequently as "readers." Approximately 50% of all men and women between the ages of 18 and 24 bought at least one book in 1997, while only 40% of all adults 65 and older purchased a book during that same time. In contrast, 56% of adults between the ages of 25 and 54 purchased at least one book during that year (Dortch, 1998). In all age cohorts, women significantly outnumber men as book buyers for all types of books (Dortch, 1998).

The typical U.S. household spent about $160 on reading materials in 1990 (U.S. Bureau of the Census, 1991) or about half what the same households spend on television and related expenses. While the amount of money spent increased with household income, the percentage of money remained relatively stable at about 0.5% of the household budget. In 1997, the expenditures for reading material were highest for the 45 to 54 cohort; about 65% of women and 47% of men in that age cohort purchased at least one book (Dortch, 1998). Consumer book sales fell about 4% between 1996 and 1997, according to the Association of American Publishers (Dortch, 1998).

Research into the reading habits of elderly people suggests that they spend less time reading books than they do reading magazines or newspapers (Danowski, 1975; Kent & Rush, 1976; McEnvoy & Vincent, 1980). McEnvoy and Vincent (1980) found that people 50 years old and older are much less likely to read books than are younger adults; in fact, people 65 years old and older account for 25% of all the nonreaders surveyed, even though that group only represents 13% of the total sample. McEnvoy and Vincent (1980) and Kent and Rush (1976) also found that older people who live alone read more books than do adults living with others. Reading did not seem to be negatively influenced by other leisure activities, including television use.

Magazine and newspaper readers tend to read to increase their knowledge, whereas book readers read for pleasure as well as to gain knowledge. This research on book readership suggests that people do not read books to fulfill social or interpersonal needs or to provide informational needs, but most often books are used to escape reality and to learn about one's self. In general, people prefer to use nonmedia sources (e.g., friends) to fulfill their social needs, and they typically rely on the media for social needs when other, more interpersonal sources, are unavailable.

Newspaper Reading

While consumer perceptions of the educational value, coverage, and efficiency of newspapers decreased between 1960 and 1980 (Bower, 1985), in 1994 50% of all adults read a paper everyday, nearly 73% of adults 18 years old and older read a newspaper at least a few times a week, and nearly 87% of this group read a newspaper at least once a week (National Opinion Research Center, 1997).

Newspaper readership is significantly and positively related to age, education, and income (National Opinion Research Center, 1997; Schramm & White, 1949) and is negatively related to TV viewership (Mediamark Research, 1991; National Opinion Research Center, 1997). While reading in general declines with age, newspaper readership steadily increases across the life span (American Newspaper Publishers Association [ANPA], 1973; Burgoon & Burgoon, 1980; Chaffee & Wilson, 1975) until the age of 70 (Chaffee & Wilson, 1975; Doolittle, 1979; National Opinion Research Center, 1997). The decline in newspaper readership at this age has been attributed to vision problems associated with aging (Salisbury, 1981). Visual acuity begins to decline gradually beginning at about the age of 40, and by the age of 70 few individuals have normal eyesight without correction (Botwinick, 1977). In addition, nearly 25% of elderly people have cataracts (Botwinick, 1977; Fozard, Wolf, Bell, McFarland, & Podolsky, 1977), which is another vision problem that causes the time spent reading to decline with age.

In 1973 the American Newspaper Publishers Association (ANPA) surveyed readers and found that newspaper readership increases with age, just as television watching increases with age. They report that 67% of people 18 to 34, 83% of adults 35 to 64, and 84% of adults 65 and older read a newspaper on a regular basis (ANPA, 1973). The General Social Survey (National Opinion Research Center, 1997) indicated that these trends are consistent throughout the 1970s, 1980s, and 1990s. Throughout these three decades, 30.4% of adults 18 to 24, 44.6% of adults 25 to 54, 57.1% of adults 55 to 64, 75.3% of adults 55 to 70, and 75.0% of adults 71 and older reported reading a newspaper daily (National Opinion Research Center, 1997).

As in their television program preferences, elderly people tend to prefer informative newspaper articles more than entertainment, and they are least likely to read the comics and sports. Chaffee and Wilson (1975) observed that public affairs, news, and political articles are frequently read, and the ANPA survey (1973) found that letters to the editor, obituaries, crime stories, public welfare stories, and health stories are also frequently read. Because elderly women significantly outnumber elderly men, the differences in content preference such as sports-column readership may reflect a gender difference and not an intergenerational difference.

Burnett (1991) also found newspaper readership to vary according to the income levels of elderly adults. Specifically, he found that affluent elderly men read the news section, business section, travel section, and magazine section of the newspaper more than do less affluent men. In addition, affluent elderly men are more likely to read *USA Today* and the *Wall Street Journal* than are elderly men with a more moderate income. Elderly women do not read the sports section or the business section of the newspaper, nor do they read the *Wall Street Journal*, but affluent elderly women are more likely to read the news section, food section, lifestyle section, and travel section than less affluent women. They are also more likely to read the *USA Today*, but are less likely to read the advertising supplement than are less affluent elderly female newspaper readers.

Magazine Reading

Unlike newspaper readership, which tends to increase with age or at least remain fairly stable from the middle adult years to the later years of life, magazine readership tends to decline with age (ANPA, 1973; Harris & Associates, 1975; Time Buying Services, 1986) and then drop off dramatically at the age of 70 (Chaffee & Wilson, 1975). Danowski (1975) found that elderly people spend about 30 minutes a day reading magazines. This estimate is somewhat higher than the estimates of marketing research on magazine consumption, which suggests men and women over the age of 65 spend just over 16 minutes a day reading magazines (Time Buying Services, 1986).

Magazine readership surveys reveal that magazine readers are generally affluent and well educated (Doolittle, 1979). Although elderly people spend less time reading magazines than do almost any other age group, the more wealthy and better-educated elderly people prefer magazines as a news source more than their less educated and less affluent counterparts do (Doolittle, 1979). Somewhat surprisingly, McEnvoy and Vincent (1980) found that the price of reading material does not seem to keep elderly people from reading. Although elderly people tend to purchase paperback books, the price of reading materials is relatively unrelated to reading.

Mundorf and Brownell (1990) compared magazine readership of college-age and elderly adults and found differences in magazine preferences. In addition, gender differences can account for some of the differences in preferences that could be due to age. For example, almost 94% of the college-age men sampled read *Sports Illustrated*, while 46.9% of the elderly men did. However, while 29% of the college-age women read *Sports Illustrated*, only about 2.5% of the elderly women read it on a regular or occasional basis. Mundorf and Brownell (1990) report that *TV Guide* is the only magazine widely read by both age cohorts.

Burnett (1991) also examined the magazine readership of elderly adults and found that affluent elderly people read many more magazines than do less affluent elderly people. Affluent elderly men are more likely to read *Business Week, Newsweek, Time, New Yorker, U.S. News & World Report, Forbes, Fortune, Money,* and *National Geographic* than are less affluent elderly men. The only magazine that moderate-income elderly men are more likely to read than are more affluent elderly men is *Field & Stream.* There are no differences in the likelihood of reading *People, Sports Illustrated, TV Guide, Reader's Digest* or tabloids such as the *National Enquirer.* Moderate-income women are more likely to read *Family Circle* and more affluent elderly women are more likely to read *Newsweek, Time, U.S. News & World Report, Money,* and *National Geographic* than are less affluent elderly women.

In a painstakingly careful and thorough investigation of magazine use in America, Frank and Greenberg (1980) categorized the public into 14 groups. The elderly group closely resembles the U.S. census data for people 65 years old and older; they were predominately women (71%) and were an average of 61 years old, with 40% of the group being retired (in contrast with about 15% of the total population being retired). In addition, 35% of the elderly group were widowed and only 18% had children still living at home. The group was somewhat disadvantaged educationally. Thirty-one percent of the group had the equivalent of a grammar school education or less, 60% had graduated from high school, and about 9% had graduated from college. Frank and Greenberg (1980) found that elderly people read very few magazines compared to the total adult population. In fact, elderly people read fewer magazines than any of the other 14 adult groups except for the alienated or "detached" adult category, which is typified by having few interests or activities and little chance that their needs are going to be met through the media.

The 10 magazines read most often by elderly people were *Reader's Digest* (30.8% of elderly people read this magazine regularly), *TV Guide* (21.6%), *Better Homes and Gardens* (21.6%), *Good Housekeeping* (20.1%), *Family Circle* (18.7%), *McCalls* (15.2%), *Ladies Home Journal* (14.5%), *Women's Day* (14.3%), *Home and Garden* (10.5%), and *National Geographic* (8.9%). The magazines read least included automotive magazines, African American magazines, business and finance magazines, fashion magazines, mechanics magazines, men's magazines, outdoor magazines, and sports magazines. Frank and Greenberg (1980) suggested that some elderly readers read *True Romance* to battle loneliness and *Newsweek* to keep informed.

In a more recent examination of the reading habits of the elderly, Robinson and Skill (1995) identified the most popular magazines of elderly adults as *Reader's Digest, TV Guide, Better Homes & Garden, National Geographic, Good Housekeeping, Family Circle, Ladies Home Journal, McCall's, Time,* and *Woman's Day.* This obviously reflects the large number of women in this age cohort. The top-ranked magazines for the 55 to 64 age cohort are quite similar to those of the 65 and older age cohort, but differ significantly from the 18 to 34 cohort. Only *McCall's* and *Woman's Day* were dropped from the list and were replaced by *People* and *Newsweek.*

FILM AND VCR VIEWING

Meyersohn's (1961) study suggested that movie attendance decreases with age. The General Social Survey (National Opinion Research Center, 1993) data on film attendance clearly supported Myersohn's claim. Nearly 90% of the 18 to 24 year olds surveyed reported seeing at least one film within the past year. Nearly 80% of the 25 to 54 cohort had attended a movie and just over 55% of the 55 to 64 cohort had gone to a theater to see a film. In contrast, just 38.3% of the elderly adults surveyed reported attending a movie within the past year.

Handel (1950) found that, consistent with their other media content preferences, elderly people prefer informational films to comedy and horror-mystery films. Not surprisingly, however, data from Market Opinion Research (1975, as cited in Atkin, 1976) found that only 4% of the 3,000 elderly people surveyed said movies are an important leisure activity. In contrast, 67% reported that television was an important leisure activity, 45% said that visiting others was important, and 39% reported that reading was important.

While VCRs are used for many things in addition to watching movies at home, it is safe to say this is a very common use. In 1997, approximately 82% of all U.S. households had at least one VCR (Brunner, 1998) and in 1992 more than $40 million was spent on video rentals (Robinson, 1993). While VCR use among elderly people is growing, the General Social Survey (National Opinion Research Center, 1993) data on VCR use in 1992 clearly indicate that elderly people are far less likely to use a VCR than are younger people. Just over 65% of the 18 to 24 cohort had recently used a VCR and nearly 70% of the 25 to 54 cohort had used a VCR. In sharp contrast, only 48% of the 55 to 64 cohort had used a VCR and less than 31% of the 65 and older cohort had used a VCR in the past year.

COMPUTER USE

SeniorNet is a nonprofit organization with over 140 learning centers and over 27,000 members across the United States. SeniorNet members are 50 years old and older and dedicated to providing other older adults access to computer technology and computer training in a variety of areas, including desktop publishing, word processing, Internet access, e-mailing, and financial planning. SeniorNet is the result of a research project funded in 1986 by the Markle Foundation to determine whether telecommunications and computers enhance the lives of older adults. Since then, elderly SeniorNet volunteers have taught over 100,000 adults 50 years old and older a variety of computer skills.

In addition to training and access, SeniorNet also operates two discussion groups that older people can access through America Online (keyword: SeniorNet) and the World Wide Web. These discussions cover a wide variety of topics and are open to the public. Membership in SeniorNet is not a requirement for participation—all older people are welcome to participate. On the Web, the discussion boards are called the SeniorNet RoundTables and can be found at the following URL: *http://www.seniornet.org.*

In an effort to determine the extent to which elderly people use computers in their daily lives, SeniorNet recently conducted a survey (Adler, 1996). The telephone survey of adults 55 years old and older was completed in November 1995 and underwritten by a grant from the Intel Corporation. The results of the survey clearly demonstrate that many elderly people have adopted this technology and increasing numbers have become enthusiastic users of computers.

Adler (1996) reported that in November 1995, 30% of adults 55 to 75 owned a computer. Just 16 months earlier, only 21% of this cohort reported owning a personal computer. This represents a 40% increase in computer ownership in 16 months. Nearly one third of the men 65 to 74 owned a personal computer and 23% of these 75 years old or older owned a computer. In addition to being more likely to own a computer, male seniors were much more likely to use an online service to access the Internet or send e-mail. This trend held true regardless of whether the seniors were married.

Not surprisingly, older people who were college graduates were much more likely to own a personal computer than their less well-educated counterparts. In fact, 53% of the older people with a college degree reported owning a computer, while only 22% of the respondents with some college education owned a computer. Only 7% of the older people who had not completed high school owned a computer in November 1995.

The most common use of the computer was word processing. Over 80% of older people reported using their computers for word processing, 60% to play games, 54% to manage their personal finances, 34% for desktop publishing, and 28% to access an online service. While only 17% of all older computer owners reported using an online service to access the Internet or send e-mail, 38% of those with a college degree reported being online. Keep in mind that in 1998, approximately 37% of all households in the United States reported being connected to the Internet ("37 Percent," 1999).

Adler (1996) wrote that one of the major reasons reported by elderly people for using personal computers is the ability to send and receive e-mail. This ability to communicate with their children and grandchildren, many of whom live in another city, is seen by many as a significant advantage of the personal computer. Similarly, many older people report that access to the Internet allows them to obtain financial information that is superior to and more convenient than other sources of financial information. Older women in particular find the availability of many different newspapers to be a significant advantage of going online. For many older people, the ability to gain access to health information is a factor that increases their likelihood of going online.

It is common in many older households that one person is the primary computer user and his or her partner may not use the computer at all. Generally, it is the man who is the computer user and the woman who is less likely to use the computer. However, previous work experience seems to account for much of this gender difference. In addition, many older women report they would be more interested in purchasing and using a computer if they believed they would have access to computer-training courses.

SUMMARY

Elderly people spend much of their day watching television. They watch more television than do any other age group of viewers and, although they enjoy entertainment programming a great deal, they watch shows that provide information at rates higher than do younger adults. While we might expect decreased mobility, economic difficulties, sensory decline, and decreased opportunities for social interaction to contribute to high levels of television use, the preference for informative programming is significant and has been offered as evidence refuting disengagement theory. People trying to disengage from society would not seem likely to be interested in C-SPAN, local politics, news, current events, or public affairs, and elderly people certainly demonstrate high levels of interest in these types of programs.

It is also clear that many elderly individuals use personal computers to stay socially integrated. Programs such as Senior Net provide skill training and help elderly people to fulfill their interpersonal needs. At the same time, communicating via computer can remedy many of the barriers elderly people face in interpersonal encounters. Personal computers and the Internet can also provide younger people with direct interpersonal experience with elderly people —making them less dependent on the media for information about aging and elderly people. Younger adults may not know the age of the elderly individual they find themselves chatting with until they have already formed an initial impression that is not age based. Further, these young people may be less inclined to hold ageist attitudes if they have had successful interpersonal contact with elderly adults.

Knowing that elderly people spend a significant amount of their time with the mass media and knowing their content preferences provides researchers with some insights into how elderly people spend their day, and what their interests and their needs are. Listening to talk shows on the radio, reading a daily newspaper, and sending e-mail to loved ones are all indications of the effort that many elderly adults make to remain engaged in society and to maintain their social networks. Perhaps those who argue for disengagement as a theory of aging have mistaken a reduction in opportunity for engagement with a reduction in interest.

Keep in mind, however, that elderly people are a heterogeneous group. The TV programming preferences, magazine preferences, radio listening preferences, and film preferences of elderly people vary with income, education level, and gender, just as the viewing habits of younger adults, teens, and children do. This highlights the need for adopting a life-span developmental perspective to understand the process of growing older.

■ REFERENCES

Adler, R. P. (1996). *Older adults and computers: Report of a national survey.* [On-line]. Available: *http://www.seniornet.org/research/survey2.html*

American Newspaper Publishers Association. (1973, April 26). *News and editorial content and readership of the daily newspaper.* (News Research Bulletin, 1120). Washington, DC: Author.

Atkin, C. (1976). Mass communication and aging. In H. Oyer & E. Jayne Oyer (Eds.), *Aging and communication* (pp. 99–118). Baltimore, MD: University Park Press.

Atkin, D. & LaRose, R. (1991). Cable access: Market concerns amidst the marketplace of ideas. *Journalism Quarterly, 68*(3), 354–362.

Barton, R. (1977). Soap operas provide meaningful communication for the elderly. *Feedback, 19*, 5–8.

Berkman, L., & Syme, S. (1979). Social networks, host resistance, and mortality. *American Journal of Epidemiology, 109*, 186–204.

Beville, H. (1985). *Audience ratings.* Hillsdale, NJ: Lawrence Erlbaum Associates.

Bleise, N. (1982). Media in the rocking chair: Media uses and functions among the elderly. In G. Gumpert & R. Cathcart (Eds.), *Intermedia: Interpersonal communication in a media world* (2nd ed, pp. 624–634.) New York: Oxford University Press.

Bogart, L. (1972). Negro and white media exposure: New evidence. *Journalism Quarterly, 49*, 15–21.

Botwinick, J. (1977). Intellectual abilities. In J. Birren & K. Schaie (Eds.), *Handbook of the psychology of aging* (pp. 580–605). New York: Van Nostrand Reinhold.

Bower, R. (1973). *Television and the public.* New York: Holt, Rinehart & Winston.

Bower, R. (1985). *The changing television audience in America.* New York: Columbia University Press.

Brunner, B. (Ed.). (1998). *Information please almanac.* Boston, MA: Houghton Mifflin.

Burgoon, J., & Burgoon, M. (1980). Predictors of newspaper readership. *Journalism Quarterly, 57*(4), 589–596.

Burnett, J. (1991). Examining the media habits of the affluent elderly. *Journal of Advertising Research, 31*(5), 33–41.

Chaffee, S., & Wilson, D. (1975, April). *Adult life cycle changes in mass media usage.* Paper presented at the annual meeting of the Association for Education in Journalism, Ottawa, Canada.

Danowski, J. (1975, Nov.). *Informational aging: Interpersonal and mass communication patterns at a retirement community.* Paper presented at the meetings of the Gerontological Society, Louisville, KY.

Davis, R. (1971). Television and the older adult. *Journal of Broadcasting, 15,* 153–159.

Davis, R. (1984). *Television and the aging audience.* Los Angeles: University of Southern California, Andrus Gerontology Center.

Davis, R., & Davis, J. (1985). *TV's image of the elderly: A practical guide for change.* Lexington, MA: Lexington Books.

Davis, R., & Kubey, R. (1982). Growing old on television and with television. In National Institute of Mental Health, *Television and behavior: Ten years of scientific progress and implications for the eighties* (Vol 2, pp. 201–208) (DHHS Publication No. ADM 82–1195). Washington, DC: U.S. Government Printing Office.

Davis, R. & Westbrook, G. (1985). Television in the lives of the elderly: Attitudes and opinions. *Journal of Broadcasting and Electronic Media, 29,* 209–214.

DeGrazia, S. (1961). The uses of time. In R. Kleemeier (Ed.), *Aging and leisure.* New York: Oxford University Press.

Doolittle, J. (1979). News media use by older adults. *Journalism Quarterly, 56*(2), 311–345.

Dortch, S. (1998, May). Ready readers, reluctant readers. *American Demographics, 20,* 8–13.

Faber, R., Brown, J., & McLeod, J. (1979). Coming of age in the global village: Television and adolescence. In E. Wartella (Ed.), *Children communicating: Media and development of thought, speech, and understanding* (pp. 215–249). Beverly Hills, CA: Sage.

Faminghetti, R. (Ed.). (1998). *The world almanac & book of facts.* Mahwah, NJ: World Almanac Books.

Fozard, J., Wolf, E., Bell, B., McFarland, R., & Podolsky, S. (1977). Visual perception and communication. In J. Birren & K. Schaie (Eds.), *Handbook of the psychology of aging* (pp. 497–534). New York: Van Nostrand Reinhold.

Frank, R., & Greenberg, M. (1980). *The public's use of television.* Beverly Hills, CA: Sage.

Gerbner, G., Gross, L., Signorelli, N., & Morgan, M. (1980). Aging with television: Images on television drama and conceptions of social reality. *Journal of Communication, 30*(1), 37–47.

Goodman, R. (1990). Television news viewing by older adults. *Journalism Quarterly, 67*(1), 137–141.

Gordon, C., Gaitz, C., & Scott, J. (1976). Leisure and lives: Personal expressivity across the life span. In R. Binstock & E. Shanas (Eds.), *Handbook of aging and the social sciences* (pp. 310–341). New York: Van Nostrand Reinhold.

Handel, L. (1950). *Hollywood looks at its audience.* Urbana, IL: University of Illinois Press.

Harris & Associates, Inc. (1975). *The myth and reality of aging in America.* Washington, DC: The National Council on Aging.

Harwood, J. (1997). Viewing age: Lifespan identity and television viewing choices. *Journal of Broadcasting & Electronic Media, 41,* 203–213.

Hoar, J. (1961). A study of free time activities of 200 aged persons. *Sociology and Social Work, 45,* 157–163.

Kagan, P. (1998, March 16). *Marketing New Media, The Cable Industry at a Glance.* [On-line]. Available: *http://www.ncta.com/dir_current.html.*

Katz, E., Gurevitch, M., & Haas, H. (1973). On the use of mass media for important things. *American Sociological Review, 38,* 164–181.

Kent, K., & Rush, R. (1976). How communication behavior of older persons affects their public affairs knowledge. *Journalism Quarterly, 53*(1), 40–46.

Korzenny, F., & Neuendorf, K. (1980). Television viewing and the self concept of the elderly. *Journal of Communication, 30,* 71–80.

Kubey, R. (1980). Television and aging: Past, present, and future. *Gerontologist, 20,* 16–35.

Lull, J. (1980). Family communication patterns and the social uses of television. *Communication Research, 7,* 319–334.

McEnvoy, G., & Vincent, C. (1980). Who reads and why? *Journal of Communication, 30*(1), 134–140.

Mediamark Research Inc. (1991). *Audio & video equipment & leisure activities.* New York: Author.

Meyersohn, R. (1961). A critical examination of commercial entertainment. In R. Kleemeier (Ed.), *Aging and leisure* (pp. 243–272). New York: Oxford University Press.

Mundorf, N. & Brownell, W. (1990). Media preferences of older and younger adults. *Gerontologist, 30*(5), 685–692.

National Opinion Research Center. (1993). *General social survey* [Machine-readable data file]. Chicago: Author.

National Opinion Research Center. (1997). *General social survey* [Machine-readable data file]. Chicago: Author.

Parker, E., Barry, D., & Smythe, D. (1955). *The television-radio audience and religion.* New York: Harper & Row.

Phillips, L. W., & Sternthal, B. (1977). Age differences in information processing: A perspective on the aged consumer. *Journal of Marketing Research, 12*(4), 444–457.

Robinson, J. (1972). Toward defining the functions of television. In E. Rubinstein, G. Comstock, & J. Murray (Eds.), *Television and social behavior: Vol. 4. Television in day-to-day patterns of use* (pp. 568–602). Washington, DC: U.S. Government Printing Office.

Robinson, J. (1981). Television and leisure. *Journal of Communication, 31,* 120–130.

Robinson, J. (1993). As we like it. *American Demographics, 15*(2), 44–51.

Robinson, J., & Skill, T. (1995). The invisible generation: Portrayals of the elderly on prime-time television. *Communication Reports, 8*(2), 111–119.

Salisbury, P. (1981). Older adults as older readers: Newspaper readership after age 65. *Newspaper Research Journal, 3*(1), 38.

Schiffman, L. (1971). Sources of information for the elderly. *Journal of Advertising Research, 11*(5), 33–37.

Schramm, W. (1969). Aging and mass communication. In M. Riley, J. Riley, & M. Johnson (Eds.), *Aging and society: Vol.2. Aging and the professions* (pp. 352–375). New York: Russell Sage

Schramm, W., & White, D. (1949). Age, education and economic status: Factors in newspaper reading. *Journalism Quarterly, 26,* 150–158.

Schrieber, E., & Boyd, D. (1980). How the elderly perceive television commercials. *Journal of Communication, 30,* 61–70.

Simmons Market Research Bureau (1991). *The 1990 study of media and markets*. New York: Author.

Simmons Market Research Bureau (1996). *The 1995 study of media and markets*. New York: Author.

Spring, J. (1993). Seven days of play. *American Demographics, 15*(3), 50–55.

Steiner, G. (1963). *The people look at television*. New York: Knopf.

37 percent of U.S. households now in Internet (1999, Feb. 1). *Springfield News and Sun*, p. A18

Time Buying Services. (1986). *TV Dimensions '86*. New York: Author.

Time Buying Services. (1989). *TV Dimensions '89*. New York: Author.

Universal Almanac. (1991). Harrisburg, VA: The Banta Co.

U.S. Bureau of the Census. *Population profile of the United States: 1991*. (Current Population Reports, Series P–23, No. 173), Washington, DC: U.S. Government Printing Office.

Wenner, L. (1976). Functional analysis of TV viewing for older adults. *Journal of Broadcasting, 20*, 77–88.

Zorn, E. (1987, December). Radio news: Alive and struggling–Debt, deregulation, and info-bits. *Washington Journalism Review, 9*(10), 16–18.

CHAPTER 5

Mass Communication Theory and Media Portrayals of Elderly People

I t is suggested in chapter 4 that elderly people spend a great deal of time watching television, listening to the radio or recorded music, reading, and using personal computers. Concern over such use patterns stems from the belief that media use impacts the user in a variety of different ways. This chapter provides several theoretical frameworks for better understanding how media use might affect elderly people, as well as younger media-consumers.

This chapter is divided into three sections. The first section provides a historical overview of media effects theories. Section two extends this discussion of the impact of the mass media and outlines five current theories of media effects. The final section focuses on how elderly people are portrayed in the media, specifically on how elderly people are portrayed on television, in newspapers and magazines, and in advertisements; and on some implications of these portrayals.

85

MASS COMMUNICATION THEORY: AN OVERVIEW

Historical Effects Theories

This overview of media effects theories begins with the hypodermic needle model. The hypodermic needle model or bullet theory posits powerful effects from mere exposure to a mediated message. Based in a tradition of mechanistic stimulus–response psychological thought—the bullet theory suggests that a message (a stimulus) presented to an audience produced an almost standardized, automatic effect (a response) on audience members. Felsenthal (1981) summarized the theory aptly when he wrote: "Communication was seen as a magic bullet that transferred ideas or feelings or motivations almost automatically from one mind to another" (p. 24). Although the bullet theory is not commonly accepted today, knowledge of the theory helps in understanding the theories that have developed after it.

On October 30, 1938, Orson Welles, broadcasting on CBS radio, told listeners that Martians had landed and were destroying an area just outside Grover Mills, New Jersey. What sounded to listeners like a typical radio news broadcast was really a performance by Welles and the Mercury Theatre on the Air. Many people panicked, actually believing there had been an invasion and that large mechanical monsters were running amok. While the details of this historical radio broadcast have since been called into question, it is easy to see why the bullet theory or hypodermic needle model of media effects was a credible theory. It seemed to many people in 1938 that a message describing a Martian invasion was presented to the listening audience and that the audience was directly affected.

The hypodermic needle model of media effects considers the mass media to be all-powerful and capable of influencing audience members in one easy step. Exposure to a mediated message automatically resulted in some specific effect. It was thought that audience members could do little if anything to protect themselves against the mass media. Born in a time when propaganda was a common fear, this theory of powerful effects seemed a reasonable explanation for successful and otherwise counterintuitive social influence campaigns.

Although the notion of an all-powerful mass media is all too commonly accepted today, most mass communication scholars are now skeptical of the bullet theory. In fact, researchers in the

1940s carefully examined the bullet theory and found little evidence to support the theory.

Perhaps the most important piece of research suggesting the mass media was not all-powerful was offered by Lazarsfeld, Berelson, and Gaudet (1948) in *The People's Choice*, a test of the hypodermic needle model in an election in Erie County, Ohio. Specifically, Lazarsfeld and his colleagues examined how mediated campaign messages influenced the election. Although the mass media did have some influence on the way people voted, the researchers felt that the majority of influence on the voters came from interpersonal conversations and *not* as a direct effect of the mass media. In fact, media influence was thought to be considerably less influential than interpersonal conversation. A great many people today believe this to be true, and most textbooks state unequivocally that the mass media has less impact on people than interpersonal communication.

Lazarsfeld and his colleagues noticed that the mass media provided information about the election to the members of an audience who were already interested in the election. Furthermore, it was found that many people went to knowledgeable parties, called "opinion leaders," to get even more information about the election. Thus, it appeared to Lazarsfeld that the media affected some people directly, but those people initially disinterested in politics were more influenced by their conversations with opinion leaders than they were by their exposure to mediated campaign messages. Lazarsfeld concluded that informal social relationships are an important consideration in determining how a message will affect an audience member. Stated simply, interpersonal communication and relationships determine, in part, the effects of the mass media. It was left to subsequent mass communication theorists to consider the relationship between mass and interpersonal communication in explaining media effects.

Lazarsfeld, Berelson, and Gaudet (1948) discovered that mere exposure did not explain the effects of the mass media. They found that the mass media was not very effective in changing attitudes and that people tended to recall, attend to, and expose themselves to messages that were consistent with attitudes they already held. These findings helped mark the change from a powerful effects perspective to a more limited effects approach to studying media influence. The term *limited effects* is particularly appropriate because theorists today realize that, in addition to media exposure, many other factors must be considered to understand media effects.

In an attempt at summarizing the known, limited effects of the mass media, Klapper (1960) published *The Effects of Mass Communication.* Essentially, Klapper concluded that mediated messages do not normally cause much change in audience attitudes or behavior. Klapper argued that although a mediated message could result in significant change, most often mediated messages strengthen attitudes that audience members already hold and reinforce behavior patterns that already exist. In short, Klapper pointed out that mediated messages are just one part of the influence process. Other factors such as group processes and norms, cultural norms and values, opinion leadership, family and peer influence, personality characteristics of audience members, and the selective nature of perception must *all* be considered if media effects are to be understood.

The limited effects model points in the direction that current mass communication effects theories are heading. Audience members are now seen as actively participating in the mass communication situation through the selection of content and the interpretation of that content based on factors such as their past experience, individual life situation, group affiliations, and aspirations. We have moved from a model of communication effects in which the only variable of importance was exposure to a model in which many factors must be considered. The message, the perceived characteristics of source, the channel or medium, and receivers characteristics must all be considered to understand media effects.

Current Effects Theories

Social Learning Theory. Perhaps the most widely accepted explanation for media effects is social learning theory (Bandura, 1977, 1986). While previous theories such as the hypodermic needle model suggested that people learned through direct experience and a process of trial and error, Bandura suggested people could learn vicariously through the observation of others. In fact, Bandura (1977) contended that anything that can be learned from direct experience can be learned vicariously and that in many cases learning observationally is more efficient than the trial-and-error process of direct experience learning.

Learning vicariously means that an individual can learn by watching others behave, and part of this process may entail the imitation of the behavior performed by a model. Even though social learning theory has been used quite successfully to explain imitative behavior, Bandura was quite clear to note that observational learning and imitation are not the same. Social learning goes far beyond the notion that audience members may imitate models or characters on television. Audience members can also learn the consequences of a particular behavior by watching what happens to the model when they perform that particular behavior. Thus, an audience member may learn a new behavior vicariously and not perform the behavior until a situation arises that suggests the behavior might be beneficial in attaining a particular goal.

From the social learning theory perspective, television portrayals are significant sources of information for a variety of reasons. The primary reason is the pervasiveness of the media and the astronomical number of potential models. While much research demonstrated that television's influence is not as strong as other agencies of socialization, particularly interpersonal sources, there is compelling evidence that audience members can learn through observation of television (Bandura, 1965, 1973, 1986; Bandura, Blanchard, & Ritter, 1969; Bandura, Ross, & Ross, 1963a; Dail & Way, 1985; DeFleur & DeFleur, 1967; Gerbner, Gross, Signorelli & Morgan, 1980, 1986; Gerson, 1966; Greenberg, Hines, Buerkel-Rothfuss, & Atkin, 1980; Passuth & Cook, 1985; Robinson, 1972; Weaver & Wakshlag, 1986).

Generally, symbolic modeling (watching a model on film or videotape) is almost as effective as watching a live model (Bandura, 1973; Bandura & Mischel, 1965; Bandura et al., 1963a) and just as effective when multiple symbolic models are used (Bandura & Menlove, 1968). The effectiveness of observational learning is further improved when the audience watches a model and physically participates (Bandura et al., 1969). Research on observational learning clearly indicates that the relative effectiveness of a model is influenced by a host of factors. People are more likely to be influenced by a model if they find themselves in situations or circumstances that are similar to those they have viewed on television (Berkowitz & Geen, 1966, 1967; Dail & Way, 1985; Doob & Macdonald, 1979; Geen & Berkowitz, 1967; Gerbner, Gross, Signorelli, & Morgan, 1986), when portrayals are perceived as being realistic (Feshbach, 1972), when the model is reinforced for the behavior (Bandura, Ross, & Ross, 1963b), when the model is of high status (Turner & Berkowitz, 1972), and when there are multiple models demonstrating a behavior (Bandura & Menlove, 1968). In addition, audience members are more likely to be influenced by a model if they perceive the model to be competent (Baron, 1970; Rosenbaum & Tucker, 1962), similar to them in attitude (Baron, 1970), and of the same gender (Perry & Bussey, 1979), and if the model behaves consistently over time (Fehrenbach, Miller, & Thelen, 1979). In cases of inconsistent behavior, children tend to be influenced by the model's nonverbal behavior more than by the verbal behavior (Bryan, Redfield, & Mader, 1971; Bryan & Walbek, 1970).

These effects are not merely short-term aberrations. Bandura and Menlove (1968) found these cognitive and behavioral changes to last a month after the experiment ended. In addition to the many studies that have demonstrated that people learn new information from the mass media, research has also shown that media portrayals can increase altruistic behavior in children (Ahammer & Murray, 1979; Tower, Singer, Singer, & Biggs, 1979), influence the rate of self-reinforcement for task success (Bandura & Kupers, 1964), reduce phobic reactions to dogs (Bandura, Grusec, & Menlove, 1967) and snakes (Bandura et al., 1969), and help treat adults with sexual problems (Bandura, 1986).

The valence (positive or negative direction of the behavior), salience (importance of the behavior to the storyline), and context (humorous or serious) of the behavior are important considerations in the analysis of portrayals on television. As Bandura (1986) pointed out, when programs report detailed accounts of some target behavior and portray the consequences of such actions as positive, even if the positive outcomes are transitory and the deviant action is later punished, people learn the antisocial behavior. The ultimate negative consequences can be easily forgotten or misunderstood by some audience members and others may attribute the failure to unrelated factors (e.g., bad luck).

Given these circumstances, Bandura (1986) posited that viewers can easily acquire faulty beliefs when they learn from observation. Faulty observations can be the result of inaccurate or insufficient information, faulty logic, or poor cognitive skills. In the words of Bandura (1977), "Beliefs about the prevailing conditions of reinforcement can outweigh the influence of experienced consequences" (p. 166).

This is consistent with a growing body of evidence that suggests that when an individual is relatively dependent on a source of information, there is a higher likelihood of being influenced by that source (DeFleur & DeFleur, 1967; Gerson, 1966; Greenberg & Dervin, 1970; Robinson, Skill, Nussbaum, & Moreland, 1985; Tolley, 1973; Weaver & Wakshlag, 1986). Of course, in situations where other sources of information are available (e.g., peers, parents, or church) the mass media is still used by audience members (Dail & Way, 1985; Gerbner, Gross, Signorelli & Morgan, 1980; Greenberg, Hines, et al., 1980).

Comstock, Chaffee, Katzman, McCombs, and Roberts (1978) pointed out that television resembles religion in the communication of values and interpretations of the world, but differs in that television does not generally do so in an explicit manner. Bandura's work and the research supporting his theory clearly demonstrated that the implicit nature of portrayals does not necessarily decrease the impact of the portrayals. In some respects, the implicit nature of the portrayals may increase the effectiveness of the messages.

Cultivation Hypothesis. Gerbner (1969) suggested that people watching television are acquiring a view of the "real world" that is shaped by the pervasive themes in the television content they view. According to Gerbner, people do not intentionally or voluntarily adopt attitudes based on the information provided by a single television program; rather, they acquire TV views of reality that are based on underlying cultural themes that occur throughout television programming. Thus, audience members do not simply learn negative information about elderly people from negative portrayals; rather, audience members cultivate a conception of reality that is informed by a myth-like theme such as "the elderly are a vanishing breed" or "live fast, die young, and leave a pretty corpse." Such themes are rampant throughout television.

Unlike many earlier effects theories, the cultivation hypothesis suggests that the effects of television content are not a result of mere exposure, but rather a function of repeated exposures to common themes. That is to say, people are affected by television content not because they have watched a violent program, but because violence is so common on television that people begin to expect the world to be as violent as it has been portrayed on television. The effect of this portrayed violence, according to Gerbner, is not an increase or decrease in the likelihood of an audience member actually behaving in a violent manner. The effect of viewing so much violence is that viewers begin to feel anxious, fearful, and alienated because they perceive the real world to be as violent as it is portrayed on television.

The age of the actors and models on television provides a simple example of a theme that occurs throughout fictional and nonfictional programming. Gerbner, Gross, Signorelli, and

Morgan (1980) examined prime-time television programming and found that most characters are between 25 and 45 years old and only 2.3% of the characters are 65 years old or older. According to the cultivation hypothesis, people who view a lot of television (heavy viewers) should begin to think that not very many elderly people exist in the world and, perhaps even worse, that they are somehow of less consequence because they are not often depicted.

Gerbner and his colleagues also observed that older characters are more likely to be depicted as bad people. They also reported that 80% of the older women and 70% of the older men depicted on television are "not held in high esteem or treated courteously" (Gerbner, Gross, Signorelli, Morgan, 1980, p. 45) and that older characters are more likely to be shown as eccentric or foolish than are younger characters.

Knowing how elderly people are portrayed on television, Gerbner and his colleagues devised a questionnaire asking people about the health and longevity of older people. They found that the more people watch television, the more they view elderly people in negative and unfavorable terms. Specifically, they found that heavy viewers feel older people are less bright, less open-minded, less alert, and less efficient. Generally, these viewers regard elderly people as a vanishing breed. Further, they found that the younger the age group, the stronger the prejudice, presumably because younger people rely more on the media than they do on personal experience for information about elderly people. Similar attitudes were observed in a sample of about 600 sixth to ninth graders. Interestingly, watching television was not found to be related to any positive perceptions of elderly people.

To summarize, the cultivation hypothesis suggests that heavy and light television viewers differ in their conceptions of what the world is like. Those differences in worldview are a function of pervasive or common themes running throughout television programming and the other mass media. The evidence indicates that a cultivation effect exists, but that the cultivation effect may be enhanced or reduced by factors such as direct experience and education. While our understanding is not yet complete, it appears that audience members can develop or cultivate conceptions of reality based on the way people, places, and things are portrayed on television.

Agenda Setting. Shaw and McCombs (1977) describe the agenda setting function of the mass media as follows:

Considerable evidence has accumulated that editors and broadcasters play an important part in shaping our social reality as they go about their day-to-day task of choosing and displaying news.... This impact of the mass media—the ability to affect cognitive change among individuals, to structure their thinking—has been labeled the agenda setting function of the mass media. Here may lie the most important effect of mass communication—its ability to mentally order and organize our world for us. In short, the mass media may not be successful at telling us what to think, but they are stunningly successful at telling us what to think about. (p. 5)

Discussed as early as 1922 by Lippman in *Public Opinion*, agenda setting differs from previously discussed theories of media influence because agenda setting does not focus on what information people may learn from the mass media. Rather, agenda setting refers to the ability of the mass media to influence audience members' levels of awareness about issues. The most basic premise of agenda setting—that the more prominently an issue is portrayed in the media, the more importance or salience an audience member will attribute to that issue—has received a good deal of support (Brosius & Kepplinger, 1990; Eaton, 1989; Iyengar & Kinder, 1987; Mackuen, 1981; McCombs & Shaw, 1972; Shaw & McCombs, 1977; Smith 1987).

The research suggests that audience agendas are more likely to be set when the issue is unobtrusive than when the issue interferes in people's daily lives (Blood, 1981; Weaver, Graber, McCombs, & Eyal, 1981; Winter & Eyal, 1981; Zucker, 1978). Thus, young people with grandparents living in another city may well be susceptible to having their agenda about elderly people set by the mass media. Further, we know that when people have a high level of interest in a topic and high levels of uncertainty about that topic (often called the need for orientation), individuals are more likely to have their agenda set by the prominence an issue receives in the mass media (Shaw & McCombs, 1977). Thus, adults with parents who are growing older may have a high level of interest in issues facing elderly people and little expertise in the area. Again, such people may be at an increased risk for having their agenda set by the mass media. This means that audience members may not be alerted to the most important problems facing elderly people unless these problems are emphasized by the mass media. And, obviously, if trivial or biased issues are the focus of the mass media, the opportunity for the mismanagement of scarce social resources is increased.

Many writers observed that news reported in the mass media is event biased. *Event biased* means that things that are reported on the news tend to be events (e.g., the opening of a bridge or a car accident) rather than issues that are nonevents (e.g., starvation in America). Thus, an event such as an elderly person being evicted may make the news on a slow news day, but an elderly person feeling lonely is not news. Consequently, it would be quite difficult, for instance, to convince taxpayers to provide computer conferencing equipment for institutionalized elderly people to supplement interpersonal conversation because, among other reasons, too many people do not understand the importance of conversation to health. And such issues are rarely, if ever, addressed on the news. If the agenda being set by the mass media is inaccurate, such an agenda may serve to impede social progress and lead researchers and policy makers in the wrong direction.

Uses and Gratification Perspective. The uses and gratifications perspective offers still another way of looking at media effects. Uses and gratifications researchers examine not how a message influences the attitudes and behavior of an audience member, but instead how an audience member uses the mass media to meet his or her needs. From the uses and gratifications perspective, media use is a goal-directed effort focused upon satisfying specific needs—just as sleep, hobbies, or interpersonal contact may be used to fulfill needs. Audience members actively select the particular medium (e.g., television) and the content they consume (e.g., *60 Minutes*) based on the needs that they are trying to fulfill (e.g., environmental surveillance). In fact, according to this perspective, audience members are so active in the process that they actually shape or interpret the messages in ways that increase the likelihood of their needs being met. Thus, the same message will be interpreted quite differently by different audience members, depending on their needs (Katz, Blumler, & Gurevitch, 1974). While researchers use various lists of needs, most typologies suggest that people have the need to understand their environment, to experience pleasurable emotional feelings, to feel some level of self-esteem, to be socially integrated with others, and to escape the tensions of everyday life (Katz, Gurevitch, & Haas, 1973).

Bleise (1982) interviewed 214 elderly adults in an attempt to determine what purpose or functions the mass media provide for elderly people. Ten uses and gratifications were identified; to a supplement or substitute for interpersonal interaction; to gather content for interpersonal interactions; to form or reinforce self-perceptions and to gather information about societal perceptions of various groups of people; to learn appropriate behaviors, including age-appropriate behavior; to provide intellectual stimulation and challenge (e.g., game shows); to provide a less costly substitute for other media; to provide networking and mutual support; to provide self-improvement (e.g., exercise programs and language lessons); to provide entertainment; and to provide "company" and safety (p. 575).

Bleise's (1982) data supported Schramm's (1969) contention that the mass media may be used as a functional alternative to interpersonal relationships and conversation. Graney and Graney (1974) call this phenomenon the substitution hypothesis and suggest that elderly people substitute the mass media for interpersonal interaction when face-to-face interaction is unavailable. Eighty-nine percent of Graney's subjects reported using the mass media just as the substitution hypothesis predicted. Approximately 17% reported using the mass media as nearly a complete replacement for interpersonal contact, 32% reported moderate levels of substitution, and 40% reported occasional substitutions of the mass media for interpersonal interaction. Other research supported this hypothesis (Bierig & Dimmick, 1979; Cassata, 1967; Graney, 1974, 1975; Turow, 1974; Wenner, 1976), but it appears the mass media are used as a substitute for interpersonal contact when other functional alternatives are unavailable.

Bleise's (1982) findings supported Meyersohn's (1961) contention that the mass media are used to provide topics for future conversations. Bleise found that over 40% of her subjects use their media experiences as topics in conversation, with almost 30% saying they sometimes watch particular shows to talk about them with friends. Over 50% reported using the media to fend off loneliness and as mediated company. Over 40% said they use the media to keep up with the world around them because such topics did come up in conversation and they did not want to appear ignorant of world events. Danowski (1975) found similar results, concluding that elderly people use the media to gain knowledge and see new things, as well as to provide informational content for use in conversation.

Recall from chapter 1, that disengagement theory postulates that elderly people want to disengage from society as society disengages from them. Bleise (1982) reports that not one subject reported wanting to disengage from social activity and that even relatively isolated subjects reported wanting more social interaction. It appears that, although elderly people may sometimes substitute face-to-face interaction with the mass media, 93% of the subjects that were forced into this substitution due to isolation were moderately to extremely dissatisfied with the media as a replacement for real interaction. This may help explain the disparity in findings about the substitutive uses of the mass media.

Finally, Bleise (1982) found that the telephone is an important functional alternative to face-to-face interaction for many elderly people. Nearly 90% of elderly people report using the telephone to check on their friends' health and well-being, and 97% think telephone conversations were as good or better than face-to-face conversations. This finding is also inconsistent with disengagement theory.

Dependency Model. Perhaps the most broad-based and sociological of the effects theories is Ball-Rokeach and DeFleur's (1976) dependency model. The dependency model examines the tripartite relationship between the mass media, the audience, and society. In offering an explanation of media effects, DeFleur and Ball-Rokeach (1982) wrote:

> This general societal system sets important limitations and boundaries on the media system and has considerable impact on its characteristics, information-delivery functions, and operating procedures. The societal system also has enormous impact upon persons; it gives rise to mechanisms that inhibit arbitrary media influence, such as individual differences, membership in social categories, and participation in social relations. The societal system also operates to create needs within persons that facilitate media alteration effects, namely the needs to understand, act in, and escape in fantasy from one's world. Finally, the interdependencies of the society's social systems and its media shape how people can and do develop dependencies on the media to satisfy these needs, thereby setting the media effects process into motion. (p. 251)

Ball-Rokeach and DeFleur suggest that, when people are dependent or reliant on the mass media to fulfill a need (e.g., for information about the world around or as a surrogate friend), the likelihood of the media influencing an individual is increased. The potential for media influence increases because the audience member has no alternative source for the information and in such cases the individual is said to be dependent on the media. Media dependence occurs when traditional agencies of socialization are no longer available or relevant. For example, Gerson (1966) found that African American school children in San Francisco who were being bussed to schools in white neighborhoods used television to learn "how to act." The traditional agencies of socialization (e.g., parents, peers, and church) were no longer helpful, and the African American school children were dependent on television for information about how they should behave in this new social situation.

The perceived needs of the audience and conditions in society also influence the creation of media content, just as economic goals of the media industry help determine the content. Thus, the tripartite relationship between the audience, the mass media, and society are mutually influencing factors. As society becomes more specialized, people become more reliant on each other. But the more specialized people become, the less they have in common with each other. These differences can result in relational and communicative difficulties. A pattern begins to emerge. Specialization leads to less commonality of experience and more dependence on one another's specialties. Because there is little opportunity for interaction and little commonality of experience due to job specialization, television has become the great homogenizer of society. Television provides people with common experiences, things to talk about, and information about otherwise unfamiliar groups of people. A sympathetic or reasonably accurate portrayal of a group often leads to some degree of empathy with that group and its members' needs. Elderly people are no different from other groups. Unfortunately, as people grow older and their roles change, they often become less well integrated into society. As interpersonal contact diminishes, their reliance on the media to fulfill their needs increases and may serve to legitimize the negative stereotypes about aging that exist. It was once argued that as America as a society grows older, TV portrayals of elderly people and attitudes toward elderly people would change (Burnett, 1991; Dail, 1988; Gerbner, Gross, Signorelli, & Morgan, 1980). Research by Robinson and Skill (1995) suggested that these changes have not yet occurred.

MEDIA PORTRAYALS

Many researchers have studied how elderly people are portrayed in the mass media. While this section will focus primarily on television portrayals of elderly people, social scientists have examined how elderly people are portrayed in a variety of different contexts. Davies (1977), Palmore (1971), and Richman (1977) examined how elderly people are depicted in jokes; Smith (1979) looked at magazine cartoons, and Demos and Jache (1981) examined birthday cards; Gantz, Gartenberg, and Rainbow (1980) and Kvasnicka, Beymer, and Perloff (1982) examined magazine advertisements; and Francher (1973) investigated TV advertisement. Still other researchers have examined popular magazines (Nussbaum & Robinson, 1986), literature (Loughan, 1977; Sohngen, 1977), letters to the "Dear Abby" advice column (Gaitz & Scott, 1975), literature for children and adolescents (Blue, 1978; Seltzer & Atchley, 1971), poetry (Sohngen & Smith, 1978), and newspapers (Buchholz & Bynum, 1982; Evans & Evans, as cited in Peterson & Karnes, 1976; MacDonald, 1973). In general, media portrayals of the elderly have been stereotypical and often either perpetuate common myths about aging or do little to dispel such myths.

Television Portrayals

Hacker (1951) explained the importance of television portrayals and argues that groups and individuals of low social status receive less frequent and less favorable treatment on television than people of higher status. Hacker's thesis that social status can be predicted by levels of exposure and the favorability of the portrayal has received considerable support. For example, Mertz (1970) found that elderly characters are underrepresented in comparison with the census figures. Since then, nearly every study that has examined TV portrayals of the elderly has concluded that fewer than 5% of the characters on prime-time television are 65 years old or older (Ansello, 1978; Arnoff, 1974; Downing, 1974; Gerbner, Gross, Signorelli, & Morgan, 1980; Greenberg & Collette, 1997; Greenberg, Korzenny, & Atkin, 1980; Levinson 1973; Northcott, 1975; Robinson & Skill, 1995; Signorelli & Gerbner, 1977). In fact, the two most recent large scale content analytic examinations of prime time television report that less than 3% of the characters on fictional prime-time programming are 65 years old or older (Greenberg & Collette, 1997; Robinson & Skill, 1995). When census figures are used as a benchmark, elderly characters are clearly represented at a rate that is much lower than their presence in society. When other character age cohorts are used as a benchmark, similar results are observed (Greenberg & Collette, 1997; Robinson & Skill, 1995).

Examinations of elderly characters on other types of TV programming indicate that the elderly are portrayed relatively infrequently on children's cartoons (Levinson, 1973). Further, the elderly are not very likely to appear on game shows as either contestants or audience members (Danowski, 1975).

Petersen (1973) found that elderly women are much less frequently found on television than are elderly men, and Arnoff (1974) suggested that for every elderly woman on television there are three elderly men. In fact, even though elderly women greatly outnumber elderly men in the United States (about 36% of women are widowed by the age of 65), according to Petersen's (1973) findings, elderly women appear on TV shows once every 4 or 5 hours, whereas elderly men appear every 20 minutes or so.

In an examination of the 1990 prime-time programming, Robinson and Skill (1995) found there had been some improvement in this area. During 1975, about 3.4% of all characters were elderly women (Greenberg, Korzenny, et al., 1980). By 1990, 4% of all characters were elderly women (Robinson & Skill, 1995). This is not, of course, a large increase. It is also interesting to note that during this time frame the number of characters that were elderly men actually decreased from 4.8% of all characters to 1.8% (Robinson & Skill, 1995).

In addition to their being underrepresented on TV, elderly characters are generally relegated to roles of lesser prominence. Robinson and Skill (1995) report that only 8.8% of elderly characters were cast in a major or central role in the 1990 sample. In contrast, Northcott (1975) found that 28.6% of elderly characters occupied leading roles in 1974. In fact, Robinson and Skill (1995) suggest that elderly people are only about half as likely to occupy a central role as other adult characters.

Elderly people are not only underrepresented on TV and cast in roles of lesser prominence, but they are also portrayed as stereotypes. Mertz (1970) reported that 82% of elderly characters appearing on TV are "stereotypical characterizations." Other studies reported similar findings (Arnoff, 1974; Danowski, 1975; Gerbner, Gross, Signorelli, & Morgan, 1980; Levinson, 1973; Northcott, 1975; Petersen, 1973; Signorelli & Gerbner, 1977). Arnoff (1974) found that elderly characters are likely to be cast as evil characters and seldom as heroes. Northcott (1975) observed that when elderly people are shown, they often have problems and are reliant on younger people for help. Harris and

Feinberg (1977) reported that the likelihood of romantic involvement is very low for elderly characters and Signorelli and Gerbner (1977) suggested that elderly people are often portrayed as being unattractive and unhappy.

Of course, not all portrayals are negative. Harris and Feinberg (1977) conclude that elderly people are most commonly found on comedy shows and on informational, public affairs, and talk shows. Elderly people, especially elderly women, fare much better on soap operas (Barton, 1977; Downing, 1974; Ramsdell, 1973). Elderly women on soaps are potent, influential, and central to the plot of the show, and they are more likely to be sought after for advice by younger characters. Older men, on the other hand, are most favorably depicted on news programs and talk shows (Harris & Feinberg, 1977). In addition, Petersen (1973) found elderly people are shown as fairly active, in good health, and independent. Kubey (1980) reminds us, however, to be aware of the use of reverse stereotypes. When an elderly individual is portrayed unrealistically, the audience tends to interpret the portrayal as comical and this results in the reinforcement of the commonly held stereotype.

Because television can reinforce existing attitudes and can contribute to the cultivation of unfavorable perceptions of elderly people, stereotypical portrayals are potentially very problematic. Americans fear aging and already hold stereotypes about growing old. And although all studies did not conclude that the elderly are poorly or inaccurately depicted, very few concluded that portrayals are positive. Finally, very few characters on television are elderly and that trend does not seem to be changing. Arguments that television characters will grow older as the demography of the United States changes have not yet received empirical support (Robinson & Skill, 1995).

Newspaper Portrayals

Despite the considerable time that elderly people spend reading newspapers, very few researchers have examined the way that newspapers portray elderly people. In one of the few examinations of this topic Evans and Evans (cited in Peterson & Karnes, 1976) reported that the amount of coverage of elderly people in five metropolitan daily newspapers did not increase from 1965 to 1975. MacDonald (1973) examined a Midwestern newspaper and found the number of articles about elderly people did increase between 1963 and 1973; unfortunately, this increase reflected a rise in the number of condescending and stereotypical articles on elderly people, not articles that presented balanced or even accurate information about the realities of growing old.

Broussard, Blackmon, Blackwell, Smith, and Hunt (1980) examined 10 daily metropolitan newspapers and concluded that the amount of space devoted to articles about elderly people is disproportionately low compared to the number of elderly people in the United States. While elderly people are somewhat underrepresented, as measured by column inches, Broussard and his colleagues reported that 65% of the articles are written in a primarily neutral tone and 31% are written in a positive tone.

Shivar (1982) studied Israeli newspapers and concluded that, "Although the quantitative representations of the elderly in the newspapers analyzed is generally fair, age seems to be significantly related to the ways characters are presented by the press, in terms of form and substance alike" (p. 95). A high percentage of the articles contain caricatures of elderly people and few carry actual pictures. Often elderly people are found in institutional settings. In addition, elderly people appear in articles in which the outcome is more negative for them than for their younger counterparts. As Shivar (1982) cautioned, however, a high percentage of most newspaper stories end negatively and many of the people portrayed in newspaper articles are atypical—hence newsworthy.

Buchholz and Bynum (1982) examined the *New York Times* and the *Daily Oklahoman* from 1970 to 1978. After examining a variety of factors, including elderly people's images or roles and the article's orientation or theme, Buchholz and Bynum found that "the two newspapers pictured the elderly more favorably than the media critics might lead one to believe" (p. 87). They argue that most of the articles balance negative images with positive images. In fact, Buchholz and Bynum suggest that if reader attention factors such as headline size, article length, and page placement are considered, there are more positive than negative stories, and, in addition, the positive stories are more prominently displayed.

Furthermore, the articles tend to portray elderly people as leading active lives. Forty-four percent of the articles depict elderly people as active, 30% depict them as passive, and 25% describe them as being neither active nor passive. Again, the active-role articles received more prominent display over the 8-year period, although the article positioning and the positive portrayal of activity may be due to the event bias so prevalent in newspapers. That's the good news.

The bad news is that the newspapers did not do a good job of informing readers about the problems facing elderly people. In fact, 97% of the stories about elderly people are obituaries, pieces about public policy and legislation concerning elderly people, retirement notices, anniversaries, and stories about fraud in government programs for elderly people. Less than 3% of the articles are about significant issues facing elderly people (e.g., health, retirement, housing, crime, employment, transportation, income, or demographic changes in the United States). In contrast, almost 25% of the articles are obituaries, compelling Buchholz and Bynum (1982) to write that "The surest way for the aged to get into the news columns was to die" (p. 86).

If, as previous research indicates, elderly people have high informational content needs and an increased reliance on the mass media for information about the world around them, the fact that very few articles address issues identified by gerontologists as being significant to successful adaptation to aging is surely an important finding. Because, as the research by Buchholz and Bynum (1982) further suggested, newspaper coverage is not improving and articles are mostly written about elderly crime victims or sensational events that just happen to include older people as part of the background, the problems facing this segment of our society will continue to be ignored. Further research on this problem should be a high priority in our social policy. The media are not serving its elderly constituency well.

The fact that such important information sources are failing is of considerably more consequence than whether fictional portrayals of the elderly are positive or negative. In this instance, one does not need to postulate a complex cognitive theory to explain the potential effects. If the information is not useful or available, elderly and younger people alike are not being well served.

Magazine Portrayals

While elderly people do not spend a great deal of time reading magazines, many other adults spend significant leisure time with periodicals. In one investigation, Nussbaum and Robinson (1986) examined the way that elderly people are portrayed in popular magazines. After analyzing popular magazine articles between 1970 and 1979, Nussbaum and Robinson concluded that as the 1970s progressed, attitudes toward elderly people did not improve and, in fact, became increasingly negative. Further, as the decade passed, the articles did less and less to try to shatter existing stereotypes.

Although elderly people were not portrayed as being completely helpless, old age was portrayed as being a less satisfying time of life and the process of aging was more closely associated with death as the decade progressed. Sixty percent of the magazine articles stressed medicine or some aspect of the medical model as the remedy for problems associated with aging. In addition, the articles did not present the elderly people's families as serving a primary helping role for them.

In general, most of the articles portrayed elderly people negatively. Fifty percent portrayed elderly people as being cantankerous, slow, sad, senile, stubborn, and lonely. On a more positive note, nearly 35% of the articles portrayed elderly people as being wise, loving, talkative, trustworthy, cheerful, and kind. Five percent of the articles portrayed elderly people as being lazy or cold; no articles mentioned compassionate or humorous old people.

In short, magazine portrayals of elderly people are similar to those in newspapers. When it was offered, advice for successful adaptation to aging was often inconsistent with gerontological research and often inconsistent with the preferences expressed by elderly people when they are asked about their coping strategies and tactics (Cicirelli, 1979). Elderly people are most often depicted in a neutral or negative light. Finally, little is done to combat the stereotypes of aging and elderly people that already exist in society.

Research into portrayals of elderly people in popular magazine advertisements yielded similar results. Gantz et al. (1980) examined magazine advertisements and found that elderly people are poorly represented. They reported far fewer elderly models than the proportion of elderly people in the population; only 5.9% of the advertisements contain elderly people, and only 3.1% of all the people shown are elderly.

Kvasnicka et al. (1982) conducted a similar study of magazines typically read by elderly people and magazines written specifically for the elderly reader. After examining the advertisements in *Better Homes and Gardens*, *McCalls*, *Reader's Digest*, and *TV Guide* (the most popular magazines of people 65 or older in 1980), they found only slight increases in the number of elderly models; 4.1% of the models were elderly and only 8.0% of the advertisements contained an elderly model. In *Fifty Plus, Modern Maturity, Retirement Life,* and *Retirement Living* (magazines with a large circulation, geared toward an elderly audience), 77% of the advertisements contained at least one elderly model, and over 72% of the models were elderly. In these advertisements, the elderly models were vigorous and active. Travel, golf, bicycling, and swimming were common activities in the advertisements. While some scholars argue that the number of elderly people in specialized magazines is an improvement, others contend that such active advertising portrayals may contribute to a less positive concept of self (cf. Korzenny & Neuendorf, 1980; Kvasnicka et al. 1982; Schreiber & Boyd, 1980) and unrealistic expectations about growing old. The media have put little effort into reversing ageist stereotypes in our society. Media portrayals may even promote ageist attitudes, negative attitudes toward aging, and perhaps also a decreased likelihood of planning for retirement.

SUMMARY

Hacker's (1951) contention that individuals of low social status receive less frequent and less favorable treatment in the mass media than people of higher status has received a great deal of support over the years. Even though elderly people spend more time with the media than any other age cohort, media portrayals of elderly people are too infrequent, often stereotypical, and too often demonstrate a lack of concern for the problems of aging and elderly people. The event bias of the media results in an overemphasis of catastrophes as news and often ignores the problems facing elderly people. Perhaps aging issues are not covered particularly well because aging itself is not a newsworthy event. It is a process that takes place over time and processes do not lend themselves to easy analysis or quick-fix cures.

Several authors argued that television programs will include more elderly characters in prime-time programming and that these programs will address problems facing elderly people as the age of the American public increases. These expected changes have not yet occurred in fictional prime-time programming (Robinson & Skill, 1995). Whatever the root causes of these problems may be, it is becoming increasingly clear that the cause is not simply economics, as was once believed. Space aliens, angels, and animated characters have a better chance of being cast in a central role on a prime-time television program than an elderly adult.

It has also been argued that, as elderly people represent an increasingly larger proportion of the consumer public, we can expect more elderly actors in commercials in response to the "graying of America." Such changes will be welcome because they may reduce ageist stereotypes in the mass media and, perhaps, improve the public's knowledge of the issues facing elderly people by providing information about the process of aging.

Although Buchholz and Bynum (1982) conclude that elderly people are depicted in newspapers "more favorably than the media critics might lead one to believe" (p. 87), there is little reason to rejoice. Concentrating less on events that involve elderly people and more on the real problems and issues facing them may be a better way to serve the public interest and help set a reasonable agenda for legislators and voters alike.

From a social learning theory perspective, because there are so few elderly characters on television and in the other media, there are very few models for the elderly audience member to emulate. Given the dependency elderly characters seem to have on younger characters, the problem-solving strategy most commonly employed on prime-time television may well be "ask someone younger to do it for you." Obviously this is problematic.

Further, younger audience members are likely to learn stereotyped information about the elderly from the mass media. Given the potential for less interpersonal contact with grandparents because of the mobility of U.S. society, this may result in increased reliance or dependency on the media for information about elderly people by younger audience members. These circumstances also enhance the likelihood of audience members cultivating a view of aging that is not veridical.

Based on research discussed in chapter 2 (Langer 1983; Langer & Abelson, 1974; Langer & Benevento, 1978), it is clear that attitudes about aging and elderly people significantly impact the quality of life of elderly people. Such labeling or stigmatization may alter a person's perceptions and evaluations of behavior (Langer & Abelson, 1974), as well as influencing task performance (Langer & Benevento, 1978). When people are labeled negatively, their behavior is evaluated differently than when the same behavior is performed by people who have been labeled positively. We also know that when people are labeled negatively, their task performance decreases. The implications of such findings are clear. The question becomes, then: where do people get their attitudes about aging and growing older? Although the mass media is not the sole source of information available to audience members, the widespread use and availability of the media makes it a natural place to look for insight into the creation and maintenance of such attitudes.

The media serve positive functions for elderly people as well. Elderly people prefer media with informative content, and it seems likely that they prefer such information because their interpersonal networks often disintegrate. Further, the use of the mass media to supply parasocial relationships, to reduce loneliness, and otherwise cope with the decline in interpersonal contact, can be viewed as positive. Although the functional alternative of choice may be interpersonal contact, for many elderly people the mass media may still significantly improve the quality of their lives by providing surrogate or parasocial relationships.

Bleise (1982) contended that the media are only used as a replacement for real people when there are few if any alternatives. When lifelong roles are taken away, interpersonal networks diminish, economic difficulties arise, and health problems become more common, elderly people may become reliant on relatively passive ways of passing the time. At the same time, such passivity may not be the intent of the elderly individual. Elderly people's interest in informative content, reaching out via a computer and the Internet, and participating in talk radio programming all suggest that this seeming passivity may be a strategy for coping with aging, but may not be the preferred method of managing the problems associated with aging.

■ REFERENCES

Ahammer, I. M., & Murray, J. P. (1979). Kindness in the kindergarten: The relative influence of role playing and prosocial television in facilitating altruism. *International Journal of Behavioral Development, 2*, 133–157.

Ansello, E. F. (1978, November). *Broadcast images: The elderly woman in television.* Paper presented at the Annual Meeting of the Gerontological Society, Dallas, TX.

Arnoff, C. (1974). Old age in prime time. *Journal of Communication, 24*, 86–87.

Ball-Rokeach, S., & DeFleur, M. (1976). A dependency model of mass-media effects. *Communication Research, 3*, 3–21.

Bandura, A. (1965). Influence of models' reinforcement contingencies on the acquisition of imitative responses. *Journal of Personality and Social Psychology, 1*, 589–595.

Bandura, A. (1973). *Aggression: A social learning analysis*. Englewood Cliffs, NJ: Prentice Hall.

Bandura, A. (1977). *Social learning theory*. Englewood Cliffs, NJ: Prentice Hall.

Bandura, A. (1986). *Social foundations of thought and action: A social cognitive theory*. Englewood Cliffs, NJ: Prentice Hall.

Bandura, A., Blanchard, E. B., & Ritter, B. J. (1969). Relative efficacy of modeling therapeutic changes for inducing behavioral, attitudinal, and affective changes. *Journal of Personality and Social Psychology, 13,* 173–199.

Bandura, A., Grusec, J. E., & Menlove, F. L. (1967). Vicarious extinction of avoidance behavior. *Journal of Personality and Social Psychology, 5,* 16–23.

Bandura, A., & Kupers, C. J. (1964). The transmission of patterns of self-reinforcement through modeling. *Journal of Abnormal and Social Psychology, 69,* 1–9.

Bandura, A., & Menlove, F. L. (1968). Factors determining vicarious extinction of avoidance behavior through symbolic modeling. *Journal of Personality and Social Psychology, 8,* 99–108.

Bandura, A., & Mischel, W. (1965). Modification of self-imposed delay of reward through exposure to live and symbolic models. *Journal of Personality and Social Psychology, 2,* 698–705.

Bandura, A., Ross, A. D., & Ross, S. A. (1963a). Imitation of film-mediated aggressive models. *Journal of Abnormal and Social Psychology, 66,* 3–11.

Bandura, A., Ross, A. D., & Ross, S. A. (1963b). Vicarious reinforcement and imitative learning. *Journal of Abnormal and Social Psychology, 67,* 601–607.

Baron, R. A. (1970). Attraction toward the model and the model's competence as determinants of adult imitative behavior. *Journal of Personality and Social Psychology, 14,* 345–351.

Barton, R. (1977). Soap operas provide meaningful communication for the elderly. *Feedback, 19,* 5–8.

Berkowitz, L., & Geen, R. G. (1966). Film violence and the cue properties of available targets. *Journal of Personality and Social Psychology, 3,* 525–530.

Berkowitz, L., & Geen, R. G. (1967). Stimulus qualities of the target of aggression: A further study. *Journal of Personality and Social Psychology, 5,* 364–368.

Bierig, J., & Dimmick, J. (1979). The late night radio talk show as interpersonal communication. *Journalism Quarterly, 56*(1), 92–96.

Bleise, N. (1982). Media in the rocking chair: Media uses and functions among the elderly. In G. Gumpert & R. Cathcart (Eds.), *Intermedia: Interpersonal communication in a media world* (2nd ed., pp. 624–634). New York: Oxford University Press.

Blood, R. W. (1981). *Unobtrusive issues in the agenda-setting role of the press*. Unpublished doctoral dissertation, Syracuse University, Syracuse, NY.

Blue, G. (1978). The aging as portrayed in realistic fiction for children: 1945–1975. *Gerontologist, 18,* 187.

Brosius, H. B., & Kepplinger, H. M. (1990). The agenda-setting function of television news: Static and dynamic views. *Communication Research, 17,* 183–211.

Broussard, E., Blackmon, C., Blackwell, D., Smith, D., & Hunt, S. (1980). News of aged and aging in 10 metropolitan dailies. *Journalism Quarterly, 57*(2), 324–327.

Bryan, J. H., Redfield, J., & Mader, S. (1971). Words and deeds about altruism and the subsequent reinforcement powers of the model. *Child Development, 42,* 1501–1508.

Bryan, J. H., & Walbek, N. H. (1970). Preaching and practicing generosity: Children's actions and reactions. *Child Development, 41,* 329–353.

Buchholz, M., & Bynum, J. (1982). Newspaper presentation of America's aged: A content analysis of image and role. *Gerontologist, 22*(1), 83–88.

Burnett, J. (1991). Examining the media habits of the affluent elderly. *Journal of Advertising Research, 31*(5), 33–41.

Cassata, M. (1967). *A study of the mass communications behavior and the social disengagement behavior of 177 members of the Age Center of New England.* Unpublished doctoral dissertation, Indiana University, Bloomington, IN.

Cicirelli, V. (1979, May 31). *Social services for the elderly in relation to the kin network* (Report to the NRTA-AARP), Washington DC: Andrus Foundation.

Comstock, G., Chaffee, S., Katzman, N., McCombs, M., & Roberts, D. (1978). *Television and human behavior.* New York: Columbia University Press.

Danowski, J. (1975, Nov.). *Informational aging: Interpersonal and mass communication patterns at a retirement community.* Paper presented at the meetings of the Gerontological Society, Louisville, KY.

Dail, P. W. (1988). Prime-time television portrayals of older adults in the context of family life. *Gerontologist, 28,* 700–706.

Dail, P. W., & Way, W. L. (1985). What do parents observe about parenting from prime-time television? *Family Relations, 34,* 491–499.

Davies, L. (1977). Attitudes toward aging as shown by humor. *Gerontologist, 17,* 220–226.

DeFleur, M., & Ball-Rokeach, S. (1982). *Theories of mass communication* (4th ed.). New York: Longman.

DeFleur, M. L., & DeFleur, L. B. (1967). The relative contribution of television as a learning source for children's occupational knowledge. *American Sociological Review, 32,* 777–789.

Demos. V., & Jache A. (1981). When you care enough: An analysis of attitudes toward aging in humorous birthday cards. *Gerontologist, 21,* 209–215.

Doob, A. N., & Macdonald, G. E. (1979). Television viewing and fear of victimization: Is the relationship causal? *Journal of Personality & Social Psychology, 37*(2), 170–179.

Downing, M. (1974). Heroine of the daytime serial. *Journal of Communication, 24,* 130–137.

Eaton, H. (1989). Agenda-setting with bi-weekly data on content of three national media. *Journalism Quarterly, 66,* 942–948.

Fehrenbach, P. A., Miller, D. J., & Thelen, M. H. (1979). The importance of consistency of modeling behavior upon imitation: A comparison of single and multiple models. *Journal of Personality & Social Psychology, 37*(8), 1412–1417.

Felsenthal, N. (1981). *Mass communications* (2nd ed.). Chicago: Science Research Associates.

Feshbach, S. (1972). Reality and fantasy in filmed violence. In J. P. Murray, E. A. Rubinstein, & G. A. Comstock (Eds.), *Television and social behavior:*

Vol 2. Television and social learning (pp. 318–345). Washington, DC: U.S. Government Printing Office.

Gaitz, C., & Scott, J. (1975). Analysis of letters to "Dear Abby" concerning old age. *Gerontologist, 15,* 47–50.

Gantz, W., Gartenberg, H., & Rainbow, C. (1980). Approaching invisibility: The portrayal of elderly in magazine advertisements. *Journal of Communication, 30,* 56–60.

Geen, R. G., & Berkowitz, L. (1967). Some conditions facilitating the occurrence of aggression after the observation of violence. *Journal of Personality, 35,* 666–667.

Gerbner, G. (1969). Toward "cultural indicators": The analysis of mass mediated public message systems. In G. Gerbner, et al. (Eds.), *The analysis of communication content* (pp. 123–132). New York: Wiley.

Gerbner, G., Gross, L., Signorelli, N., & Morgan, M. (1980). Aging with television: Images on television drama and conceptions of social reality. *Journal of Communication, 30*(1), 37–47.

Gerbner, G., Gross, L., Signorelli, N., & Morgan, M. (1986). Living with television: The dynamics of the cultivation process. In J. Bryant & D. Zillman (Eds.), *Perspectives on media effects* (pp. 17–40). Hillsdale, NJ: Lawrence Erlbaum Associates.

Gerson, W. (1966). Mass media socialization behavior: Negro-white differences. *Social Forces, 45,* 40–50.

Graney, M. (1974). Media use as a substitute activity in old age. *Journal of Gerontology, 29,* 322–324.

Graney, M. (1975). Communication uses and the social activity constant. *Communication Research, 2,* 347–366.

Graney, M., & Graney, E. (1974). Communication activity substitution in aging. *Journal of Communication, 24,* 88–96.

Greenberg B., & Dervin, B. (1970). *Use of the mass media by the urban poor.* New York: Praeger.

Greenberg, B., & Collette, L. (1997). The changing faces on TV: A demographic analysis of network television's new seasons, 1966–1992. *Journal of Broadcasting & Electronic Media, 41,* 1–13.

Greenberg, B. S., Hines, M., Buerkel-Rothfuss, N., & Atkin, C. (1980). Family role structures and interactions on commercial television. In B. S. Greenberg (Ed.), *Life on television: Content analysis of U.S. TV drama* (pp. 149–160). Norwood, NJ: Ablex.

Greenberg, B. S., Korzenny, F., & Atkin, C. K. (1980). Trends in the portrayal of the elderly. In B. S. Greenberg (Ed.), *Life on television: Content analysis of U. S. TV drama* (pp. 23–33). Norwood, NJ: Ablex.

Hacker, H. (1951). Women as a minority group. *Social Forces, 30,* 39–44.

Harris A., & Feinberg, J. (1977). Television and aging: Is what you see what you get? *Gerontologist, 17,* 464–468.

Iyengar S., & Kinder, D. R. (1987). *News that matters: Agenda-setting and priming in a television age.* Chicago: University of Chicago Press.

Katz, E., Blumler, J., & Gurevitch, M. (1974). Uses of mass communication by the individual. In W. Davison & F. Yu (Eds.), *Mass communication research* (pp. 11–35). New York: Praeger.

Katz, E., Gurevitch, M., & Haas, H. (1973). On the use of mass media for important things. *American Sociological Review, 38,* 164–181.

Klapper, J. (1960). *The effects of mass communication.* New York: Free Press.

Korzenny, F., & Neuendorf, K. (1980). Television viewing and the self concept of the elderly. *Journal of Communication, 30,* 71–80.

Kubey, R. (1980). Television and aging: Past, present, and future. *Gerontologist, 20,* 16–35.

Kvasnicka, B., Beymer, B., & Perloff, R. (1982). Portrayals of the elderly in magazine advertisements. *Journalism Quarterly, 59*(4), 656–658.

Langer, E. (1983). *The psychology of control.* Beverly Hills, CA: Sage.

Langer, E., & Abelson, R. (1974). A patient by any other name … : Clinician group differences in labeling bias. *Journal of Consulting and Clinical Psychology, 42,* 4–9.

Langer, E., & Benevento, A. (1978). Self-induced dependence. *Journal of Personality and Social Psychology, 36,* 886–893.

Lazarsfeld, P., Berelson, B., & Gaudet, H. (1948). *The people's choice.* New York: Columbia University Press.

Levinson, R. (1973). From Olive Oyle to Sweet Polly Purebred: Sex role stereotypes and televised cartoons. *Journal of Popular Culture, 9,* 561–572.

Lippmann, W. (1922). *Public opinion.* New York: Macmillan.

Loughan, C. (1977). Novels of senescence: A new naturalism. *Gerontologist, 17,* 79–84.

MacDonald, R. (1973, November). *Content analysis of perceptions of aging as represented by the news media.* Paper presented at the meetings of the Gerontological Society, Miami Beach, FL.

Mackuen, M. B. (1981). *More than news: Media power in public affairs.* Beverly Hills, CA: Sage.

McCombs, M. E., & Shaw, D. L. (1972). The agenda-setting function of mass media. *Public Opinion Quarterly, 36,* 176–187.

Mertz, R. (1970, May). *Analysis of the portrayal of older Americans in commercial television programming.* Paper presented at the annual meeting of the International Communication Association, Chicago, IL.

Meyersohn, R. (1961). A critical examination of commercial entertainment. In R. Kleemeier (Ed.), *Aging and leisure.* New York: Oxford University Press.

Northcott, H. (1975). Too young, too old—age in the world of television. *Gerontologist, 15,* 184–186.

Nussbaum, J., & Robinson, J. (1986). Attitudes toward aging. *Communication Research Reports, 1,* 21–27.

Palmore, E. (1971). Attitudes toward aging as shown in humor. *Gerontologist, 11,* 181–186.

Passuth, P., & Cook, F. (1985). Effects of television viewing on knowledge and attitudes about older adults. A critical reexamination. *The Gerontologist, 25*(1), 69–77.

Perry, D. G., & Bussey, K. (1979). The social learning theory of sex differences: Imitation is alive and well. *Journal of Personality and Social Psychology, 37,* 1699–1712.

Petersen, M. (1973). The visibility and image of old people on television. *Journalism Quarterly, 50,* 569–573.

Peterson, D., & Karnes, E. (1976). Older people in adolescent literature. *Gerontologist, 16,* 225–231.

Ramsdell, M. (1973). The trauma of TV's troubled soap families. *Family Coordinator, 22,* 299–304.

Richman, L. (1977). The foolishness and wisdom of age: Attitudes toward the elderly as reflected in jokes. *Gerontologist, 17,* 210–219.

Robinson, J. (1972). Toward defining the functions of television. In E. Rubinstein, G. Comstock, & J. Murray (Eds.), *Television and social behavior: Vol.4. Television in day-to-day patterns of use* (pp. 568–602). Washington, DC: U.S. Government Printing Office.

Robinson, J., & Skill, T. (1995). The invisible generation: Portrayals of the elderly on prime-time television. *Communication Reports, 8*(2), 111–119.

Robinson, J., Skill, T., Nussbaum, J., & Moreland, K. (1985). Parents, peers, and television characters: The use of comparison of others as criteria for evaluating marital satisfaction. In E. Lange (Ed.), *Using the media to promote knowledge and skills in family dynamics* (pp. 11–15). Dayton, OH: Center for Religious Telecommunications.

Rosenbaum, E., & Tucker, I. F. (1962). Competence of the model and the learning of imitation and nonimitation. *Journal of Experimental Psychology, 63,* 183–190.

Schramm, W. (1969). Aging and mass communication. In M. Riley, J. Riley, & M. Johnson (Eds.), *Aging and society: Vol. 2. Aging and the professions* (pp. 252–275). New York: Russell Sage.

Schrieber, E., & Boyd, D. (1980). How the elderly perceive television commercials. *Journal of Communication, 30,* 61–70.

Seltzer, M., & Atchley, R. (1971). The concept of old age: Changing attitudes and stereotypes. *Gerontologist, 11,* 226–230.

Shaw, D., & McCombs, M. (1977). *The emergence of American political issues.* St. Paul, MN: West.

Shivar, D. (1982). The portrayal of the elderly in four Israeli daily newspapers. *Journalism Quarterly, 59*(1), 92–96.

Signorelli, N., & Gerbner, G. (1977). *The image of the elderly in prime-time network drama* (Report No. 12). Philadelphia: University of Pennsylvania, Annenberg School of Communications.

Smith, D. (1979). The portrayals of elders in magazine cartoons. *Gerontologist, 19,* 408–412.

Smith, K. (1987). Newspaper coverage and public concern about community issues. *Journalism Monographs, No. 101.*

Sohngen, M. (1977). The experience of old age as depicted in contemporary novels. *Gerontologist, 17,* 70–78.

Sohngen, M., & Smith, R. (1978). Images of old age in poetry. *Gerontologist, 18,* 181–186.

Tolley, H., Jr., (1973). *Children and war: Political socialization to international conflict.* New York: Teachers College Press.

Tower, R. B., Singer, D. B., Singer, J. L., & Biggs, A. (1979). Differential effects of television programming on preschoolers' cognitive, imagination, and social play. *American Journal of Orthopsychiatry, 49,* 265–281.

Turner, C. W., & Berkowitz, L. (1972). Identification with film aggressor (overt role taking) and reactions to film violence. *Journal of Personality and Social Psychology, 21,* 256–264.

Turow, J. (1974). Talk show radio as interpersonal communication. *Journal of Broadcasting, 18,* 171–179.

Weaver, D., Graber, D. A., McCombs, M. E., & Eyal, C. H. (1981). *Media agenda-setting in a presidential election: Issues, images, and interests.* New York: Praeger.

Weaver, J., & Wakshlag, J. (1986). Perceived vulnerability to crime, criminal victimization experience, and television viewing. *Journal of Broadcasting and Electronic Media, 30,* 141–158.

Wenner, L. (1976). Functional analysis of TV viewing for older adults. *Journal of Broadcasting, 20,* 77–88.

Winter, J. P., & Eyal, C. H. (1981). Agenda-setting for the civil rights issue. *Public Opinion Quarterly, 45,* 376–383.

Zucker, H. G. (1978). The variable nature of news media influence. In B. D. Ruben (Ed.), *Communication Yearbook 2* (pp. 225–240). New Brunswick, NJ: Transaction Book.

CHAPTER 6

Work, Leisure, and Retirement

T his chapter focuses on the communicative issues surrounding work, leisure, and retirement. During adulthood, work and family represent an individual's greatest involvements, and changes or transitions in one often have effects on the other. In spite of these interconnections between family and work, most of the issues relating to work, leisure, and retirement such as income and poverty (Lohmann & Lohmann, 1983), have little to do with communication and social interaction, and are outside the scope of this book. Some issues, such as the factors influencing the decision to retire and the impact of retirement on health, are discussed here only in terms of the roles played by communication and social relationships. The discussion focuses on the communicative and social factors in a person's adjustment to retirement and how interpersonal relationships affect retirement satisfaction, and the role communication plays in these processes.

Included in this are gender differences in people's reactions to retirement; special consideration is given to women's retirement and to preretirement activities. In addition, the relationship between leisure and communication will be discussed.

113

Leisure, both for retired and gainfully employed elderly individuals, plays an important role in life quality and our communicative relationships with others.

The concept of retirement is relatively recent. Industrialization led to a large number of people moving from an agricultural lifestyle to one of working for wages. In nonindustrial nations today, elderly individuals are not likely to ever retire (Holmes & Holmes, 1995). In industrialized nations, retirement has been a common practice among all social classes for only the last 60 years.

In industrialized nations, the number of people retiring is rapidly increasing (Cox, 1985; Szinovacz & Ekerdt, 1994), whereas the number of people working is not increasing at the same rate. For this reason, retirement and its effects have become a concern for numerous researchers and architects of social policy. Some argue that retirement is a stigmatizing activity. Weiss (1977) likened retirement to a "death-watch." In the United States, however, retirement is gaining increasing acceptance (Back, 1977; Quadagno & Hardy, 1996). Although many Americans hold a strong work ethic, most of those same people believe that hard-working people should be rewarded with leisure time before and after retirement. Because many of the fears associated with retirement have not been supported empirically, the labeling of retirement as a life "crisis" has been called into question (Gayda, Vacola, & Leger, 1984; MacBride, 1976). In short, American society views retirement more negatively than it really is (Sheppard, 1976).

One ostensible rationale for mandatory retirement policies has been that the work skills in elderly people deteriorate. Generally, the data do not support this belief (Salthouse & Maurer, 1996; Sonin & Layner, 1979; Sterns & McDaniel, 1994). Older workers are more consistent and experienced (Sheppard, 1976), and they demonstrate greater accuracy and attention to detail (McFarland & O'Doherty, 1959) than do younger workers. In addition, older workers are less likely to incur on-the-job injuries (Sterns & McDaniel, 1994). Although their cognitive abilities may begin to decline, older workers can compensate for the decline by relying on their extensive job experience and knowledge in order to perform effectively (Salthouse & Maurer, 1996). For these reasons and others, many elderly individuals remain in the workforce, even after they have officially retired (Beck, 1985; Blau, Oser, & Stephens, 1983). Some researchers have advocated this sort of engagement or re-engagement in the workforce as a mechanism for creating and maintaining social relationships, generating income, and staying active (Kouri, 1984).

An individual's decisions about retirement are influenced by a number of communicative factors. The attitudes of one's family and friends, particularly of one's children, spouse, and neighbors, play an important role in the retirement decision (Atchley, 1976; Szinovacz & Ekerdt, 1994). Family support is needed for a decision to retire (Kimmel, Price, & Walker, 1978), although numerous other factors also influence this decision (Beehr, 1986). Other important family considerations include timing retirement to meet the needs of both members of dual-career couples and the need to provide care for an ailing spouse or elderly parent or for grandchildren (Szinovacz & Ekerdt, 1994). Hobbies and other leisure activities are needed to fill the time that used to be consumed by work (Kremer, 1984–1985), although it is important to note that many elderly people report not having enough time to do all the things they want to do.

Any discussion of retirement must also take into consideration the meaning of work in modern society. Work, especially for men, is an intimate part of one's identity (Blau, 1973). The working role is linked to power and perceived desirability (Back, 1977). Again, this is especially true for men; however, work and retirement are becoming much more salient issues for women than they used to be.

WORK

The older population is a growing portion of the population, but a declining portion of the labor force. In 1970, individuals over 55 made up 19% of all adult workers, while in 1993 that percentage had dropped to 13% (U.S. Census Bureau, 1996). Over half of the elderly people who are in the workforce work part-time. Although the percentage of older workers is declining, their numbers are increasing (Salthouse & Maurer, 1996). Very little research has focused on the advantages and disadvantages of employing older workers. Stereotypes about older workers being slower, less efficient, and less up-to-date certainly abound (Shea, 1991), but empirical research has not examined the consequences of these stereotypes on the ability of older workers to maintain or acquire jobs. The U.S. Congress passed the Age Discrimination in Employment Act (ADEA) in 1967 to prohibit workplace discrimination based on age. Social scientific research has found that employers seriously underestimate the strengths and capacities of older workers and that, when given the opportunity to perform, older workers perform their job roles far better than expected (Riley & Riley, 1991). One of the most pernicious stereotypes of elderly workers is their inability to adopt new technologies. Research has consistently demonstrated this stereotype to be false (Riley & Riley, 1991).

The acceptance of negative stereotypes of older workers may be influenced by an organization's corporate culture. Different organizations have different attitudes toward older employees. Long, DeJoy, Javidi, and Javidi (1997) conceptualized a framework for describing organizational cultures that accounts for these types of differences. Some organizations are more task-focused. This type of organization values getting the job done as efficiently and quickly as possible. Employees are treated like cogs in a wheel—the assumption is that employees do not have unique abilities and are easily replaced. Other organizations, however, are more worker-focused. This type of organization values the individual employee's qualities, including his or her experience. This latter type of organization is more amenable to using the skills of older employees. Unfortunately for older workers in the United States, the businesses tend to be more task- than worker-focused.

The labor market encourages older workers to move out of the labor force through financial incentives and downsizing of the labor force (Quadagno & Hardy, 1996). These work disincentives have been specifically designed to encourage older workers to take early retirement (Quadagno & Hardy, 1991). Older workers who have moved out of the workforce are more likely to be unable to find new employment or must settle for part-time positions (Quadagno & Hardy, 1996).

The communicative world of the older adult worker has not been examined. The consequences for older workers of being forced out of the labor market have not been specifically addressed; however, financial stress associated with unemployment may affect marital and other relationships on many important levels. Leisure activities during a period of undesired retirement may be interpreted in a different light than they would in a desired retirement. We turn next to leisure, focusing on the leisure activities of retired individuals.

WHAT IS LEISURE?

Dumazedier (1967) defined *leisure* as nonwork activity in which people engage during their free time for the purpose of relaxation, entertainment, or personal development. Kelly (1982) and Kelly, Steinkamp, and Kelly (1986) extended this definition of leisure to include activities chosen for their own sake. Burrus-Bammel and Bammel (1985) wrote that "the time left over when existence and subsistence necessities of life have been taken care of is classified as leisure" (p. 31). Mancini and Sandifer (1994) argued that it is through leisure activities that relationships are enhanced, with attachments being formed and maintained by shared enjoyment of activities. This last line of thinking reflects the perspective of this book—relationships are created through communication; communication itself often provides a form of entertainment. Gerontologists have studied the leisure activities of elderly people for nearly 5 decades (Atchley, 1976; Burrus-Bammel & Bammel, 1985; Havighurst, 1957; Kelly, 1982; Palmore, 1979). Burrus-Bammel and Bammel (1985) offered an excellent review of the leisure literature.

Several theories of leisure have been advanced to help explain why individuals behave as they do during their leisure time. The first theory of leisure dates to ancient Greece and the writings of Aristotle. "For Aristotle, everything in life was related to leisure since leisure was the goal of all activity" (Burrus-Bammel & Bammel, 1985, p. 849). Leisure activities were considered to be just as important as any work-related activity.

A second theory of leisure, the compensatory theory, asserts that work or job-related activity is the major activity of one's life. Leisure enables an individual to behave in ways that free him or her from the shackles of the job and provides opportunities to break out of the job routine.

A third and opposing theory of leisure holds that "Leisure is a 'spillover' from work and that experiences sought in leisure parallel work activity and complement it" (Burrus-Bammel & Bammel, 1985, p. 849). Individuals with very exciting jobs are likely to have very exciting leisure activities, whereas individuals with dull jobs are likely to have very unexciting leisure activities.

A fourth theory, the personal community theory, stresses the importance of an individual's social network in his or her leisure activity. If an individual is very comfortable with a certain group of friends or family members, then whatever those friends or family members enjoy during their leisure time is what the individual will enjoy during his or her leisure time. This theory may be problematic for elderly people, whose close social network may no longer be living.

Finally, Burrus-Bammel and Bammel (1985) look to the writings of Dumazedier (1967), whose theory views leisure as not only relaxation or a departure from work, but as a way of broadening the life of the individual. Leisure can be challenging and can produce knowledge throughout the life span. One should never underestimate the creative nature of leisure and the spiritual renewal that is often associated with leisure.

These theories of leisure do not, for the most part, stress the life-span nature of leisure: Leisure activity develops and changes throughout the course of one's life. Thus, elderly people have had a lifetime to perfect and adapt their leisure activities. Perhaps the most significant aspect of an elderly individual's life in U.S. society that can impact leisure is the inevitability of retirement. It is important to note that retirement does not equal leisure. Those who are not retired can spend a great deal of time engaged in leisure activities. The reverse is also true: Those who are retired may spend very little time engaged in leisure activities. After all, some elderly individuals in this society are forced to spend all of their time providing for their survival needs and have no time for leisure.

Functions of Leisure Activity

The significance of leisure in later life is not so much dependent on how elderly people spend their leisure time as it is on the consequences of the leisure activity for their lives. This section focuses on how leisure functions for elderly people and whether leisure serves a communication function.

Kelly (1982) and Kelly et al. (1986) discuss three functions of leisure for the elderly population. The first function of leisure is simply as a time filler. When an individual retires, he or she is left with at least 8 hours of each former workday to fill with some kind of activity. Leisure can function to take the place of what was once job-related time. In this sense, leisure can be a very important adaptive mechanism in a traumatic time. A second function of leisure for elderly people is the opportunity for "effectual action in the years when work and family commitments have lessened" (Kelly et al. 1986, p. 531). Parenting may no longer be an appropriate role, and leisure provides the opportunity to fill this lost role with similar meaningful activity. Grandparenting, for instance, is often perceived as more of a leisure activity than a well-defined job activity. The third function of leisure activity for elderly people is to provide the context in which important relationships are developed and expressed. Leisure, then, by its very nature can be a pure communication event. The following three examples of leisure activity—watching television, playing poker, and learning about computers—which on the surface appear to be noninterpersonal, can be quite intensive interpersonal experiences.

Watching television is often a solitary act. Yet, as discussed in chapter 4, the information in the television program can provide those who watch television with something to talk about. Watching television, then, can become a precommunicative act. Indeed, if an elderly individual complains about not having anything to talk about or feeling left out of conversations that deal with current events, one cure for this complaint is for him or her to spend some time watching television. Paradoxically, time spent alone in front of the television can lead to socially fulfilling interactions.

Playing poker is another rich communicative experience. Not only are several other individuals needed before a game can begin, but, also after the game is over, the winners and losers have plenty to discuss and to explain. The entire context of the poker environment is social. Stone and Kalish (1981) observed many strong relationships inside a poker establishment that continued "beyond the parking lot."

The stereotype of a "computer nerd" in U.S. society is an individual who would rather interface with a computer terminal than with a human being. This is far from the truth. Anyone who has taken instruction in computers knows how much information must be shared by individuals in the class. If computer learners are not doing well, they need others by their side, constantly helping. If computer learners are doing very well, they will be called on by those who desperately need their help. Computer classes are quite rich in communicative behavior. In addition, computers are high technology that is future oriented. Thus, elderly people who take the time to learn about computers are simultaneously developing practical skills and conversational skills with which the younger generation are familiar. This can lead to intergenerational relationships based on an interest in computers.

There is an additional benefit of computer-related leisure activities. Maxwell and Silverman (1970), Danowski and Sacks

(1980), and Robinson and Wallace (1984), argued that the ability to use the technological and informational resources of a society is a significant indicator of social status. Further, increasing such abilities should result in an increase in the social status of elderly people; Danowski and Sacks (1980) offered some empirical support for this claim. In addition, the use of computers for activities such as e-mail and chat rooms provides older individuals with an opportunity to remain connected with their larger social network and to develop new relationships with those who have similar interests.

Leisure Activities of Elderly People

One way to understand leisure within the elderly population is to simply list and describe the various activities associated with leisure in later life and discuss how these activities are different from the leisure activities of other segments of the population. Several key studies of older individuals reveal that the two most popular leisure activities for elderly people are visiting friends and watching television (Kubey, 1980; McAvoy, 1979; Moss & Lawton, 1982; Peppers, 1976). Other activities reported frequently by elderly people include traveling, reading, fishing, walking, gardening, doing hobbies, driving, attending club meetings, and caring for animals.

These lists of leisure activities are somewhat interesting, but how these activities change throughout the life span is more informative. A study by Kelly et al. (1986) investigated the changing levels of leisure activities throughout an individual's life span. Two activities showed a major decline with increasing age: exercise and sport activities, and outdoor recreation. These two activities, however, are currently receiving considerable attention in U.S. society, and the benefits of participating in physical exercise are beginning to influence the elderly population. The major conclusion of the Kelly et al. (1986) study was that "later life leisure demonstrates considerable continuity with earlier adult periods" (p. 533). Although it is true that physical exercise declines with increasing age, family, social, and home-based activities remain stable well into old age.

Two articles in the gerontological literature that report on the leisure activities of older people are particularly enlightening. Stone and Kalish (1981) wrote about gambling, specifically poker, and elderly people who frequent the poker tables at clubs in Gardena, California. Interviews conducted with the elderly participants of the nightly poker games reveal that the primary reason for venturing to these clubs is the pure enjoyment of gambling. "Gambling unconsciously revives childhood fantasies of grandeur and activates rebellion against the reality principle, in favor of the pleasure principle" (Stone & Kalish, 1981, p. 35). The gambling clubs provide a social atmosphere that is preferred to that in senior centers. It is exciting, one can survive on one's wits, and, if skillful, one can make some money.

Furlong and Kearsley (1986) wrote about computer instruction for older adults, finding that "computers offer the potential to enrich the lives of older people by providing intellectual stimulation and improved access to information" (p. 32). The elderly individuals who enroll in the computer workshops are very positive about their experiences with computers. Surprisingly, elderly people describe programming (an area that completely baffles at least one of the authors of this book) as the most enjoyable area of the workshop. Furlong and Kearsley (1986) did not observe any differences in learning across age groups. "The elder learned at about the same rate, made similar mistakes, and were equally enthusiastic about what they learned" (p. 34).

Older individuals are adopting computer technology in greater numbers, although men are adopting it faster than women (Mundorf, Bryant, & Brownell, 1997). Senior sites, such as SeniorNet and CyberSenior, are growing in number and in the number of visitors. Older individuals enjoy making new friends online and those with Internet access report less isolation (Mundorf et al., 1997).

Variables Affecting Leisure

It is quite obvious that everyone does not enjoy the same leisure activities or have the same amount of leisure time. This is as true for individuals in their teens as it is for individuals in their 70s. Burrus-Bammel and Bammel (1985) did an excellent job of reviewing the many variables that affect leisure behavior; several of their findings will be summarized here.

An initial variable that affects leisure is work orientation and occupation. The results of numerous studies indicate that those individuals who have a very high work orientation permit their work to influence their leisure activity. Parker (1976) stated that some executives in U.S. society enjoy work so much that they make no distinction between work and leisure. For these people, retirement can present a problem if they do not find satisfying ways to fill the increased amount of leisure time (Kelly, 1982; Kelly et al. 1986). In addition, those individuals who have professional occupations have the greatest variety of leisure activities, whereas individuals with less creative jobs tend to have less creative leisure activities.

Financial independence is a second variable that influences leisure activity. Income level has been directly related to activity level. In U.S. society, more money equals more leisure options. In addition, leisure time is more appealing to those with higher incomes. If one exists at or below the poverty level, leisure is not a major part of one's life.

Time is also a variable that influences leisure. Retirement brings with it more free time. This free time can be used for leisure activities. However, many elderly individuals cite not having enough time to do all they want to do as a major problem with their lives.

An obvious variable that affects participation in leisure activity is health and mobility. In order to participate in a variety of leisure activities good health is a necessity. "Lack of ability was mentioned by the elderly as their most important problem in trying to participate in preferred activities" (Burrus-Bammel & Bammel, 1985, p. 852). Those individuals who perceive themselves as healthy tend to participate in a wide variety of leisure activities. The additional consideration of mobility can impact leisure. Transportation is a major problem for some elderly people. A large majority of elderly people often find themselves dependent on others for transportation. If transportation is not available, then leisure activities will be limited.

Cheek, Field, and Burdge (1976) reported that the most common recreation unit is the family. In U.S. society, people spend a great deal of leisure time with their families, so if an elderly individual is married with children and grandchildren, that elderly person will spend a good deal of his or her leisure time with his or her family. Problems arise, however, when a spouse dies and children move away. Many elderly people prefer to spend their leisure time with members of their own age group. Thus, friendship is an important determinant of leisure activity. Families and friends have a major impact on the lives of elderly people (see chapters 7–10).

Many other variables can also have an influence upon leisure activity. Age, educational level, place of residence, ethnic group, and perceived status are only a few of the variables that gerontologists relate to leisure. The environment in which people live often dictates the appropriate leisure activity. If an individual is not lucky enough to live in a city with a major-league franchise, that person cannot attend major-league games regularly. In the very same way, a person's background or location can prevent him or her from exercising many leisure options. If a person grows up in western Pennsylvania, where body surfing is impossible on the Ohio River, he or she will discover that the competence needed to body surf remains a mystery. On the other hand, Hawaiians, who can learn to body surf as children, cannot drive to Three Rivers Stadium and take in a Pirates game on a regular basis. The influence of these variables on choice of leisure activity remain throughout one's life-span.

ADJUSTING TO RETIREMENT

The age at which individuals retire is highly variable. A person might enter the military at the age of 18 and retire with 20 years of service at the age of 38. Another person might retire from one job at the age of 65 and begin a new career in which he or she remains active for many years. Many older people actually move in and out of retirement, retiring from a full-time job and then starting a new job, which may or may not be related to their previous employment, on a full-time or part-time basis (Hardy, 1991). These individuals may choose to be out of the labor force for a period of time and then re-enter the working world as it meets their new lifestyles. Individuals who choose to retire when they are younger than 65 are more likely to pursue additional employment after this event than are workers who wait until they reach the age of 70 to retire from full-time employment for the first time. About half of men who retire from full-time employment begin a part-time job shortly thereafter (Quadagno & Hardy, 1996). Younger individuals (under 65) who do not choose to retire, but who leave employment due to external factors, are more likely to desire re-employment (Hardy, 1991). Individuals who want to remain actively employed, however, may face difficulties in securing a paid position due to health limitations, family demands, and age discrimination on the part of potential employers.

Most people do adjust to or come to terms with retirement (Kremer, 1984–1985). Some of the important variables affecting this adjustment include activities with friends and family, feelings about rest and tranquility, and activities that fill up free time (Kremer, 1984–1985). Generally, elderly people can cope well with the discontinuity posed by retirement and even look forward to it (Atchley, 1977).

Retirement serves as an important rite of passage, one that brings out both memories and dreams (Savishinsky, 1995). In a longitudinal study, Savishinsky (1995) followed 26 people as they approached retirement and for the first 3 years following that event. Ceremonies that signify this passage may be formal or informal. Formal ceremonies are usually organized by the employer. Most retirees found these events relatively unsatisfying, although they felt compelled to attend. The ritual seemed hollow, especially for those who attended ceremonies along with several other retirees from the same organization. Even more disconcerting, for those who had been forced into early retirement due to economic reasons, no official ceremony marked their departure. Those individuals who had an informal ceremony found that these were often quite rewarding events, helping them to review their past and contemplate their future. Informal events were perceived as more meaningful because the retiree had been involved in developing the guest list, intimate friends and family were included, and gifts were selected that reflected the individual. Many of the retirees in this study traveled for a period shortly after retirement. These individuals felt that they had successfully made the transition from their work routine to their retired routine by taking some time to separate not only from work, but home and the community. Going away and coming back helped them to adjust to their new identity.

One factor that may influence the adjustment to retirement is relocation. A large number of older adults have migrated to the sunbelt (Hazelrigg & Hardy, 1995). Some relocate before retirement in order to take advantage of the warmer climate and develop a network, while others make the move after retirement. The adjustment to retirement is often made easier by the support of families and friends; however, moving to a new community may disrupt established support networks and require the development of a new friendship network. Individuals who have a difficult time developing new friendships may feel isolated. In addition, the geographic relocation may move the retirees closer to or further from children, affecting whether children will be available for participation in leisure activities.

A relocation after retirement need not be to a far-away state, but could be to a local retirement community. Adjusting to retirement in these communities results when a new normative system develops. Among the residents, qualities such as trust, friendliness, and concern for others are more highly valued than former achievements or occupational status (Perkinson, 1980). Those residents who "keep going" are the ones who lack self-pity, keep mentally alert and aware, and are willing to help others. These individuals are seen as having made a "good adjustment." New roles develop, including alternate work roles (committee memberships and volunteer activities); family roles (represented by supportiveness and helping toward fellow residents); and leisure roles. The importance of leisure roles in retirement has been pointed out frequently (e.g., Fly, Reinhart, & Hamby, 1981), although leisure is not solely a retirement activity. Satisfaction with retirement communities is linked to social interaction (Holmes & Holmes, 1995). Opportunities to interact with others and build a sense of community, a sense of "we-ness" or common culture, increase a person's satisfaction with the retirement community.

How one adjusts to retirement will be affected by whether the decision to retire is voluntary or involuntary. Those retiring voluntarily often have little or no difficulty adjusting (Atchley, 1982). When an individual's retirement is motivated by family events (e.g., in order to provide care for an elderly parent or grandchildren), the retirement can be seen as untimely, which makes adaptation more difficult (Szinovacz, 1989). Early retirement is associated with more negative effects when an individual's retirement is motivated by poor health, although ethnic minorities feel the need to continue working until their health levels are much worse than do European Americans (Stanford, Happersett, Morton, Molgaard, & Peddecord, 1991).

Preretirement Activities

Another factor that may affect successful adjustment to retirement is preretirement "grooming" activities. For instance, interacting with a close friend who is retired seems to make the transition to retirement an easier one (Evans, Ekerdt, & Bosse, 1985). This friendship can ease some of the uncertainty about retirement and demonstrate to the person that relationships with others are possible after retirement. Seeking advice and information about retirement decreases uncertainty (Simpson, Back, & McKinney, 1966b).

Significant others also help determine preretirement attitudes (Cox & Bhak, 1978–1979), which, in turn, affect adjustment. Focusing on this specifically, Atchley (1975) argued that the key to adjusting to retirement lies in one's hierarchy of personal goals. Interpersonal negotiation with one's significant others helps determine this hierarchy. The soon-to-be retired person shares his or her thoughts and feelings with others and gets feedback from them. The person may get support or resistance from others; belittlement by others will make retirement more difficult (Camerini, 1983).

Participation in preretirement training can be beneficial because it helps to increase information (Kremer & Harpaz, 1984). This training may help counter the unrealistically high expectations about retirement held by some people (McDermott, 1982). And the training also seems to have some positive effects on the social and communicative aspects of retirement, in that those who have gone through such training are more satisfied with their family relationships in retired life (Kamouri & Cavanaugh, 1986), particularly with their contact with grandchildren (Harpaz & Kremer, 1981).

Satisfaction with Retirement

Adjusting to retirement, of course, is not necessarily the same thing as enjoying it or being satisfied with it. Generally, most retired people *are* satisfied with their retirement. There are several variables that seem to help determine an individual's satisfaction with retirement. One such variable—and an important one—is activity level, particularly interpersonal interaction (Beveridge, 1980; Graney, 1975; Rowe, 1983). Perceived social usefulness is also a facilitator of satisfaction with retirement (Graney, 1975), as is involvement in organizations (Dorfman, Kohout, & Heckert, 1985) and household tasks (Keith & Dobson, 1979). Dorfman and his colleagues also found that the quality of one's interpersonal relationships and the receiving of aid from confidants and relatives helped build satisfaction with retirement.

Two other noncommunication variables should also be mentioned as determinants of retirement satisfaction: previous satisfaction with one's job and income. The more satisfied one was with one's job, the less satisfied one is with retirement (McDermott, 1982). Satisfaction is not related, however, to the comparison of one's retirement income to one's preretirement income, but to the absolute level of one's retirement income (Maxwell, 1985). Even if a person does not have as much money as he or she used to have, the person will be satisfied as long as he or she has enough to get by.

Effects of Retirement

Implicit in our discussion of adjustment to and satisfaction with retirement has been the effects of retirement. Quite a bit of research addresses this issue, and some of it has implications for the understanding of communication and elderly people. Research shows, most generally, a great deal of continuity between preretirement and postretirement life (Beehr, 1986), although retirement does not affect everyone the same way (Maddox, 1966). To provide an overall picture of the effects of retirement, we summarize here some of the findings of the Duke longitudinal study (Palmore, 1981). The study found that:

1. Retirement does not have major effects on income—a person is likely to be poor after he or she retires only if that person has always been poor.
2. Retirement is more likely to be caused by poor health than to cause poor health.
3. Retirement does not cause mental illness.
4. Retirement does not lead to a decline in life satisfaction for most people.
5. Retirement leads to little decline in social activity for most people.

Palmore (1981) also concluded that the "Most negative effects of retirement were either temporary or relatively minor" (p. 43) and that "Retirement appears to have a small *positive* effect on happiness once other social variables are taken into account" (p. 45, emphasis original). Palmore added that involuntary mandatory retirement has some negative effects, but these are quickly overcome. In a summary study of six longitudinal data sets examining the consequences of retirement, Palmore, Fillenbaum, and George (1984) again concluded that retirement has few effects on health, social activity, and life satisfaction. Atchley (1982), however, did find that retirement reduces activity level to a certain extent, but not negatively.

Most retirees feel little loss of involvement in society with retirement, especially if they are healthy and were highly involved with their jobs prior to retirement (Back & Guptill, 1966). That finding may contradict what many would expect. It is not completely consistent with the finding by Blau (1973) that demoralization sometimes occurs as a result of the role loss that can come with retirement. Role loss is less likely to occur if one has been feeling alienated from one's job. Demoralization and role loss are associated with the loss in self-esteem that can come with retirement. For some, retirement causes them to question the meaning of their existence and leads to self-denigration and feelings of inadequacy (Blau, 1973). This sort of reaction is possible because the interpersonal relationships that people experience at work contribute to their self-identity and to the amount and diversity of information that they have about themselves and others (McDermott, 1982). The loss of a social network from work removes a recurring source of affirmation and denies a major source of self-reflexive activity (McDermott, 1982). Retired people now have fewer opportunities for self-knowledge by comparing their behavior to the behavior of others. The self-concept may also be hurt by the feelings of uselessness that can come with retirement (Camerini, 1983).

Role loss has been discussed widely in retirement research literature (e.g., Chambre, 1984). Longitudinal research, however, has shown that role loss in retirement is a less important predictor of social participation than is one's prior level of participation, one's family network size, and one's personal characteristics (Wan & Odell, 1983). Researchers also know that *job deprivation*, that is, the feeling of being deprived because of the lack of a job, is not as frequent in retirement as might be believed (Goudy, Burke, Powers, & Keith, 1982).

For a few people, loneliness is a consequence of retirement (Blau, 1973), but the likelihood of this is related in part to marital status. Most elderly individuals spend some time in solitude, but this is not a wholly negative experience for them (Larson, Zuzanek, & Mannell, 1985). This is especially true of those who have the regular companionship of a spouse. And the amount of loneliness experienced may be a function of the intensity of friendships during working years. One study found that the loneliness of retired military personnel was a cost of the intensity of friendships that they had developed during their active service (Little, 1981). They had developed such intense friendships while in the service that the friendships were sorely missed during retirement.

There is no question that some social relationships are disrupted by retirement, unless one's social group is also retired (Blau, 1973). If this is the case, retirement may be welcomed and may actually help friendships. Other researchers have suggested that phased retirement may make the sudden disruption of work and social relationships easier to handle (Kaminski-Da Roza, 1985), and that the disruption of social networks is most likely when an individual moves to a different residence around the same time as retirement (Kahana & Kahana, 1983), although moving is, in actuality, only rarely related to retirement (Atchley, 1977).

A relationship that is not disrupted per se by retirement is the marital relationship. Marital difficulties may result from a new 24-hour-a-day relationship in which unresolved conflicts, unsatisfactory patterns of interaction, poor communication, and inadequate sharing come to light (Bradford, 1979). These problems cannot be ignored as easily as they were before retirement. Other factors, such as the prestige (or lack of prestige) of the spouse's former occupation no longer affect marital satisfaction after retirement (Cassidy, 1985). In spite of these potentially negative changes, most couples adapt successfully to retirement (Szinovacz & Ekerdt, 1994). The effects of retirement on marital partners will be discussed in more detail later in this chapter.

Interaction with other family members is also affected by retirement. Retirement usually leads to an increase in the amount of time spent with the family (Farakhan, Lubin, & O'Connor, 1984), although not as great an increase as many believe (Keith, Goudy, & Powers, 1984). More time spent with children and satisfaction with this time have been found to be associated with less depression (Farakhan et al., 1984). Although retirement increases the amount of time available to be spent with family, increased contact may not be satisfactory (Szinovacz & Ekerdt, 1994). If retirement was prompted by the need to provide care for family members or if the family makes unreasonable demands on the retired person's or couple's time, then the retirement experience can be spoiled (Brubaker & Brubaker, 1992; Miller & Cavanaugh, 1990; Vinick & Ekerdt, 1991). In addition, postretirement relocations may enhance or undermine increased familial contact (Cuba, 1992; Cuba & Longino, 1991). Generally, retired individuals have stronger needs for love and association with others than do people at other points in the life span (Romsa, Bondy, & Blenman, 1985) and this may influence any relocation decision. The amount of social involvement that one has during retirement, however, is likely to be similar to the amount one had while working—if a person had few social involvements before retirement, such involvements probably would not be built up after retirement (Simpson, Back, & McKinney, 1966a).

Another effect of retirement, although not clearly a communication or social interaction variable, is the death rate. One study found that the death rate increases after retirement (Haynes, McMichael, & Tyroler, 1977). A later study, however, found that the death rate increases after retirement *only* for those people who greatly decrease their interaction with friends and their other activities after retirement (Cameron & Persinger, 1983). Thus, the death rate after retirement is associated with communication and social interaction. Communication can be good for you!

Other research has also examined the social relationships and retirement of elderly people. Overall, sociability is negatively linked with infirmity and with the use of the mass media as a pasttime (Andersson & Walck, 1982). Connectedness of temporal experience (seeing the present as being connected to the past and future) also leads to higher social integration (Levy, 1978).

Although the *quantity* of interaction is not crucial to understanding adaptation to aging and retirement (Connor, Powers, & Bultena, 1979), researchers have found that social relationships are helpful for adaptation. For instance, one study found that retirement leads to diminished life satisfaction only when a change in marital status (i.e., divorce) occurs around the same time as the retirement, and that marital relations are a more important determinant of life satisfaction than is retirement (Gayda et al. 1984).

In one way, of course, retirement presents a new opportunity—an opportunity to develop a social life outside of work and family (Beveridge, 1980). Many retired individuals look at retirement in just this way. But the family continues to be important for most retirees. This leads to a question that has been raised by researchers, but has yet to be adequately studied: What happens to family relationships when younger people have to support retired old people? This concern will be addressed in chapter 9.

Marital Relationships and Retirement

Although leisure activities are important for the adjustment to retirement, a second and perhaps even more significant determinant of adjustment to retirement is the marital relationship. Atchley (1982) and others suggested that high marital satisfaction facilitates adjustment to retirement. This, of course, makes sense—if a person likes his or her spouse and marital relationship, that person will be more interested in spending time with his or her spouse after retirement. Support from one's spouse and family makes the adjustment to retirement easier (Howard, 1982; Szinovacz & Ekerdt, 1994). Activities and interaction with family and friends help fill the time that one now has available (Kremer, 1984–1985; MacLean, 1980, 1983).

While many couples anticipate postretirement problems and changes in activities, they find that they experience fewer problems than anticipated (Vinick & Ekerdt, 1992). Comparing older couples (husbands were 54 or older) in which the husband was or was not retired, Ekerdt and Vinick (1991) found relatively few marital complaints and no significant differences between husband-working and husband-retired couples. Wives in both groups desired more attention to housework, more communication, and more signs of appreciation, whereas husbands desired more sexual activity. Overall, retirement was seen as neither a benefit nor a hindrance to marital adjustment.

Szinovacz and Ekerdt (1994) summarized the research on retirement and marital quality, finding no large effects overall, but that couples experience both negative and positive changes. On the negative side, wives report problems with their husbands' being around all the time, a lack of privacy, and too much togetherness. Husbands report dismay at their wives' humdrum routines and narrow interests. Conversely,

> Positive changes brought about by retirement include increased freedom to develop joint endeavors, increased companionship, fewer time pressures, and a more relaxed atmosphere at home. Spouses engaging in joint decision making and shared activities are especially likely to benefit from retirement. In addition, support from the spouse, confirmation of the retiree's self-concept, and adjustment to the retired spouse's needs seem important prerequisites for marital adjustment after retirement (Szinovacz & Ekerdt, 1994, p. 386).

Gender Differences

Retirement does not affect all people in the same way. There are ethnic differences in responses to retirement, although they are few (Farakhan et al., 1984; Jackson & Gibson, 1985). Very little research focused on retirement and family linkages across cultural contexts (Dorfman, 1992; Hatch, 1991; Taeuber, 1990). In addition, only limited research was conducted on the impact of retirement on homosexual or cohabiting couples, and on those who are divorced or never married (Barresi & Hunt, 1990; Lipman, 1986). There are also different responses depending upon the length of retirement (Cherry, Zarit, & Krauss, 1984). More research has been devoted to gender differences in response to retirement than to any other variable. Most of the retirement research, of course, has focused on men. It has often been assumed that retirement is less important to women because work is less important to them. This assumption, as we shall show, is not only sexist, but it is not always supported by the data.

There are gender differences in the predictors of adjustment to retirement. For men, these predictors include age, education, occupational status, health, and increased interaction with friends. For women, the only significant predictor of the effects of retirement is age (George, Fillenbaum, & Palmore, 1984). Men and women also differ in their preretirement attitudes (Behling & Merves, 1985). Women tend to express more concern over social relationships after retirement than do men (Fox, 1977).

While retirement has positive and negative effects for both men and women, the outcomes are different. The outcomes of retirement for men include decreased participation in formal organizations, increased time spent in extra-work activities, and decreased life satisfaction. But for women, retirement is associated with increased time spent in hobbies and household tasks, increased perceptions of social worth, and increased perceptions of internal control (George et al., 1984). And women, because of lifetime patterns of work and family obligations, are less able to retire with economic security than are men (O'Rand, 1983). No consistent differences, however, seem to emerge between men and women in adjustment to retirement (Gratton & Haug, 1983).

One very interesting study explored the impact of retirement on the sexual identities of older men and women (Starker, 1980). Starker observed patterns of game playing in a senior center in New York City. She found that, during their work careers, men spent a lot of time away from home, and women tended to regard the home as their personal domain. Retirement by the husbands threatens the wives' need for personal space. In retirement, separate spaces were maintained by men and women at the senior center. The men tended to monopolize the better, high-prestige places, whereas the women had low-prestige places.

Marital status affects retirement differently for men and women. Formerly married women, for instance, are less likely to have adequate pensions than are other individuals and may have more difficulty with retirement. Never-married women, however, embrace retirement (Keith, 1985). Keith's data indicated that the commonly held view that work substitutes for family ties for never-married women, making retirement more difficult for them, is not accurate. Retired married women have more primary relations than do married men, and spouseless men have the fewest primary relations of any group (Longino & Lipman, 1981). Spouseless women receive more emotional, social, and instrumental support from family members than do spouseless men. Women's investment in maintaining family ties appears to pay off in later life (Longino & Lipman, 1981). Widows who retain preretirement friends and social contacts report higher life satisfaction than those who do not (Dorfman & Moffett, 1987) and adapt to retirement more successfully when they maintain greater contact with relatives (Szinovacz, 1992). Unmarried men, however, are more likely to lack close kin relationships and, therefore, sense a greater loss from decreased interaction with work colleagues (Szinovacz, 1992).

Women's Retirement. Retirement is a broader issue for women than it is for men. "Men retire from their jobs, certainly a major disruption, but women retire from their families, largely through widowhood, losing not only their jobs but also their primary support system and source of identity" (Livson, 1983, p. 134). As previously discussed, all of this support is not lost, but retirement for women can certainly be devastating if one includes the notion of retirement from the family. The other retirement research does not take this broad perspective on retirement, but focuses instead only on retirement from paid employment outside the home.

Life satisfaction appears to be higher for working older women than for retired older women (Riddick, 1985). Retired older women are also more concerned about power and status and are less inclined toward affiliation and peers than are working older women or older homemakers (Richardson, 1985). Richardson speculated that women's reaction to retirement is different than men's because of the prevailing inequities in status and income between them, particularly in the later years.

With the increasing number of dual-career couples, joint timing of retirement has become a greater issue (Szinovacz & Ekerdt, 1994). These couples attempt to time their retirement in relation to each other, unless the woman retires due to family caregiving needs (Hurd, 1990; O'Rand, Henretta, & Krecker, 1992) or needs to continue working for financial reasons (Szinovacz & Ekerdt, 1994). Studies show that women make their decisions about retirement differently than do men. Although one study found that husbands take their wives' employment status into account when making retirement decisions (Anderson, Clark, & Johnson, 1980), most research shows that husbands exert a stronger influence on their wives' decisions than wives do on their husbands' decisions. A wife's decision about retirement is strongly influenced by her husband's retirement (Shaw, 1984; George et al., 1984; Gratton & Haug, 1983). One *New York Times* article ("As more men ... ," 1986) cited numerous examples of wives who continue working after their husbands have retired. Some husbands are threatened by this and demand that their wives stop working, but the wives do not always comply. One researcher cited in this article noted that husbands state, "My wife supported my decision to retire," (p. C1) whereas women say, "He pressured me to retire" (p. C1). Many other husbands welcome their wives' continuing to work. As one such husband puts it, "it works out well for both of us. It's the first time in 40 years that I can stay in bed and wave goodbye to my wife" ("As more men ... ," 1986, p. C1). Most wives are younger than their husbands, and many have taken time off from paid employment to raise families. As a result, their careers may be in full swing at the time that the husband decides to retire, so it certainly makes sense that retirement would occur at different times. Research has yet to examine, however, the change in roles necessitated when the husband retires and the wife keeps working. Does the man, who is now at home most of the time, take over the household tasks—cooking, cleaning, and so forth? Does the woman, who may now be a more important source of income, have more decision-making power than she did in the past? Numerous questions like these should be examined by future researchers.

One other consideration should be briefly mentioned at this point—wives' satisfaction with their husbands' retirement. The early investigations of this issue found that half of the wives studied were sorry that their husbands had retired, but these tended to be working-class wives whose husbands were in poor health and who had unhappy marriages prior to retirement (Heyman & Jeffers, 1968). Consistent with this finding was that of Kerckhoff (1966), who concluded that retiring husbands look forward to retirement more and experience more satisfaction with retirement than do their wives. The retired husbands did become more involved in household tasks, and this was welcomed by wives in the middle and upper strata. Working-class wives were less companionate and more authoritarian in their orientations, and expected more exclusive control over the house. They did not respond favorably to the husbands' new involvement. Both the husbands and wives in these marriages saw the men's involvement in the household as undesirable after a while, but the husbands continued to do it. This led to conflict—guilt for him and irritation for her. While researchers may speculate that these reactions have changed as (some) marriages have become more egalitarian, research has yet to provide definitive answers.

SUMMARY

Some of the social-interaction issues surrounding work, leisure, and retirement for elderly people have been outlined in this chapter. The research cited herein indicated that retirement is becoming more accepted and should not be considered to be a crisis in one's life. This is true even though work is an intimate part of one's identity. Adjustment to retirement is associated with the development of alternate roles and learning to cope with discontinuity. It is influenced by marital and family relationships, and by friendships. Satisfaction with retirement seems to increase as activity increases. In particular, social interaction increases retirement satisfaction. Social interaction and activity even decrease the death rate for retirees! Retirement has both positive and negative effects on elderly individuals. Notable among these is the disruption of social relationships. As work relationships become less important, family and marital relationships become more important. More opportunities open up for developing new relationships in retirement. If the marriage has been bad all along, the problems may come to the fore during retirement.

Researchers also know that there are some gender differences in retirement. In particular, husbands affect their wives' retirement decisions and retirement experience. And a wife is not always thrilled that her husband has chosen to retire. Some preretirement activities influence adjustment to retirement; training, seeking information, support from significant others, and having a retired friend all help preretirees. Some leisure activities or replacement activities to fill the time vacuum created by retirement also help the adjustment from working to retirement.

The chapters that follow focus further on relationships with spouses, family, and friends that sometimes become more important to retired individuals than to those who are still working.

■ REFERENCES

Anderson, K., Clark, R. L., & Johnson, T. (1980). Retirement in dual-career families. In R. L. Clark (Ed.), *Retirement policy in an aging society* (pp. 109–127). Durham, NC: Duke University Press.

Andersson, L., & Walck, C. (1982). Some factors relating to sociability: A structural equation model approach. *Reports from the Laboratory for Clinical Research, 164,* 13.

As more men retire early, more women work longer. (1986, April 3). *New York Times,* p. Cl.

Atchley, R. C. (1975). Adjustment to loss of job at retirement. *International Journal of Aging and Human Development, 6,* 17–27.

Atchley, R. C. (1976). *The sociology of retirement.* Cambridge, MA: Schenkman.

Atchley, R. C. (1977). Retirement: Continuity or crisis? In R. Kalish (Ed.), *The later years: Social implications of gerontology* (pp. 136–142). Monterey, CA: Brooks/Cole.

Atchley, R. C. (1982). Retirement: Leaving the world of work. *The Annals of the American Academy of Political and Social Science, 464,* 120–131.

Back, K. W. (1977). The ambiguity of retirement. In E. W. Busse & E. Pfeiffer (Eds.), *Behavior and adaptation in late life* (pp. 78–98). Boston: Little, Brown.

Back, K. W., & Guptill, C. S. (1966). Retirement and self-ratings. In I. H. Simpson & J. C. McKinney (Eds.), *Social aspects of aging* (pp. 120–129). Durham, NC: Duke University Press.

Barresi, C. M., & Hunt, K. (1990). The unmarried elderly: Age, sex, and ethnicity. In T. H. Brubaker (Ed.), *Family relationships in later life* (2nd ed., pp. 169–192). Newbury Park, CA: Sage.

Beck, S. H. (1985). Determinants of labor force activity among retired men. *Research on Aging, 7,* 251–280.

Beehr, T. A. (1986). The process of retirement: A review and recommendations for future investigation. *Personnel Psychology, 39,* 31–55.

Behling, J. H., & Merves, E. S. (1985). Preretirement attitudes and financial preparedness: A cross-cultural and gender analysis. *Journal of Sociology and Social Welfare, 12,* 113–128.

Beveridge, W. E. (1980). Retirement and life significance: A study of the adjustment to retirement of a sample of men at management level. *Human Relations, 33,* 69–78.

Blau, Z. S. (1973). *Old age in a changing society.* New York: New Viewpoints.

Blau, Z. S., Oser, G. T., & Stephens, R. C. (1983). Older workers: Current status and future prospects. *Research in the Sociology of Work, 2,* 101–124.

Bradford, L. P. (1979). Emotional problems in retirement and what can be done. *Group and Organizational Studies, 4,* 429–439.

Brubaker, E., & Brubaker, T. H. (1992). The context of retired women as caregivers. In M. Szinovacz, D. J. Ekerdt, & B. H. Vinick (Eds.), *Families and retirement* (pp. 222–235). Newbury Park, CA: Sage.

Burrus-Bammel, L. L., & Bammel, G. (1985). Leisure and retirement. In J. E. Birren and K. W. Schaie (Eds.), *Handbook of the psychology of aging* (pp. 848–863). New York: Van Nostrand Reinhold.

Camerini, M. (1983). Condizione marginale e communicazione. *Studi di Sociologia, 21*, 370–377.

Cameron, K. A., & Persinger, M. A. (1983). Pensioners who die soon after retirement can be discriminated from survivors by postretirement activities. *Psychological Reports, 53*, 564–566.

Cassidy, M. L. (1985). Role conflict in the postparental period: The effects of employment status on the marital satisfaction of women. *Research on Aging, 7*, 433–454.

Chambre, S. M. (1984). Is volunteering a substitute for role loss in old age? An empirical test of activity theory. *The Gerontologist, 24*, 292–298.

Cheek, N. H., Field, D. R., & Burdge, R. I. (1976). *Leisure and recreation places.* Ann Arbor, MI: Ann Arbor Science.

Cherry, D. L., Zarit, S. H., & Krauss, I. K. (1984). The structure of postretirement adaptation for recent and longer-term women retirees. *Experimental Aging Research, 10*, 231–236.

Connor, K., Powers, E., & Bultena, G. (1979). Social interaction and life satisfaction: An empirical assessment of late-life patterns. *Journal of Gerontology, 34*, 116–121.

Cox, H. G. (1985). Retirement trends and issues. *Contemporary Education, 57*, 8–13.

Cox, H., & Bhak, A. (1978–1979). Symbolic interaction and retirement adjustment: An empirical assessment. *International Journal of Aging and Human Development, 9*, 279–286.

Cuba, L. (1992). Family and retirement in the context of elderly migration. In M. Szinovacz, D. J. Ekerdt, & B. H. Vinick (Eds.), *Families and retirement* (pp. 205–221). Newbury Park, CA: Sage.

Cuba, L., & Longino, C. F., Jr. (1991). Regional retirement migration: the case of Cape Cod. *Journal of Gerontology: Social Sciences, 46*, S33–S42.

Danowski, J., & Sacks, W. (1980). Computer communication and the elderly. *Experimental Aging Research, 6*, 125–135.

Dorfman, L. T. (1992). Couples in retirement: Division of household work. In M. Szinovacz, D. J. Ekerdt, & B. H. Vinick (Eds.), *Families and retirement* (pp. 159–173). Newbury Park, CA: Sage.

Dorfman, L. T., Kohout, F. J., & Heckert, D. A. (1985). Retirement satisfaction in the rural elderly. *Research on Aging, 7*, 577–599.

Dorfman, L. T., & Moffett, M. M. (1987). Retirement satisfaction in married and widowed rural women. *The Gerontologist, 27*, 215–221.

Dumazedier, J. (1967). *Toward a society of leisure.* London: Collier.

Ekerdt, D. J., & Vinick, B. H. (1991). Marital complaints in husband-working and husband-retired couples. *Research on Aging, 13*, 364–382.

Evans, L., Ekerdt, D. J., & Bosse, R. (1985). Proximity to retirement and anticipatory involvement: Findings from the normative aging study. *Journal of Gerontology, 40*, 368–374.

Farakhan, A., Lubin, B., & O'Connor, W. A. (1984). Life satisfaction and depression among retired black persons. *Psychological Reports, 55,* 452–454.

Fly, J. W., Reinhart, G. R., & Hamby, R. (1981). Leisure activity and adjustment in retirement. *Sociological Spectrum, 1,* 135–144.

Fox, J. H. (1977). Effects of retirement and former work life on women's adaptation in old age. *Journal of Gerontology, 32,* 196–202.

Furlong, M., & Kearsley, G. (1986). Computer instruction for older adults. *Generations, 11,* 32–34.

Gayda, M., Vacola, G., & Leger, J. M. (1984). Sante mentale et premieres annees de la retraite. *Annales Medico-Psychologiques, 142,* 423–431.

George, L. K., Fillenbaum, G. G., & Palmore, E. (1984). Sex differences in the antecedents and consequences of retirement. *Journal of Gerontology, 39,* 364–371.

Goudy, W. J., Burke, S. C., Powers, E. A., & Keith, P. M. (1982, August). *Job deprivation among older men: A nonmetropolitan test.* Paper presented at the 10th World Congress of the International Sociological Association, Mexico City, Mexico.

Graney, M. (1975). Happiness and social participation in aging. *Journal of Gerontology, 30,* 701–706.

Gratton, B., & Haug, M. R. (1983). Decision and adaptation: Research on female retirement. *Research on Aging, 5,* 59–76.

Hardy, M. A. (1991). Employment after retirement: Who gets back in? *Research on Aging, 13,* 267–288.

Harpaz, I., & Kremer, Y. (1981). Determinants of continued and discontinued participation in preretirement training: An Israeli case study. *Journal of Occupational Psychology, 54,* 213–220.

Hatch, L. R. (1991). Informal support patterns of older African-American and white women: Examining effects of family, paid work, and religious participation. *Research on Aging, 13,* 144–170.

Havighurst, R. J. (1957). The leisure activities of the middle aged. *American Journal of Sociology, 63,* 152–162.

Haynes, S. G., McMichael, A. J., & Tyroler, H. A. (1977). The relationship of normal, involuntary retirement to early mortality among U.S. rubber workers. *Social Science and Medicine, 11,* 105–114.

Hazelrigg, L. E., & Hardy, M. A. (1995). Older adult migration to the Sunbelt: Assessing income and related characteristics of recent migrants. *Research on Aging, 17,* 209–234.

Heyman, D. K., & Jeffers, F. C. (1968). Wives and retirement: A pilot study. *Journal of Gerontology, 23,* 488–496.

Holmes, E. R., & Holmes, L. D. (1995). *Other cultures, elder years* (2nd ed.). Thousand Oaks, CA: Sage.

Howard, J. H. (1982). Adapting to retirement. *Journal of the American Geriatrics Society, 30,* 488–500.

Hurd, M. D. (1990). The joint retirement decision of husbands and wives. In D. A. Wise (Ed.), *Issues in the economics of aging* (pp. 231–258). Chicago: University of Chicago Press.

Jackson, J. S., & Gibson, R. C. (1985). Work and retirement among the black elderly. *Current Perspectives of Aging and the Life Cycle, 1,* 193–222.

Kahana, E., & Kahana, B. (1983). Environmental continuity, futurity, and adaptation of the aged. In G. D. Rowles & R. J. Ohta (Eds.), *Aging and mi-*

lieu: Environmental perspectives on growing old (pp. 205–228). New York: Academic Press.

Kaminski-Da Roza, V. (1985). Phased retirement: An experiential view. *Activities, Adaptation and Aging, 6,* 9–30.

Kamouri, A. L., & Cavanaugh, J. C. (1986). The impact of preretirement education programmes on workers' preretirement socialization. *Journal of Occupational Behaviour, 7,* 245–256.

Keith, P. M. (1985). Work, retirement, and well-being among unmarried men and women. *The Gerontologist, 25,* 410–416.

Keith, P. M., & Dobson, C. D. (1979, August). *Occupation, household roles and adjustment of older men.* Paper presented at the annual convention of the Rural Sociological Society, Burlington, VT.

Keith, P. M., Goudy, W. J., & Powers, E. A. (1984). Salience of life areas among older men: Implications for practice. *Journal of Gerontological Social Work, 8,* 67–82.

Kelly, J. R. (1982). *Leisure.* Englewood Cliffs, NJ: Prentice-Hall.

Kelly, J. R., Steinkamp, M. W., & Kelly, J. R. (1986). Later life leisure: How they play in Peoria. *The Gerontologist, 86,* 531–557.

Kerckhoff, A. C. (1966). Norm-value clusters and the "strain toward consistency" among older married couples. In I. H. Simpson & J. C. McKinney (Eds.), *Social aspects of aging* (pp.133–137). Durham, NC: Duke University Press.

Kimmel, D. C., Price, K. F., & Walker, J. W. (1978). Retirement choice and retirement satisfaction. *Journal of Gerontology, 33,* 575–585.

Kouri, M. K. (1984). From retirement to reengagement: Young elders forge new futures. *The Futurist, 18,* (3), 35–42.

Kremer, Y. (1984–1985). Predictors of retirement satisfaction: A path model. *International Journal of Aging and Human Development, 20,* 113–121.

Kremer, Y., & Harpaz, I. (1984). Anticipatory socialization toward occupational retirement. *Journal of Sociology and Social Welfare, 11,* 558–584.

Kubey, R. W. (1980). Television and aging: Past, present, and future. *The Gerontologist, 20,* 16–33.

Larson, R., Zuzanek, J., & Mannell, R. (1985). Being alone versus being with people: Disengagement in the daily experience of older adults. *Journal of Gerontology, 40,* 375–381.

Levy, S. M. (1978). Some determinants of temporal experience in the retired and its correlates. *Genetic Psychology Monographs, 98,* 181–202.

Lipman, A. (1986). Homosexual relationships. *Generations, 10*(4), 51–54.

Little, R. W. (1981). Friendships in the military community. *Research in the Interweave of Social Roles, 2,* 221–235.

Livson, F. B. (1983). Changing sex roles in the social environment of later life. In G. D. Rowles & R. J. Ohta (Eds.), *Aging and milieu: Environmental perspectives on growing old* (pp.131–152). New York: Academic Press.

Lohmann, R., & Lohmann, N. (1983). Aging and the social policy milieu. In G. D. Rowles & R. J. Ohta (Eds.), *Aging and milieu: Environmental perspectives on growing old* (pp. 17–28). New York: Academic Press.

Long, L. W., DeJoy, D. A., Javidi, M. N., & Javidi, A. N. (1997). Cultural views and stereotypes of aging in American organizations. In H. S. N. Al-Deen (Ed.), *Cross-cultural communication and aging in the United States* (pp. 125–142). Mahwah, NJ: Lawrence Erlbaum Associates.

Longino, C. F., Jr., & Lipman, A. (1981). Married and spouseless men and women in planned retirement communities: Support network differentials. *Journal of Marriage and the Family, 43,* 169–177.

MacBride, A. (1976). Retirement as a life crisis: Myth or reality? A review. *Canadian Psychiatric Association Journal, 21,* 547–556.

MacLean, M. J. (1980). Personal major events and reactions to retirement: Preliminary findings. *Canadian Counsellor, 14,* 83–87.

MacLean, M. J. (1983). Differences between adjustment to and enjoyment of retirement. *Canadian Journal on Aging, 2,* 3–8.

Maddox, G. L. (1966). Retirement as a social event in the United States. In J. C. McKinney & F. T. deVyver (Eds.), *Aging and social policy* (pp. 119–135). New York: Appleton-Century-Crofts.

Mancini, J. A., & Sandifer, D. M. (1994). Family dynamics and the leisure activities of older adults: Theoretical viewpoints. In R. Blieszner & V. H. Bedford (Eds.), *Aging and the family: Theory and research* (pp. 132–147). Westport, CT: Praeger.

Maxwell, N. L. (1985). The retirement experience: Psychological and financial linkages to the labor market. *Social Science Quarterly, 66,* 22–33.

Maxwell, R., & Silverman, P. (1970). Information and esteem: Cultural considerations in the treatment of the aged. *Aging and Human Development, 1,* 161–194.

McAvoy, L. (1979). The leisure preferences, problems, and needs of the elderly. *Journal of Leisure Research, 11,* 40–47.

McDermott, V. (1982, November). *The role of interpersonal processes in adjusting to retirement.* Paper presented at the annual convention of the Speech Communication Association, Washington, DC.

McFarland, R. A., & O'Doherty, B. M. (1959). Work and occupational skills. In J. E. Birren (Ed.), *Handbook of aging and the individual* (pp. 452–502). Chicago: University of Chicago Press.

Miller, S. S., & Cavanaugh, J. C. (1990). The meaning of grandparenthood and its relationship to demographic, relationship, and social participation variables. *Journal of Gerontology: Psychological Sciences, 45,* P244–P247.

Moss, M., & Lawton, M. P. (1982). Time budgets of older people: A window on four lifestyles. *Journal of Gerontology, 37,* 115–123.

Mundorf, N., Bryant, J., & Brownell, W. (1997). Aging and infotainment technologies: Cross-cultural perspectives. In H. S. N. Al-Deen (Ed.), *Cross-cultural communication and aging in the United States* (pp. 43–62). Mahwah, NJ: Lawrence Erlbaum Associates.

O'Rand, A. M. (1983). Loss of work and subjective health assessment in later life among men and unmarried women. *Research in Sociology of Education and Socialization, 4,* 265–286.

O'Rand, A. M., Henretta, J. C., & Krecker, M. L. (1992). Family pathways to retirement. In M. Szinovacz, D. J. Ekerdt, & B. H. Vinick (Eds.), *Families and retirement* (pp. 81–98). Newbury Park, CA: Sage.

Palmore, E. (1979). Predictors of successful aging. *The Gerontologist, 16,* 444–446.

Palmore, E. (1981). *Social patterns in normal aging: Findings from the Duke longitudinal study.* Durham, NC: Duke University Press.

Palmore, E., Fillenbaum, G. C., & George, L. K. (1984). Consequences of retirement. *Journal of Gerontology, 39,* 109–116.

Parker, S. (1976). *The sociology of leisure.* New York: International Publications Service.

Peppers, L. G. (1976). Patterns of leisure and adjustment to retirement. *The Gerontologist, 16,* 441–446.

Perkinson, M. A. (1980). Alternate roles for the elderly: An example from a midwestern retirement community. *Human Organization, 39,* 219–226.

Quadagno, J. S., & Hardy, M. (1991). Regulating retirement through the Age Discrimination in Employment Act. *Research on Aging, 13,* 470–475.

Quadagno, J. S., & Hardy, M. (1996). Work and retirement. In R. H. Binstock & L. K. George (Eds.), *Handbook of aging and the social sciences* (4th ed., pp. 325–345). San Diego, CA: Academic Press.

Richardson, V. (1985). Status concerns among retired women: Implications for social work practice. *Journal of Applied Social Sciences, 9,* 177–186.

Riddick, C. C. (1985). Life satisfaction for older female homemakers, retirees, and workers. *Research on Aging, 7,* 383–393.

Riley, J. W., Jr., & Riley, M. W. (1991). Social science and the ADEA. *Research on Aging, 13,* 458–462.

Robinson, J., & Wallace, S. (1984, May). *Computer conferencing: A supplement to face-to-face interaction for the elderly.* A paper presented at the annual meeting of the International Communication Association, San Francisco.

Romsa, G., Bondy, P., & Blenman, M. (1985). Modeling retirees' life satisfaction levels: The role of recreational, life cycle and socioenvironmental elements. *Journal of Leisure Research, 17,* 29–39.

Rowe, A. R. (1983). Retirement and subjective chance. *International Journal of Contemporary Sociology, 20,* 95–101.

Salthouse, T. A., & Maurer, T. J. (1996). Aging, job performance, and career development. In J. E. Birren & K. W. Schaie (Eds.), *Handbook of the psychology of aging* (4th ed., pp. 353–364). San Diego, CA: Academic Press.

Savishinsky, J. (1995). The unbearable lightness of retirement: Ritual and support in a modern life passage. *Research on Aging, 17,* 243–259.

Shaw, L. B. (1984). Retirement plans of middle-aged married women. *The Gerontologist, 24,* 154–159.

Shea, G. (1991). *Managing older employees.* Oxford, England: Jossey-Bass.

Sheppard, H. L. (1976). Work and retirement. In R. H. Binstock & E. Shanas (Eds.), *Handbook of aging and the social sciences* (pp. 286–309). New York: Van Nostrand.

Simpson, I. H., Back, K. W., & McKinney, J. C. (1966a). Attributes of work, involvement in society, and self-evaluation in retirement. In I. H. Simpson & J. C. McKinney (Eds.), *Social aspects of aging* (pp. 55–74). Durham, NC: Duke University Press.

Simpson, I. H., Back, K. W., & McKinney, J. C. (1966b). Exposure to information on, preparation for, and self-evaluation in retirement. In I. H. Simpson & J. C. McKinney (Eds.), *Social aspects of aging* (pp. 90–105). Durham, NC: Duke University Press.

Sonin, M. Y., & Layner, K. A. (1979). O trudosposobnosti nauchnykh rabotnikov poxhilogo vozrasta. *Sotsiologicheskie Issledovaniya, 6,* 130–133.

Stanford, E. P., Happersett, C. J., Morton, D. J., Molgaard, C. A., & Peddecord, K. M. (1991). Early retirement and functional impairment from a multi-ethnic perspective. *Research on Aging, 13,* 5–38.

Starker, K. Z. (1980). "Male and female created He them": Sex-identity in old age. *Centerpoint, 3*(3–4), 91–103.

Sterns, H. L., & McDaniel, M. A. (1994). Job performance and the older worker. In S. Rix (Ed.), *Older workers: How do they measure up.* Washington, DC: American Association of Retired Persons.

Stone, K., & Kalish, R. A. (1981). Of poker, roles, and aging. In R. Kastenbaum (Ed.), *Old age on the new scene* (pp. 26–37). New York: Springer.

Szinovacz, M. (1989). Retirement, couples, and household work. In S. J. Bahr & E. T. Peterson (Eds.), *Aging and the family* (pp. 33–58). Lexington, MA: Lexington Books.

Szinovacz, M. (1992). Social activities and retirement adaptation: Gender and family variations. In M. Szinovacz, D. J. Ekerdt, & B. H. Vinick (Eds.), *Families and retirement* (pp. 236–253). Newbury Park, CA: Sage.

Szinovacz, M., & Ekerdt, D. J. (1994). Families and retirement. In R. Blieszner & V. Bedford (Eds.), *Aging and the family: Theory and research* (pp. 375–400). Westport, CT: Praeger.

Taeuber, C. (1990). Diversity: The dramatic role. In S. A. Bass, E. A. Kutza, & F. M. Torres-Gil (Eds.), *Diversity in aging* (pp. 1–45). Glenview, IL: Scott, Foresman.

U.S. Census Bureau. (1996). *65+ in the United States.* (U.S. Census Bureau, Current Populations Reports, Special Studies, P23–190). Washington, DC: U.S. Government Printing Office.

Vinick, B. H., & Ekerdt, D. J. (1991). The transition to retirement: Responses of husbands and wives. In B. B. Hess & E. Markson (Eds.), *Growing old in America* (4th ed., pp. 305–317). New Brunswick, NJ: Transaction.

Vinick, B. H., & Ekerdt, D. J. (1992). Couples view retirement activities: Expectation vs. experience. In M. Szinovacz, D. J. Ekerdt, & B. H. Vinick (Eds.), *Families and retirement* (pp. 129–144). Newbury Park, CA: Sage.

Wan, T. T., & Odell, B. G. (1983). Major role losses and social participation in older males. *Research on Aging, 5,* 173–196.

Weiss, D. (1977). L'insertion sociale des retraites: Interest et limites de la post-activite. *Revue francaise des Affaires sociales, 31*(4), 77–121.

CHAPTER 7

Aging and the Family: Marital Relationships

*T*he next three chapters discuss a topic of concern to all human beings, young or old: the family. This chapter focuses on the successful conjugal, or marital, relationship, chapter 8 discusses marital relationships that end in divorce, remarriage, and widowhood; and in addition the single life and the dating and courtship patterns of elderly people. Chapter 9 looks at older people's relations with other family members.

After a discussion of the functions of the family, this chapter first focuses on the impact of marriage on the quality of life and various aspects of an individual's life. Then it moves to a discussion of the characteristics that appear to be associated with successful (happy) as opposed to unsuccessful (unhappy) marriages. It should be noted that long-term marriages are inherently later-life marriages; however, late-life marriages need not be long-term marriages. Although, a 40-year-old individual could not have been married for 40 years, a married 65-year-old individual could be celebrating a 1st or 40th wedding anniversary. The marriages discussed in this chapter are primarily long-term first marriages.

FUNCTIONS OF THE FAMILY

There are a variety of myths about the family—what it used to be like, what it should be like, and so forth. As is the case with many myths, most American myths about the family are based more in fantasy than in reality. While people sometimes think that the family of yesteryear was much more caring than today's family, particularly toward elderly people, the data do not seem to support this idea. Certainly within the United States, multigenerational families in one household have *never* been the norm. As Decker (1980) pointed out, the American family has always formed around the conjugal (husband–wife) bond rather than the consanguineal (blood) bond. In colonial times, older individuals were more likely to help younger family members (through setting them up on farms and so forth) than younger members were likely to help older people. The exception to this was when a mother was widowed. In this case, the mother was usually taken in by one of her married children if she did not have the resources to care for herself. Indeed, such care was often specified in the father's will (Decker, 1980). In most cases, however, older individuals have generally preferred to live independently and care for themselves as long as possible.

Until the Industrial Revolution, most younger people were more dependent on older people than vice versa. Age was respected and given status. After the Industrial Revolution, of course, younger people were no longer as dependent on older parents to set them up financially on a farm or in a family business. Younger people could go to work and make their own way. Old age came to be held in less esteem, and the cult of youth began.

Even today, however, it is usually inaccurate to assume that the problems of elderly people are caused by their cold, uncaring children who will not allow their parents to live with them, shipping the parents off to nursing homes to die. Most older people live with a spouse (Treas, 1977) and prefer to be independent. Few older people want financial support from their children. Like most people, elderly people do not want to be dependent. People who do not live with a spouse usually choose to live by themselves, and their morale is not hurt (Treas, 1975).

Thus, family living arrangements in the United States have not changed from an extended family, in which grandparents live with children and grandchildren, to a nuclear unit of just husband, wife, and children. The family, except in certain ethnic groups, has always taken the form of a nuclear unit. Today, of course, the nuclear family is more likely to be split, or blended, than it was in the past. But although the form taken by the family has changed only slightly, the functions served by the family have changed more dramatically.

In the past, the family served a variety of functions, including child rearing, financial support, socialization, and emotional bonding and nurturance. Many experts now argue that it is no longer essential for the family to provide such assistance because other agencies will take over if necessary (Decker, 1980; Lasch, 1977; Livson, 1977). Socialization is provided by peers and schools, and the state will assist with child rearing and financial support. Many social critics fear that the family's sole responsibility has become the fulfilling of emotional needs. By reducing the number of functions the family serves, Lasch (1977) believed, the family's importance and ability to provide emotional support is lessened.

As Fitzpatrick and Badzinski (1995) pointed out, the establishment of a norm for high expressivity in family interaction is a very risky proposition. Although openness and expressivity are valuable and an important part of relational development, too much openness is still too much openness. Bochner (1982) argued quite convincingly that expressiveness and protectiveness, two functions of communication in ongoing relationships, are potentially contradictory. Through expressiveness, people can hurt those for whom they care. Therefore, complete openness and expressiveness is probably unrealistic and unwise. There are some things that people would rather not know, and the establishment of a high-expressivity norm might erode the balance between expressiveness and protectiveness. We will return to the notion of expressiveness in late-life relationships in a subsequent portion of this chapter.

There are limitations in the research on marriage and elderly people that should be mentioned. Most of this research has been demographic. Researchers have investigated the impact of numerous demographic variables, such as sex, age, ethnic background, and location, of late-life marriages. Although this information may be interesting, it does little to help the understanding of what actually happens in these marriages. It gives no understanding of the *process* of building and keeping together a relationship. It is obviously no small undertaking to keep a marriage together for 30, 40, 50, or more years, but statistics indicate that, because people are now living longer than they did in the past, one out of five couples will celebrate their

50th wedding anniversary (Ade-Ridder & Brubaker, 1983; Gilford, 1986). How do people do it? The research sheds little light on this question. We will discuss the small amount of relevant research that does exist, and from there on we will be forced to speculate.

MARRIAGE AND THE QUALITY OF LIFE

Research consistently reports that one of the primary predictors of global well-being and satisfaction with life is marital status (Huyck, 1994). Overall, married men are more satisfied than married women, and married individuals are more satisfied than unmarried ones. Quirouette and Pushkar Gold (1995) argued that marital happiness rather than marital status itself is the primary predictor of well-being, but because so many older marriages are relatively happy, marital status functions in much the same way as does marital happiness in affecting life satisfaction and well-being. Important gender differences exist in this relationship between marriage and life satisfaction. Women appear to be more strongly affected by the quality of their marriages and their levels of marital adjustment (Quirouette & Pushkar Gold, 1995). This gender difference may reflect different expectations about marriage, especially among the current cohort of elderly people. Women carry more responsibility for emotional well-being, whereas men are more responsible for financial security. The success or failure of their marriage may then seem to reflect on the wife's abilities to adjust to her marital partner and create a happy home life, thus fulfilling her role expectations.

Most of the early research on the impact of marital status on the quality of life was not very encouraging. These studies indicated growing disenchantment in the later years of marriage. Typical of this line of research was a study by Blood and Wolfe (1960) that found that the quality of the conjugal relationship decreases with age. More specifically, Pineo (1961) found more and more complaints and less and less idealization of both the partner and the relationship as couples grew older. He argued that the decreased satisfaction is due to unforeseen changes in people that occur over the years. The reasons that they had decided to marry had deteriorated. Others suggested that the "empty nest" syndrome is responsible for lower satisfaction ratings in later years. In contrast to this, Livson (1977) concluded that there is more stress in the anticipation of children leaving home than in actually experiencing it.

Later research, however, found other developmental trends in marital quality. Many argued that the early research was not longitudinal and that the decrease in marital satisfaction has to do with other factors, such as deteriorating health and retirement, that affect one's evaluation of the quality of life. For instance, Deutscher (1968) studied both upper-middle-class and lower-middle-class families in the Kansas City area and found that only three of the couples saw postparental life as clearly negative. The remainder felt their life was better than it had been. They described this time of their lives as being a time of freedom, when they could let their hair down and had less work to do. They also reported better relationships in postparental life than in the parenting years, and a sense of accomplishment and contentment. Stinnett, Carter, and Montgomery's (1972) study confirmed these findings.

Most research is fairly consistent in indicating that the earliest years of marriage—the honeymoon—are the happiest (Troll, 1982). After this time, there is some evidence of decreasing satisfaction during the childrearing years, followed by an up-swing in satisfaction (Rollins & Feldman, 1970) in later life. For instance, Burr (1970) found the lowest feelings of life quality are in the years when the children were in school. More specifically, Schumm and Bugaighis (1986) determined that there is a serious decline in satisfaction during these years for a small number of women who are working full time and have little time to talk about daily matters with their husbands.

Some argued for a "second honeymoon" after children leave home (Steere, 1981). Steere also pointed out, however, that dissatisfied couples have probably divorced by this time, so they could not have participated in the research. Couples who have stayed together may find it in their interest to convince themselves they *are* happy—after all, they have such an investment in each other and the relationship that it would make them uncomfortable to accept the fact that it has become a negative experience. Definitions and expectations for marriage may influence an individual's evaluation of success in a marriage. The current elderly cohort married and have stayed married. Part of their marital satisfaction may be linked to the fact that they stayed together, thus fulfilling their marital expectations (Mares & Fitzpatrick, 1995).

Just because one member of a relationship is happy or unhappy does not necessarily mean that the other member will feel the same, of course. Troll (1982) cited studies indicating that middle-aged women are not as happy with their husbands as are older or younger women, and middle-aged men realize that they do not meet their wives' needs. These women are less hopeful about finding affection and warmth in their relationships. And older men are more satisfied by their marriages than are older women. In this study, the men felt they were not getting enough respect, and the women felt they were not getting enough communication (Stinnett, Carter, & Montgomery, 1972). Gender differences in happiness make some sense in light of the evidence indicating that women are typically the dyad members who must make the most adjustments and changes in order for a marriage to continue (Ahammer, 1973; Quirouette & Pushkar Gold, 1995). If an individual has been forced to adjust and change, and he or she feels that his or her partner has not made the same sort of accommodations, the individual may not feel satisfied with the relationship. Overall, however, most recent evidence indicates a fairly high amount of satisfaction in older marriages.

Other research looked at the impact of marital status on the quality of life for elderly people. Marital status seems to be an important variable for elderly people because, after children leave and people retire, the marital relationship becomes a focal point. In summarizing the research on the effects of marital status, Gilford (1986) concluded that older people are better off if they are married because married elderly individuals typically have higher incomes, more emotional support, and more social integration than those who are not married. Gilford argued that married older people are less vulnerable than unmarried people. Other research has indicated that married older people are less sensitive to changes in the number of elderly neighbors (Rosow, 1967), have more primary relationships (Longino & Lipman, 1981), are better adjusted (Pihlblad & McNamara, 1965), have better health (Palmore, 1981), are happier (Altergott, 1985), have a lower suicide rate (Kastenbaum & Aisenberg, 1972), have less depression and anxiety (Livson, 1983), and have fewer psychoneurotic symptoms (Busse & Eisdorfer, 1970) than do unmarried (divorced, separated, widowed, and never-married) people. Altergott (1985), however, found that being married limits an individual's involvement with others, although not because of the time spent with the spouse.

It should be noted that one study found that marital status is *not* the most important variable in determining life satisfaction.

Mouser, Powers, Keith, and Goudy (1985) concluded that, when such variables as having a confidant, being affiliated with a voluntary organization, and having personal resources such as good health are taken into account, marital status does not seem to make any difference in life satisfaction. They also found several other variables that did not make a difference in the life satisfaction of a marriage relationship: parenthood, employment status, size of friend network, and amount of friend interaction. In an earlier study, however, Lee (1978) concluded that marriage improves morale in later life even holding constant such variables as gender, age, length of marriage, education, health, satisfaction with standard of living, and employment status. To further complicate this relationship, Hutchinson (1975) found that marital status makes a difference in morale and life satisfaction for those above the poverty line, but not for those below the poverty line.

Generally, then, the majority of the research seems to indicate that most people who are married are happier than are most people who are not married. The marital relationship provides self-concept confirmation for people at a time when, because of retirement and other role changes, confirmation is sorely needed (Atchley, 1980; Blau, 1973). Blau also argued that this function can put a great deal of strain on the marital relationship because it puts pressure on the spouse to be the sole source of confirmation for the partner. He suggested that people with friends as well as a spouse are better off in this regard.

CHARACTERISTICS OF OLDER MARRIAGES

Convergence

There has been some research, although not a great deal, on determining just what older marriages are like. This research examines a variety of different variables, but the variable that has probably received the most investigation has been role differentiation or task specialization. Traditionally, there are certain behaviors that were societally defined as being appropriate for wives (childrearing, housekeeping, etc.) and certain behaviors that were usually delegated to husbands (taking out the garbage, mowing the lawn, "bringing home the bacon," etc.). Some experts studying marriages among elderly people have argued that this changes with time. Role differentiation and task specialization become minimized in the later years of marriage, leading to increased convergence of tasks. The evidence on this question is somewhat inconclusive (Brubaker, 1985). Whereas Steere (1981) cited several studies indicating these patterns do become more idiosyncratic (less determined by gender roles), Troll (1982) found studies showing increasing specialization by gender from early marriage to retirement. Further, she argued that retired husbands do not work around the home any more than they did prior to retirement. Troll felt that, in terms of role differentiation, more changes have taken place in ideology than in actual behavior. Brubaker (1985) found some support for Troll's position. This study concluded that, although male and female expectations about task division are similar and show less gender differentiation when observed over time, the actual tasks show fairly traditional assignments. The exception to this was that 50% of the men in the study did do some housecleaning. In this study, the men expected to share in traditionally feminine tasks, but neither men nor women expected the women to share in traditionally masculine tasks. The husbands in this study did do more traditionally feminine tasks if the wife was in poor health.

One related study found a difference in lower-class as compared with middle-class marriages. Dobson (1983) indicated that lower-class couples do not show more husband involvement in household tasks after retirement, although middle-class couples do show more involvement. These husbands did do more traditionally masculine tasks around the house after retirement than they did before they retired, and this led to less stress for the wives. Many people in this study argued that neither dyad member should be responsible for tasks such as shoveling snow or mowing the lawn. Whereas the research, then, seems to indicate some examples of less-extreme role differentiation in later marriages, the changes could not quite be called role convergence. The importance of this line of research was stressed by Lowenthal and Robinson (1976), who suggested that those with rigid role definitions in their marriages have more trouble adjusting to retirement, and by Livson's (1983) argument that androgyny, or less-extreme role differentiation, leads to more successful aging. Livson also suggested that these changing sex roles will be easier for later age cohorts.

Dobson (1983) cited a variety of studies on the question of increasing or decreasing gender role differentiation in older marriages. She summarized her review with, "Conclusions from such research are necessarily tentative, but several authors argue that the differentiation between male and female sex-role definitions diminishes in old age" (p. 116). Of course, gender differentiation is diminishing in society as a whole, and this undoubtedly, influences the expectations that marital partners have for one another's participation in task-oriented activities.

In addition to the convergence of gender roles, researchers have examined increasing congruence over time in other areas of marital life. Kerckhoff (1966), for instance, discovered increased similarity between dyad members over time on parent–child norms, division of labor, acceptance of the value of change, and conflict between children's mobility and family values. He noted, however, that the magnitude of the changes was not great. Similarly, Ahammer (1973) cited evidence that in happy marriages people become more similar with time. This may occur because those who are more similar demand less change of each other and reinforce the existing behavior systems. Lauer, Lauer, and Kerr (1995) found that highly satisfied older couples agree on a variety of issues, including family finances, recreation, religion, demonstration of affection, sexual relations, proper behavior, philosophy of life, ways of dealing with in-laws, aims and goals in life, amount of time to spend together, making major decisions, household tasks, leisure activities, and career decisions.

Another kind of similarity that has been investigated by researchers is instrumentality as compared with expressiveness. Instrumentality and expressiveness are important communicative behaviors. In a communicative sense, *instrumentality* refers to communicating for a purpose—to get information across to another person. *Expressiveness* refers to communicating because of the speaker's need or desire to talk about something, but the receiver of the message does not necessarily need to hear the information. If something is bothering an individual, and he or she feels a need to talk about it, that individual is communicating expressively. In intimate relationships, people frequently engage in expressive communication. We speculate that, if behaviors are becoming more expressive in general, communication may also be changing. Reminiscing is, in many cases, an example of expressive communication. Researchers do know that reminiscing becomes more common in the later years (Butler, 1968).

The convergence of expectations about expressiveness in marriage is influenced by societal changes. During the 1900s, American expectations regarding expressiveness have changed drastically (Mares & Fitzpatrick, 1995). Couples in the 1920s talked very little, except to manage day-to-day household affairs. In the 1960s and 1970s, expectations shifted, placing more emphasis on sharing feelings and being more open and egalitarian in discussions. In addition, the number of taboo topics diminished significantly. These societal changes make it more difficult to compare current marriages of young, middle-aged, and older adults; however, some differences appear to be linked to the length of marriage rather than to cohort differences. For example, older longer-married couples spend less time talking about their relationship itself and self-disclosing. Less expressive talk may be evident because the older couple has spent many years together and the two people know each other fairly well, having "worked out" any marital differences.

Overall, the evidence is mixed as to whether older couples engage in more instrumental talk than expressive talk, or vice versa (Mares & Fitzpatrick, 1995). Typically, men have taken on the more instrumental, task-oriented roles, and women have had the primary responsibility for the expressive, emotion-sharing behaviors. Several studies suggested that this difference, too, becomes minimized over time. Indeed, there is some indication that wives become more assertive and instrumental and husbands more affiliative and expressive in the later years of marriage (Chiriboga & Thurner, 1975; Grunebam, 1979; Gutmann, 1975; Levinson, 1978; Lowenthal & Chiriboga, 1972; Neugarten & Gutmann, 1958). Several other authors, however, concluded that both husbands and wives become more expressive as they grow older (Cumming, 1963; Lipman, 1961, 1962; Lowenthal & Robinson, 1976; Troll, 1971). In either case, there is a trend toward similarity. In the first group of studies, husbands and wives start at opposite extremes and move toward each other; in the second group, husbands and wives both move in the same direction—toward expressiveness.

This trend toward convergence during marriage may reflect the couple's adapting to each other over the years and finding more common ground, as indicated by the number and variety of issues on which they agree. Zietlow and Sillars (1988) examined conflict resolution strategies across age groups. Young adult couples used highly engaged strategies (e.g., openly and directly dealing with issues). Middle-aged couples used more analytical strategies (e.g., problem-solving and solution-oriented comments). Older couples used avoidance strategies (e.g., changing the topic, making abstract and hypothetical remarks). While acknowledging the possibility of cohort differences, Zietlow and Sillars argued that at least some of the differences in conflict resolution style reflect the length of marriage and older couples' having resolved most of their significant differences. The older couples in this study rated the topics of conflict as relatively unimportant; therefore avoidance strategies seemed reasonable because in their minds the topic really did not require resolution. Over time, couples develop not just more similar attitudes, but also develop more implicit and idiomatic styles that reflect their large knowledge base of each other (Sillars & Wilmot, 1989).

Overall, then, marital partners become more like each other as time passes. They tend to agree on major issues affecting their marriage and their family. As couples spend years together, they find ways to manage any conflict that arises (or they divorce) and come to know each other extremely well. Research also shows that couple's IQs converge with age (Eichorn, Hunt, & Honzik, 1981).

Most of the other changes in relationships identified by research have been brought about through communication. This is because relationships are created through communication, as discussed in chapter 3; they do not spring out of nowhere. If older marital partners become more similar or change in other ways, they create these changes through dyadic communication.

Berger and Kellner (1964), in a very provocative article, described this process of coming together, or creating a shared reality. Berger and Kellner began with the assumption that all reality is socially created. By this they meant that how each person sees reality is determined through that person's interactions with others. They argued that when a couple gets married they begin creating a new view of reality—a conjoint reality. This new, shared reality is created through conversations between the marital partners. They talk about how things are, what people are like, what is good and what is bad, how life works, and so forth. Gradually, they begin creating a shared (conjoint) view of what the world is like. Over the years, this shared reality grows until they agree on more and more things and become more similar in some ways. As children come along, the parents teach them this new view of reality. Children, in the early years, usually accept the view of reality that they are taught by their parents. When parents see children accepting their view of reality, it gives the parents more confidence in this view. They begin to think, "Our view of reality must be correct because all of us believe it." At the same time, the couple is developing friendships that help confirm their view of reality. Berger and Kellner described children and friends as a "supporting chorus." They cited evidence indicating that premarital friendships gradually deteriorate and new friendships replace them. These new friendships are more likely to support how the couple now sees the world. The people in the couple naturally seek out these friendships because they find such friendships confirming for them and their marriage. Throughout this process, the people in the couple have been creating a new, conjoint reality. As they see the world more similarly, they are becoming more similar. Berger and Kellner provided, then, a theoretical explanation for the findings on convergence.

Other Characteristics of Older Marriages

Although few studies have focused on communication in older marriages, some do compare conversations in older and younger dyads. Treas (1975) found that older couples focus their conversations differently than do younger couples. In later life, couples talk about their kids much less than they do when they are younger. They also are more likely to focus on rather conventional topics such as church, home upkeep, and health. Some of these differences, of course, may be cohort differences and may not hold up in longitudinal research.

Troll (1982) also concluded that there is a great deal of concern about and discussion of health in middle-age and older marriages. In particular, women exhibit considerable concern about their husbands' health—they are more concerned about their husbands' health than they are about their own.

These topics of conversation are closely related to the themes of older marriages that have been identified by Huyck and Hoyer (1982):

1. Older marriages are a good welfare system—they are the first line of care and also help ward off loneliness.
2. Older marriages lead to people who are healthier, have better morale, and are better-off financially.
3. Older marriages have less passion and more conventionality and concern for health than do younger marriages.

Possibly, the overriding theme of older marriages is that they have experienced and continue to experience a variety of transitions. Successful marriages make successful transitions. Later-life couples have had to adapt to children leaving the home, to retirement, and to health problems (Mares & Fitzpatrick, 1995). Recall that marital satisfaction is highest during the early years, dips during the child-bearing and child-rearing years, and then increases again. Once the children have left the home, the couple begins to focus on each other as a couple again. The role that the marital partner plays in adapting to retirement is discussed in chapter 6. Issues regarding health, communication, and aging are addressed more fully in chapter 12, but the consequences of caregiving for the marital relationship will be touched on here.

The notion of helping in older marriages (Theme 1 in the list) has been the focus of some research interest. Troll (1982) concluded that, as might be expected, wives usually take care of husbands. This probably relates to the fact that wives are usually younger than their husbands, a fact that will be discussed in a bit more detail subsequently. In an overall study of the family and support, Johnson (1983) determined that "the most comprehensive and unstressful support was provided by a spouse" (p. 377). However, Burke and Weir (1982) found that older couples exhibited less helping activity toward one another than they had in the past and that there was a decrease in communication about tensions and problems. Older wives, they found, seek the help of someone else instead of their husbands. Burke and Weir, however, were focusing on helping in regard to handling stress, rather than helping as a physical behavior. Their findings, combined with Johnson's (1983) conclusions, seem to indicate that couples might be better off seeking help from each other.

Although most older individuals are healthy, when health problems do arise, the person most likely to offer assistance is an individual's spouse. Of the individuals providing informal caregiving, 36% are spouses (Mares & Fitzpatrick, 1995). How any particular couple adapts to caregiving is influenced by the nature of the couple's relationship (Grand, Grand-Filaire, & Pous, 1995). Based on whether couples have unspoken contracts and the level of egalitarianism in their relationship, couples can be placed into one of four categories: associative, conflictual, unilateral contractual, or mutually advantageous contractual.

Associative couples have an egalitarian balance of power and no unspoken contract. The individuals in an associative couple focus most of their efforts outside the relationship—on work or other family members. When a disability occurs, each individual is likely to attempt to deal with the situation on his or her own or to turn to other members of the social network for assistance.

Conflictual couples have a nonegalitarian balance of power and no unspoken contract, with one partner the dominated and the other the dominator. The dominated has had little control over his or her life to this point and cannot expect his or her partner to provide much assistance. The dominator, however, expects his or her dominated partner to step in and efficiently attend to the dominator's needs, as has been the pattern of their lives.

Unilateral contractual couples have a nonegalitarian balance of power and an unspoken contract, with one partner the provider and the other the beneficiary. The provider usually has a history of taking care of others and handles any problems that arise should the beneficiary become disabled. If the roles are reversed, however, problems may ensue. The beneficiary is ill-equipped to provide care and may even downplay any health problems of the provider. The extended social network must step in to make sure that the provider receives care.

Mutually advantageous contractual couples have an egalitarian balance of power and an unspoken contract. The individuals in a mutually advantageous couple have a history of "coping together," and they face any and all challenges with a united front. They are likely to have negotiated tasks throughout the history of their marriage and will continue to do so as they manage the redistribution of responsibilities in light of a disability. In addition, they are least likely to turn to outside sources and will go to great lengths in order to manage by themselves and remain in their home.

While this typology was constructed from a sample of rural French farming couples, its applicability reaches beyond that specific group. Individuals in a couple develop styles for coping with life's problems and are likely to continue to exhibit these same styles throughout their history together. Obviously, some of these couple types appear to be more successful in adapting to a disability than others, depending on which member of the dyad suffers the limitations.

In their summary of caregiving between marital partners, Mares and Fitzpatrick (1995) noted that women caregivers are less satisfied with their marital relationship and feel more stress, but successfully adapt to their role. Couples with successful coping strategies are more successful at coping with the attendant problems of illness and disability.

Power differences in older marriages may be an issue even when illness and disability are not factors. Smith (1965) argued that men have more power in older marriages because of the scarcity of older men. This finding may, however, be somewhat outdated in light of societal changes in gender roles. Somewhat more recently, Treas (1975) concluded that women acquire more power with increasing age. One may speculate that this trend has increased since Treas's study because more and more older women have now been in the workforce at some time in their lives and may be more independent than women were in the past. Independence and power may be associated. One of the biggest changes that the couple may have to manage is a shift in power that may occur as a result of one partner's illness, particularly as the degree of impairment increases.

Power, of course, is a somewhat nebulous concept. It is generally defined as the potential to influence others and the environment. When power is actualized, it becomes control. Recall from chapter 3 that control is an important communication concept because control is carried out through communication.

Types of Older Couples

Over the years, researchers have made a number of attempts to categorize families and couples into various typologies. Many of these were inadequate because they were based only on couples who came in for therapy or on samples that were biased in some other way. Some research on couple types, however, has focused on middle-aged or older couples and, thus, is of interest here. In 1965, Cuber and Haroff developed a rather provocative typology based on their research with middle-aged couples. Consistent with the earlier research of Pineo (1961), they concluded that the most common type of couple in the middle years is *devitalized*—characterized by unexcited dependency. The second most common type is *conflict-habituated* couples, who have become very used to fighting with each other and are very good at it; the partners in these couples know exactly how to hurt each other. The next most common type is *passive-congenial*, a relationship of convenience in which the partners get along well enough. Finally, some couples are *vital*—couples characterized by a great deal of sharing, intimacy, and interdependence.

Recall that many studies have shown that marital satisfaction decreases in the middle age and then increases again in the later years. Cuber and Haroff's findings, then, may not be typical of older marriages. Indeed, that is exactly what Atchley and Miller (1983) found. Their research indicated that devitalized couples, the most common type in the earlier study, are not common in older couples. They discovered that it was more helpful to categorize older couples according to their similarity in family orientation, particularly on the value placed on close family ties and on intimacy. The most common type of couple is *divergent*, in which the partners do not totally agree on these two values. The second most common couple is *integrated*, in which both close family ties and an intimate marital relationship are valued. This is followed by couples who are *family-centered*, in which the most importance is placed on the value of close family ties. The last two types of couples are relatively rare: *self-centered*, in which neither family ties nor intimacy are valued, and *couple-centered*, in which intimacy is valued but close family ties are not. *Divergent* couples typically have one member who is family-centered and one who is integrated (valuing both family ties and intimacy). All in all, this presents a much more positive view of older marriages than was indicated by Cuber and Haroff's study. All of Atchley and Miller's couples were happy except for the few who were self-centered, or couple-centered.

Huyck (1994) reported different styles that influence individuals' experiences of their marriages, but did not propose a formal typology. Some individuals focus primarily on the marital relationship, some on the general family, and others on activities outside the family and marriage. Marital partners need not agree on their focus. The reported satisfaction with the marital relationship varied across these different styles, indicating that no one style is preferable. One can imagine, however, that conflicts might arise when marital partners disagree as to what the focus of their union should be.

Characteristics of Successful and Unsuccessful Marriages

Most of the studies mentioned so far have been simply descriptive. That is, they have just tried to identify what older marriages are like. Some research, however, has looked at how these characteristics and others relate to the *success* of the marriage. Atchley and Miller's (1983) findings about couple types, previously noted, is an example of this type of study. Of course, the definition of successful marriages may vary depending on the criteria used to evaluate success (Mares & Fitzpatrick, 1995). For the current cohort of elderly people, success may equal survivorship because they expected to marry for life, no matter what problems might arise. As partners age, the definition of success may change as the couple comes to emphasize shared experiences and interdependence over individual fulfillment (Mares & Fitzpatrick, 1995).

A number of studies looked at the impact of various inequities on marital happiness and success. For instance, Smith (1965) found that high marital adjustment is associated with a more democratic or egalitarian power structure rather than with a patriarchal or matriarchal one; it is better to share power than to monopolize it. Atchley (1980) also concluded that happily married couples demonstrate more interdependence and equality than unhappily married couples. Brubaker (1985) found that higher marital satisfaction correlates with a less traditional division of labor around the house, both in terms of actual and expected behavior. And Atchley (1980) suggested that egalitarianism makes marriages more expressive, and expressive marriages are more successful.

In another study of inequity, Keith and Schafer (1985) found that older husbands frequently feel overbenefitted in their marriages and perceive there to be inequity because of this. They concluded that equity is a component of support in a relationship, and that it provides some protection from stress, strain, and depression. In a more recent study, Peterson (1995) found similar results. Husbands felt particularly overbenefitted during the child-rearing years, but thought the relationship was fairly equitable before having children and after the children left home. About half of the wives felt the relationship had been equitable throughout. Wives who felt underbenefitted reported feeling the relationship was equitable before they had children. Overall, men and women agreed that men are generally overbenefitted and women are generally underbenefitted in marriage.

Keith, Schafer, and Wacker (1995) found that less-equitable relationships are less stable, which is resolved by balancing out the gains or dissolving the relationship. Individuals in long-term marriages acknowledge that inequities are inevitable in marriage, but that these inequities are relatively short-lived and should average out in the long run.

In a rather interesting study, Busse and Eisdorfer (1970) found that equality of ages between spouses was associated with less happiness. Unhappy couples also had a wife who was mentally superior to the husband. In these unhappy couples, the wives tended to talk more frequently, were more responsive to their environment, were more adaptable, and were more imaginative and accurate in their perceptions than were their husbands. The partners in these less happy marriages had more psychoneurotic symptoms and less-frequent sex. The couples in the study, however, were not terribly unhappy.

Age differences were also examined in a study by Foster, Linger-Vartabedian, and Wispe (1984). They found that marriage to a younger woman is associated with a longer life for men. They speculated that this may be due to self-selection factors (healthier men may be more inclined to marry younger women), or that the factors leading to longevity may be enhanced by marriage to a younger woman. This would also certainly relate to the findings mentioned earlier that indicated that women usually take care of their husbands.

Other difficulties occurring in older marriages seem to fall into three groups: (a) menopause or aging-related disabilities, although Livson in a 1977 study pointed out that menopause is much more benign than is generally believed; (b) a self-perception of being a failure in some way; and, (c) an inability to fill the new gap in the relationship. The term *new gap* refers to the gap in a relationship that occurs because something that has kept the relationship intact is now missing. Deutscher (1968) observed that husbands and wives who remain in marriages because of the children (and not because of their spousal relationships) find themselves with a huge gap in their relationships once the children leave home. Deutscher also found that the postparental years are more crucial for the wife than for the husband because the husband is more likely to still be working. Wives' evaluations tend to be more extreme in these years than husbands' evaluations.

Gilford (1986) delineated the possible sources of strain in older marriages: a decline in joint activities, fewer expressions of love and commitment, and frequent disagreements. Some of the disagreements may relate to the change from instrumentality to expressiveness, noted earlier. If the husband and wife change in contradictory directions, disagreements are more likely. Finally, Gilford pointed out that health problems and caregiving can cause strains. Few older people confide in others about these problems, however.

Finally, Atchley (1980) concluded that most older marriages are happy and satisfying—but a few are hostile. In these hostile marriages, each partner feels that his or her spouse is the cause of *all* the troubles. Because from our perspective, all problems are relational, remedying this hostility will be difficult. When a person views his or her partner's behavior as being the problem, the person is not accepting a share of the responsibility for the relationship. From the relational perspective, people behave the way they do because of the relationships they are in. If a husband thinks his wife nags him too much, from the relational perspective he should look at the reasons his behavior encourages his wife to nag. This is, of course, not to say the wife is not at all responsible. Both parties create the relationship through their communicative behavior, and any problems that occur in the relationship occur because of the way both parties behave together. In chapter 8, this will be extended to include the impact of divorce, dating, remarriage, singlehood, and widowhood on elderly people.

When asked what makes for an enduring relationship, couples in long-term marriages (45–64 years of marriage) indicated that they liked and enjoyed each other, they had a strong sense of commitment to each other and to the relationship, they looked for the humor in a situation, and they had a high level of agreement on important matters regarding their life together (Lauer, Lauer, & Kerr, 1995). When experts rated marriages as highly satisfactory, the common elements of those relationships were a strong affective commitment to the partner and not a utilitarian arrangement, lack of avoidance of conflict, and a reluctance to expect perfection from the partner (Huyck, 1994). Although there is no simple prescription for a successful long-term marriage, it would appear that shared values, a commitment to each other, realistic expectations, and open (but not too open) communication are important contributing factors.

SUMMARY

It should be apparent that families of yesteryear were no more caring than families are today. Contrary to popular belief, multigenerational households have never been the norm in the United States, and elderly people have always preferred to live independently of their children, whenever possible. Today much of the support that elderly people receive is provided by their families, although there have been some changes in the types of support the families provide.

We point out that most of the research on later-life marriages has been demographic, rather than focusing on the process of building a relationship. Yet, the research suggests that marriage and quality of life are related. Although the early research on older marriage indicated disenchantment, recent research is more likely to show an upswing in satisfaction after the children leave home. Men tend to be happier than women, however. Overall, married people are happier and better off than divorced, widowed, or never-married people There is some evidence, although surely not conclusive, that indicates increasing convergence between older husbands and wives on such characteristics as role differentiation, instrumentality as opposed to expressiveness, values, and so forth. Much of the data indicate that older men still do not engage in many feminine tasks, but that some increasing similarity of men and women does occur over the years. Berger and Kellner's (1964) perspective on marriage and the construction of a shared reality helps to explain this phenomenon.

Other studies found that older couples focus their conversations differently than do younger couples, have different themes in their marriages, and provide less help to each other. In addition, men have more power in older marriages. Various types of older couples are discussed. It was pointed out that successful (happy) older marriages typically have few inequities, are more expressive, and have wives who are younger and not mentally superior to their husbands. Sources of strain in older marriages are also noted. Overall, most older marriages are happy.

■ REFERENCES

Ade-Ridder, L., & Brubaker, T. H. (1983). The quality of long-term marriages. In T. H. Brubaker (Ed.), *Family relationships in later life* (pp. 21–30). Beverly Hills, CA: Sage.

Ahammer, I. M. (1973). Social-learning theory as a framework for the study of adult personality development. In P. B. Baltes & K. W. Schaie (Eds.), *Life-span developmental psychology: Personality and socialization* (pp. 253–284). New York: Academic Press.

Altergott, K. (1985). Marriage, gender and social relations in later life. In W. A. Peterson & J. Quadagno (Eds.), *Social bonds in later life* (pp. 51–70). Beverly Hills, CA: Sage.

Atchley, R. C. (1980). *The social forces in later life* (3rd ed.). Belmont, CA: Wadsworth.

Atchley, R. C., & Miller, S. J. (1983). Types of elderly couples. In T. H. Brubaker (Ed.), *Family relationships in later life* (pp. 77–90). Beverly Hills, CA: Sage.

Berger, P., & Kellner, H. (1964). Marriage and the construction of reality. *Diogenes, 46*, 1–24.

Blau, Z. S. (1973). *Old age in a changing society.* New York: New Viewpoints.

Blood, R. O., & Wolfe, D. N. (1960). *Husbands and wives: The dynamics of married living.* New York: The Free Press.

Bochner, A. P. (1982). On the efficacy of openness in close relationships. In M. Burgoon (Ed.), *Communication yearbook 5* (pp. 109–124). New Brunswick, NJ: Transaction Books.

Brubaker, T. H. (1985). Responsibility for household tasks: A look at golden anniversary couples aged 75 years and older. In W. A. Peterson & J. Quadagno (Eds.), *Social bonds in later life* (pp. 27–36). Beverly Hills, CA: Sage.

Burke, R., & Weir, T. (1982). Husband-wife helping relationships as moderators of experienced stress: "The mental hygiene" function in marriage. In H. McCubbin (Ed.), *Family stress, coping and social support* (pp. 221–238). Springfield, IL: Thomas.

Burr, W. R. (1970). Satisfaction with various aspects of marriage over the life cycle: A random middle class sample. *Journal of Marriage and the Family, 32,* 29–37.

Busse, E. W., & Eisdorfer, C. (1970). Two thousand years of married life. In E. Palmore (Ed.), *Normal aging* (pp. 266–269). Durham, NC: Duke University Press.

Butler, R. N. (1968). The life review: An interpretation of reminiscence in the aged. In B. Neugarten (Ed.), *Middle age and aging* (pp. 486–496). Chicago: University of Chicago Press.

Chiriboga, D., & Thurner, M. (1975). Concept of self. In M. Lowenthal, M. Thurner, & D. Chiriboga (Eds.), *Four states of life* (pp. 62–83). San Francisco: Jossey-Bass.

Cuber, J. F., & Haroff, P. B. (1965). *The significant Americans.* New York: Meredith.

Cumming, E. (1963). Further thoughts on the theory of disengagement. *International Social Science Journal, 15,* 377–393.

Decker, D. L. (1980). *Social gerontology.* Boston: Little, Brown.

Deutscher, I. (1968). The quality of postparental life. In B. Neugarten (Ed.), *Middle age and aging* (pp. 263–268). Chicago: University of Chicago Press.

Dobson, C. (1983). Sex-role and marital-role expectations. In T. H. Brubaker (Ed.), *Family relationships in later life* (pp.109–126). Beverly Hills, CA: Sage.

Eichorn, D. H., Hunt, J. V., & Honzik, M. P. (1981). Experience, personality, and IQ: Adolescence to middle age. In D. H. Eichorn, J. A. Clausen, N. Haan, M. P. Honzik, & P. H. Mussen (Eds.), *Present and past in middle life* (pp. 89–116). New York: Academic Press.

Fitzpatrick, M. A., & Badzinski, D. M. (1995). All in the family: Interpersonal communication kin relationships. In M. L. Knapp & G. R. Miller (Eds.), *Handbook of interpersonal communication* (2nd ed., pp. 726–771). Thousand Oaks, CA: Sage.

Foster, D., Linger-Vartabedian, L., & Wispe, L. (1984). Male longevity and age differences between spouses. *Journal of Gerontology, 39,*117–120.

Gilford, R. (1986). Marriages in later life. *Generations, 10*(4), 16–20.

Grand, A., Grand-Filaire, A., & Pous, J. (1995). Aging couples and disability management. In J. Hendricks (Ed.), *The ties of later life* (pp. 55–72). Amityville, NY: Baywood.

Grunebam, H. (1979). Middle age and marriage: Affiliative men and assertive women. *American Journal of Family Therapy, 7*(3), 46–50.

Gutmann, D. L. (1975). Parenthood: Key to the comparative psychology of the life cycle. In N. Datan & L. Ginsberg (Eds.), *Development psychology: Normative life crises* (pp. 167–184). New York: Academic Press.

Hutchinson, I. W., III (1975). The significance of marital status for morale and life satisfaction among lower-income elderly. *Journal of Marriage and the Family, 37,* 287–293.

Huyck, M. H. (1994). Marriage and close relationships of the marital kind. In R. Blieszner & V. H. Bedford (Eds.), *Aging and the family: Theory and research* (pp. 181–200). Westport, CT: Praeger.

Huyck, M. H., & Hoyer, W. J. (1982). *Adult development and aging.* Belmont, CA: Wadsworth.

Johnson, C. L. (1983). Dyadic family relations and social support. *The Gerontologist, 23,* 377–383.

Kastenbaum, R., & Aisenberg, R. (1972). *The psychology of death.* New York: Springer.

Keith, P. M., & Schafer, R. B. (1985). Equity, role strains and depression among middle aged and older men and women. In Q. A. Peterson & J. Quadagno (Eds.), *Social bonds in later life* (pp. 37–49). Beverly Hills, CA: Sage.

Keith, P. M., Schafer, R. B., & Wacker, R. (1995). Outcomes of equity/inequity among older spouses. In J. Hendricks (Ed.), *The ties of later life* (pp. 9–19). Amityville, NY: Baywood.

Kerckhoff, A. C. (1966). Norm-value clusters and the "strain toward consistency" among older married couples. In I. H. Simpson & J. C. McKinney (Eds.), *Social aspects of aging* (pp. 133–137). Durham, NC: Duke University Press.

Lasch, C. (1977). *Haven in a heartless world.* New York: Basic Books.

Lauer, R. H., Lauer, J. C., & Kerr, S. T. (1995). The long-term marriage: Perceptions of well-being in older couples. In J. Hendricks (Ed.), *The ties of later life* (pp. 35–41). Amityville, NY: Baywood.

Lee, G. R. (1978). Marriage and morale in later life. *Journal of Marriage and the Family, 40,* 131–139.

Levinson, D. (1978). *The seasons of a man's life.* New York: Knopf.

Lipman, A. (1961). Role conceptions and morale of couples in retirement. *Journal of Gerontology, 16,* 267–271.

Lipman, A. (1962). Role concepts of couples in retirement. In C. Tibbitts & W. Donahue (Eds.), *Social and psychological aspects of aging* (pp. 475–483). New York: Columbia University Press.

Livson, F. B. (1977). Coming out of the closet: Marriage and other crises in middle age. In L. Troll, J. Israel, & F. Israel (Eds.), *Looking ahead* (pp. 81–92). Englewood Cliffs, NJ: Prentice-Hall.

Livson, F. B. (1983). Changing sex roles in the social environment of later life. In G. D. Rowles & R. J. Ohta (Eds.), *Aging and milieu: Environmental perspectives on growing old* (pp. 131–152). New York: Academic Press.

Longino, C. F., Jr., & Lipman, A. (1981). Married and spouseless men and women in planned retirement communities: Support network differentials. *Journal of Marriage and the Family, 43,* 169–177.

Lowenthal, M. F., & Chiriboga, D. (1972). Transition to the empty nest: Crisis, challenge or relief? *Archives of General Psychiatry, 26,* 8–14.

Lowenthal, M. F., & Robinson, B. (1976). Social networks and isolation. In R. H. Binstock & E. Shanas (Eds.), *Handbook of aging and the social sciences* (pp. 432–456). New York: Van Nostrand Reinhold.

Mares, M.-L., & Fitzpatrick, M. A. (1995). The aging couple. In J. F. Nussbaum & J. Coupland (Eds.), *The handbook of communication and aging research* (pp. 185–205). Mahwah, NJ: Lawrence Erlbaum Associates.

Mouser, N. F., Powers, E. A., Keith, P. M., & Goudy, W. J. (1985). Marital status and life satisfaction: A study of older men. In W. A. Peterson & J. Quadagno (Eds.), *Social bonds in later life* (pp. 71–90). Beverly Hills, CA: Sage.

Neugarten, B. L., & Gutmann, D. L. (1958). Age-sex roles and personality in middle age: A thematic apperception study. *Psychological Monographs, 72*(17), 1–33.

Palmore, E. (1981). *Social patterns in normal aging: Findings from the Duke longitudinal study.* Durham, NC: Duke University Press.

Peterson, C. C. (1995). Husbands' and wives' perceptions of marital fairness across the family life cycle. In J. Hendricks (Ed.), *The ties of later life* (pp. 43–53). Amityville, NY: Baywood.

Pihlblad, C. T., & McNamara, R. L. (1965). Social adjustment of elderly people in three small towns. In A. M. Rose & W. A. Peterson (Eds.), *Older people and their social world* (pp. 49–73). Philadelphia: Davis.

Pineo, P. C. (1961). Disenchantment in the later years of marriage. *Marriage and Family Living, 23,* 3–11.

Quirouette, C., & Pushkar Gold, D. (1995). Spousal characteristics as predictors of well-being in older couples. In J. Hendricks (Ed.), *The ties of later life* (pp. 21–33). Amityville, NY: Baywood.

Rollins, B. C., & Feldman, H. (1970). Marital satisfaction over the family life cycle. *Journal of Marriage and the Family, 32,* 2–28.

Rosow, I. (1967). *Social integration of the aged.* New York: The Free Press.

Schumm, W. R., & Bugaighis, M. A. (1986). Marital quality over the marital career: Alternative explanations. *Journal of Marriage and the Family, 48,* 165–168.

Sillars, A. L., & Wilmot, W. W. (1989). Marital communication across the life span. In J. F. Nussbaum (Ed.), *Lifespan communication* (pp. 225–253). Hillsdale, NJ: Lawrence Erlbaum Associates.

Smith, J. E. (1965). Family interaction patterns of the aged: A review. In A. M. Rose & W. A. Peterson (Eds.), *Older people and their social world* (pp. 143–161). Philadelphia: Davis.

Steere, G. H. (1981). The family and the elderly. In F. J. Berghorn & D. E. Schafer (Eds.), *The dynamics of aging* (pp. 289–309). Boulder, CO: Westview Press.

Stinnett, N., Carter, L. M., & Montgomery, J. E. (1972). Older persons perceptions of their marriages. *Journal of Marriage and the Family, 34,* 665–670.

Treas, J. (1975). Aging and the family. In D. S. Woodruff & J. E. Birren (Eds.), *Aging* (pp. 92–108). New York: Van Nostrand.

Treas, J. (1977). Family support systems for the aged. *The Gerontologist, 17,* 486–491.

Troll, L. E. (1971). The family of later life: A decade review. *Journal of Marriage and the Family, 33,* 263–290.

Troll, L. E. (1982). *Continuations: Adult development and aging.* Monterey, CA: Brooks/Cole.

Zietlow, P. H., & Sillars, A. L. (1988). Life-stage differences in communication during marital conflicts. *Journal of Social and Personal Relationships, 5,* 223–245.

CHAPTER 8

Aging and the Family: Relational Lifestyle Changes

*I*n chapter 7 we discuss the literature on marital relationships and elderly people. Chapter 8 extends this discussion, covering divorce, dating, remarriage, singlehood, and widowhood and their implications for elderly people.

DIVORCE

It is generally believed that the divorce rate is rapidly increasing. The divorce rate peaks for people in their mid-twenties and declines with advancing age (Decker, 1980). People of every age seem more and more likely to see divorce as a viable option (Hennon, 1983). About 15,000 men and women over the age of 65 were divorced during the year 1995 (U.S. Census Bureau, 1996). In 1990, about 5% of both men and women over 65 reported they had divorced and not remarried, with that number estimated to rise to a little over 6% in the year 2000 (U.S. Census Bureau, 1996).

Unfortunately, only a small amount of research has been conducted on divorce in older marriages. From the research that has been done, a few conclusions can be drawn:

1. Older divorced people are less happy than younger divorced people (Troll, 1982).
2. Divorce is a particular problem for displaced home-makers (Troll, 1982), who suffer both economically and in terms of self-esteem from the divorce (Huyck & Hoyer, 1982).
3. The younger people are when they first marry, the more likely they are to divorce (Troll, 1982).
4. Divorced women are much worse off than divorced men (Troll, 1982).
5. Divorced people are frequently worse off than are widowed people (Hennon, 1983).

Finding Number 5 deserves some elaboration, because it may go against commonsense notions. It is argued that, at least for the current cohort of elderly, divorce is more difficult than widowhood because widowhood is a well-defined role with established norms, especially as one ages. It does not bring with it the shame that divorce can often bring. Although the stigma of divorce is disappearing among younger people, this change has been slower among elderly people. Elderly divorcees feel more alienated and restricted socially. They receive less social support than do widows. This may be complicated by feelings of ambivalence toward their ex-spouses, which brings with it adjustment problems. Health problems are more frequent among divorced older people because not only are their ex-spouses not likely to provide care, but friendship patterns and relationships with their children may change and make care from them less likely (Hennon, 1983). Relationships with children are rarely hurt by widowhood, but they can be damaged by divorce. The consequences that divorce has on relationships with children, especially for fathers, will be discussed in chapter 9. In addition, friendship patterns and networks may be hurt because unattached people, particularly among women, may be seen as rivals (Blau, 1973).

According to one study, life satisfaction ratings are (from highest to lowest) married men, widowed women, married women, widowed men, never-married women, never-married men, divorced women, and divorced men (Altergott, 1985). Similarly, the suicide rate is lowest for married individuals, followed by never-married, widowed, and divorced individuals, in that order. Rates are somewhat higher for men than for women, but the pattern remains the same. The suicide rate is lower for those who have children, especially for women (Kastenbaum & Aisenberg, 1972).

Divorce, of course, is not totally negative. Many times, divorce is a welcome alternative to an untenable situation. In these cases, feelings about divorce are likely to be mixed—they include relief, mourning, shame, and pride in autonomy (Huyck & Hoyer, 1982). These findings are echoed in a thorough study on divorce (Hennon, 1983). Hennon found that divorce may be either shattering or seen as an opportunity and that:

1. Divorced people are less likely to help their children financially or to exchange financial advice with their children.
2. Divorced people have lower incomes.
3. Divorced people may have strained relationships with their children and are less integrated into kin networks.
4. Divorced people are more independent, but they are less satisfied with their financial situations and have more money worries.
5. Divorced people are less religious.
6. Divorced people are more satisfied with their health than are widowed individuals, and they feel that they have fewer problems than they did when they were married.

The problems that these people had when they were married no doubt led to the divorces. Escape from a problem-ridden situation has many advantages. It must be noted, however, that Hennon's study included only women, and it did not include those who were newly divorced or widowed. The people in the study had all adjusted to their situation to some degree. And Hennon concluded that women handle divorce better than men do, even though they are worse off financially than men.

Most divorced people remarry. Divorce does not usually indicate dissatisfaction with the institution of marriage, only with the particular marriage that has ended. In order to remarry, older individuals must find new partners. We thus turn to the issues of dating and courtship.

DATING AND COURTSHIP

Dating has implications not only for the divorced, but also the never-married and the widowed (who are discussed in more detail later in the chapter). Dating is, for the most part, an American innovation (Troll, 1982). It has traditionally been something in which youth participated. But, as there are more and more single people of all ages, dating and courtship are becoming a somewhat more widespread phenomenon. And, as Bulcroft and Bulcroft (1985) pointed out, "In a world of shrinking social roles, dating relationships in late life may have heightened importance" (p. 116).

Dating requires health, mobility, and money—things that some older people may lack to a certain degree (Bulcroft & Bulcroft, 1991; Huyck & Hoyer, 1982). Courtship is also different in some ways for older people. One difference is the limited availability of men. Men are much more likely than women to continue dating in their later years because of the number of potential partners available (Bulcroft & Bulcroft, 1991).

Another difference is the goal of dating. Whereas dating in younger life is frequently a prelude to mate selection, this is not necessarily the case for older people. They do not have the pressures to get married that younger people may experience. Indeed, the pressures may be not to marry. Bulcroft and Bulcroft (1985), however, found that many older people still use dating to find a mate, even without the usual social pressures. In a more recent study with a larger sample, Bulcroft and Bulcroft (1991) found that the overall likelihood of dating declines with age, along with the individuals' perceptions of their likelihood to ever marry or cohabitate with a significant other.

Thus, mate selection is only one of the motives for dating by older people. Even though many people in Bulcroft and Bulcroft's (1985) study did not feel they would marry the person they were currently dating, they felt that dating gave them a chance to meet other potential dating partners. Additional motives for dating include wanting an exchange of intimacies, the use of the dating relationship as a vehicle to remain socially active, and an opportunity to practice interacting with people of the opposite sex. Two other motives are relevant for women, wanting prestige and maintaining a stable identity. Some older women report that their identity is dependent on being involved with a man. In contrast, many other women report a reluctance to give up the new-found freedom they have since their divorce or partner's death. This reaction is more common in women (who may have never had such freedom before) than it is in men. Although one might expect the companionship found in dating to reduce loneliness, Bulcroft and Bulcroft (1991) found that dating is not re-lated to happiness or depression.

Dating also appears to be more varied in older life—elderly people on dates engage in a wider variety of activities than younger people typically do (Bulcroft & Bulcroft, 1985). And dating older people are likely to move the relationship along a bit more rapidly than youngsters because they feel they have less time left. They do not have time for playing games.

Huyck and Hoyer (1982) pointed out that love does not change as people age, but sex becomes less important. How-ever, Treas (1975) cited a study of 51-to-60-year-old women that indicates that 40% of the divorcees and 25% of the widows re-ported postmarital coitus. And Bulcroft and Bulcroft's (1985) interviews indicated that sexuality is a vital part of the dating relationship and that sexual intercourse is expected from the dating partner, typically by the fourth or fifth date. Of those older individuals who report having a "steady," 90% report sex-ual activity with that partner (Bulcroft & Bulcroft, 1991). Cer-tainly, sex is more important to older people than many younger people blindly believe.

Older people are less likely to go out looking for someone to date than are younger people. Vinick (1978) pointed out that a majority of the remarried couples she interviewed had been in-troduced by a mutual friend or relative, or they had known each other when one or both were married. Two of the couples in the study had even been related by marriage. Others had met in public places by chance, and several others had met in settings provided especially for senior citizens. Vinick reported that people who are actively involved with others and who get out of the house more have a better chance of meeting others to date; mobility encourages dating.

Bulcroft and Bulcroft's (1985) findings about where older people meet dating partners were a bit different from Vinick's findings. They reported that older people tend to meet each other through more formal means, such as clubs and organiza-tions, and that few meet through friends. They also found that organizational membership and contact with siblings is related to a greater likelihood to date, but that religious activity and contact with children is not (Bulcroft & Bulcroft, 1991).

The studies did concur, however, on who initiates the rela-tionship. Bulcroft and Bulcroft (1985) found that none of the older women they interviewed had ever asked a man out on a date, nor had any of the men been asked out by a woman. Vinick (1978) also reported that the men typically took the initiative in developing and sustaining the relationship. Many of the couples she interviewed reported that the relationship seemed to evolve naturally. One woman said, "[But] as he came, I kind of missed him when he didn't come, see? ... The more we saw of each other, the better we liked each other. It just worked into something" (p. 361). This statement reflects how all dating works, and how all relationships are built regardless of the age of the people. This process was described most lucidly by Bolton (1961). His perspective was also based on in-depth interviews with couples after their relationship was well developed, although he interviewed only younger couples. He found that relationships are not predetermined by the background characteristics, such as similarity and complementarity, that people bring to a relationship. Instead, the relationship is determined by what people *do* once they get there—how they *communicate* with each other. In particular, he described processes called "escalators," which move the relationship forward much as an electronic escalator in a mall moves people throughout the shopping complex. If one wants, one can always turn around and go back down the up-escalator or up the down-escalator. But it's a lot easier to keep going the same direction that the escalator is running than it is to turn around and go the opposite direction. Escalators in relationships function similarly. Examples are tying together one another's daily schedules, making statements of commitment to each other or to outsiders, idealizing the other person, and fantasizing about the relationship. Once these processes have started, they move the relationship forward and make it a little bit more difficult to back away from the relationship.

Obviously, in the interview statement, "it just worked into something," the "just" is misleading. A relationship does not "just" develop; it develops through the communication of the two people involved. This is equally true of the relationships of older and younger people. Relationship development is a *process*.

REMARRIAGE

Recall that widows have lower life satisfaction than do people who are married. Remarried people have a feeling of life satisfaction that is somewhere between these two (Mouser, Powers, Keither, Goudy, 1985). Most older individuals getting married are entering remarriages—only 6% are first-time unions (Treas & Van Hilst, 1976). It seems that 78% of older brides and grooms marry widowers and widows rather than never-married people, although there is a growing trend toward choosing a partner with a similar marital background regardless of whether they have been married before (Treas & Van Hilst, 1976). Huyck and Hoyer (1982) argued that second marriages are about as happy as first marriages, but they are more likely to end in divorce if the marriage is unhappy. Apparently, once an individual has learned that divorce is a viable option and that one will survive it, it is easier to use it as an alternative again.

Treas (1975) also argued that, although late marriages are rare, they are frequently successful. Those people who are most satisfied with their previous unions are more predisposed to remarriage. Because men are usually more satisfied with their previous relationships (Treas, 1975), it may not be surprising that the percentage of men remarrying is much higher than is the percentage of women remarrying. The remarriage interval is one half as long for men as it is for women. Another consideration in remarriage is that males have more potential partners from which to select a new mate. In 1990, only 2 out of every 1000 widowed women remarried, but 14 out of every 1000 widowed men did (U.S. Census Bureau, 1996). Hoyt (1980) also found that older women are especially critical of men and have no desire to make the accommodations necessary for a new relationship.

There are many barriers to remarriage. One such barrier for older women is that there simply are fewer men available for marriage. Additional forces work against leading older people to remarriage (Treas & Van Hilst, 1976). Children are frequently a particularly strong barrier to remarriage. If the person is widowed, his or her children may want the deceased parent to be respected and sanctified, and they may fear that this will not happen if the surviving parent remarries. The children may feel that the deceased parent may be forgotten after a remarriage. There are also likely to be concerns about estates and inheritances with remarriages. If the elderly person is divorced, his or her children may not want someone else trying to take the place of their mother or father. Especially for women, the presence of children hurts their chances of remarriage (Huyck & Hoyer, 1982; Troll, 1982).

Children are not the only a barrier to remarriage. Some people do not remarry because they feel that it would be disloyal to their first spouse (Huyck & Hoyer, 1982). On a related note, jealousy of the previous spouse on the part of a potential new partner can also get in the way of remarriage (Huyck, & Hoyer, 1982). Vinick (1978) reported even more negative feedback in this regard from an individual's friends than from his or her offspring.

Another barrier to remarriage is that many times elderly people have stereotypes about other elderly individuals that make them reluctant to remarry. If they think that most other elderly individuals (themselves excepted, of course) are senile and in ill health, they will be reluctant to undertake another union (Vinick, 1978). Women, particularly, may be reluctant to remarry, although they may in some ways also be more ready to remarry than are men (Troll, 1982), because they know that they have a good chance of having to care for an ailing spouse (Huyck & Hoyer, 1982).

One of the conditions necessary for remarriage is likely to be approval of the couple's offspring (Treas, 1975). The other conditions identified by Treas include a desire for companionship, love, and adequate income for both parties. Atchley (1980) adds that both the bride and the groom must be well adjusted for the union to be successful. Older individuals are more likely to remarry when they are in better health and are not living with a relative or friend (Bulcroft, Bulcroft, Hatch, & Borgatta, 1989). There are some gender differences, however, in what men and women look for in their remarriages. Men are more likely than women to look for companionship and care in remarriages (Huyck & Hoyer, 1982; Vinick, 1978).

The older the divorced or widowed person and the longer it has been since he or she ended or lost his or her previous marriage, the less likely the person is to remarry (Bulcroft et al. 1989). When people do remarry, they frequently select partners who remind them of their first mates. Remarriages are most likely (and most successful) among those who have known each other for a long time prior to the union (McKain, 1969). Generally, the reasons for remarriages include desiring companionship, having mutual and lasting affection and regard, feeling anxiety about health, and not wanting to depend on one's children (Troll, 1982). Generally, older couples choose the same romantic customs as do younger couples for their weddings and honeymoons.

Despite the factors that lead older individuals to remarriage, there are some individuals who never remarry. Bell (1979) categorized these:

1. *The bitter*: "He'll/She'll be as bad as the old one was!"
2. *The frightened*: "I don't want to risk another personal failure."

3. *The overdemanding*: "I can't find anyone who fits my requirements."
4. *The rejected*: "I can't find anyone who will have me."
5. *The adjusted*: "I have accepted being single and enjoy it."

Type 5, the adjusted no-longer-married individual, is likely to be similar in some ways to the person who has never been married. Although this group accounts for a rather small percentage of the population, the number of never-married individuals is large enough to warrant some discussion.

SINGLEHOOD

Although many have lamented the paucity of research on marriage and elderly people and on divorce and elderly people, there is a plethora of research in those areas compared with what can be found on the topic of singlehood for older people who have never been married. A larger percentage of older individuals who are not married are single because their partner has died than because they have never married. In 1993, 14% of older men were widowers and 48% of older women were widows (U.S. Census Bureau, 1996), compared to about 4% of both elderly men and women who never married (U.S. Census Bureau, 1996).

In the best discussion of singlehood in older age, Gubrium (1976) drew a distinction between isolation and desolation. Isolation is a physical state of aloneness, but does not bring with it the loneliness and negativity of desolation. He pointed out that most never-married older people are not desolate, they are simply more isolated than are most other people. While older single people are isolated, they have always been so. They are used to it and are not really lonely. Troll (1982) echoed this. Indeed, never-married older people resent the commonly held assumption that they are lonely.

The data indicate that, although most older people think about isolation, dependence, death, and loneliness fairly frequently, never-married older people do not (Gubrium, 1976). Their status involves independence, continuity, and minimal social involvements. This early development of independence is particularly helpful in older age, when many people need independence but do not have it.

Although never-married people may miss some of the benefits of marital and familial relationships, they also miss some of the disadvantages. They are much less likely to go through the pain and suffering of grief and bereavement (Atchley, 1980; Gubrium, 1976; Troll, 1982), for instance. Finally, Troll (1982) pointed out that never-married women are usually better off than are never-married men. This is consistent with the information cited earlier indicating that divorce is harder for men than it is for women and that men take widowhood harder than do women.

WIDOWHOOD

Women over 65 years old are nearly as likely to be widowed as they are to be married, divorced, or never married, and for women over 75 the percentage of widows rises to two thirds (U.S. Census Bureau, 1996). Older men are more likely to be married than widowed, with about 14% of men over 65 widowed and less than 25% of men 75 and over widowed (U.S. Census Bureau, 1996). These differences are accounted for by greater longevity among women, combined with the tendency of men to marry younger women. The mean age for widows is 56 years old (Atchley, 1994). Indeed, in their 50s, American women are more likely to be divorced and remarried or widowed than still married to their first husband (Safilios-Rothschild, 1977).

Grieving

Silverman (1986) pointed out that bereavement changes a person irrevocably—one cannot cure grief. It is a time of numbness, longing, sorrow, and depression that frequently brings with it weight loss, insomnia, and irritability (Treas, 1975). The grief is not less if the death was expected, but expected grief does seem to be shorter in duration (Troll, 1982). Troll also found that 35% of widows and widowers were depressed one month after their spouses' death, and 17% were still depressed 1 year later.

The bereaved person is likely to be avoided because his or her presence reminds others of death (Lesnoff-Caravaglia, 1984). This may be accompanied by pressures not to grieve for too long. All of these factors are especially troublesome for younger widows and widowers. The research consistently indicates that it is harder to be a younger widow or widower than an older one, although the chances of remarriage are better for younger people (Troll, 1982).

In a rather interesting piece, Silverman (1986) argued that one has to learn to be a widow or widower—one has to work at it. Other widowed individuals can provide advice and role models to facilitate this. Indeed, Heinemann (1983) broke down widowhood into component phases of mourning and adaptation. Further, widowhood includes both "grief work" (i.e., dealing with one's grief) and "reality testing" (attempting to function independently, without the spouse). It is not a simple process.

Effects of Widowhood

Because widowhood is a rather devastating experience, its effects are likely to be notable. One effect, of course, is loneliness (Palmore, 1981), although several studies pointed out that loneliness seems to be less of a problem for widows and widowers now than it was in the past (Atchley, 1980; Lopata, 1979). Widowers are more likely to commit suicide than are those who are married (Altergott, 1985). But most widows and widowers adapt (Lopata, 1979), and those who are widowed have a lower rate of institutionalization than do those who are divorced or never-married (Litwak, 1985). Furthermore, the results of the most thorough studies of the effects of aging, the Duke longitudinal studies, indicated that widowhood does not usually produce long-term, seriously negative effects (Palmore, 1981). This study also concluded that widowhood is more stressful in middle age than in old age, but even in middle age there are no serious, long-term effects. The consensus of a number of studies, then, is that individuals are highly resilient and generally recover from the loss of a spouse, even though this is a significant loss (O'Bryant & Hansson, 1994). For some people, however, widowhood brings relief and adjustment, especially for those who have been suffering with a spouse's long-term illness or disability.

Economic change does sometimes occur with widowhood. Huyck and Hoyer (1982) write that the worst effects for women are economic. A lower income brings with it less social participation and greater loneliness. They add that the parent of a dependent child is hardest hit by widowhood. This parent not only has to cope with economic problems, but they also have to cope with the child's as well as his or her own grief.

Morgan (1981) found, however, that the conclusion that widowhood has negative economic repercussions was based only on cross-sectional studies. She concluded from longitudinal data that the data "fail to demonstrate a significant decline in income or financial well-being upon the death of spouses.... Widowhood is not the major cause of poverty in this group" (p. 899). This is likely to be moderated by some other factors, of course. The increased perception among widows and widowers that they have limited financial resources can also increase stress and anxiety (O'Bryant & Hansson, 1994).

Becoming a widow(er) affects not only the individual, but his or her entire social support network (Pellman, 1995). The widowed have the most primary group resources and receive the most help of all groups. Litwak's (1985) findings indicated that help was received by 34% of the widowed, compared to 16% of the marrieds, 20% of the divorced, 24% of the separated, and 26% of the never-marrieds. Treas (1975) added that oldest and youngest children are especially obligated to help. But all the help does not come from the children. Heinemann (1985) found that kin and friends both provide support, although the support differs. Relatives give socioemotional assurance, financial aid, and provide a source of identity. Frailties and vulnerabilities are more accepted by family members. Friends, on the other hand, provide mutual gratification (as opposed to families, where the gratification is more one-sided), socialization, and opportunities for socializing. Friends also serve as confirmation of one's identity—a more subtle role than serving as an original source of identity. Friendships require more reciprocity and assertiveness, and foster self-worth and a sense of accomplishment. Economic vulnerability does not hurt these friendships; however, the friends in this case are likely to be in the same boat. Heinemann found that the family relationships were usually stronger than the friendships.

Lopata (1977, 1979) also found that, whereas friends are important for a widow, they do not replace the spouse or children. In Lopata's (1977) study, surprisingly few women emphasized friends as important sources of support. Their friendships are generally companionate, rather than comforting. This study found that, although 90% of the widows find their friends helpful, the friends are not strong contributors to support systems, other than providing social support. And most widows do not engage in a lot of social activities. The friends do not even provide strong emotional support, serve as the main confidants of the widows, or provide a sense of identity or confirmation. Friends, however, do give the widows a feeling of acceptance.

It also appears that friends from the past can serve a different function for the widow than new friends. New friends who are also widowed help one cope, whereas older friends help keep memories alive (Litwak, 1985). Some continuity of relationships also helps people maintain a sense of identity, something that becomes particularly important during widowhood, when identity changes in some very basic ways (Blau, 1973). But good friends made after widowhood are typically other widowed individuals who can help one cope (Lopata, 1979).

In the most thorough study of friendship in widowhood, Lopata (1977) found the following three types of women: (a) those who keep their old friends and develop new friendships; (b) those who keep their old friends and do not develop any new ones; and, (c) those who never had any friends and do not develop any after widowhood. The third type, the friendless widow, tends to be someone who is not originally from the area and has not had time to make friends because of many burdens at home. This person typically has lived near many relatives in the past, and does not know *how* to make friends. They believe that relatives are the only true friends. Only a portion of the people falling into this group even want to make friends, but this portion also lacks the confidence to initiate the relationship.

The second type, the woman with prewidowhood friends but not new friends, is more likely to be younger and working. The friendships include few with men; any cross-sex friendships are with men who are a part of couples, and whose wives have initiated the relationship. These widows do not see the friends as frequently as they had when the husband was still living. Lopata described steps in a process that typically occurs in these situations: (a) the widow's grieving makes friends uncomfortable, (b) the widows do not respond to any friendly advances that are made, (c) relations become strained, (d) the widow's low self-confidence makes her overly sensitive, and (e) the friends drift apart. Additionally, the widows feel like "fifth wheels" around other couples. Couples typically drop widows as friends. The same does not happen to widowers. Blau (1973) elaborated on this process by noting that conversations with married friends change with widowhood. Normally, the men talk "guy talk" and the women talk "girl talk." Now, one of the people does not have anyone with whom to talk. So the same-sex pair change their topics of conversation so as not to exclude the third person. The resulting conversation is not as gratifying for any of them. Finally, some friends who are not widowed do not want to face their own future by spending a lot of time with a widow (Atchley, 1980).

The first type of widow in Lopata's (1977) study was the widow who develops new postwidowhood friendships. These people tend to be more educated and have higher incomes. Some cross-sex friends are included in their network. Other work also emphasized the importance of other widows as new friends for widows (e.g., Silverman, 1986). Generally, however, it appears that most widows are not isolated (Altergott, 1985). One half of the widows in Lopata's (1979) study reported no significant change in themselves or their social lives since their spouse had died. Social contacts are particularly well maintained if the people stayed in the same neighborhood after the death. Blau (1981) cited several studies indicating that, after the age of 70, married people are less socially active than widowed people, probably because there are more widows by that time.

Not only is social participation with friends affected by widowhood, but interaction patterns with the family are typically affected as well. There is some controversy in the literature over these changes, however. For instance, Anderson (1984) found that ties with children (which are based in part on obligation) are not much affected by widowhood, but ties with siblings and other kin are affected. At the same time, Morgan (1984) concluded that the "average frequency of interaction with available kin increases for both married and widowed persons over time, with the greatest increase among women who become widowed. The total number of contacts, in contrast, decreases for both widows and widowers" (p. 323). The notion of frequency of interaction was also examined by Gibbs (1985), who concluded that people in the widow's social support network, particularly family, must be available and frequently engage in interaction with the widow. A large number of visitors is not necessary if they visit frequently and are concerned. Gibbs also found that family contact is not always emotionally satisfying.

Heinemann (1983) described the process that typically occurs in the families of widows. Beginning at the time of death, bereavement brings the families closer together. At this point, female relatives take over most services for the widowed, and male relatives typically take over funeral arrangements, finances, insurance matters, and so forth. After a while, the relatives gradually return to their own family obligations and contact with in-laws, in particular, declines.

As time goes on, the family helps the widow know when she has grieved long enough. This is important because guidelines for mourning are ambiguous in our culture. Some widows resent the pressure to stop grieving and to give up the role of "wife." They perceive family members who make such suggestions as uncaring. Friction can also result when other family members try to do too much for the widow or if it becomes evident that those providing help see it as a strain. Strain can result if too much or poor advice is given to the widow. Heinemann's research indicated that much of the advice given to widows was *not* helpful and much was contradictory. Conflicts emerge, especially with in-laws.

Children become particularly important for most widows, although siblings take on an important role for the childless widow. Nieces and nephews sometimes play this role for the childless widow, but not without resentment. Because the parent–child relationship is based on affection, gratitude, guilt, and desire for approval (Heinemann, 1983), the resulting relationships vary in quality. They are usually not reciprocal. The widow is invited to activities, but is not asked to participate in the planning, and so forth. This lack of involvement frequently leads to dissatisfaction (although this is rarely voiced) for the widows. High filial expectations are rarely met, also leading to dissatisfaction.

Typically, relationships with children are renegotiated after widowhood. Widows usually become closer to daughters, although they are more likely to move in with sons (Atchley, 1980). Widows who move in with children do so as a last resort, however (Lopata, 1973). They do not want to be involved in conflicts about running the house and do not want to raise more children. They also find it difficult to be second in command when they are used to running their own home. This renegotiation of roles occurs through the communication between the widowed parents and their children.

Widows who still have children in the home find that this keeps them going, but provides more strain in the long run. They are sometimes so busy with the children that they do not have time to grieve.

Overall, the data seem to indicate that interactions with the family increase immediately after the death of a spouse, and then decrease gradually (Lopata, 1973). The exception to this is contact with children.

Other Problems

The stressfulness of widowhood is affected by the circumstances surrounding the death of the spouse. For instance, Lopata (1979) found that suicides have the most aftereffects, whereas violent deaths are the hardest with which to cope. Widowhood is also made more difficult by anxiety about one's own death (Lesnoff-Caravaglia, 1984).

Several studies examined some of the other problems encountered by widows (Heinemann, 1983; Lopata, 1979; Troll, 1982). This list of problems includes making funeral arrangements, handling finances, dealing with loneliness, not having enough opportunity to grieve, feeling a lack of emotional support, having a lack of daily help or contacts after the funeral, having a fear of crime now that the person is alone, experiencing difficulty in maintaining the house and the car, finding transportation, lacking sex, and having difficulties in decision making and child rearing. Finally, Lesnoff-Caravaglia (1984) added that sexism makes widowhood (a likely eventual state for many women) even more difficult. Because women (especially in the current cohort of elderly women) have rarely had an opportunity to develop the skills necessary for self-sufficiency, they find it more difficult to do so when they are widowed and have no choice. For instance, Treas (1975) pointed out that widowhood is especially hard for a woman who does not drive.

The difficulties surrounding decision making for widowed individuals are exacerbated by the loss of the partner with whom major life decisions were discussed and considered (O'Bryant & Hansson, 1994). The widowed may feel reluctant to make necessary decisions like selling the house, especially if a decision might conflict with family or the deceased partner's expectations (Lund, Caserta, & Dimond, 1993).

One of the major determinants of an individual's moving to a nursing home is his or her marital status. Older couples tend to manage on their own, even when they are developing physical or cognitive limitations, by compensating for one another's losses. The loss of a spouse may result in the need for the surviving partner to move to a nursing home because he or she can no longer manage on his or her own (O'Bryant & Hansson, 1994). Such a move results in an even more dramatic re-ordering of the individual's life than does the loss of the spouse itself.

Widowers Compared to Widows

Most of the research that has been presented so far has been based on women because widowhood is much more common for women than it is for men. Some writers, however, compared widowhood for men with widowhood for women.

Although Treas (1975) suggested that widowhood may be even more devastating for men than for women, Atchley (1980) concluded that there are no definitive data showing that it is harder for men or for women. Although it may be harder on women economically, men are more likely to become socially isolated as a result of widowhood. There are several reasons for this. First of all, the mother is usually the one who brings the family together and without her presence, the family does not see the widower as frequently (Heinemann, 1983). Women also have more mutuality and intimacy in their other friendships, which makes it easier to adjust to widowhood. Men find intimacy only in marriage (Lowenthal & Robinson, 1976). Men rely on their wives as confidants, so when their wives are gone they have no one with whom they can share their feelings (Strain & Chappel, 1982). While widowers may have more friends than widows, these friendships are typically much less close. Widowers also have less interaction with their friends and neighbors than do widows. Because there are fewer widowers than widows, the role of widower is much more vague and does not solidify groups. Men also find it more difficult to grieve because they are less used to showing their emotions and to dealing with their emotions (Atchley, 1980). Many men feel uncomfortable about the competition that now exists for their affections among the larger number of unmarried women their age. Finally, many widowers are ill-prepared to take care of themselves and a house. This inability to perform simple household tasks is frustrating to the widower, but the ability to accomplish such tasks is not fulfilling (O'Bryant & Hansson, 1994).

All of these factors combine to make a devastating experience for widowers. Few widowers move in with their children or other relatives, but they remarry five times as frequently as do widows (Palmore, 1981). They are typically less involved in religious activities than are widows (Troll, 1982), but participate more frequently in clubs and other organizations (Huyck & Hoyer, 1982). Huyck and Hoyer also cited evidence indicating more negative symptoms of disorganization in widowers: suicide, physical illness, mental illness, alcoholism, and accidents.

Some widowers lose the will to live. Like women, widowed men are expected to preserve the memory of their deceased spouse and not show an interest in other women. Rarely, however, do they take this advice for very long (Atchley, 1980). Most widowers return to normal routines quickly and begin to date not too long after their spouse's death (Heinemann, 1983).

Coping with Widowhood

Whether it happens to a man or a woman, widowhood is not an easy experience with which to cope. Some suggestions can be made to facilitate the coping process, however. Lopata (1979) pointed out that widowed individuals have three primary resources: possessions, people, and themselves. On a related note, Atchley (1980) added that how people cope with widowhood depends on whether they base their identity on their job roles (which usually leads them to become more involved with their jobs), their personal qualities (which leads them to become more involved with family and friends), or their possessions (which requires changes in behavior only if the person's financial status has changed). He pointed out that some renegotiation of identity may be necessary, especially before remarriage will be possible. Widowed people vary in adaptation, depending on how important their role as spouse was to them (Troll, 1982). Treas (1975) provided some suggestions for other family members to facilitate this adaptation. Family members need to:

1. Build the widow's competence and confidence—do not encourage dependency.
2. Encourage the widow to postpone major decisions for a while.
3. Assume some of the deceased person's responsibilities for awhile.
4. Allow the widow to attend and ministrate to them.
5. Maintain a supportive interpersonal relationship with the widow.

Silverman (1986) added to this list that widowed individuals need to know that grief is normal, that it is rarely based on guilt, and that other widows can be helpful. Churches and voluntary associations may be helpful, as well as women's groups where widows do not encounter the stigma of the lone woman (Atchley, 1980).

Glick, Weiss, and Parkes (1974) identified five patterns of reorganization in the life of a widowed person during the first year of bereavement:

1. Remarriage.
2. Organization of life around close supportive relationships with kin.
3. Organization of life around a nonmarital relationship with a member of the opposite sex.
4. Organization of life independent of close relationships with anyone except children.
5. Lack of organization—chaos.

Fortunately, Pattern 5 is not observed very frequently.

The role of widow or widower has typically included keeping the memory of the dead spouse alive, not being interested in people of the opposite sex, and engaging in activities with other widows and with one's children (Atchley, 1980). As some of the patterns in the list indicate, this is no longer always the case. Regardless of which pattern is used, one problem experienced by most widowed individuals is breaking ties with the deceased. Heinemann (1983) pointed out this difficulty, and other work indicated that many people still "consult" the deceased spouse by considering his or her values when making decisions (Atchley, 1980).

The difficulty of breaking ties with the deceased is also manifested through the sanctification of the spouse. Although positive memories of the spouse can be supportive (Lopata, 1979), sanctification can be based on guilt and may then be dysfunctional (Heinemann, 1983). Some depression in widowhood may also be based on guilt (Huyck & Hoyer, 1982). This sanctification and guilt make remarriage less likely (Heinemann, 1983). Lopata's (1979, 1981) research indicated that sanctification is less likely for women who have had a difficult time in marriage, particularly due to minority status, inadequate education, and low income.

At some point, most widowed individuals begin to develop new roles for themselves. While some may hold on to the past, most move on to reorganize their lives (O'Bryant & Hansson, 1994). In fact, for some widowed individuals, their new status may provide them with an opportunity to discover their own identity separate from their identity within a couple. Women who have been in abusive marriages may find this time to be particularly liberating (O'Bryant & Hansson, 1994). Widowhood, then, is a very difficult time for anyone to go through. But most people survive it with few long-term negative effects.

SUMMARY

Marriages that are not happy are more likely to end in divorce today than in the past. Divorce is harder on older people and on women (although women handle it better), and it may even be harder than widowhood. Divorced people frequently remarry.

In order to remarry, divorced people must find a new partner. Older people, like younger people, use dating for mate selection, even though they do not have the same pressures to marry. Other motives for dating, such as the need for companionship, are also noted. Sex is important in older dating relationships. The relationships are typically initiated by the men. The process of relationship development is also discussed.

All dating among older individuals does not lead to remarriage. Remarriage when it occurs is much more common for men than for women. Remarriage is usually successful once the barriers to it, particularly opposition from the individuals' children and friends, are overcome. There are many reasons, however, why older people do not want to remarry.

Some older people, of course, have never married at all. These never-married people are usually somewhat isolated, but are not desolate or lonely; and they resent the assumption that they are. In some ways, never-marrieds are happier because they do not have to cope with the pain and tragedy of a relationship that has ended through divorce or death.

The last section of this chapter focuses on widowhood: the statistical likelihood of its occurrence, the process of grieving, and the effects of widowhood, including loneliness, economic hardship, the use of support networks, and the types of interaction with friends as compared with family. The types of friendship patterns among the widowed, with some thoughts on how friendships with couples change after widowhood, are discussed. Most widows are not isolated, although family contacts with kin other than children decrease after the funeral. Some pressures occur in family relationships after widowhood and family roles are renegotiated.

Widows are also contrasted with widowers. This discussion indicates that men find widowhood harder than women and that men remarry rather quickly. The research on the difficulty of widowhood for men as compared with women is inconclusive, however. Some thoughts about coping with widowhood and the difficulty of breaking ties with the deceased and the problem of sanctification of the deceased are also discussed.

■ REFERENCES

Altergott, K. (1985). Marriage, gender and social relations in later life. In W. A. Peterson & J. Quadagno (Eds.), *Social bonds in later life* (pp. 51–70). Beverly Hills, CA: Sage.

Anderson, T. B. (1984). Widowhood as a life transition: Its impact on kinship ties. *Journal of Marriage and the Family, 46*, 105–114.

Atchley, R. C. (1980). *The social forces in later life* (3rd ed.). Belmont, CA: Wadsworth.

Atchley, R. C. (1994). *Social forces and aging* (7th ed.). Belmont, CA: Wadsworth.

Bell, R. (1979). *Marriage and family interaction* (5th ed.). Homewood, IL: Dorsey.

Blau, Z. S. (1973). *Old age in a changing society.* New York: New Viewpoints.

Blau, Z. S. (1981). *Aging in a changing society.* New York: Franklin Watts.

Bolton, C. D. (1961, August). Mate selection as the development of a relationship. *Marriage and Family Living, 23*, 234–240.

Bulcroft, K., & Bulcroft, R. (1985). Dating and courtship in later life: An exploratory study. In W. A. Peterson & J. Quadagno (Eds.), *Social bonds in later life* (pp. 115–128). Beverly Hills, CA: Sage.

Bulcroft, R. A., & Bulcroft, K. A. (1991). The nature and functions of dating in later life. *Research on Aging, 13*, 244–260.

Bulfcroft, K., Bulcroft, R., Hatch, L., & Borgatta, E. F. (1989). Antecedents and consequences of remarriage in later life. *Research on Aging, 11*, 82–106.

Decker, D. L. (1980). *Social gerontology.* Boston: Little, Brown.

Gibbs, J. M. (1985). Family relations of the older widow: Their location and importance in her social life. In W. A. Peterson & J. Quadagno (Eds.), *Social bonds in later life* (pp. 91–104). Beverly Hills, CA: Sage.

Glick, I. O., Weiss, R. S., & Parkes, C. M. (1974). *The first year of bereavement.* New York: Wiley.

Gubrium, J. F. (1976). Being single in old age. In J. F. Gubrium (Ed.), *Times, roles and self in old age* (pp. 179–197). New York: Human Sciences.

Heinemann, G. D. (1983). Family involvement and support for widowed persons. In T. H. Brubaker (Ed.), *Family relationships in later life* (pp. 127–148). Beverly Hills, CA: Sage.

Heinemann, G. D. (1985). Interdependence in informal support systems: The case of elderly, urban widows. In W. A. Peterson & J. Quadagno (Eds.), *Social bonds in later life* (pp. 165–186). Beverly Hills, CA: Sage.

Hennon, C. B. (1983). Divorce and the elderly: A neglected area of research. In T. H. Brubaker (Ed.), *Family relationships in later life* (pp. 149–172). Beverly Hills, CA: Sage.

Hoyt, L. (1980, November). *Determinants of aged female sexuality.* Paper presented at the 33rd annual scientific meeting of the Gerontological Society, San Diego, CA.

Huyck, M. H., & Hoyer, W. J. (1982). *Adult development and aging.* Belmont, CA: Wadsworth.

Kastenbaum, R., & Aisenberg, R. (1972). *The psychology of death.* New York: Springer.

Lesnoff-Caravaglia, G. (1984). Widowhood: The last stage in wifedom. In G. Lesnoff-Caravaglia (Ed.), *The world of the older woman* (pp. 137–143). New York: Human Sciences.

Litwak, A. (1985). *Helping the elderly: The complementary role of informal networks and formal systems.* New York: Guilford.

Lopata, H. Z. (1973). *Widowhood in an American city.* Cambridge, MA: Schenkman.

Lopata, H. Z. (1977). The meaning of friendship in widowhood. In L. Troll, J. Israel, & F. Israel (Eds.), *Looking ahead* (pp. 93–105). Englewood Cliffs, NJ: Prentice-Hall.

Lopata, H. Z. (1979). *Women as widows: Support systems.* New York: Elsevier-North Holland.

Lopata, H. Z. (1981). Widowhood and husband sanctification. *Journal of Marriage and the Family, 43,* 439–450.

Lowenthal, M. F., & Robinson, B. (1976). Social networks and isolation. In R. H. Binstock & E. Shanas (Eds.), *Handbook of aging and the social sciences* (pp. 432–456). New York: Van Nostrand Reinhold.

Lund, D. A., Caserta, M. S., & Dimond, M. F. (1993). The course of spousal bereavement in later life. In M. S. Stroebe, W. Stroebe, & R. O. Hansson (Eds.), *Handbook of bereavement* (pp. 240–254). New York: Cambridge University Press.

McKain, W. (1969). *Retirement marriage.* Storrs, CT: University of Connecticut Press, Agricultural Experiment Station.

Morgan, L. A. (1981). Economic change at midlife widowhood: A longitudinal analysis. *Journal of Marriage and the Family, 43,* 899–907.

Morgan, L. A. (1984). Changes in family interaction following widowhood. *Journal of Marriage and the Family, 47,* 323–331.

Mouser, N. F., Powers, E. A., Keith, P. M., & Goudy, W. J. (1985). Marital status and life satisfaction: A study of older men. In W. A. Peterson & J. Quadagno (Eds.), *Social bonds in late life* (pp. 71–90). Beverly Hills, CA: Sage.

O'Bryant, S. L., & Hansson, R. O. (1994). Widowhood. In R. Blieszner & V. H. Bedford (Eds.), *Aging and the family: Theory and research* (pp. 440–458). Westport, CT: Praeger.

Palmore, E. (1981). *Social patterns in normal aging: Findings from the Duke longitudinal study.* Durham, NC: Duke University Press.

Pellman, J. (1995). Widowhood in elderly women: Exploring its relationship to community integration, hassles, stress, social support and social support seeking. In J. Hendricks (Ed.), *The ties in later life* (pp. 75–85). Amityville, NY: Baywood.

Safilios-Rothschild, C. (1977). Sexuality, power, and freedom among older women. In L. Troll, J. Israel, & F. Israel (Eds.), *Looking ahead* (pp. 162–166). Englewood Cliffs, NJ: Prentice-Hill.

Silverman, P. R. (1986). *Widow to widow.* New York: Springer.

Strain, L. A., & Chappel, N. L. (1982). Confidants: Do they make a difference in quality of life? *Research on Aging, 4,* 479–502.

Treas, J. (1975). Aging and the family. In D. S. Woodruff & J. E. Rirren (Eds.), *Aging* (pp. 92–108). New York: Van Nostrand.

Treas, J., & Van Hilst, A. (1976). Marriage and remarriage rates among older Americans. *The Gerontologist, 16,* 132–135.

Troll, L. E. (1982). *Continuations: Adult development and aging.* Monterey, CA: Brooks/Cole.

U.S. Census Bureau. (1996). *65+ in the United States.* (U. S. Census Bureau Current Populations Reports, Special Studies, P23–190). Washington, DC: U.S. Government Printing Office.

Vinick, B. H. (1978). Remarriage in old age. *The Family Coordinator, 27,* 359–363.

CHAPTER 9

Aging and the Family: Parents, Grandparents, and Siblings

T he aging family is a complex system of interdependent relationships. The previous two chapters focused on marriage as a very significant relationship for an elderly individual. This chapter focuses on three additional important and unique family relationships for elderly people: the elderly parent–adult child relationship, the grandparent–grandchild relationship, and the sibling relationship. These family relationships will each be discussed separately, but this does not indicate that these relationships operate independently. Each family relationship, including the spouse relationship, affects and is affected by all of the other family relationships. People with living grandparents, parents, and brothers or sisters know that their relationships with their parents can affect their relationships with their grandparents and their siblings. The unnatural separation of the family relationships in this chapter is done for convenience, and the reader should be mindful of the interdependence and complexity of the system of family relationships that exist for each individual.

THE ELDERLY PARENT–ADULT CHILD RELATIONSHIP

Many negative myths abound in our society concerning the elderly parent–adult child relationship. One myth places unnecessary blame on adult children for abandoning their elderly parents by moving far away from them, never contacting them, and placing their parents into prison-like nursing homes. Another myth places blame upon elderly parents, who sap the economic as well as psychological strength of their children by always wanting the children to sacrifice their own lives in order to give aid to their parents. These myths are not only destructive, but they are very far from the truth.

Study after study showed that the great majority of the elderly who have children (anywhere from 78–90%) see or speak with their children by telephone at least once a week (Cicirelli, 1983a, 1983b; Riley and Foner, 1968; Shanas, 1979; Troll, 1971; Troll, Miller, & Atchley, 1979). In addition, the quality of the elderly parent–adult child relationship is quite good. Cicirelli (1981) reported that nearly 90% of adult children state that they feel "close" or "very close" to their elderly parents. Although research rather consistently shows that parents feel a stronger sense of attachment to their children than children report towards their parents across the life span, these feelings remain relatively high for all parties (Giarrusso, Stallings, & Bengtson, 1995). Indeed, research indicates that the parent–child relationship is strong and vital throughout the entire life span (Atchley, 1983). Parents and children alike acknowledge the strong reciprocal effect that they have on one another throughout their lives (Suitor, Pillemer, Keeton, & Robison, 1994). They continue to provide each other with assistance, affection, and companionship throughout the life span (Logan & Spitze, 1996; Rossi & Rossi, 1990). The myth of an alienation of adult children from their elderly parents is just not true.

For their own part, elderly parents have a great need to remain independent from their adult children. This is obvious when one considers that the great majority of elderly people maintain their own households and respect the separate lives of their adult children (Atchley, 1980; Decker, 1980). The myth of elderly parents constantly begging for time, affection, and money from their children is not true.

The elderly parent–adult child relationship can sometimes last up to 90 years. Researchers have long asked the question: Why does this relationship endure? Two theories have been advanced to help understand and explain the dynamic character-istics of this lifelong relationship. Bengtson, Olander, and Haddad (1976) proposed a model of family solidarity based primarily on sociological work that was written originally as an attempt to explain small-group solidarity. Cicirelli (1983a, 1983b) tested life-span attachment theory as originally proposed by Bowlby (1979, 1980). Life-span attachment theory has its roots in the psychological tradition of social research. Each of these theories will be discussed.

Intergenerational Solidarity

The theory of intergenerational solidarity was proposed to de-scribe and to explain the special relationship that adults have with their elderly parents (Bengtson et al., 1976). Three key factors compose the solidarity that exists in the elderly par-ent–adult child relationship. The first factor is association. The more the elderly parent is associated with the adult child, the more solidarity exists in the relationship. Within the literature, association has been typically defined as close interpersonal contact and residential proximity.

A second factor playing a key role in the amount of solidarity found in the elderly parent–adult child relationship is affection. Bengtson and his colleagues argued that helping behavior is the key signal of affection within the relationship. The crucial element of helping within this approach is the giving of the help. Adult children have a sense of obligation—a duty—to help their parents. This filial obligation is heightened when parents are in the most need of help.

The third factor related to family solidarity is the ability of adult children and elderly parents to reach agreement on values, beliefs, and opinions. Any behavior that aids this consen-sus promotes solidarity. Thus, both children and parents must accept the role changes of retirement and other aspects of aging to promote consensus. In addition, communication must take place to foster consensus between the generations, especially when there is a lack of shared experiences.

Intergenerational solidarity theory proposes that the elderly parent–adult child relationship will remain strong as long as as-sociation, affection, and consensus remain strong. Research over the past 40 years supports many of the claims of intergenerational solidarity theory (Bengtson, 1995). However, one major study undertaken by Atkinson, Kivett, and Campbell

(1986) found very little support for this theory. Their research questioned the role of affect and consensus in the elderly parent–adult child relationship. Researchers may need to reexamine the importance of such concepts as filial obligation and shared norms as key elements in the elderly parent–adult child relationship.

Life-Span Attachment Theory

A second theory, life-span attachment theory, was advanced to explain the lifelong nature of the parent–child relationship (Cicirelli, 1983a, 1983b). Originally formulated to address mother–infant interaction, attachment theory was extended by Bowlby (1979, 1980) to the elderly parent–adult child relationship. "Attachment refers to an emotional or affectional bond between two people; essentially it is being identified with, in love with, and having desire to be with another person" (Cicirelli, 1983b, pp. 815–816). Attachment is an internal feeling that parents and children feel for one another. This feeling can lead to attachment behaviors.

Child psychologists have studied the attachment of infants to their parents for some time. Bowlby (1979, 1980) and Cicirelli (1983a, 1983b) argued that attachment feelings and behaviors follow people throughout their lives. As adults, people's feelings of closeness toward their elderly parents are manifestations of attachment. Residential proximity, frequent visits and phone calls, letter writing, and caregiving are all behaviors associated with attachment in adulthood.

Life-span attachment theory as applied to the helping behavior of older adults was studied extensively by Cicirelli (1983b). He found that feelings of attachment by adult children lead directly to caregiving behavior. Cicirelli speculated that adult children may increase their attachment to their elderly parents as the parents become older. This increased attachment makes it more likely that the adult child will detect the parent's need for help and, at the same time, it increases the likelihood that help will be given.

Holmes and Holmes (1995), as cultural anthropologists, did not study life-span attachment directly. They argued, however, that cultures that encourage warm and supportive parenting styles also exhibit warm and supportive attitudes towards their elderly members. Life-span attachment theory supports the idea that people develop attachments and learn how to treat others in childhood. These attitudes are then extended throughout the life span.

Functions of the Elderly Parent–Adult Child Relationship

The two theories presented here are sound explanations of why the parent–child relationship remains vital throughout the life span. The utility of this relationship for elderly people, however, has yet to be discussed. Two major functions of the elderly parent–adult child relationship emerge from the social scientific literature. The first function concerns the affective nature of the relationship. The second function centers on the mutual aid provided in the elderly parent–adult child relationship.

Affect Function. No matter what age they are, all human beings strive to be close to other human beings. Henderson (1980), Mueller (1980), Cohler (1983), and countless others stressed the importance of extensive close networks of relationships throughout people's adult years. The parent–child relationship can serve as one type of close relationship for the elderly individual.

The importance of the affective function of the elderly parent–adult child relationship for the elderly parent can be found in two studies concentrating on childless elderly people. Singh and Williams (1982) surveyed close to 1000 elderly individuals. Of this sample, approximately 20% were childless. Compared to those elderly individuals who had children, childless elderly people were significantly less satisfied with their family life. In addition, the least satisfied of elderly people were those in the oldest cohort. Beckman and Houser (1982) extended these results and found that "childless widows had lower overall well-being and were more lonely and dissatisfied with their lives than were widows with grown children" (p. 249). A third study indicated that elderly people with more than one child report qualitatively superior patterns than elderly people with only one child (Kivett & Atkinson, 1984). These results highlight the basic affective nature of the parent–child relationship for the elderly parent.

It is common to think that parenting ends once the child leaves home. But even after their children are grown, parents have a sense of a continuing role as parent, although the content of the role changes when children are adults (Blieszner & Mancini, 1987). The parent–child relationship can be a good, close relationship throughout the entire life span as the relationship undergoes a series of transitions. Alpert and Richardson (1980) wrote about family-stage theory and considered parenting to be a five-stage process. The final stage in the parenting process is the parent–adult child stage. Transitions that influence the parent–adult child relationship include such events as the child moving out of the parent's home, getting married, and becoming a parent himself or herself, as well as the parent's retiring, being widowed, or having health problems (Boyd, 1989; Suitor et al., 1994). Some researchers pointed to the time of the last child leaving home as depressing for the parents, especially for older women (Bart, 1970). Other research, however, suggested that independence from children is greeted by relief and satisfaction among women (Harkins, 1978; Lowenthal & Chiriboga, 1972; Rollins & Feldman, 1970). Stressful events in the life of either the parent or child often bring them closer together as they help each other through these adjustments. One of the most important aspects of the affective nature of the parent–adult child relationship is that closeness in this long-standing relationship provides a sense of continuity as the parent and child manage transitions in their lives (Henwood, 1995).

Although parents and adult children continue to feel close to one another, they also prefer to remain independent of each other. Because the elderly parent and the adult child remain independent, they maintain contact out of affection for each other rather than out of obligation alone. The maintenance of contact by choice rather than obligation has become more important, compared to historical times when children were financially dependent on parents and therefore required to "stay close" in order to inherit the family farm or other resources (Suitor et al., 1994). Sussman and Burchinal (1962a, 1962b) made a very convincing argument that, as people age, they become more involved with their families than with other types of activities. Studies of the general population agree that the elderly parent–adult child relationship remains close for the vast majority throughout their life spans (Cicirelli, 1983a). Although there are actually four possible dyads involved in this relationship (mother–daughter, mother–son, father–daughter, and father–son), research suggested that the mother–daughter dyad is the closest (Cicirelli, 1983a; Troll, 1986; Troll et al., 1979). Shanas (1979) reported that adult daughters are more likely to live close to their mothers, are likely to visit more often, and are more likely to give help when needed. Troll et al. (1979) go so far as to say that in Western societies, mothers and daughters hold the family together throughout the life span.

It is evident that the elderly parent–adult child relationship can be characterized as an affectionate, warm relationship. Because of the affective nature of the relationship, there is bound to be a certain level of and tolerance for interpersonal conflict. Some researchers suggest that closeness and conflict are recurring themes and an inherent part of the parent–child relationship (Boyd, 1989; Henwood & Coughlan, 1993; Suitor et al., 1994). While conflict may arise, the parent and child also discover ways of managing conflict at a tolerable level (Henwood & Coughlan, 1993). Brody (1985) and Cicirelli (1981) reported that, as elderly parents age and begin to "demand" help from the adult children, negative feelings enter into the parent–child relationship. Prior to the declining health of the parent, minor conflicts can occur, mostly "centered on one party's criticism of, or intrusion into, the other's habits or activities" (Cicirelli, 1983a, p. 34). For the most part, however, the elderly parent-adult child relationship is a close, affectionate, and stable relationship that is rewarding for the elderly parent as well as for the adult child.

Mutual Aid.   A second major function of the elderly parent–adult child relationship deals with mutual aid. Ample evidence exists that mutual helping between parents and their children is a lifelong phenomenon (Cicirelli, 1981, 1983a; Spitze & Logan, 1992; Troll, 1986; Troll et al., 1979). "In general, parents give more services and money to their children throughout their life, and children give more emotional support, household help, and care during illness" (Troll 1986, p. 23).

Ward (1996) reported that elderly parents often provide more aid to their adult children than vice versa. Housekeeping, babysitting, food preparation, and help with finances are part of the day-to-day aid that elderly parents give to their children. In fact, older parents give three times more assistance to their children than they receive until about the age of 75. After a parent reaches the age of 75, children give more assistance than they receive, but parents typically are still providing some level of assistance in return.

A fascinating study by Bankoff (1983) provides evidence that adult children need parental support not only for day-to-day living but also during times of crisis. Perhaps the greatest crisis faced by a middle-aged individual is the death of a spouse. The average age of widowhood in U.S. society is 56 years. Bankoff (1983) reasoned that elderly parents are uniquely suited to provide the empathy and nurturance to their adult children that they need to endure the loss of a spouse. Widows who receive little or no parental support have a very difficult time adjusting to the tragedy—no matter how much support they receive from other individuals.

The time comes, however, when the responsibility of giving aid in the parent–child relationship shifts from the parent to the child. When a parent becomes ill or for some reason faces loss in his or her ability to cope with life, the adult child begins to provide services for the parent. The literature is rich with studies showing that when parents have physical or emotional needs, adult children are there to provide for those needs (Cicirelli, 1981; Troll, 1986). The primary caregiver in a great majority of these situations is a daughter who lives nearby and has kept in close touch with the parent (Cicirelli, 1983a).

Excellent reviews on the adult child as helper exist in the gerontological literature (Cicirelli, 1981; Fisher, 1985; Litwak, 1985; Shanas, 1979). Variables such as residential proximity, attachment, filial obligation, economic well-being, number of children, parental attitudes toward receiving help, and type of aid needed influence the aid that can be given by adult children. Still, the literature is quite clear. Today, more than ever before, adult children "provide more care and more difficult care over a much longer time than such children did in the 'good old days'" (Troll, 1986, p. 83).

Parental Divorce and the Parent–Child Relationship

If a parent becomes frail, children readily step in to provide instrumental and emotional support. Families, mostly spouses and children, provide most of the support provided to elderly people in the United States. If an individual's parents have divorced and a parent has not remarried, the child typically will become responsible for the parent's care because a spouse is not available to provide these services. Studies of divorce consistently show that men have less interaction with their children, even in the children's adult years (Bulcroft & Bulcroft, 1991). Divorced fathers over 55 have less contact, through visits, phone calls, and letters, than do mothers. Men who were divorced when their children were younger and whose ex-wives remarried have even less contact with their children. Widowhood does not have a similar impact on the father–child relationship. Bulcroft and Bulcroft (1991) found that divorce has an extremely negative effect on the father–child relationship, but did not negatively impact the mother–child relationship. The long-term cost of divorce for men is restricted contact with their children in later life. This loss of contact may be particularly problematic for men if they should need care giving in their later years because their children are not a source of support (Mares & Fitzpatrick, 1995).

Conclusion

The societal myth of alienation in the elderly parent–adult child relationship is simply not true for the vast majority of aging family members. The parent–child relationship remains vital throughout life. This relationship functions to serve the affect needs and the aid needs of both the elderly parent and adult child. Communication plays a critical role in defining the nature of the parent–child relationship as the members manage the social stress and strains of life (Henwood, 1995).

THE GRANDPARENT–GRANDCHILD RELATIONSHIP

An increasingly important family relationship that is beginning to receive a great deal of attention by social scientists is the grandparent–grandchild relationship. This relationship is of special importance to the family for a number of reasons. First, the elderly population is growing; thus, there is a greater potential for an elderly individual to become a grandparent during his or her lifetime. Currently, 94% of the individuals over the age of 65 who are parents are also grandparents and nearly 50% are great-grandparents (Hooyman & Kiyak, 1991). Second, the age at which individuals are becoming grandparents can be anywhere from 30 years old to over 80. People are becoming grandparents at increasingly younger ages and the grandparent–grandchild relationship can now last for several decades. Of course, this long period of overlap in lifetimes means that a grandchild may be a newborn or a retiree. Third, the grandparent role has become clearly distinct from the parent role. This is due mainly to the societal norm that people cease childbearing in the third decade of life. Thus, an individual is not likely to be simultaneously a grandparent and a parent of a young child (Troll, 1980).

Many myths have been generated in American society concerning the behavior of grandparents. Bengtson and Robertson (1985) explored the nature and importance of the grandparent role in the modern family; the major features of grandparenting are highlighted here. One must keep in mind, however, the complexity of this relationship in the context of the family system. The brief treatment of this important relationship in this book is in no way meant to downplay the significance of grandparenting within the modern family.

Styles of Grandparenthood

Neugarten and Weinstein (1964) realized the importance of grandparenting for elderly individuals and introduced the concept of styles of grandparenthood to help understand the diverse nature of such a complex role. Prior to this investigation, it was a commonly held belief that grandparenting was a simple role, with some individuals being good grandparents, while others simply had no time for it. Troll (1981) summarized the Neugarten-and-Weinstein styles of interaction for grandparents:

1. *Formal:* An orientation that maintains clearly demarcated lines between parent and grandparent, with an occasional gift or minor service.
2. *Fun-seeker:* A leisure orientation, characterized by grandparental self-indulgence and mutuality of pleasure.
3. *Surrogate parent:* An orientation in which the grandparent, almost always the grandmother, substitutes for the children's mother if she is employed or otherwise unable to care for her child.
4. *Reservoir of family wisdom:* An orientation in which the grandparent, more often the grandfather, fills a role reminiscent of the traditional power role described by Apple (1956).
5. *Distant figure:* An orientation in which the grandparent emerges "from the shadows" ritually and fleetingly.

The most popular styles of interaction for grandfathers and grandmothers are the formal and fun-seeker styles. Younger grandparents have more diverse styles of interacting within the family, whereas older grandparents are typically formal and distant (Neugarten & Weinstein, 1964).

Wood and Robertson (1976) conceptualized the grandparent role based on the belief that "attitudes and expectations of the role derive from two major sources: those that are determined almost exclusively by social or normative factors and meet the needs of society, and those that stem from personal forces within the individual and meet his (*sic*) needs" (p. 245). Their four grandparent styles are (a) apportioned, (b) individualized, (c) symbolic, and (d) remote. Grandparents in the *apportioned* group are high in personal needs and high in social needs. Grandparents in the *individualized* group are high in personal needs and low in social needs. Wood and Robertson (1976) reported that grandparents in these two groups are older, are less educated, have more grandchildren, and engage in more activities with them. Grandparents in the *symbolic* group are low in both personal and social needs. The grandparents in this style are younger and more involved with community events and friends than with their grandchildren. Grandparents in the *remote* group have little if any contact with their grandchildren.

An additional attempt to classify grandparenting styles (Kivinck, 1981) presented five styles: centrality, valued elder, immortality, reinvolvement, and indulgence. It was assumed that each grandparent manifested some of the behaviors of each style.

These three attempts to classify grandparenting styles all share the notion that some grandparents are more involved in family interaction than other grandparents. The underlying assumption of this approach to classifying styles of grandparenting is that certain styles are related to successful aging or relational satisfaction. At this time, no scientific evidence has been advanced to link certain styles of grandparenting interaction to positive aging outcomes. However, it is important to note that these researchers identified the grandparenting role as a complex system of interactional styles; there is more than one way to behave as a grandparent.

Matthews and Spray (1985) advanced an intriguing proposition that grandchildren do not react to the role of grandparent but instead to each individual person fulfilling grandparenthood. "The grandchildren indicated that their attachments were not to grandparents in general, but to specific ones" (Matthews & Spray, 1985, p. 625). They stated that to understand the grandparent–grandchild relationship, researchers must begin to treat each relationship as unique and to consider the influence of other family members in the relational system. Grandchildren see their relationships with their grandparents as important to their lives, with enjoyment, emotional ties, and obligation playing roles in how they define the significance of the relationship (Roberto & Stroes, 1995). Matthews and Spray (1985) felt that 5, 6, or even 100 styles of grandparenting will never fully grasp the complex nature of the grandparental relationships in a family.

Functions of Grandparenting

Kornhaber (1985) argued that "a great many grandparents have given up emotional attachments to their grandchildren. They have ceded the power to determine their grandparenting relationship to the grandchildren's parents and, in effect, have turned their backs on an entire generation" (p. 159). The victims of this "new social contract" are the children who become scornful of elderly people and fearful of becoming old. Kornhaber (1985) made a strong case that grandparents have given up any significant function they might have within the family. He advocated the rejection of the "new social contract" and the reestablishment of the three-generation family.

The radical description of the present state of grandparenting by Kornhaber, although well-intentioned, does not necessarily find support in the gerontological literature (Cherlin & Furstenberg, 1986). The research evidence overwhelmingly supports a strong attachment between grandparents and their grandchildren. Cherlin and Furstenberg reported a strong sense of obligation on the part of grandparents, as well as grandchildren and children, to keep a close "in touch" relationship. These close relationships serve both generations with an opportunity for continuity and interconnectedness in their lives (McKay, 1993). McKay (1993) suggested that grandparents help provide guidance to their grandchildren through narratives of their life stories, which help the younger generation by conveying insights about life, reinforcing for both generations the continuity of life. In contrast to these close relationships, Troll (1983) referred to the grandparent as the "family watchdog," who subscribes to a norm of noninterference during times of normality, but who is able and willing to comfort during times of crisis.

The consensus of research supports the view that grandparents serve important functions in the family and not the view that grandparents have abandoned their grandchildren. Grandparents serve as a source of social support and assist in the socialization of their grandchildren.

As mentioned previously, grandparents step in to provide assistance during times of crisis (Robertson, 1994). Grandparents not only provide child care for parents who are working outside the home, but will take on the responsibilities of primary caregiver if parents are unable to fulfill their obligations. Grandparents provide a sense of security and continuity to grandchildren during the divorce of the parents. Grandparents serve as liaisons between adolescents or young adults and their parents (McKay & Caverly, 1995). Grandparents also receive social support from their grandchildren, helping to create a family definition as a system of mutual reciprocity across the life span (Langer, 1995).

Grandparenting and Socialization. Grandparents play a role in socializing their grandchildren not only by passing on cultural and historical values, but also by serving as role models for younger generations (Robertson, 1994). An important element of the grandparents' roles in the family is generating and maintaining a sense of family connectedness and continuity. Grandchildren report that their grandparents have played an important role in the development of their values (Roberto & Stroes, 1995).

There is some evidence to suggest that grandmothers have different functions in the family than grandfathers. Hagestad (1978) found that grandmothers are more likely to have warm close relationships with their grandchildren, whereas grandfathers were more concerned with jobs and financial matters. In addition, Thomas (1982) reported that grandfathers are more interested in playing with mature grandchildren, whereas grandmothers speak of offering advice to these mature grandchildren. In one investigation, however, Thomas (1986) reported that grandfathers as well as grandmothers "endorsed relatively high levels of responsibility for grandchildren's care and for offering child-rearing advice" (p. 422). Although Thomas (1995) found no gender differences on the level of perceived responsibility for grandchildren, the centrality of the relationship in their lives, their sense of re-involvement with the past, or the value of sharing wisdom, grandmothers reported greater satisfaction in their relationships with grandchildren and grandfathers placed greater stress on generational extension and indulging grandchildren. From the grandchild's perspective, young adults report having engaged in more activities with their grandmothers and that grandmothers have a greater influence on their value development, except in the areas of political beliefs and work ethic (Roberto & Stroes, 1995).

Age may also be a factor within the grandparent–grandchild relationship. Troll (1983) reported that "grandparents in their fifties, sixties and seventies were more likely to say good things about their grandchildren, whereas those in their forties and eighties were more likely to be critical" (p. 69). Thomas (1986) found young grandparents more willing to offer childrearing advice. The effect of a grandchild's age on the grandparent–grandchild relationship is unclear. The few studies that have been done report contradictory results and do not study grandchildren beyond adolescence.

Several other factors may influence the grandparent–grandchild relationship. The most important of these is, first of all, the acceptance of the grandparent role by the grandparent. The role of grandparent is a nonvoluntary one, depending on the actions of another. Individuals in their 30s typically do not think of themselves as grandparents but may, in fact, find themselves in that role. The second factor is the grandparent–parent relationship, which can have significant effects on the grandparent–grandchild relationship. The grandparent can often function as a mediator between the child and his or her parent. If a grandparent and a parent do not get along, the grandchild is less likely to have frequent contact with that grandparent. Another factor is physical proximity (Hodgson, 1995). Physical proximity increases the frequency of face-to-face contact, and frequent contact during the grandchild's early years establishes a closer relationship that is then easier to maintain during the grandchild's adult years. Finally, Troll (1983), Cherlin and Furstenberg (1986), and others mentioned the divorce of parents as an important factor influencing the grandparent-grandchild relationship.

Grandparenting After Divorce. Once parents divorce, the role of the grandparent can change drastically. As mentioned previously, the grandparent may serve as a source of continuity and stability during the time of the divorce. Grandparents also provide moral support to their grandchildren as the family is being redefined through divorce, preferring to provide short-term support and not take on a long-term responsibility (Robertson, 1994). The opportunity, however, to give support depends on whether the grandparent is the parent of the custodial parent (McKay & Caverly, 1995). If the mother has custody, the paternal grandparents may have a difficult time maintaining regular contact with their son's children; maternal grandparents, however, may become more involved in their grandchildren's lives. The increase in involvement may be multiplied if the mother returns to her parents' home with her children.

In 1998, almost 4 million children under the age of 18 lived in the home of one of their grandparents (U.S. Census Bureau, 1998). For about half of these children, one of their parents also lived in the home. Obviously, living in the same household increases opportunities for contact and influences the interaction among the generations. The responsibility for discipline and caregiving, however, falls to the grandparent when a parent is not also in the home—which is true for nearly 1.5 million children. Creighton (1991) called grandparents "silent saviors" when they take responsibility for their grandchildren because of the unavailability of the parents, especially when it is due to drug abuse or other criminal activity. Grandparents who are serving as the primary caregivers for their grandchildren often place less emphasis on their own physical and emotional health in order to protect the security of their grandchildren (Robertson, 1994). Commitment to the family outweighs their personal plans and goals.

The increasing number of divorces and remarriages has led to blended families, including step-grandparents (Trygstad & Sanders, 1995). Sixty percent of all remarriages involve an adult with physical custody of one or more child; however, step-grandparents and step-children are often unclear as to how they should relate to one another or even what they should call each other. This step relationship is influenced by all the other factors that have been discussed, as well as the factors influencing how families blend together. Factors such as the age of the child when the remarriage occurred; the grandparent's attitude toward the remarriage, the step-parent, and his or her child; and the frequency of contact determine how the step-grandparent and step-grandchild define their relationship.

Conclusion

Grandparenting is a role that many people will one day fill. Research evidence strongly suggests that grandparents have satisfying relationships with their grandchildren. Although the grandparents may not want to take an active role in childrearing or derive any pleasure from such a role, "still, grandparents play an important emotional and symbolic role, providing valued, affectionate, informal relationships and serving as symbols of family continuity" (Cherlin & Furstenberg, 1986, p. 28).

THE SIBLING RELATIONSHIP

Of the four major relationships within the aging family (the spouse relationship, the elderly parent–adult child relationship, the grandparent–grandchild relationship, and the sibling relationship), the sibling relationship has received the least scholarly attention. Most of the scientific explorations of sibling relationships concentrated on children and adolescents (Cicirelli, 1972; Irish, 1964; Sutton-Smith & Rosenberg, 1970). Yet, the sibling relationship can have the longest duration of any family relationship and can also be the most egalitarian of all the relationships entered into throughout life (Cicirelli, 1980).

Affect Between Siblings

Evidence from several studies indicated that over 80% of elderly individuals have at least one living brother or sister (Adams, 1968; Cicirelli, 1979, 1980; Clark & Anderson, 1967); this proportion is expected to continue at least through the Baby Boom generation (McKay & Caverly, 1995). In addition, Cicirelli (1980) and Scott (1983) reported that siblings maintain frequent contact with one another in later life. Although some social scientists suggested a decline in sibling contact with increasing age (Rosenberg & Anspaugh, 1973), others suggested that siblings renew their relationships as their own children mature and leave home (Cicirelli, 1980). In this way, the sibling relationship is more like a friendship than an involuntary family relationship (McGhee, 1985).

More important than the frequency of interaction between siblings may be the closeness felt in the sibling relationship. Cicirelli (1977) stated that the "elderly feel closer to siblings than to other relatives, except their own children. This is especially true for elderly who are married with no children, widowed or divorced or never married" (p. 317). In another investigation, Cicirelli (1979) found that approximately 65% of the elderly individuals studied reported "close" or "very close" relationships with at least one sibling. Changes in the sense of closeness with siblings are likely to occur throughout the life span, with high levels of closeness during childhood, greater distance during early adulthood, and then again greater closeness during the middle and late years of life (Bedford, 1994). McGhee (1985) suggested that the closeness felt by elderly siblings toward one another may be a result of common concerns about aging because siblings are typically of similar age. Atchley (1991) suggested that sibling relationships are more highly valued in later years because of similarities in life experiences and as the need for emotional support increases.

The vast majority of older adults report a positive relationship with at least one of their siblings (Bedford, 1994). The affective nature of the sibling relationship may depend to some extent, however, on the sex of the sibling. Of the three sibling dyads, Cumming and Schneider (1961), Shanas (1973), Allan (1979), Cicirelli (1980), and McGhee (1985) found the closest relationships between elderly sisters, the next closest relationship between elderly brothers and sisters, and the most distant relationship between elderly brothers. Gold (1989) reported that 85% of white middle-class sibling dyads with at least one sister feel close, while 63% of dyads with brothers report the same level of closeness. For African American sibling dyads, however, gender differences do not seem to be important, with 95% reporting close relationships (Gold, 1990). Connidis and Davies (1992) also reported that relationships with sisters become particularly important in later years. These gender differences have been questioned by Scott (1983), who reported "the sibling that respondents tended to have the most contact with and to feel close to was just as frequently a brother as it was a sister for both sexes" (p. 61).

Functions of the Sibling Relationship

The functions of the sibling relationship have not, as yet, received much attention within the scholarly journals. Bedford (1994) reported that siblings are an important source of emotional and instrumental support during the later years. Cicirelli (1977) stated that the sibling relationship can involve encouraging, building morale, counseling in time of crisis, serving as confidant, and supplying information. Evidence from Cicirelli's (1977) investigation indicated that sisters provide emotional support for their elderly brothers, and challenge and stimulation for their elderly sisters. Other researchers suggested that sibling relationships can function as a helping relationship in times of bad health, poor finances, or emotional stress (Troll, 1980). Siblings become particularly important for older individuals who are divorced, never married, or widowed (Bedford, 1994; Connidis & Davies, 1992).

Siblings also provide each other with a sense of continuity through their shared family histories and experiences (Cicirelli, 1993). The interwoven nature of their kin network supports a sense of belonging to a family that reaches into the past as well as the future (Bedford, 1994).

Sibling rivalry and competition are major functions of this family relationship in youth and adolescence (Sutton-Smith & Rosenberg, 1970). The rivalry between brothers, between sisters, or between brothers and sisters is said to prepare people for later competition and to build character. No evidence has been found to suggest that sibling rivalry continues throughout the life span (Allan, 1979; Ross & Milgram 1992). Conflict between older siblings, however, does occur. Usually the conflicts that arise stem from ongoing struggles (that is, they reflect a long-standing pattern) or are related to situational stresses (Bedford, 1994); one such stress siblings must cope with is the decline of their parents' health. In addition, they at times behave in a manner consistent with current notions of sibling rivalry.

The changing demographics across the life span have significant effects on the sibling relationship in a number of ways. First, as the average life span increases, parents are living longer; therefore, siblings must cope with their parent's death while they are reaching old age themselves. Second, as the childless rate for individuals increases, sibling relationships are being called on to serve the functions typically handled by adult children. Finally, as the divorce rate remains high, half- or step-brothers and half- or step-sisters become part of an individual's life and must be integrated into the family system.

Conclusion

The sibling relationship is the best example of a life-span developmental relationship. Evidence suggests that siblings stay in contact throughout their entire lives. In addition, this relationship remains close and can function to support the physical, social, and emotional needs of elderly people. Because of the changing dynamics of the elderly family, sibling relationships may take on greater significance for future generations.

OTHER FAMILY RELATIONSHIPS

The family relationships discussed so far are primary relationships. One should not forget, however, that other family relationships exist and that some people spend a great deal of time and involvement in other extended family relationships. One such relationship involves great-grandparents. Atchley (1980) estimated that 40% of the elderly people in U.S. society are great-grandparents. Research has yet to uncover the consequences of four-generation families. However, Atchley speculated that a relationship between young children and great-grandparents may be problematic because of the very active nature of young children and the advanced age of great-grandparents.

The major functions of the primary relationships, affect and aid, can also be served by aunts, uncles, cousins, nephews, nieces, and in-laws. Robins and Tomanec (1962) reported that individuals list aunts, uncles, and cousins as close family members. Troll (1982) stated that extended family members can have important roles during family ritual occasions. It is the nature of U.S. society to invite extended family members to weddings, funerals, and special holiday celebrations. A close relationship to extended family members may serve elderly people well, as these relationships provide additional sources of help. But at the same time, elderly people can become overwhelmed with the number of relationships and become involved in too many problems in an extended family.

SUMMARY

Three primary family relationships for elderly individuals are reviewed in this chapter. The elderly parent–adult child relationship is an active, close relationship. Elderly individuals see their children quite frequently, feel close to their children, yet wish to remain independent from their children for as long as possible. Life-span attachment theory and intergenerational solidarity theory help in the understanding of the life-span nature of this relationship. The elderly parent-adult child relationship serves two major relational functions, an affect function and a mutual-aid function.

An increasingly important relationship in the family is the grandparent–grandchild relationship. The complexity of the grandparent role is obvious when one considers the various styles with which grandparents interact with their grandchildren. Arguments persist in the literature as to whether or not grandparents have lost their emotional bond with the family. The evidence suggests that grandparents are quite close to their grandchildren and can function within the family in both an emotional and a supportive capacity.

Sibling relationships have not as yet received a great deal of research attention. Siblings appear to keep in contact throughout their life span with high affect and a willingness to help, especially when adult children are not available. The true life-span nature of the sibling relationship makes it an interesting as well as important relationship within the aging family.

Myths persist in American society concerning the alienation of the family from its elderly members. A great majority of scholarly evidence rejects these myths and shows family relationships to be quite viable throughout the life span.

■ REFERENCES

Adams, B. N. (1968). *Kinship in an urban setting.* Chicago: Markham.

Allan, G. (1979). Sibling solidarity. *Journal of Marriage and the Family, 39,* 177–184.

Alpert, J. L., & Richardson, M. S. (1980). Parenting. In L. W. Poon (Ed.), *Aging in the 1980s* (pp. 441–454). Washington, DC: American Psychological Association.

Apple, D. (1956). The social structure of grandparenthood. *American Anthropologist, 58,* 656–663.

Atchley, R. C. (1980). *The social forces in later life: An introduction to social gerontology* (3rd ed.). Belmont, CA: Wadsworth.

Atchley, R. C. (1983). *Aging: Continuity and change.* Belmont, CA: Wadsworth.

Atchley, R. C. (1991). Family, friends, and social support. In *Social forces and aging* (pp. 150–152). Belmont, CA: Wadsworth.

Atkinson, M. P., Kivett, V. R., & Campbell, R. T. (1986). Intergenerational solidarity: An examination of a theoretical model. *Journal of Gerontology, 41,* 408–416.

Bankoff, E. A. (1983). Aged parents and their widowed daughters: A support relationship. *Journal of Gerontology, 38,* 226–230.

Bart, P. (1970). Mother Portnoy's complaint. *Transaction, 8,* 69–74.

Beckman, C. J., & Houser, B. B. (1982). The consequences of childlessness on the social-psychological well-being of older women. *Journal of Gerontology, 37,* 243–250.

Bedford, V. H. (1994). Sibling relationships in middle and old age. In R. Blieszner & V. H. Bedford (Eds.), *Aging and the family: Theory and research* (pp. 201–222). Westport, CT: Praeger.

Bengtson, V. L. (1995). Afterword: Six controversies in current research on adult intergenerational relationships. In V. L. Bengtson, K. W. Schaie, & L. M. Burton (Eds.), *Adult intergenerational relations: Effects of societal change* (pp. 297–309). New York: Springer.

Bengtson, V.L., Olander, G. & Haddad, A. A. (1976). The generation gap and aging family members: Toward a conceptual model. In J. J. Gubrium (Ed.), *Time, roles and self in old age* (pp. 237–263). New York: Human Sciences.

Bengtson, V. L., & Robertson, J. F. (1985). *Grandparenthood*. Beverly Hills, CA: Sage.

Blieszner, R., & Mancini, J. (1987). Enduring ties: Older adults' parental role and responsibilities. *Family Relations, 36,* 176–180.

Bowlby, J. (1979). *The making and breaking of affectional bonds.* London, England: Tavistock.

Bowlby, J. (1980). *Attachment and loss: Vol.3. Loss, stress and depression.* New York: Basic Books.

Boyd, C. J. (1989). Mothers and daughters: A discussion of theory and research. *Journal of Marriage and the Family, 51,* 291–301.

Brody, E. (1985). Parent care as a normative family stress. *The Gerontologist, 25,* 19–29.

Bulcroft, K. A., & Bulcroft, R. A. (1991). The timing of divorce: Effects on parent-child relationships in later life. *Research on Aging, 13,* 226–243.

Cherlin, A., & Furstenberg, F. F. (1986). Grandparents and family crisis. *Generations, 10,* 26–28.

Cicirelli, V. G. (1972). The effect of sibling relationships on concept learning of young children taught by child teachers. *Child Development, 43,* 282–287.

Cicirelli, V. G. (1977). Relationship of siblings to the elderly person's feelings and concerns. *Journal of Gerontology, 32,* 317–322.

Cicirelli, V. G. (1979). *Social services for the elderly in relation to the kin network* (Report to the NRTA-AARP). Washington, DC: Andrus Foundation.

Cicirelli, V. G. (1980). Sibling relationships in adulthood: A life span perspective. In L. W. Poon (Ed.), *Aging in the 1980s* (pp. 455–462). Washington, DC: American Psychological Association.

Cicirelli, V. G. (1981). *Helping elderly parents: The role of adult children.* Boston: Auburn House.

Cicirelli, V. G. (1983a). Adult children and their elderly parents. In T. H. Brubaker (Ed.), *Family relationships in later life* (pp. 47–62). Beverly Hills, CA: Sage.

Cicirelli, V. G. (1983b). Adult children's attachment and helping behavior to elderly parents: A path model. *Journal of Marriage and the Family, 45,* 815–823.

Cicirelli, V. G. (1993). Sibling relationships in adulthood. *Marriage and the Family Review, 16,* 291–310.

Clark, M., & Andersen, B. (1967). *Culture and aging.* Springfield, IL: Thomas.

Cohler, B. J. (1983). Autonomy and interdependence in the family of adulthood: A psychological perspective. *The Gerontologist, 23,* 33–39.

Connidis, I. A., & Davies, L. (1992). Confidants and companions: Choices in later life. *Journal of Gerontology, 47,* S115–S122.

Creighton, L. L. (1991, December 16). The silent saviours. *U. S. News and World Report*, pp. 80–89.

Cumming, E., & Schneider, D. M. (1961). Sibling solidarity: A property of American kinship. *American Anthropologist, 63*, 498–507.

Decker, D. L. (1980). *Social gerontology: An introduction to the dynamics of aging*. Boston: Little, Brown.

Fisher, C. R. (1985). Elderly parents and the caregiving role: An asymmetrical transition. In W. A. Peterson & J. Quadango (Eds.), *Social bonds in later life: Aging and interdependence* (pp. 105–114). Beverly Hills, CA: Sage.

Giarrusso, R., Stallings, M., & Bengtson, V. L. (1995). The "intergenerational stake" hypothesis revisited: Parent-child differences in perceptions of relationships 20 years later. In V. L. Bengtson, K. W. Schaie, & L. M. Burton (Eds.), *Adult intergenerational relations: Effects of societal change* (pp. 227–263). New York: Springer.

Gold, D. T. (1989). Sibling relationships in old age: A typology. *International Journal of Aging and Human Development, 28*, 37–51.

Gold, D. T. (1990). Late-life sibling relationships: Does race affect typological distribution? *The Gerontologist, 30*, 741–748.

Hagestad, G. O. (1978, July). *Patterns of communication and influence between grandparents and grandchildren in a changing society*. Paper presented at the World Congress of Sociology, Uppsala, Sweden.

Harkins, E. B. (1978). Effects of empty nest transition on self-report of psychological and physical well being. *Journal of Marriage and the Family, 40*, 547–558.

Henderson, S. A. (1980). A development in social psychiatry: The systematic study of social bonds. *The Journal of Nervous and Mental Disease, 168*, 63–68.

Henwood, K. L. (1995). Adult parent-child relationships: A view from feminist and discursive social psychology. In J. F. Nussbaum & J. Coupland (Eds.), *Handbook of communication and aging research* (pp. 167–183). Mahwah, NJ: Lawrence Erlbaum Associates.

Henwood, K. L., & Coughlan, G. (1993). The construction of "closeness" in mother-daughter relationships across the lifespan. In N. Coupland & J. F. Nussbaum (Eds.), *Discourse and lifespan identity* (pp. 121–214). Newbury Park, CA: Sage.

Hodgson, L. G. (1995). Adult grandchildren and their grandparents: the enduring bond. In J. Hendricks (Ed.), *The ties of later life* (pp. 155–170). Amityville, NY: Baywood.

Holmes, E. R., & Holmes, L. D. (1995). *Other cultures, elder years* (2nd ed.). Thousand Oaks, CA: Sage.

Hooyman, N., & Kiyak, H. A. (1991). *Social gerontology: A multidisciplinary perspective* (2nd ed.). Boston: Allyn & Bacon.

Irish, D. P. (1964). Sibling interaction: A neglected aspect in family life research. *Social Forces, 42*, 269–288.

Kivett, V. R., & Atkinson, M. P. (1984). Filial expectations, association, and helping as a function of number of children among older rural-transitional parents. *Journal of Gerontology, 39*, 499–503.

Kivinck, H. (1981). Grandparenthood and the mental health of grandparents. *Aging and Society, 1*, 365–391.

Kornhaber, A. (1985). Grandparenthood and the "New Social Contract." In V. L. Bengtson & J. F. Robertson (Eds.), *Grandparenthood* (pp. 159–172). Beverly Hills, CA: Sage.

Langer, N. (1995). Grandparents and adult grandchildren: What do they do for one another? In J. Hendricks (Ed.), *The ties of later life* (pp. 171–179). Amityville, NY: Baywood.

Litwak, E. (1985). *Helping the elderly: The complementary roles of informal networks and formal systems.* New York: Guilford.

Logan, J. R., & Spitze, G. D. (1996). *Family ties: Enduring relations between parents and their grown children.* Philadelphia: Temple University Press.

Lowenthal, M. F., & Chiriboga, D. (1972). Transition to the empty nest: Crisis, challenge, or relief? *Archives of General Psychology, 26,* 814.

Mares, M. L., & Fitzpatrick, M. A. (1995). The aging couple. In J. F. Nussbaum & J. Coupland (Eds.), *The handbook of communication and aging research* (pp. 185–205). Mahwah, NJ: Lawrence Erlbaum Associates.

Matthews, S. H., & Spray, J. (1985). Adolescent's relationships with grandparents: An empirical contribution to conceptual clarification. *Journal of Gerontology, 40,* 621–626.

McGhee, J. C. (1985). The effects of siblings on the life satisfaction of the rural elderly. *Journal of Marriage and the Family, 47,* 85–91.

McKay, V. C. (1993). Making connections: Narrative as the expression of continuity between generations of grandparents and grandchildren. In N. Coupland & J. F. Nussbaum (Eds.), *Discourse and lifespan identity,* (pp. 173–185). Newbury Park, CA: Sage.

McKay, V. C., & Caverly, R. S. (1995). Relationships in later life: The nature of inter- and intragenerational ties among grandparents, grandchildren, and adult siblings. In J. F. Nussbaum & J. Coupland (Eds.), *The handbook of communication and aging research* (pp. 207–225). Mahwah, NJ: Lawrence Erlbaum Associates.

Mueller, D. (1980). Social networks: A promising direction for research on the relationship of the social environment and psychiatric disorder. *Social Science and Medicine, 14A,* 147–161.

Neugarten, B. L., & Weinstein, K. K. (1964). The changing American grandparent. *Journal of Marriage and the Family, 26,* 199–204.

Riley, M. W., & Foner, A. (1968). *Aging and society: Vol.1. An inventory of research findings.* New York: Russell Sage.

Roberto, K. A., & Stroes, J. (1995). Grandchildren and grandparents: Roles, influences, and relationships. In J. Hendricks (Ed.), *The ties of later life* (pp. 141–153). Amityville, NY: Baywood.

Robertson, J. F. (1994). Grandparenting in an era of rapid change. In R. Blieszner & V. H. Bedford (Eds.), *Aging and the family: Theory and research* (pp. 243–260). Westport, CT: Praeger.

Robins, L., & Tomanec, M. (1962). Closeness to blood relatives outside the immediate family. *Marriage and Family Living, 24,* 340–346.

Rollins, B. C., & Feldman, H. (1970). Marital satisfaction over the family life cycle: A reevaluation. *Journal of Marriage and the Family, 32,* 20–28.

Rosenberg, G. S., & Anspach, F. (1973). Sibling solidarity in the working class. *Journal of Marriage and the Family, 35,* 108–113.

Ross, H. G., & Milgram, J. I. (1992). Important variables in adult sibling relationships: A qualitative study. In M. E. Lamb & B. Sutton-Smith

(Eds.), *Sibling relationships: Their nature and significance across the lifespan* (pp. 225–249). Hillsdale, NJ: Lawrence Erlbaum Associates.

Rossi, A. S., & Rossi, P. H. (1990). *Of human bonding: Parent-child relations across the life course.* New York: Aldine de Guyter.

Scott, J. P. (1983). Siblings and other kin. In T. H. Brubaker (Ed.), *Family relationships in later life* (pp. 47–62). Beverly Hills, CA: Sage.

Shanas, E. (1973). Family-kin networks and aging in cross-cultural perspective. *Journal of Marriage and the Family, 35,* 505–511.

Shanas, E. (1979). The family as a social support system in old age. *The Gerontologist, 19,* 169–174.

Singh, B. R., & Williams, J. S. (1982). Childlessness and family satisfaction. *Research on Aging, 3,* 218–227.

Spitze, G., & Logan, J. R. (1992). Helping as a component of parent-adult child relations. *Research on Aging, 14,* 291–312.

Suitor, J. J., Pillemer, K., Keeton, S., & Robison, J. (1994). Aged parents and aging children: Determinants of relationship quality. In R. Blieszner & V. H. Bedford (Eds.), *Aging and the family: Theory and research* (pp. 223–242). Westport, CT: Praeger.

Sussman, M. B., & Burchinal, L. (1962a). Kin family network: Unheralded structure in current conceptualizations of family functioning. *Marriage and Family Living, 24,* 231–240.

Sussman, M. B., & Burchinal, L. (1962b). Parental aid to married children: Implications for family functioning. *Marriage and Family Living, 24,* 320–332.

Sutton-Smith, B., & Rosenberg, B. G. (1970). *The sibling.* New York: Holt, Rinehart & Winston.

Thomas, J. L. (1982). *The development of grandparents' relationships with their grandchildren: An exploratory study.* Unpublished doctoral dissertation, West Virginia University, Morgantown.

Thomas, J. L. (1986). Age and sex differences in perceptions of grandparenting. *Journal of Gerontology, 41,* 417–423.

Thomas, J. L. (1995). Gender and perceptions of grandparenthood. In J. Hendricks (Ed.), *The ties of later life* (pp. 181–193). Amityville, NY: Baywood.

Troll, L. E. (1971). The family of later life: A decade review. *Journal of Marriage and the Family, 33,* 263–290.

Troll, L. E. (1980). Grandparenting. In L. W. Poon. (Ed.), *Aging in the 1980s* (pp. 475–481). Washington, DC: American Psychological Association.

Troll, L. E. (1982). *Continuations: Adult development and aging.* Monterey, CA: Brooks/Cole.

Troll, L. E. (1983). Grandparents: The family watchdogs. In T. H. Brubaker (Ed.), *Family relationships in later life* (pp. 63–76). Beverly Hills, CA: Sage.

Troll, L. E. (1986). Parents and children in later life. *Generations, 10,* 23–25.

Troll, L., Miller, S. J., & Atchley, C. (1979). *Families in later life.* Belmont, CA: Wadsworth.

Trygstad, D. W., & Sanders, G. F. (1995). The significance of stepgrandparents. In J. Hendricks (Ed.), *The ties of later life* (pp. 209–224). Amityville, NY: Baywood.

U.S. Census Bureau. (1998). *Household and family characteristics* (pp. 20–515). [On-line] Available: *www.census.gov*

Ward, R. A. (1996). Which is the dependent generation? In J. R. Logan & G. D. Spitze (Eds.), *Family ties: Enduring relations between parents and their grown children* (pp. 28–55). Philadelphia: Temple University Press.

Wood, V., & Robertson, J. (1976). The significance of grandparenthood. In J. Gubrium (Ed.), *Time, roles, and self in old-age* (pp. 278–304). New York: Human Sciences.

CHAPTER 10

Friendship and Aging

O ne of the greatest compliments any individual can pay another individual in Western society is to call that person a friend. Most people have friends and they seem to be able to distinguish friends from nonfriends; yet, for the social scientist, the concept of "friend" has not been easy to explain or to research. This chapter explores friendship and aging. In order to accomplish this task, the friend relationship is first defined and friendship is distinguished from kinship. Next, the functions of friendship for elderly people are explored. Finally, current research reflecting the nature of friendship in the older population is described.

THE FRIEND RELATIONSHIP

The discipline of communication has generally done a very poor job conceptualizing and researching the friend relationship. With the exception of some notable work done by William Rawlins, one must look primarily to the field of sociology for a general understanding of friendship. European sociologists have actively studied friendship and have attempted to distinguish the friend relationship from family relationships. In this section, we rely on the work of Allan (1979) for a definition of the friend relationship in Western culture.

American society defines the family very clearly. Family members are those individuals who have the same "blood" or who are linked by marriage. In the previous three chapters, several of the more intimate family relationships are discussed. The friend relationship is not so easy to categorize. "The term friend is only applied to people who have a personal relationship that is qualitatively of a particular sort. It is the active relationship itself that is the most important factor in deciding whether someone can or cannot be labeled a friend" (Allan, 1979, p. 34).

If a person were asked to gather 15 of his or her friends, a great deal would be known about the quality of the relationships that the person has with those 15 individuals. If, on the other hand, the person were asked to gather 15 family members, nothing would be known about the quality of the relationship that he or she has with those individuals. The term friend is a relational term in that it connotes a qualitative meaning about the relationship. The term itself gives meaning to the relationship.

The study of friendship would be much simpler if family members could not be friends. However, if one asks a small child who his or her "best friend" is, more than likely the answer is his or her mother. Likewise, if a married individual is asked to name his or her best friend, a common response would be to name that person's spouse as best friend. Thus, in some instances family members are considered friends. However, one must keep in mind that not all family members are friends.

Allan (1979) distinguished a friend relationship from a family relationship in three ways. First, "friendship is a personal relationship in that it is seen as involving individuals as individuals and not as members of groups or collectivities" (Allan, 1979, p. 38). Friendship, in this sense, lacks the formality of role positions. A friend who plays a certain formal role in an organization cannot be replaced by another individual who plays a similar role. Thus, if a person has a friend who happens to be an accountant and that friend is lost, another accountant does not necessarily have to replace that individual as the person's friend. The lack of a formal role position permits individuals to "be themselves." Within a friendship one can be genuine and get to know the "real self" of the other individual.

A second characteristic of a friend is the voluntary nature of the relationship. Friendship is based on the free choices and selections of each individual in the relationship. Allan (1979) stated that friends are achieved rather than ascribed. Because of the voluntary nature of friendship, it is assumed that the relationship is enjoyable; a friend is someone who is sought out for enjoyment. The relationship is enjoyed for its own sake beyond the activities of the relationship. Many people have friends with whom they participate in certain role activities. For instance, they sing together in a choir or play together in some sport. They are able to separate the enjoyment derived from the activity from the enjoyment derived from the friend relationship. A final indication of the voluntary nature of friendship is the role chance plays in the friendship. People consider themselves to have control over choosing their friends. Therefore, friend relationships are not "chance" relationships. "You meet people by chance, live near them by chance, even work with them by chance, but you do not form a friendship by chance" (Allan, 1979, p. 43).

A third important characteristic of friendship is the nonexploitive nature of friendship. Friendships are formed for their own sake, not for some ulterior motive. Friends can certainly help one another or rely on each other in times of need, but one does not form a friendship just to receive help. Two ideas that are important to the nonexploitative nature of friendship are reciprocity and symmetry. If one individual seeks aid, it is inevitable that the individual receiving aid will want to reciprocate and help his or her friend in return when the opportunity arises. Through reciprocity, the symmetry of the relationship is maintained. Unlike many family relationships, status distinctions do not exist in friendships.

A major conceptual complexity when attempting to understand the entire domain of friendship is determining how individuals classify and distinguish "best friend" from "just a friend" or from "acquaintances." The vast majority of social scientific research considers only best friends. "If a relationship is not characterized by strong emotional attachment, feelings of empathy, mutual sympathy and understanding, it is immediately classified as something other than a full friendship and removed from consideration" (Allan, 1979, p. 36). Very little is known about friendships that are not considered to be best friend relationships. All that researchers can state is that not all friends are best friends and that these less-intimate relationships may function in ways quite different from our best-friend relationships.

Researchers do know something about the communication that characterizes friend relationships. Rawlins (1983a, 1983b, 1992, 1995) identified three sets of *dialectics* that are likely to occur in friendships and that appear to be particularly salient in older adult friendships. A *dialectic* refers to two factors that are contradictory but that are both essential to the development of a close relationship. Rawlins believed that friendships are achieved through ongoing communication that must be used to manage the tension between the two ends of these dialectical poles.

The first dialectic he described is expressiveness versus protectiveness. In friendships, people need to be open and self-disclosing, but sometimes this openness and disclosure can hurt the friend. This is where protectiveness becomes important. People also have a need to protect their friends—to not hurt them. For example, if something about a friend bothers an individual, he or she, may want to mention it to the friend. But doing so may hurt the friend. There is, therefore, a dialectic or contradiction between expressiveness and protectiveness in friendships.

The second dialectic Rawlins labelled the dialectic of conjunctive freedoms. This describes the balance people try to achieve in their friendships between the freedom to be independent and the freedom to be dependent. While people are able to depend on their friends, they are also able to behave independently. People must balance the level of interdependence that they develop in their friendships.

The third dialectic Rawlins labelled the dialectic of judgment and acceptance. People expect their friends to have unconditional love for them; yet they also want them to tell them when they are making fools of themselves. Therefore, a tension exists between friends not judging people for their actions and letting them know when they should modify their behavior in order to attain their social goals.

LATER-LIFE FRIENDSHIPS

Friendship is a relationship that can also be described as a true life-span phenomenon. Some people, those who are very lucky, have friends for 60, 70, or even 80 years. These lifelong friends are their closest confidants and understand them as no others can. To grasp the complexity of friendship in old age, one must first realize that the length of a person's life can affect the quality of friendships. Because the vast majority of research attempting to describe friendships has concentrated on children and adolescents, rarely has the longevity of the friend relationship been considered to be a significant factor in describing friendship. For elderly people, however, a relationship history has developed and this history is a key ingredient for understanding the relationship. The history of the relationship itself will more than likely be the best explanation of the friendship.

Unique Factors in Later-Life Friendships

While some elements of friendship remain the same across the life span, such as the lack of formal roles and the voluntary and nonexploitive nature of the relationship, some characteristics change as people age. Nussbaum (1994) and Patterson, Bettini, and Nussbaum (1993) found that older adults report many more levels of closeness in their friendships than do younger adults. Younger adults make clearer distinctions between best friends and all other friends, while older adults differentiate between best friends with several levels of closeness. In this relational stratification, then, older individuals place adult friendships along a continuum of intimacy, with several different levels of best friends. In addition, with old age, consistent and frequent communicative contact may not be as important for maintaining the level of closeness in the relationship as it is for younger adults. Older adults report remaining extremely close to long-term friends even when they have not seen each other for years.

Matthews (1986a) noted three other factors that make friendship in later life unique: (a) the physical reality of illness and death; (b) the long shared histories of individuals, and, (c) the importance of having friends one's own age. The first factor that Matthews (1986b) described as unique in later-life friendship is death and disease. As individuals age, the likelihood of one friend witnessing the death of the other friend increases. One sad fact of aging is the possibility of living beyond many of one's friendships. The death of a friend is a devastating event. The death of the friend obviously changes the immediate relationship, but, not so obviously, it affects all the relationships within the friendship network. Death may influence the closeness of other relationships, or it can tear some friendships apart. The inevitability of death can also change the way an individual interacts with a friend. Because the probability of death increases as one ages, there is a greater likelihood that each interaction may be the last. This inevitability can produce disengaging behavior that helps an individual cope prior to the actual death of his or her friend. Disease is also a factor that may affect lifelong friendships. The physical or mental deterioration of one friend can limit the ability of the friendship to remain active. Matthews (1986a) stated that these physical and mental changes in friends can affect the content of the relationship. Although each partner may still consider the other a friend, they are no longer able to act as friends. A friend whose hearing has deteriorated cannot communicate the way he or she did a decade earlier. The disease can affect the equalness of the relationship and drastically change it. Because of the inherent nature of equality in friendships, it can become uncomfortable for one member of the friendship to have to rely on the other member and feel that he or she cannot reciprocate in kind (Rawlins, 1995).

The second major factor Matthews (1986a) described affecting friendship in later life is the existence of extended populated biographies. As individuals age, they carry a wealth of relationship experiences with them. These relational experiences act as populated biographies. It is important to note that the past relationships of an individual affect the present relationships of the individual. The past relationships can make meeting new people easy if there is some common historical connection between the individual and the new acquaintances. For example, adaptation to a new residence in later life can be made easier if the older individual can find a historical connection through another friend between himself or herself and the individuals who live in the new neighborhood or retirement village. In addition, long friendships can be enhanced by the lifelong duration of the relationship. The common experiences shared throughout a lifetime can strengthen the quality of the friendship.

A third factor that distinguishes friendship in later life from friendship in one's younger years is that elderly people inhabit a different position in the age structure of society than do other individuals. The majority of individuals surrounding elderly people are from younger cohorts. Elderly people, then, in an effort to maintain their friendship network, are often forced to interact with younger individuals. Social scientists point to age similarity as a major factor influencing friendships, although the range of ages that is considered to define age peers becomes larger with age. Thus, elderly people are in a culturally unnatural position. Matthews (1986a) stated that elderly individuals often do not consider younger individuals to be friends. The "friend" label is not easily given to a relationship involving a younger individual and an elderly individual.

Friendship Styles in Later Life

Matthews (1983a, 1983b, 1986a, 1986b) studied friendship across the life span and described several styles of friendship. She defined a friendship style as "the expectations about friendship built up through the life course that are brought to old age" (Matthews, 1986a, p. 257). Three distinct styles of friendship and a fourth that is a combination of two styles were described at some length by Matthews (1986b). A short description of these styles can help understanding friendship in the elderly population.

Following extensive interviews with over 60 elderly individuals, Matthews (1986a, 1986b) identified the first friendship style as the *Independents*. These elderly individuals did not identify specific individuals as friends but alluded to circumstances when friendship was important. Friendship is an absolute commitment for people who are independents. Often individuals are not considered friends once they have lost contact. Friendship is very special and people who are independents only have room for one or two friends at a time. "In old age the independents continued to be affected primarily by the circumstances that surround them" (Matthews, 1986b, pp. 128–129). The environment provides people who are independents with "friendly interactions," but those interactions come and go.

The second style of friendship that emerged from the interviews was the *Discerning* style. "Informants who were classified as discerning were least affected by the current circumstances of their lives with respect to whom their friends were but the most vulnerable to their friends no longer being available" (Matthews, 1986b, p. 133). If friends do not remain in contact, the discerning people will become very lonely. New friendships are not easy for discerning-style adults to develop. When friends are lost, discerning people become lonely and often remain friendless for the remainder of their lives.

A third friendship style was labeled *Discerning to Independent*. These individuals had several lifelong friends with whom, during the course of their lives, they had lost contact. These lost friendships remain a part of their lives, but the individuals now let circumstances provide friendly interactions. The individual has moved from a discerning style of close mutually dependent relationships to an independent style of circumstantial interaction.

The fourth friendship style described by Matthews (1986a, 1986b) is the *Acquisitive* style. Acquisitive individuals have friendships from their past and are open to new friendships. Often new environments provide opportunities for meeting new individuals. Acquisitive individuals maintain relationships with their old friends as well as take advantage of opportunities to make new friends.

FUNCTIONS OF FRIENDSHIP FOR OLDER PEOPLE

A significant amount of the social scientific research that concentrates on friendship and aging has attempted to outline the functions of elderly friendships. Two functions of friendship in the elderly population that have emerged are psychosocial well-being and informal support. In addition, a third function, successful adaptation to aging, is beginning to emerge.

Psychosocial Well-Being

A clear relationship exists between friendship and psychosocial well-being in the elderly population (Adams, 1967, 1986; Arling, 1976; Atchley, 1972; Larson, 1978; Lowenthal & Haven, 1968; Nussbaum, 1985; Roberto & Scott, 1986; Rosnow, 1976; Wood & Robertson, 1978). This positive relationship is stronger than the relationship between family activity and psychosocial well-being. In fact, the strongest predictor of positive psychosocial well-being in older people is having at least one confidant (Connidis & Davies, 1990, 1992; Lowenthal & Haven, 1968; Rawlins, 1995). Confidants are close friends who share in intimate communication and who care about and have a high level of involvement with each other (Rawlins, 1992). Although in chapter 9 the family is shown to function to meet the affective needs of the elderly, this affective function of family relationships has not been shown to be positively associated with well-being in older people. Friendships, on the other hand, do seem to function in a way that increases the psychosocial well-being of older people.

The social scientific literature offers four explanations for the positive relationship between friendship and the psychosocial well-being of elderly people (Adams, 1986). The first explanation centers around the concept of *homophily* (Hess, 1972; Lazarsfeld & Melton, 1959; Matthews, 1986b; Roscow, 1967). Two individuals are *homophilous* if they are the same age, have the same status, have the same ideas and habits, and live near one another. Friends tend to be homophilous and therefore have much in common. With the exception of one's spouse, who is both a family member and a friend, most of an individual's family members are not the same age, often do not share similar ideas and beliefs, and can live quite far away. The homophily shared by friends is rewarding and enhances the well-being of elderly individuals.

A second explanation for the positive relationship between friendship and the psychosocial well-being of elderly people is the voluntary nature of the relationship. Blau (1981) and Roberto and Scott (1986) stressed the importance of the mutual choice in the friendship relationship. Both partners freely choose to be friends, and this leads to equity in the relationship. Children, siblings, grandparents, and most other family relationships are neither voluntary nor equitable. The freedom associated with friendship and the inherent equity in the relationship support the well-being of elderly people.

A third explanation for the positive relationship between friendship and the psychosocial well-being of elderly people centers on the notion that "friendships involve the older person in the larger society more than family relationships do" (Adams, 1986, p. 42). Montgomery (1972), Sherman (1975), Arling (1976), Bell (1983), Nussbaum (1981), and Rawlins (1995) found that friendships tend to increase participation in more general social activities. Friends are likely to go shopping, to take a walk, to go to a ball game, or just to visit one another. These activities integrate the elderly individual into society. Thus, "the friendship relationship functions for the elderly individual as a mechanism to maintain social activity" (Nussbaum, 1983, p. 239).

A fourth explanation of the positive relationship between friendship and the psychosocial well-being of the elderly, which has pure communicative significance, was discussed by Nussbaum (1983). Citing previous work by Jourard (1971) and Wheeless (1978), Nussbaum (1983) speculated that friendship was an important arena for elderly self-disclosive behavior. Cicirelli (1983) and others reported that elderly people often do not feel comfortable discussing intimate matters with their children. Friendship gives elderly people this opportunity. Because self-disclosure has been linked to mental well-being (Jourard, 1971), friendships can function to permit self-disclosures by elderly people and, thus, increase psychosocial well-being. In addition, older individuals' psychosocial well-being is affected by the enjoyment they derive from socializing and talking to their friends (Rawlins, 1992). Rawlins (1995) believed that enjoyable interactions with friends provide an important tool for combating depression in elderly people and, therefore, for improving their sense of well-being.

Informal Social Support

The second major function of friendship for elderly individuals is the informal support generated within the friendship relationship. In chapter 9, the major helping function of some family relationships was discussed. Adult children provide an enormous amount of aid to their elderly parents. The aid, however, is tempered by an obligation to give the aid. Adult children feel an obligation to help because of their role in the family. This obligation can lead to bad feelings for both the provider and the elderly individual receiving the aid.

A growing body of literature indicates that elderly friends provide support and give aid to one another (Adams, 1986; Cantor, 1979; Hochschild, 1973; Litwak, 1985; Roscow, 1967; Shanas, 1962). Often the voluntary nature of the friend relationship makes helping much easier and guilt-free. This is especially true in equitable friendships with reciprocal giving, in which friends both give and receive aid.

Adams (1986) pointed to several norms of friendship support that help to maintain a healthy friendship. For instance, in certain circumstances it is important for the caregiver to share a similar lifestyle with the individual receiving care. A friend is more likely to share a similar lifestyle than is an adult child. This is especially true for friendships involving widows and widowers. Another norm for friends providing care is the consideration of the level of inconvenience for the caregiver. Friends will be asked to help only when it will cause them a minor inconvenience. Taking someone shopping or to a doctor's appointment are examples of how friends can provide informal support.

The key to friendship functioning as informal support rests on the voluntary nature of the relationship. One enters into a friendship willingly and offers assistance simply because one

wants to help. Family relationships have an emotional obligation that is not voluntary and therefore can lead to bad feelings.
As long as the norms of friendship helping are followed, the
friendship can function as a key informal support system.

Successful Adaptation to Aging

The previous two functions of friendship for older people are
related to successful adaptation to aging. Individuals who report more positive levels of well-being are evaluated as adapting to aging more successfully. Individuals who have sufficient
instrumental (particularly from family) and emotional (particularly from friends) social support are able to more successfully
adapt to aging and to any related limitations. Rawlins (1995)
suggested that these are not the only important functions that
friends serve in successful adaptation to aging. Long-term
friends are able to provide judgments regarding one's ability to
maintain certain activities in ways that are less detrimental than
when family members make the same judgments. Because of
the long-term nature of these life-long friendships, the friends
are likely to also be age peers who are struggling with the same
concerns. This provides older individuals with a "sounding
board" for making decisions about limiting activity or seeking
assistance without also limiting control over one's own life.
Long-term friendships can also provide a sense of continuity,
even in the face of major life changes (e.g., the death of a spouse
or relocating). Because these life-long friends' lives are interwoven, they are better able to help maintain one another's sense of
coherence about their lives.

GENDER DIFFERENCES IN ELDERLY PEOPLE'S FRIENDSHIPS

One aspect of elderly people's friendships that has received a
fair amount of research attention is the role of gender differences in elderly friendships. "Both men and women are subject
to and experience the overall normative definitions of friendships among adults in our society, but the specification of norms
differs for man and woman" (Stein, 1986, p. 262). Pleck (1975),
Maccoby and Jacklin (1974), and Stein (1986) reported not only
differences in how men and women are integrated into support
groups, but also differences regarding intimacy, sociability, af-

filiation, self-disclosure behavior, and sympathy between the friendships of men and the friendships of women.

Women tend to be better off socially in old age than men because women are more likely to have stable, intimate, and supportive friendships (Adams, 1986; Blieszner & Adams, 1992; Hess, 1979). Although the evidence at times appears to be contradictory, a majority of studies suggest that elderly men report not only fewer friendships in old age than women but friendships that are less intimate and less supportive (Adams, 1986; Blieszner & Adams, 1992; Keith, Hill, Goudy, & Powers, 1984; Stein, 1986). In fact, Booth (1972) reported that men who share intimacies or thoughts central to themselves are looked down on in U.S. society.

Lewis (1978), Pleck (1975), and Stein (1986) identified several barriers to friendships between men in U.S. society, particularly for the current cohort of elderly men. First, men are socialized to be competitive. This lessens the likelihood of an elderly man sharing his weaknesses and vulnerabilities with other individuals. Second, men lack the skills to sustain intimate friendships. Men are not taught competent friendship skills and have few role models to imitate. Third, men do not show affection toward other men in U.S. society. To be labeled an affectionate man is a stigma. Most elderly men would rather remain lonely than be ridiculed as being too close to a friend. Finally, men in this society have a need to always be in control of the relationship. This need for dominance can prohibit them from forming friendships with certain other dominant individuals. As a result, men are more likely to have work- and activity-related friendships that may be difficult to maintain after retirement (Rawlins, 1995). In addition, men are more likely to name their wives as their best friends and the people with whom they confide the most (Connidis & Davies, 1990). These factors limit the network of close intimate relationships for men.

A problem that women may face in later life is the effect of normative restrictions on cross-sex friendships (Adams, 1985, 1986). Elderly women do not have as many male friends as elderly men have female friends. The obvious reason for the discrepancy is the paucity of available elderly men. Recall that women live longer than men in the United States. Because there are more women than men, the opportunity for cross-sex friendships for elderly men is greater. Booth and Hess (1974) and Usui (1984) offered two additional reasons for elderly men enjoying more cross-sex interactions. First, men have always worked in environments that provide for cross-sex interactions.

Men, therefore, may be more comfortable in a cross-sex friendship. With more women entering the workforce, this factor may become less important as the elderly cohort includes more women who have worked outside the home. Second, "societal norms favor the development of cross-sex friendships among men to a greater extent than women" (Usui, 1984, p. 354). American society frowns upon women who know too many men. This is just as true for adolescent people as it is for elderly people. Rawlins (1982) described many of the difficulties involved in building cross-sex friendships. These difficulties can become more of a burden as people age.

HOMOSEXUALITY AND ELDERLY PEOPLE'S FRIENDSHIPS

The sexual orientation of the individuals involved in the friendship can influence who becomes friends. Although at times it does not appear to be true, homosexuality is an accepted lifestyle for millions of people in U.S. society. Yet, older people are rarely portrayed as gay men and lesbians; the media, when doing stories on homosexuality, constantly interview and photograph young gay men and lesbians. However, elderly gay men and lesbians do exist and maintain friendships throughout their lives.

What effect does sexual orientation have on the initiation, maintenance, and functions of elderly friendships? The elderly age cohort does not view homosexuality as favorably as do younger age cohorts. This negative attitude toward homosexuality can force the older gay man or lesbian to remain "in the closet" and to erect barriers to hide his or her sexual orientation. Some research suggested that gay men and lesbians achieve companionship, commitment, intimacy, ego-enhancement, and fulfillment from their friendships just as heterosexual men and women do. "In sum, the characteristics and functions of long-term relationships show many similarities between homosexuals and heterosexuals and tend to transcend the issue of sexual preference" (Lipman, 1986, p. 54).

FRIENDSHIP IN THE NURSING HOME

Circumstances force a significant minority of elderly individuals to maintain and acquire friendships in nonnormative ways. Approximately 1.5 million elderly individuals reside in nursing homes at any one time in the United States. It is assumed that the individuals placed in these homes live miserable lives. "Institutional rules, routines, and standardized nurse–patient re-relationships are presumed to strip residents of self-esteem (Lieberman, 1969; Wack & Rodin, 1978) so that they are unable to form meaningful social ties with those around them" (Restinas & Garrity, 1985, p. 376). The common notion of a nursing-home resident is an elderly individual who sits motionless waiting for visitors from the outside world.

Nursing homes do present formidable barriers to friendship formation. Residents often suffer from physical or mental limitations that prohibit normal interaction. In addition, the nursing-home environment, which strips the residents of their unique individuality and prohibits freedom of movement, creates barriers that make acquiring friends difficult. Nevertheless, Nussbaum, Robinson, and Grew (1985), Nussbaum, Holladay, Robinson, and Ragan (1986), and Restinas and Garrity (1985) viewed the nursing home as a unique environment where friendships are found and maintained.

The research evidence suggested that the nursing home can be rich with communicative interactions. Restinas and Garrity (1985) reported that residents in nursing homes make friends. The key determinants of friendship in nursing homes are lucidity, ability to speak, and ability to see. It appears that, as long as the resident has the physical and mental capacity to communicate, he or she will form friendships regardless of the barriers constructed in the nursing home.

Nussbaum (Nussbaum, 1990, 1991; Nussbaum & Robinson, 1990) found a consistent, critical link between life satisfaction and friendship for institutionalized elderly people. Although the link between friendship and life satisfaction is important for elderly people living in the community and in retirement settings, this link is particularly crucial for elderly people living in nursing homes. Older individuals who have the greatest physical and cognitive limitations, those most likely to reside in nursing homes, report a higher satisfaction with life when they also report having close friends with whom they remain in contact.

SUMMARY

The term friend gives qualitative meaning to a relationship. Friendship can be distinguished from a family relationship in several ways. First, friends involve individuals as individuals and not as members of certain groups who fulfill specific roles. Second, friendships are voluntary in nature. Third, friendships are nonexploitive.

Friendships, much like sibling relationships, can be lifelong relationships. One cannot understand friendship in older people without first grasping the history of the relationship. The friend relationship for elderly people is impacted by such factors as the recognition of more levels of intimacy within the "best friend" relationship, the ability to maintain closeness without frequent contact, death and disease, extended population biographies, and various age structures.

One way to understand the complexity of friendship in old age is to distinguish certain friendship styles used by individuals. Four styles of friendships have been discussed in the literature: the independents, the discerning, the independents to discerning, and the acquisitives.

A positive relationship exists between friendships and the psychosocial well-being of elderly people. In addition, in certain circumstances friendships function as informal support networks for the elderly. These functions also assist the individual in successfully adapting to the aging process.

Gender differences exist in elderly people's friendships. Although research is contradictory as to which gender has more friendships, it is quite clear that women have more intimate friendships in old age. Cross-sex friendships are problematic for women in U.S. society. In addition, elderly gay men and lesbians are socially active, at least within their circle, and friendships function in the same ways for gay men and lesbians as they do for heterosexual men and women.

Elderly people's friendships also exist within environments normally not associated with mainstream America. Nursing homes have been investigated and friendships grow within these institutions as well.

■ REFERENCES

Adams, B. (1967). Interaction theory and social network. *Sociometry, 30*, 69–78.

Adams, R. G. (1985). People would talk: Normative barriers to cross-sex friendships for elderly women. *The Gerontologist, 25*, 605–611.

Adams, R. G. (1986). A look at friendship and aging. *Generations, 10*, 40–43.

Allan, O. A. (1979). *A sociology of friendship and kinship*. London: Allen & Unwin.

Arling, G. (1976). The elderly widow and her family, neighbors, and friends. *Journal of Marriage and the Family, 38,* 757–768.

Atchley, R. (1972). *The social forms in later life.* Belmont, CA: Wadsworth.

Bell, R. R. (1983). *Marriage and family interaction* (6th ed.). Homewood, IL: Dorsey Press.

Blau, Z. S. (1981). *Aging in a changing society* (2nd ed.). New York: Franklin Watts.

Blieszner, R., & Adams, R. G. (1992). *Adult friendship.* Newbury Park, CA: Sage.

Booth, A. (1972). Sex and social participation. *American Sociological Review, 37,* 183–192.

Booth, A. & Hess, E. (1974). Cross-sex friendship. *Journal of Marriage and the Family, 36,* 38–47.

Cantor, M. H. (1979). Neighbors and friends. *Research on Aging, 1,* 434–463.

Cicirelli, V. G. (1983). Adult children and their elderly parents. In T. H. Brubaker (Ed.), *Family relationships in later life* (pp. 31–46). Beverly Hills: Sage.

Connidis, I. A., & Davies, L. (1990). Confidantes and companions in later life: The place of family and friends. *Journal of Gerontology, 45,* S141–S149.

Connidis, I. A., & Davies, L. (1992). Confidants and companions: Choices in later life. *Journal of Gerontology, 47,* S115–S122.

Hess, B. B. (1972). Friendship. In M. Riley (Ed.), *Aging and society: Vol. 3. A sociology of age stratification* (pp. 357–393). New York: Russell Sage.

Hess, B. B. (1979). Sex roles, friendship and the life course. *Research on Aging, 1,* 494–515.

Hochschild, A. R. (1973). *The unexpected community.* Englewood Cliffs. NJ: Prentice–Hall.

Jourard, S. M. (1971). *Self disclosure: The experimental investigation of the transparent self.* New York: Wiley.

Keith, P. M., Hill, K., Goudy, W. J., & Powers, E. A. (1984). Confidants and well-being: A note on male friendships in old age. *The Gerontologist, 24,* 318–320.

Larson, R. (1978). Thirty years of research on the subjective well-being of older Americans. *Journal of Gerontology, 33,* 109–125.

Lazarsfeld, P., & Melton, R. (1959). Friendship as social process. In M. Berger, T. Abel, & C. Page (Eds.), *Freedom and control in modern society* (pp. 18–66). Princeton, NJ: Van Nostrand.

Lewis, R. A. (1978). Emotional intimacy among men. *Journal of Social Issues, 34,* 108–121.

Lieberman, M. A. (1969). Institutionalization of the aged: Effects on behavior. *Journal of Gerontology, 24,* 330–340.

Lipman, A. (1986). Homosexual relationships. *Generations, 10,* 51–54.

Litwak, E. (1985). *Helping the elderly.* New York: Guilford.

Lowenthal, M. F., & Haven, C. (1968). Interaction and adaptation: Intimacy as a critical variable. In B. L. Neugarten (Ed.), *Middle age and aging* (pp. 390–400). Chicago: University of Chicago Press.

Maccoby, E. E., & Jacklin, C. N. (1974). *The psychology of sex differences.* Stanford, CA: Stanford University Press.

Matthews, S. H. (1983a). Analyzing topical oral biographies of old people: The case of friendship. *Research on Aging, 5,* 569–589.

Matthews, S. H. (1983b). Definitions of friendships and consequences in old age. *Aging and Society, 3,* 141–155.

Matthews, S. H. (1986a). Friendships in old age: Biography and circumstance. In V. W. Marshall (Ed.), *Later life: The social psychology of aging* (pp. 233–270). Beverly Hill, CA: Sage.

Matthews, S. H. (1986b). *Friendships through the life course: Oral biographies in old age.* Beverly Hills, CA: Sage.

Montgomery, J. E. (1972, January). The housing patterns of older families. *The Family Coordinator, 21,* (pp. 37–46).

Nussbaum, J. F. (1981). *Interactional patterns of elderly individuals: Implications for successful adaptation to aging.* Unpublished doctoral dissertation, Purdue University, West Lafayette, IN.

Nussbaum, J. F. (1983). Relational closeness of elderly: Implications for life satisfaction. *Western Journal of Speech Communication, 47,* 229–243.

Nussbaum, J. F. (1985). Successful aging: A communication model. *Communication Quarterly, 33,* 262–269.

Nussbaum, J. F. (1990). Communication within the nursing home: Survivability as a function of resident-staff affinity. In H. Giles, N. Coupland, & J. M. Wiemann (Eds.), *Communication, health and the elderly* (pp. 155–171). Manchester, England: Manchester University Press.

Nussbaum, J. F. (1991). Communication, language and the institutionalised elderly. *Ageing and Society, 11,* 149–166.

Nussbaum, J. F. (1994). Friendship in older adulthood. In M. L. Hummert, J. M. Wiemann, & J. F. Nussbaum (Eds.), *Interpersonal communication in older adulthood: Interdisciplinary theory and research* (pp. 209–225). Thousand Oaks, CA: Sage.

Nussbaum, J. F., Holladay, S., Robinson, J. D., & Ragan, S. (1986, Nov.). *The communication world of the nursing home resident: A preliminary analysis of in-depth interviews concentrating upon friendship.* Paper presented at the annual convention of the Speech Communication Association, Denver, CO.

Nussbaum, J. F., & Robinson, J. D. (1990). Communication within the nursing home. In H. D. O'Hair & G. Kreps (Eds.), *Applied communication theory and research* (pp. 353–369). Hillsdale, NJ: Lawrence Erlbaum Associates.

Nussbaum, J. F., Robinson, J. D., & Grew, D. J. (1985). Communicative behavior of the long-term health care employee: Implications for the elderly resident. *Communication Research Reports, 2,* 16–22.

Patterson, B. R., Bettini, L., & Nussbaum, J. F. (1993). The meaning of friendship across the lifespan: Two studies. *Communication Quarterly, 41,* 145–160.

Pleck, J. H. (1975). Man to man: Is brotherhood possible? In N. Glazer-Malbin (Ed.), *Old family/new family* (pp. 229–244). New York: Van Nostrand.

Rawlins, W. K. (1982). Cross-sex friendship and the communicative management of sex-role expectations. *Communication Quarterly, 30,* 353–352.

Rawlins, W. K. (1983a). Negotiating close friendship: The dialectic of conjunctive freedoms. *Human Communication Research, 9,* 255–266.

Rawlins, W. K. (1983b). Openness as problematic in ongoing friendships: Two conversational dilemmas. *Communication Monographs, 50,* 1–13.

Rawlins, W., K. (1992). *Friendship matters: Communication, dialectics, and the life course*. New York: Aldine de Gruyter.

Rawlins, W. K. (1995). Friendships in later life. In J. F. Nussbaum & J. Coupland (Eds.), *Handbook of communication and aging research* (pp. 227–257). Mahwah, NJ: Lawrence Erlbaum Associates.

Restinas, J., & Garrity, P. (1985). Nursing home friendships. *The Gerontologist, 25*, 376–381.

Roberto, K. A., & Scott, I. P. (1986). Equity consideration in the friendships of older adults. *Journal of Gerontology, 41*, 241–247.

Rosnow, I. (1967). *Social integration of the aged*. New York: The Free Press.

Rosnow, I. (1976). Status and role change through the life span. In R. Binstock & E. Shanas (Eds.), *Handbook of aging and the social sciences*. New York: Van Nostrand Reinhold.

Shanas, E. (1962). *The health of older people: A social survey*. Cambridge, MA: Harvard University Press.

Sherman, S. (1975). Patterns of contacts for residents of age segregated and age integrated housing. *Journal of Gerontology, 30*, 103–107.

Stein, P. J. (1986). Men and their friendships. In R. Lavis & R. Salt (Eds.), *Men in families* (pp. 261–270). Beverly Hills, CA: Sage.

Usui, W. M. (1984). Homogeneity of friendship networks of elderly blacks and whites. *Journal of Gerontology, 39*, 350–356.

Wack, J., & Rodin, J. (1978). Nursing homes for the aged: The human consequences of legislation-shaped environments. *Journals of Social Issues, 34*, 6–21.

Wheeless, L. R. (1978). A follow-up study of the relationships between trust, disclosure, and interpersonal solidarity. *Human Communication Research, 4*, 143–147.

Wood, Y., & Robertson, J. F. (1978). Friendship and kinship interaction: Differential effect on morale of the elderly. *Journal of Marriage and the Family, 40*, 367–375.

CHAPTER 11

Barriers To Conversation Facing Elderly People

*T*hroughout this book we suggest that there is a significant relationship between interpersonal relationships, which are a function of interpersonal communication, and the satisfaction people derive from their lives. It stands to reason, then, that people's ability to create and maintain interpersonal relationships influences their health. This is not to suggest that people with happy lives and interpersonal relationships will live forever. However, epidemiological research by Berkman and Syme (1979) certainly suggested that people without close interpersonal ties are more than twice as likely to die than their counterparts with close interpersonal ties.

The importance of the communicative relationship works in another significant way. Not only does communication play an important role in determining people's mental and physical health, but, in addition, after they become ill, their communicative relationships seem to influence how quickly they get well. Because of the complexity of these relationships, the logical connection between the barriers that elderly people and their partners face in conversation and other health communication kinds of issues must be separated. Chapter 11 identifies barriers that elderly people and their partners face in conversation, and some of the implications of these barriers. Chapter 12 extends the discussion to more traditional health communication issues, such as the patient–physician relationship and compliance with a medical regimen. Obviously, the barriers that elderly people and their partners face in conversation also influence patient-physician interaction, making an already difficult interaction even more difficult.

Before this chapter identifies some of these conversational and relational barriers, an understanding of Busse's (1969) distinction between the primary and secondary characteristics of aging is essential. Busse (1969) was one of the first gerontological theorists to recognize that many of the deficits associated with aging were really a function of things other than growing old. Busse suggested that developmental changes that result solely from the process of aging should be considered the primary characteristics of aging and that changes that occur as a result of events that occurred during the life span should be considered secondary characteristics.

More importantly, Busse advocated keeping the two types of characteristics separate for obvious reasons. There are many examples of secondary characteristics that were once thought to be primary. Intelligence is a good example. For years, people thought that elderly people experience significant cognitive deficits as a primary characteristic of aging. However, Eisdorfer and Cohen (1980) argued that, in fact, much of the supposed intellectual decline associated with aging is not really caused by aging at all. In fact, Eisdorfer and Cohen suggested that much of the cognitive decline that has been associated with aging is really caused by high blood pressure and can occur at any age.

Perhaps a second example is in order here. A person who eats a poorly balanced diet is more likely to have health problems than a person who eats a balanced diet. If the individual ends up with a heart condition after 50 years of an unbalanced diet, it is not reasonable to conclude that the heart condition is caused by age. The heart condition is actually caused by accumulated life events (e.g., in this case, the accumulated cholesterol). Thus, many of the health problems that seem to be a function of growing old are really the consequences of some other cause. These secondary factors can be quite difficult to ferret out and can significantly impair the researchers' understanding of the process of aging. It must be recognized, therefore, that the barriers facing elderly people and their conversational partners can be caused by both primary and secondary characteristics of aging.

If people's interpersonal relationships play a central role in their mental and physical health, then any barriers to the creation and maintenance of interpersonal relationships can significantly alter their health. In fact, communication and people's interpersonal relationships have been shown to influence physical and mental health, the magnitude of some illnesses, the likelihood of getting well, whether people will become institutionalized, and, to some degree, the amount of satisfaction they derive from their lives.

AGE-RELATED BARRIERS TO CONVERSATION

People's senses play important roles in their communicative interactions with others. Although the sense of smell or the sense of touch may not seem to play as significant a role as the sense of hearing, a conversation with a person who smells bad or who touches his or her conversational partner in an inappropriate fashion is a quick reminder of how important those two channels can be.

Throughout this book we suggest that a relationship is the communicative behavior between people and that such interaction is intimately related to their physical and mental well-being. Understanding the sensory decline associated with aging, then, is important because these sensory abilities significantly impact people's abilities to create and maintain interpersonal relationships.

Aging and Sight

The decline in eyesight associated with aging is known as presbyopia and generally begins at about the age of 40. Presbyopia is a thickening of the crystalline lenses of the eye, with a resulting diminished elasticity of the lenses of the eye (Corso, 1971; Kline & Scialfa, 1996; McFarland, 1968). People often compensate for this inability to focus on nearby objects by holding printed material farther away from their eyes. By the age of 50, most people notice a significant decline in their ability to see small objects and details (Bischof, 1976) and glasses are almost universally needed for reading (Botwinick, 1978). Botwinick further notes that by the age 70, fewer than 30% of elderly people have 20/20 eyesight and most do not have normal eyesight even with correction.

Presbyopia also contributes to an increased difficulty in viewing objects at a distance. Because of the thickening and diminished elasticity, the eye is less able to adapt to differing visual conditions with age (e.g., Birren, 1964; Bischof, 1976; Domey, McFarland, & Chadwick, 1960; Kline & Scialfa, 1996; McFarland, 1968).

In addition to overall problems related to seeing objects up close or at a distance, older adults note that certain losses affect their everyday activities (Kline & Scialfa, 1996). Difficulties with spatial acuity, depth perception, motion perception, and seeing in shadowed areas increase with age and are particularly difficult when managing day-to-day routines.

A somewhat less common eye problem associated with aging that greatly affects visual acuity is cataracts. Described as an eye disease in which the lens of the eye becomes opaque or "cloudy," nearly 25% of elderly people suffer from partial or total blindness from cataracts. The likelihood of another eye disease, glaucoma, also increases with age. Glaucoma is characterized by increased pressure in the eye and a hardening of the eye that leads to decreased visual acuity and can result in blindness. Although fewer than 10% of people older than 65 are in fact blind, Birren (1964) found that over half of all blindness occurs after the age of 65.

The high incidence of blindness among elderly people and decline in visual acuity associated with aging suggests that sight problems are a serious problem for elderly people. It is important to note, however, that, while vision changes are noticeable, the changes for most people are not disabling. Atchley (1985) pointed out that the vast majority of elderly people can see well enough to qualify for a license to operate an automobile.

The implications of diminished visual abilities are obvious. Sight plays an important role in our conversations with others, and even a relatively slight decrease in visual acuity affects our ability to communicate. Many of the nonverbal cues we use in conversation are visual, and a diminished capacity to process visual information makes conversation far more difficult. It is possible, however, to help a visually impaired individual compensate somewhat for sight problems by using verbal messages that can be understood without a great deal of additional visual information. For example, sarcasm is often predicated on the ability to understand subtle facial expressions or other primarily visual information. Such messages may be lost or misunderstood by people with diminished visual abilities.

Aging and Hearing

As people grow older, their ability to process aural information also decreases. The hearing loss associated with aging is known as presbycusis and results in a reduced sensitivity to higher-frequency sounds, decreased ability to discriminate among adjacent frequencies, and decreased ability to discriminate between consonants (Botwinick, 1977, 1978; Corso, 1971; Willeford, 1971). The higher-frequency consonants such as "f," "g," "s," "t," and "z" are particularly difficult for elderly people to understand (Sataloff & Vassallo, 1966).

People suffering from presbycusis describe speech as sounding "fuzzy," with the words seeming to run together even when the speech is loud enough to hear (Botwinick, 1977; Kline & Scialfa, 1996; Willeford, 1971). In general, the likelihood of hearing impairment increases dramatically after the age of 45, although deafness is still unusual for elderly people. Only about 15% of people 75 years of age or older are deaf, although another 20% or so suffer from a lesser impairment of their hearing (Darbyshire, 1984; Verbrugge, 1984).

Research suggests that speech sounds are more difficult for elderly people to hear when people speak at a fast rate, when there is some external interference—such as distortion or reverberation—and when they are under conditions of stress (Corso, 1971; Kline & Scialfa, 1996). Jarvik and Cohen (1973) suggest that hearing difficulties are compounded by the loss of confidence in the ability to hear that is common among people losing their hearing. The decreased ability to hear and the decreased confidence in the ability to hear often result in increased requests for information to be repeated in conversation or avoiding conversations altogether.

The diminished capacity to hear can greatly affect people's ability to communicate with others. Even modest hearing loss can make conversation more difficult and requires a louder and slower conversational style (Eisdorfer & Wilkie, 1972). Although some research suggested that hearing loss is not related to a reduction in social interaction (Norris & Cunningham, 1981; Powers & Powers, 1978), the evidence offered by these researchers is not very convincing. Methodological and conceptual shortcomings may have led these researchers to conclusions that are not generalizable. Norris and Cunningham (1981) suggested as much in discussing their findings. Measuring social interaction solely by the number of conversations that occur hardly captures the nuance or the importance of communication with others. In this case, then, it is probably not a safe conceptual leap to consider hearing loss as unrelated to social interaction.

A great many other factors seem likely to impact the relationship between hearing ability and social interaction. Depending on the level of hearing loss, it seems likely that diminished aural acuity significantly impacts people's ability to communicate with others. For example, Eisdorfer (1960) found that people suffering from presbycusis exhibited more withdrawn and rigid personalities than do their better-hearing counterparts. Oyer and Paolucci (1970) found support for Eisdorfer's claims. They found that husbands felt more tension in their marriages when their wives suffered severe hearing losses. Being less able to hear or having reduced confidence in the ability to hear makes conversation more trying.

Older individuals who are experiencing hearing losses will attempt to compensate through a variety of strategies. One such strategy is the reliance on their knowledge of semantics and syntactics to "fill in the gaps" (Villaume, Brown, & Darling, 1994). By anticipating the words that would typically fill a spot where they missed a word, individuals with hearing impairments can avoid asking for repetitions. Difficulties can arise, however, when the conversation does not follow well-established routines and the individual "fills in" with the wrong words.

Another strategy employed by those with hearing impairments is a greater reliance on their sight to help them interpret what others say. Commonly called "lip reading," this combining of senses often helps people with hearing deficits compensate for that sensory decline (Villaume et al., 1994). A slight impairment of sight coupled with a slight impairment of hearing can have much more of an impact on conversation than might be expected. Slight impairments in both sight and hearing can be worse than a greater impairment in either sight or hearing alone.

The decrease in confidence that often accompanies sensory deficit can be further confounded by proxemic violations during conversation. Proxemics is the study of personal space. Most people are relatively unaware that there are normative (or expected) distances between people when they stand talking to one another. These distances were first identified by Hall (1959), and the relevance of proxemics to this discussion of sensory deficits is clear. People often compensate for a reduced ability to see or to hear by standing closer to the information source. Unfortunately, such space violations are considered to be inappropriate and can make conversation unpleasant (Lawton & Nahemow, 1973).

A pattern begins to emerge. An elderly individual may have some hearing loss and some decline in the ability to see things at a distance. During previous conversations, this elderly individual has learned that he or she does not understand others as easily as before. Consequently, the individual has less confidence in his or her conversational abilities. In an attempt to compensate for these sensory deficits, the individual may try to stand a little closer to the other person to be sure he or she is hearing correctly. The conversational partner is likely to have stereotyped attitudes toward elderly people and may view this proxemic violation as being aberrant. The natural inclination is to back up and increase the conversational distance. The elderly partner again tries to reduce the distance. The younger partner in this hypothetical example may begin to send messages nonverbally that say, "I am not comfortable." Imagine adding other factors, such as the likelihood that the importance of the interaction for the elderly person is high and that the age difference makes common topics of interest fewer, and one begins to see why these "misunderstandings" between people can result in great conversational difficulty.

Aging and Message Transmission

In addition to its contribution to proxemic violations in conversation, hearing loss also contributes to difficulties in producing speech sounds (Hutchinson & Beasley, 1981). When people speak, they rely somewhat on their ability to hear as a feedback mechanism for monitoring their speech sounds. Consequently, hearing problems can contribute to speech production difficulties.

An additional problem in the transmission of messages is the increase in time it takes for elderly people to encode and decode messages. This increase in encoding and decoding time is attributed to physiological changes in the brain and a decrease in the information-processing efficiency of the central nervous system (Birren, Woods, & Williams, 1980; MacKay & Abrams, 1996; Smith, Thompson, & Michalewski, 1980; Takeda & Matsuzawa, 1985). In general, these delays in encoding and decoding efficiency are considered to be relatively minor unless there are other factors, such as an organic brain disorder, complicating the process. Notice, however, that even short delays during conversation often seem much longer than they are. This is particularly likely to be annoying when a listener attributes the cause of the delay to the negative dispositional characteristics of an elderly person.

Concurrent with delays in processing are difficulties in planning what to say, word retrieval (MacKay & Abrams, 1996), and name recall (Cohen, 1994). Difficulties with planning what to say are indicated by disfluencies (e.g., hesitations, false starts, and word repetitions; MacKay & Abrams, 1996) and affect the pace of the conversation. "Fishing" for the right word or for someone's name not only slows down the interactive processes of the conversation, but it can create uncomfortable episodes as the listener attempts to help the speaker find the words. These word-retrieval difficulties often lead the listener, and sometimes the speaker as well, to question the older speaker's competence.

Memory difficulties are not the only problems associated with message transmission. Although research on the impact of aging on verbal ability is sparse, Hutchinson and Beasley (1981) suggested that the ability to produce speech declines somewhat with age. The vocal apparatus used in speech production changes over one's life span and can contribute to further difficulties in conversation (Hutchinson & Beasley, 1981). Research suggested that the rate at which people speak decreases (Mysak, 1959; Ryan, 1972) and the pitch increases with age (Endres, Bambach, & Flosser, 1970; Hollien & Shipp, 1972; Mysak, 1959). There is some evidence that women's voices do not change as much as men's (cf., Hollien & Shipp, 1972; McGlone & Hollien, 1963; Mysak, 1959), although the data on such a gender difference are far from conclusive.

The changes in vocal-production ability associated with aging have implications that pose additional barriers to conversation. There is evidence that the changes in vocal production associated with aging are perceived to be negative and may contribute to the creation and reinforcement of ageist attitudes. In examining the impact of these paralinguistic cues on perception, Heinberg (1964) suggested that a slow speech rate is perceived to be indicative of less animation, intelligence, and extroversion. Further, men with higher-pitched voices are perceived to be more effeminate. Finally, decreased pitch variety is associated with a less dynamic personality. Slight changes in communicative abilities thus often can result in increased difficulties in face-to-face interaction.

Aging and Touch

The sense of touch is often considered to be insignificant as a channel of communication, when, in fact, touch is a very real way of communicating warmth, nurturance, understanding, and affection. About 25% of elderly people experience a decreased sensitivity to touch (Kenshalo, 1977; Thompson, Axelrod, & Cohen, 1965), although the impact of this sensory decline is not very well understood.

Haptics research demonstrated that touch is essential to human development (Frank, 1957; Klaus & Kennell, 1982; Montagu, 1971), relational development (Jourard & Rubin, 1968; Morris, 1971), and the success of health care regimens (Aguilera, 1967). Aguilera found that when nurses touch patients, the patients reported more positive attitudes toward the nurses, and engaged in more "small talk." Small talk is an important antecedent to relational development and an opportunity for health care providers to gain information about the patient.

Barnett (1972) found that touch in the clinical setting is underutilized and suggested that touch is particularly important because people's social contacts have changed and they are scared and nervous, and because touching helps build relationships. Barnett (1972) found that physicians were much less likely than nurses and other hospital workers to touch patients when they talked. This held true for physicians at all levels of training.

Geriatric nurses are much less likely to touch men and severely impaired patients (Watson, 1975). It has also been observed that women are more likely than men to initiate touching, and women are most likely to touch other women when they initiate contact (Rinck, Willis, & Dean, 1980). Because older men and the severely impaired in particular may need the "strokes," it is important for physicians and health care professionals to recognize the importance of touch to relational development and well-being. If the importance of touch is recognized, this important communicative mechanism can be used during conversations.

Aging and Reaction Time

Although not a sensory modality, *reaction time* is typically defined as the amount of time it takes an individual to respond to some stimulus. Obviously, reaction time plays an important role in the maintenance and regulation of conversation. It is generally thought that the time it takes to react to a stimulus increases with age, and there is some evidence to support this claim. In addition to primary aging factors, other secondary factors seem to account for some of the increase in reaction time that is associated with aging.

Botwinick (1977) found that increased reaction time is also a function of an increased cautiousness associated with aging. Botwinick (1977), and others, argued that elderly people place a great premium on being accurate in experimental tasks and consequently are often thought to be slower at performing a task merely because they are being more careful than their younger counterparts. Other experimental evidence supports this contention that elderly people value accuracy more than speed, preferring not to respond rather than to be wrong (Elias & Elias, 1977; Jarvik & Cohen, 1973).

It was also demonstrated that elderly people take longer to react to a stimulus if the task is not perceived to be relevant or meaningful (Arenberg, 1973; Elias & Elias, 1977), if the task is perceived to be stressful (Elias & Elias, 1977; Labouvie-Vief, 1977), if the task has little structure or direction (Botwinick, 1973; Jarvik & Cohen, 1973), if there is little motivation to perform the task (Elias & Elias, 1977), if the elderly person is fatigued (Labouvie-Vief, 1977), if there are time constraints on the task (Arenberg, 1973; Chown, 1968), or if the task is abstract in nature (Baltes & Schaie, 1974; Botwinick, 1973). This leads to the conclusion that increased reaction time is a function of both primary and secondary aging factors.

Botwinick (1978) and others argued that increases in reaction time can often be overcome with exercise, practice, and high levels of motivation. Reducing stress by communicating in a supportive fashion would also seem to be likely to help reduce reaction time in the laboratory or in conversation. Very short delays in conversation can seem like an eternity and greatly impact conversational coherence and satisfaction. If one recognizes that a slight increase in reaction time is common in conversations with elderly partners, the discomfort caused by such delays in conversation should be reduced. The reduction in stress may well alleviate some of the increase in reaction time associated with aging because the evidence suggests that stress and the fear of being evaluated increases the reaction time of elderly individuals.

Aging and Cognitive Abilities

For years people assumed that intelligence and the ability to think decline with age. Research suggests, however, that this simplistic relationship between intelligence and age is not accurate. Much of what was considered cognitive decrement due to aging was shown to be related to secondary aging factors such as illness (Jarvik & Blum, 1981; Schaie, 1975, 1996). Still other research suggested that intelligence testing is biased in favor of young people (Atchley, 1985). Finally, reexaminations of the literature concluded that previous research was fraught with methodological problems, measurement errors, and inappropriate data interpretation (Eisdorfer, 1978; Jarvik & Cohen, 1973; Savage, Britton, Bolton, & Hall, 1975).

One problem with the generalization that intelligence decreases with age is that intelligence is a complex, multidimensional phenomenon. Baltes and Labouvie (1973) suggested that as many as 20 distinct factors make up what is commonly thought of as intelligence. With so many processes making up intelligence, it seems unlikely that all dimensions would be affected in the same way by aging. Nesselroade, Schaie, and Baltes's (1972) research suggested that some dimensions of intelligence diminish with age, others remain relatively stable across the life span, and still others actually increase as people grow older. In a recent summary of this area of research, Schaie (1996) concurred with this complex view of intellectual development throughout adulthood.

Whereas some dimensions of intelligence diminish with age, these decreases are actually fairly small and seldom occur before the age of 70 (Jarvik & Bank, 1983; Palmore & Cleveland, 1976; Schaie, 1983, 1996; Schaie & Hertzog, 1983; Siegler, 1980, 1983; Siegler, McCarty & Logue, 1982; Suedfeld & Piedrahita, 1984). Further, it appears that some of the cognitive decline associated with aging can be battled with physical and mental activity (Botwinick, 1977; Elsayed, Ismail, & Young, 1980; Kohn, 1980; Kohn & Schooler, 1978; Labouvie-Vief, 1977; Schaie, 1996). In short, the evidence for cognitive decline as a consequence of growing old has been overstated. The evidence just does not support such a simplistic, negative relationship.

Why, then, have elderly people been characterized as becoming less intelligent as they grow older? One factor that has confounded researchers' understandings of the relationship between age and intelligence is that there appears to be a very significant decrease in intelligence that occurs about 5 years before death. Kleemeier (1962) coined the term *terminal drop* to describe this significant decline in cognitive ability, and terminal drop has been cited as a significant predictor of impending death (Riegel & Riegel, 1972). This decline, however, is not so much age-related as it is related to distance from death and it is influenced by health problems and a variety of social factors (Berg, 1996).

A second reason elderly people are often described as declining intellectually with age is that in the real world intelligence is inferred from behavior and not from a score on a test. Research by Cohen (1979) suggested that, even when elderly people are able to understand a spoken message as accurately as younger adults, they are in some ways less able to use that information. Cohen (1979) suggested that the elderly have more difficulty than younger adults in making inferences from information obtained in conversation. It seems likely, then, that people assume that the elderly person has lower intelligence because this disability leads to the conclusion that he or she has "missed the point."

Another aspect of real-world intelligence is everyday problem solving. Although older individuals are no less capable of problem-solving, their problem-solving strategies differ from those used by younger adults (Willis, 1996). These differences are exhibited on both the declarative and procedural levels. The *declarative level* has to do with the search for information. Older adults make less extensive searches for and use fewer pieces of information when making decisions. Much like experts in an area of knowledge, older individuals are better able to identify the few, most relevant pieces of information necessary for selecting a solution. Younger adults perform more like novices by searching for extensive information. If one measures successful decision making based on the amount of information gathered, then older adults appear to perform more poorly than do younger adults.

On the *procedural level* of problem solving, older adults tend to use top-down procedures. In this style of problem solving, prior experiential knowledge is used extensively. Through experience, older individuals have developed well-honed procedural strategies for selecting solutions. Although reliance on prior experience can simplify the task, if the procedures become too routine, poor problem solving may result when old skills are applied to new problems.

A third reason that elderly people are often described as declining intellectually is that some dimensions of intelligence do decrease with age. Intelligence is commonly divided into two types, crystallized and fluid. *Crystallized* intelligence includes the abilities and skills acquired through education and personal experience. Verbal skills, comprehension skills, and vocabulary make up crystallized intelligence and these skills remain relatively stable until the age of 70 (Botwinick, 1977; Labouvie-Vief, 1977). Fluid intelligence includes skills and abilities that are relatively unrelated to education or experience. *Fluid* intelligence refers to primarily nonverbal skills such as abstract reasoning, response time, and mathematics. Fluid intelligence begins to decline as early as 35 (Horn & Donaldson, 1980) and is thought to be a function of the decreasing efficiency of the central nervous system. Research suggested that the decline in fluid intelligence can be slowed through physical and mental activity (Elsayed et al., 1980; Kohn, 1980; Kohn & Schooler, 1978).

Because much of the meaning in a conversation is derived from nonverbal and relational information, the decline in fluid intelligence is significant. Increased difficulty in processing nonverbal information makes conversation more difficult. As it becomes more difficult to maintain and regulate a conversation, the likelihood of elderly people entering into conversations seems likely to decrease because generally people approach experiences that have been positive and avoid those that have been negative. Research into the impact of fluid intelligence on conversation is sorely needed.

Schaie (1975) summarized the research on intelligence and aging:

> Our studies strongly suggest that in the areas of intellectual abilities and skills, old people, in general, if they are reasonably healthy, have not declined but rather have become obsolete. This conclusion might be viewed as a rather negative value judgment. That is not true at all, because obsolescence can be remedied by retraining, while deterioration would be irreversible. Indeed if it can be shown that the real intellectual problem for older people is the fact they are functioning at the level they attained in their younger days, but which is no longer appropriate for successful performance in contemporary society, it follows that we may be able to do something about this situation. (p. 120)

One of the things that can be done is to recognize that, as people age, the combination of deficits in fluid intelligence, hearing, and sight are compounded further by increases in reaction time. This combination makes processing nonverbal and relational information much more difficult. Again, nonverbal and relational information is crucial to understanding conversation and in the maintenance of health.

In addition to recognizing that these deficits are occurring, one must also recognize that the difficulties are not completely insurmountable. An excellent way to slow the decline in fluid intelligence is through conversation with others. An awareness of some of the barriers facing elderly people and their partners in conversation may minimize their difficulties and increase the satisfaction they derive from interaction.

Aging and Memory

Much like the research on aging and intelligence, research into the impact of aging on memory suggests that memory is a multidimensional construct and that the relationship between age and memory is more complex than was once thought. Although the terminology may vary from study to study, there are three types of memory: sensory, short-term, and long-term. These three types of memory seem to be differentially affected by the process of aging.

Sensory memory refers to the ability to retain an image or memory of some stimuli for a very short time after exposure. The duration of such recall is typically described in fractions of a second. Interestingly enough, research suggested that, if sensory limitations do not interfere with the reception of the stimuli, sensory memory does not seem to decline with age (Baltes, Reese, & Lipsitt, 1980; Craik, 1977; Labouvie-Vief & Schell, 1982).

Short-term memory refers to the ability to retain an image or memory of some stimuli for a short time after exposure. The duration of such recall is usually described in seconds or minutes and declines somewhat with age (Botwinick & Storandt, 1974; Craik, 1977). The decline is generally not very severe, and it seems to vary with the cognitive style of the individual (Monge, 1969), the complexity of the stimuli material (Botwinick & Storandt, 1974), the speed of presentation (Arenberg & Robertson-Tchabo, 1977), the amount of stress or emotional threat the elderly person perceives (Arenberg & Robertson-Tchabo, 1977; Monge, 1969), the fear of failure (Okun, 1976), the familiarity with the recall material (Chase & Simon, 1973; Hanley-Dunn &

McIntosh, 1984), and the amount or complexity of organizing necessary to encode the information (Arenberg & Robertson-Tchabo, 1977; Craik, 1977; Craik & Rabinowitz, 1985; Macht & Buschke, 1984; McFarland, Warren, & Crockard, 1985; Rankin & Collins, 1985). Although the decline is not large and is partially a function of factors other than age, it appears that younger people have an advantage in their ability to recall information from short-term memory. Difficulties in conversation typically arise because of problems with simultaneously storing and processing information (Smith, 1996). The short-term memory decline associated with aging can make conversation more difficult, but it need not make conversation impossible. By conversing in a relaxed and nonevaluative style, affect can be generated (Nussbaum, Robinson, & Grew, 1983) and the impact of the memory deficits associated with aging may be reduced.

Long-term memory is a complex set of components, including episodic memory (memory of specific experiences), semantic memory (knowledge), and procedural memory (Smith, 1996). The decline in some components of long-term memory associated with aging is more dramatic than the decline observed in short-term memory (Craik, 1977). This decline in long-term memory is primarily attributable to encoding or organizing difficulties, the procedural component of memory (Arenberg, 1973; Arenberg & Robertson-Tchabo, 1977; Botwinick, 1973; Craik, 1977; Craik & Rabinowitz, 1985; Macht & Buschke, 1984; McFarland et al., 1985; Monge, 1969; Rankin & Collins, 1985; Smith, 1996).

Other factors contribute to the decline in long-term memory. The increase in the time it takes to retrieve information from memory (Arenberg, 1973; Cerella, 1985; Chi, 1978; Craik, 1977; Madden, 1985), the familiarity with the material being recalled (Chase & Simon, 1973; Evans, Brennan, Skorpanich, & Held, 1984; Fozard, 1980; Hanley-Dunn & McIntosh, 1984), and the learning style of the individual (Monge, 1969) impact long-term recall.

In addition, the salience or importance of the information (Arenberg, 1973; Birren, 1970; Botwinick, 1973), the motivation level of the individual (Elias & Elias, 1977), the way information retrieval is measured (Johnson, 1972; Schonfield & Robertson, 1966; Thomas, 1972), the number of things to recall (Arenberg, 1973; Botwinick, 1973; Jarvik & Cohen, 1973; Riegel, 1966), the type of task, and the task structure (Botwinick, 1973; Jarvik & Cohen, 1973) all affect the recall of information.

Although the focus has been on losses associated with aging, it should be pointed out that in some areas older adults out-perform younger adults. For example, older adults have a better narrative recall (Blanchard-Fields & Abeles, 1996). By calling on their greater experience with social knowledge structures, older adults remember story lines more accurately and in more detail than do younger adults. Older adults also have a more developed scripted knowledge of everyday activities and are better at problem appraisal and solving (Blanchard-Fields & Abeles, 1996).

The long-term memory decline associated with aging, as does the short-term memory decline, can make conversation more difficult. As with the problems involved in word and name retrieval, recall difficulties can slow down the pace of the conversation and make it difficult for information to be accurately shared. Conversely, the fact that older adults have different problem-solving strategies and social-knowledge scripts than younger adults may lead to misunderstandings because the conversants do not share the same schema. Again, using a relaxed and nonevaluative style can reduce the stress of the interaction and help to minimize problems with recall. If one acknowledges life-experience differences and explicitly states assumptions in conversations, this can help to identify areas where different schema are being used and help reduce misunderstandings.

AGING AND COMMUNICATOR STYLE

Norton (1978; 1983) defined *communicator style* as being the manner or way that a person verbally or paraverbally interacts with others. Much of how a signal should be taken or interpreted is a function of the style in which the message is communicated. The style a person employs during conversation is extremely important, not only because it provides the context within which messages are interpreted, but also because the style helps define the relationship between communicants. Characteristic styles of interaction have been examined in a variety of contexts (cf., Norton, Murray, & Arnston, 1982; Norton & Nussbaum, 1980; Weber, 1987) and play an important role in the definition of a relationship.

Nussbaum, Robinson, and Grew (1985) found that nursing personnel report intentionally altering their communicative style when they talk with the residents of nursing homes. When asked, nurses and nurse's aides said they do not communicate with residents of a nursing home in the same manner they communicate with their friends and family. Specifically, the nurses and nurse's aides report communicating in a more open, dramatic, dominant, relaxed, friendly, and attentive style with the residents.

Nussbaum et al. (1983) also found that nursing personnel who feel high levels of affinity communicate in a different style than do nurses and nurse's aides who feel lower levels of affinity toward the residents. Specifically, it was found that nurse's aides who feel high levels of affinity communicate in a more friendly and relaxed manner than other nurse's aides. Similarly, nurses who feel high levels of affinity report communicating in a more friendly manner than do other staff members.

These results suggest that staff members do not communicate with elderly residents in the same way that they communicate in their other daily conversations. Whether the residents feel that the staff members communicate in a more friendly or relaxed fashion is a question that cannot be answered at this time. Nussbaum's (1981, 1983) research strongly suggested that elderly people in nursing homes often do not view the staff as friends, but as employees paid to do a job. And they feel the nursing staff is not paid to enter into significant relationships with the residents. Whether nonnursing personnel make similar stylistic modifications has not been empirically investigated. However, the language and aging literature provides some insight into that question.

AGING AND LANGUAGE

Research suggests that people modify the language they use in conversation with elderly people. It is not surprising that people attempt to simplify their speech when they perceive their conversational partners to have diminished capacity (e.g., hearing loss) for conversation (Bates, 1975), nor is it surprising that the degree to which people will modify their speech is related to their expectation of their conversational partners' abilities (Blount, 1972; Broen, 1972; Cross, 1975; Shatz & Gelman, 1973; 1977; Snow, 1977). What is somewhat surprising is that adults also modify the amount of affect and nurturance in their voices (Rubin & Brown, 1975). In short, adults may treat elderly people as children without the accompanying caring and nurturance typical of parent–child interaction (Ferguson, 1977; Kalish & Knudtson, 1976; McTavish, 1971).

When people expect their conversational partner to be unable to comprehend normal conversational speech, there is a tendency to use simpler and more concrete words, to construct simpler and more single-word sentences, to slow the speech rate, and to exaggerate nonverbal and vocalic information (Blount, 1972; Broen, 1972; Farwell, 1975; Ferguson, 1977; Shatz & Gelman, 1973; Snow, 1972).

The consequences of this modified speech style are tremendous. When an elderly individual is perceived to have some diminished capacity (e.g., hearing loss), the younger adult is likely to communicate in simplified speech or "baby talk." The relational message being sent by the younger person may be decoded as, "You are less capable than you once were, and I have less affection for you than I once did." Because the level of simplification employed is determined by the responses of the listener and not on the conversational sophistication and speech register of the respondent (Farwell, 1975), a slow or inaccurate response may lead to an even simpler speech register in subsequent interactions.

If the elderly individual feels that he or she is being treated as a simpleton or as a child, he or she may feel anxious during conversation. Such stress and anxiety about being evaluated have been shown to be related to an increase in reaction time (Elias & Elias, 1977; Labouvie-Vief, 1977) and may contribute to further conversational difficulties.

Recall the Communication Predicament of Aging model (Harwood, Giles, Fox, Ryan, & Williams, 1993; Ryan, Giles, Bartolucci, & Henwood, 1986) from chapter 2. A downward spiral occurs when younger adults modify their speech when interacting with an older person. The older adult feels incompetent, the younger adult thinks the older adult is incompetent, and both walk away from the interaction dissatisfied and less likely to engage in future interactions.

This is not to suggest, however, that people should not simplify their speech when they talk with elderly people. Obviously, the cognitive and behavioral slowing associated with aging is a significant barrier to understanding language and to participating in conversation. Further, as Cohen (1979) demonstrated, the ability to make inferences during conversation decreases with age. Slowing down one's rate of speech, using simpler sentences, and making more explicit messages when appropriate can make conversation more pleasant and effective. Ryan, Meredith, MacLean, and Orange (1995) proposed the Communication Enhancement of Aging (CEA) model to address this need. An individual who is interacting with an older individual should be trained to recognize the individual aspects of the older person that would alert him or her to any changes that are necessary in his or her communication strategies. In this way, individualized accommodations are made when needed and the satisfaction that both parties have with the interaction will be increased.

One particular case in which simplifications to speech may be appropriate is when the older person has Alzheimer's disease (Kemper & Lyons, 1994). In individuals suffering from dementia due to Alzheimer's disease, semantic memory, which provides connections between related objects, and script knowledge, which identifies events that occur in a situation, become disorganized. Therefore, these individuals have trouble finding words, naming objects, and comprehending conversations. These individuals use more vague or empty terms, are more repetitive and redundant in their speech, and are not as likely to modify their speech to accommodate situational factors compared to healthy older adults. Simplification strategies will increase the performance of the individual with Alzheimer's by reducing memory demands and providing more contextual cues (Kemper, Anagnopoulos, Lyons, & Heberlein, 1994; Kemper, Vandeputte, Rice, Cheung, & Gubarchuk, 1995).

A critical element in the process of simplifying speech is to consider the affective and relational components of the message being transmitted. It is important that nurturance and affect are not lost in the simplification process. In addition, it is important to recognize that a slight decrease in hearing is not necessarily evidence of cognitive impairment. Unfortunately, there is a tendency for some people to respond to hearing loss or a slight increase in reaction time as if it were evidence of diminished cognitive capacity. Recall that Botwinick (1977) and Labouvie-Vief (1977) suggested that crystallized intelligence (i.e., vocabulary and comprehension) do not decrease very much with age in the absence of health problems. A relatively simplistic answer, therefore, is not necessarily evidence of a diminished information-processing capacity. In fact, a simple answer (e.g., just "Yes" or "No") may be evidence of the certainty of the speaker in his or her response.

Difficulties are more likely to arise when people of different generations have conversations. As Tamir (1982) pointed out, differences in past experiences, socioeconomic status, life stage, and a variety of other factors make the sharing or co-creation of meaning more difficult. Research suggests that young people and old people are very likely to misperceive and misunderstand one another because of these factors.

McTavish (1971) found that young adults are prone to behaving in an artificially friendly manner when in conversation with elderly partners. This less than genuine interactional style has potentially disastrous implications for relational development. This lack of genuineness in relational development results in the creation and propagation of stereotyped attitudes that further compound the difficulties of intergenerational conversation. Such interaction can also reduce the satisfaction derived from conversation, decrease the self-esteem of the participants, and cause a lack of understanding.

This lack of understanding can lead to additional significant health-related problems. The term *double bind* was coined by Bateson, Jackson, Haley, and Weakland (1956) to describe a particular type of communicative interaction typified by the presence of two or more messages that are mutually contradictory. Without delving into the intricacies of the concept, suffice it to say that Bateson and his colleagues felt that when people are put into paradoxical situations, health problems can arise. There is a substantial body of evidence that suggests that when people's interactions with others are "double binding," their mental health can suffer (cf., Jackson, 1968; Watzlawick, 1978).

In a case study by Herr and Weakland (1979), an elderly widow was put in a double bind by her children. After her husband died, the woman was told by her children that if she wanted to maintain her independence, her children would help her do so. But she would have to do what they told her to do, or they would not allow her to remain independent. The paradox in the situation is, obviously, that if she must do what someone else tells her to do, she is not independent. Consequently, whatever the mother did was a violation of one of the two messages. Although the children seemed unaware that their requests were paradoxical, the impossibility of the situation did not escape the mother.

Watzlawick (1978) pointed out the implications of being put into a double bind at any age. If the double bind is relatively inescapable and occurs over an extended period of time, people begin to distrust their senses and their feelings. In addition, they feel that they have little or no control over their lives. In the case of elderly people, as in the case of young children, the double bind presents a particular problem because of their increased reliance on others. An individual who is reliant or dependent on another for help or services cannot "leave the paradoxical relationship" easily. This is an area of research that needs further investigation. Sensory deficits and the associated loss of confidence seem to make elderly people particularly susceptible to finding themselves in double binds and perhaps less able to extricate themselves from them.

All of the factors discussed in this chapter suggest that conversational barriers exist and seem to increase with age. Some of the barriers are caused by aging, some are caused by the accumulation of life events, and some are influenced by both primary and secondary characteristics of aging. Regardless of the cause, these barriers impede conversation and can influence the interpersonal relationships of elderly people.

The interpersonal relationships of elderly people are important for all of the reasons discussed thus far. In addition, interpersonal relationships are significant because they allow elderly people to live in relative independence. Mutual assistance from friends, family members, and neighbors is often the key determinant of quality of life and life satisfaction for elderly people. The importance of the social support network, and other related health issues will be discussed at length in chapter 12.

SUMMARY

There are a great many barriers that face elderly people and their conversational partners. Some of the barriers result directly from growing old, and some of the barriers are functions of an accumulation of life events. Some are the result of stereotyped attitudes about aging and elderly people, and are little more than figments of the imagination. Regardless of the cause of the barriers, they can make conversation much more difficult. This difficulty compounds the original barriers and creates new barriers, making subsequent conversations even more difficult. These barriers, then, have the potential to significantly influence the mental and physical well-being of older adults.

Recognizing the differences in the primary and the secondary characteristics of aging and understanding the changes that result in the aging process will help one to minimize the significance of such barriers. Further, by understanding the importance of conversation, it will be easier to initiate and maintain difficult conversations. Finally, one of the best ways to combat the deficits associated with aging is through conversation with others. Although communication is not a panacea, communication does play an important role in the well-being of elderly people.

■ REFERENCES

Aguilera, D. (1967). Relationships between physical contact and verbal interaction between nurses and patients. *Journal of Psychiatric Nursing, 5,* 5–21.

Arenberg, D. (1973). Cognition and aging: Verbal learning, memory, problem solving and aging. In C. Eisdorfer & M. Lawton (Eds.), *The psychology of adult development and aging* (pp. 74–97). Washington, DC: American Psychological Association.

Arenberg, D., & Robertson-Tchabo, E. (1977). Learning and aging. In J. Birren & K. Schaie (Eds.), *Handbook of the psychology of aging* (pp. 721–749). New York: Van Nostrand Reinhold.

Atchley, R. (1985). *The social forces in later life* (4th ed.). Belmont, CA: Wadsworth.

Baltes, P., & Labouvie, G. (1973). Adult development of intellectual performance: Description, explanation, and modification. In C. Eisdorfer & M. Lawton (Eds.), *The psychology of adult development and aging* (pp. 157–219). Washington, DC: American Psychological Association.

Baltes, P., Reese, H., & Lipsitt, L. (1980). Life-span developmental psychology. In M. Rosenzweig & L. Porter (Eds.), *Annual review of psychology* (pp. 65–110). Palo Alto, CA: Annual Reviews.

Baltes, P., & Schaie, K. (1974, March). Aging and IQ: The myth of the twilight years. *Psychology Today, 7,* p. 3540.

Barnett, K. (1972). A survey of the current utilization of touch by health team personnel with hospitalized patients. *International Journal of Nursing Studies, 9,* 195–209.

Bates, E. (1975). Peer relations and the acquisition of language. In M. Lewis & L. Rosenblum (Eds.), *Friendship and peer relations.* New York: Wiley.

Bateson, G., Jackson, D., Haley, J., & Weakland, J. (1956). Toward a theory of schizophrenia. *Behavioral Science, 1,* 251–264.

Berg, S. (1996). Aging, behavior, and terminal decline. In J. E. Birren & K. W. Schaie (Eds.), *Handbook of the psychology of aging* (4th ed., pp. 323–337). San Diego, CA: Academic Press.

Berkman, L., & Syme, S. (1979). Social networks, host resistance, and mortality. *American Journal of Epidemiology, 109,* 186–204.

Birren, J. (1964). *The psychology of aging.* Englewood Cliffs, NJ: Prentice-Hall.

Birren, J. (1970). Toward an experimental psychology of aging. *American Psychologist, 25,* 124–135.

Birren, J., Woods, A., & Williams, M. (1980). Behavioral slowing with age: Causes, organization, and consequences. In L. Poon (Ed.), *Aging in the 1980s* (pp. 293–308). Washington, DC: American Psychological Association.

Bischof, L. (1976). *Adult psychology* (2nd ed.). New York: Harper & Row.

Blanchard-Fields, F., & Abeles, R. (1996). Social cognition and aging. In J. E. Birren & K. W. Schaie (Eds.), *Handbook of the psychology of aging* (4th ed., pp. 150–161). San Diego, CA: Academic Press.

Blount, B. (1972). Parental speech and language acquisition: Some Luo and Samoan examples. *Anthropological Linguistics, 14*, 119–130.

Botwinick, J. (1973). *Aging and behavior.* New York: Springer.

Botwinick, J. (1977). Intellectual abilities. In J. Birren & K. Schaie (Eds.), *Handbook of the psychology of aging* (pp. 580–605). New York: Van Nostrand Reinhold.

Botwinick, J. (1978). *Aging and behavior* (2nd ed.). New York: Springer.

Botwinick, J., & Storandt, M. (1974). *Memory related functions and age.* Springfield, IL: Thomas.

Broen, P. (1972). The verbal hearing environment of the language-learning child. *American Speech and Hearing Association Monograph, 17.*

Busse, E. (1969). Theories of aging. In E. Busse & E. Pfeiffer (Eds.), *Behavior and adaptation in later life* (pp. 11–32). Boston: Little, Brown.

Cerella, J. (1985). Information processing rates in the elderly. *Psychological Bulletin, 98*, 67–83.

Chase, W., & Simon, H. (1973). The mind's eye in chess. In W. G. Chase (Ed.), *Visual information processing* (pp. 215–281). New York: Academic Press.

Chi, M. (1978). Knowledge structure and memory development. In R. Siegler (Ed.), *Carnegie-Mellon symposium on cognition* . Hillsdale, NJ: Lawrence Erlbaum Associates.

Chown, S. (1968). Personality and aging. In K. Schaie (Ed.), *Theory and methods of research on aging* (pp. 134–157). Morgantown, WV: West Virginia University Press.

Cohen, G. (1979). Language comprehension in old age. *Cognitive Psychology, 11*, 423–429.

Cohen, G. (1994). Age-related problems in the use of proper names in communication. In M. L. Hummert, J. M. Wiemann, & J. F. Nussbaum (Eds.), *Interpersonal communication in older adulthood: Interdisciplinary theory and research* (pp. 40–57). Thousand Oaks, CA: Sage.

Corso, J. (1971). Sensory processes and age effects in normal adults. *Journal of Gerontology, 26*, 90–105.

Craik, F. (1977). Age differences in human memory. In J. Birren & K. Schaie (Eds.), *Handbook of the psychology of aging* (pp. 384–420). New York: Van Nostrand Reinhold.

Craik, F., & Rabinowitz, J. (1985). The effects of presentation rate and encoding task on age-related memory deficits. *Journal of Gerontology, 40*, 309–315.

Cross, T. (1975). Some relations between mothers and linguistic level in accelerated children. *Papers and Reports on Child Language Development, 10*, 117–135.

Darbyshire, J. (1984). The hearing loss epidemic: A challenge to gerontology. *Research on Aging, 6*, 384–394.

Domey, R., McFarland, R., & Chadwick, E. (1960). Threshold and rate of dark adaptation as functions of age and time. *Human Factors, 2*, 109–119.

Eisdorfer, C. (1960). Rorscharch rigidity and sensory decrement in a senescent population. *Journal of Gerontology, 15*, 188–190.

Eisdorfer, C. (1978). Psychophysiologic and cognitive studies in the aged. In O. Usdin & C. Hoflings (Eds.), *Aging: The process and the people* (pp. 96–128). New York: Bruner/Mazel.

Eisdorfer, C., & Cohen, D. (1980). The issue of biological and psychological deficits. In E. Borgatta & N. McCluskey (Eds.), *Aging and society: Current research and policy perspectives* (pp 49–70). Beverly Hills, CA: Sage.

Eisdorfer, C., & Wilkie, F. (1972). Auditory changes. *Journal of the American Geriatrics Society, 20,* 377–382.

Elias, M. F., & Elias, P. K. (1977). Motivation and activity. In J. Birren & K. Schaie (Eds.), *Handbook of the psychology of aging* (pp. 357–383). New York: Van Nostrand Reinhold.

Elsayed, M., Ismail, A., & Young, R. (1980). Intellectual differences of adult men related to age and physical fitness before and after an exercise program. *Journal of Gerontology, 35,* 383–387.

Endres, W., Bambach, W., & Flosser, G. (1970). Voice spectrograms as a function of age, voice, disguise, and voice imitation. *Journal of the Acoustic Society of America, 49,* 1842–1848.

Evans, G. W., Brennan, P. L., Skorpanich, M. A., & Held, D. (1984). Cognitive mapping and elderly adults: Verbal and location memory for urban landmarks. *Journal of Gerontology, 39,* 368–374.

Farwell, C. (1975). The language spoken to children. *Human Development, 18,* 288–309.

Ferguson, C. (1977). Baby talk as simplified register. In C. Snow & C. Ferguson (Eds.), *Talking to children* (pp. 219–235). New York: Cambridge University Press.

Fozard, J. L. (1980). The time for remembering. In L. Poon (Ed.), *Aging in the 1980s* (pp. 273–287). Washington, DC: American Psychological Association.

Frank, L. (1957). Tactile communication. *Genetic Psychology Monographs, 56,* 209–255.

Hall, E. (1959). *The silent language.* Garden City, NY: Doubleday.

Hanley-Dunn, P., & McIntosh, J. (1984). Meaningfulness and recall of names by young and old adults. *Journal of Gerontology, 39,* 583–585.

Harwood, J., Giles, H., Fox, S. Ryan, E. B., & Williams, A. (1993). Patronizing young and elderly adults: Response strategies in a community setting. *Journal of Applied Communication Research, 21,* 211–226.

Heinberg, P. (1964). *Voice training for speaking and reading aloud.* New York: Ronald Press.

Herr, J., & Weakland, J. (1979). Communications within family systems: Growing older within and with the double bind. In P. Ragan (Ed.), *Aging parents* (pp. 144–153). Los Angeles: University of Southern California Press.

Hollien, H., & Shipp, T. (1972). Speaking fundamental frequency and chronologic age in males. *Journal of Speech and Hearing Research, 15,* 155–159.

Horn, J. L., & Donaldson, G. (1980). Cognitive development in adulthood. In O. G. Brim, Jr. & J. Kagen (Eds.), *Constancy and change in human development* (pp. 445–529). Cambridge, MA: Harvard University Press.

Hutchinson, J., & Beasley, D. (1981). Speech and language functioning among the aging. In H. Oyer & E. Oyer (Eds.), *Aging and communication* (pp. 155–174). Baltimore: University Park Press.

Jackson, D. (1968). *Therapy, communication and change.* Palo Alto, CA: Science and Behavior Books.

Jarvik, L., & Bank, L. (1983). Aging twins: Longitudinal psychometric data. In K. Schaie (Ed.), *Longitudinal studies of adult psychological development* (pp. 40–63). New York: Guilford.

Jarvik, L., & Blum, J. (1981). Cognitive dexlines as predictors of mortality in twin pairs. In E. Palmore & F. Jeffers (Eds.), *Prediction of the life span.* Lexington, MA: D. C. Health.

Jarvik, C., & Cohen, D. (1973). A biobehavioral approach to intellectual change with aging. In C. Eisdorfer & M. Lawton (Eds.), *The psychology of adult development and aging* (pp. 220–280). Washington, DC: American Psychological Association.

Johnson, I. (1972, December). *Memory loss with age: A storage or retrieval problem.* Paper presented at the meeting of the Gerontological Society, San Juan, Puerto Rico.

Jourard, S., & Rubin, J. (1968). Self-disclosure and touching: A study of two modes of interpersonal encounter and their interrelation. *Journal of Humanistic Psychology, 8,* 39–48.

Kalish, R. A., & Knudtson, F. W. (1976). Attachment versus disengagement: A life-span conceptualization. *Human Development, 19,* 171–181.

Kemper, S., Anagnopoulos, C., Lyons, K., & Heberlein, W. (1994). Speech accommodation to dementia. *Journal of Gerontology, 49,* 223–229.

Kemper, S., & Lyons, K. (1994). The effects of Alzheimer's dementia on language and communication. In M. L. Hummert, J. M. Wiemann, & J. F. Nussbaum (Eds.), *Interpersonal communication in older adulthood: Interdisciplinary theory and research* (pp. 58–82). Thousand Oaks, CA: Sage.

Kemper, S., Vandeputte, D., Rice, K., Cheung, H., & Gubarchuk, J. (1995). Speech adjustments to aging during a referential communication task. *Journal of Language and Social Psychology, 14,* 40–59.

Kenshalo, D. (1977). Age changes in touch, vibration, temperature, kinesthesis, and pain sensitivity. In J. Birren & K. Schaie (Eds.), *Handbook of the psychology of aging* (pp. 562–579). New York: Van Nostrand Reinhold.

Klaus, M., & Kennell, J. (1982). *Parent-infant bonding.* St. Louis, MO: Mosby.

Kleemeier, R. (1962). Intellectual changes in the senium. *Proceedings of the Social Statistics Section of the American Statistics Association, 1,* 290–295.

Kline, D. W., & Scialfa, C. T. (1996). Visual and auditory aging. In J. E. Birren & K. W. Schaie (Eds.), *Handbook of the psychology of aging* (4th ed., pp. 181–203). San Diego, CA: Academic Press.

Kohn, M. (1980). Job complexity and adult personality. In N. Smelser & E. Erickson (Eds.), *Themes of work and love in adulthood* (pp. 193–210). Cambridge, MA: Harvard University Press.

Kohn, M., & Schooler, C. (1978). The reciprocal effects of substantive complexity of work and intellectual flexibility: A longitudinal assessment. *American Journal of Sociology, 84,* 24–52.

Labouvie-Vief, G. (1977). Adult cognitive development: In search of alternative interpretations. *Merrill-Palmer Quarterly, 23*(4), 227–263.

Labouvie-Vief, G., & Schell, D. (1982). Learning and memory in later life. In B. Wolman (Ed.), *Handbook of developmental psychology* (pp. 828-846). Englewood Cliffs, NJ: Prentice-Hall.

Lawton, M., & Nahemow, L. (1973). Ecology and the aging process. In C. Eisdorfer & M. Lawton (Eds.), *The psychology of adult development and aging* (pp. 619–714). Washington, DC: American Psychological Association.

Macht, M., & Buschke, H. (1984). Speed of recall in aging. *Journal of Gerontology, 39,* 439–443.

MacKay, D. G., & Abrams. L. (1996). Language, memory, and aging: Distributed deficits and the structure of new-versus-old connections. In J. E. Birren & K. W. Schaie (Eds.), *Handbook of the psychology of aging* (4th ed., pp. 251–265). San Diego, CA: Academic Press.

Madden, D. J. (1985). Age related slowing in the retrieval of information from long-term memory. *Journal of Gerontology, 40*, 208–210.

McFarland, C., Warren, L., & Crockard, J. (1985). Memory for self-generated stimuli in young and old adults. *Journal of Gerontology, 40*, 205–207.

McFarland, R. (1968). The sensory and perceptual processes in aging. In K. Schaie (Ed.), *Theory and methods of research on aging* (pp. 9–52). Morgantown, WV: West Virginia University Press.

McGlone, R., & Hollien, H. (1963). Vocal pitch characteristics of aged women. *Journal of Speech and Hearing Research, 6*, 164–170.

McTavish, T. (1971). Perceptions of old people: A review of the research, methodologies, and findings. *The Gerontologist, 11*, 90–101.

Monge, R. (1969). Learning in adult years set or rigidity. *Human Development, 12*, 131–140.

Montagu, M. F. A. (1971). *Touching: The human significance of the skin.* New York: Columbia University Press.

Morris, D. (1971). *Intimate behaviour.* New York: Random House.

Mysak, E. (1959). Pitch and duration characteristics of older males. *Journal of Speech and Hearing Research, 2*, 46–54.

Nesselroade, J., Schaie, K., & Baltes, P. (1972). Ontogenetic and generational components of structural and quantitative change in adult cognitive behavior. *Journal of Gerontology, 27*, 222–228.

Norris, M., & Cunningham, D. (1981). Social impact of hearing loss in the aged. *Journal of Gerontology, 36*, 727–729.

Norton, R. (1978). Foundation of a communicator style construct. *Human Communication Research, 4*, 99–112.

Norton, R. (1983). *Communicator style: Theory, applications and measures.* Beverly Hills, CA: Sage.

Norton, R., Murray, E., & Arnston, P. (1982). Communication connections to health: Talking about it may help. In L. Pettegrew, P. Arnston, D. Bush, & K. Zoppi (Eds.), *Straight talk: Explorations in provider and patient interaction* (pp. 53–58). Louisville, KY: Humana.

Norton, R., & Nussbaum, J. (1980). Dramatic behaviors of the effective teacher. In D. Nimmo (Ed.), *Communication yearbook IV* (pp. 565–579). New Brunswick, NJ: Transaction Books.

Nussbaum, J. (1981). *Interactional patterns of elderly individuals: Implications for successful adaptation to aging.* Unpublished doctoral dissertation, Purdue University, West Lafayette, IN.

Nussbaum, J. (1983). Relational closeness of elderly interaction: Implications for life satisfaction. *The Western Journal of Speech, 47*, 229–243.

Nussbaum, J., Robinson, J., & Grew, D. (1983, May). *Nursing staff-resident communication within the long-term health care facility.* Paper presented at the International Communication Association, Dallas, TX.

Nussbaum, J., Robinson, J., & Grew, D. (1985). Communicative behavior of the long-term health care employee: Implications for the elderly resident. *Communication Research Reports, 2*, 16–22.

Okun, M. (1976). Adult age and cautiousness in decision. *Human Development, 19*, 220–233.

Oyer, E., & Paolucci, B. (1970). Homemakers' hearing losses and family integration. *Journal of Home Economics, 62*, 257–262.

Palmore, E., & Cleveland, W. (1976). Aging, terminal decline, and terminal drop. *Journal of Gerontology, 31,* 76–81.

Powers, J., & Powers, E. (1978). Hearing problems of elderly persons: Social consequences and prevalence. *ASHA, 20,* 79–83.

Rankin, J., & Collins, M. (1985). Adult age differences in memory elaboration. *Journal of Gerontology, 40,* 451–458.

Riegel, K. (1966). Development of language: Suggestions for a verbal fallout model. *Human Development, 9,* 97–120.

Riegel, K., & Riegel, R. (1972). Development, drop, and death. *Developmental Psychology, 6,* 306–319.

Rinck, C., Willis, F., & Dean, L. (1980). Interpersonal touch among residents of homes for the elderly. *Journal of Communication, 30,* 44–47.

Rubin, K., & Brown, I. (1975). A life-span look at person-perception and its relationship to communicative interaction. *Journal of Gerontology, 30*(4), 461–468.

Ryan, E. B., Giles, H., Bartolucci, G., & Henwood, K. (1986). Psycholinguistic and social psychological components of communication by and with the elderly. *Language and Communication, 6,* 1–24.

Ryan, E. B., Meredith, S. D., MacLean, M. J., & Orange, J. B. (1995). Changing the way we talk with elders: Promoting health using the Communication Enhancement Model. *International Journal of Aging and Human Development, 41,* 87–105.

Ryan, W. (1972). Acoustic aspects of the aging voice. *Journal of Gerontology, 27,* 265–268.

Sataloff, J., & Vassallo, L. (1966). Hard-of-hearing senior citizens and the physician. *Geriatrics, 21,* 182–186.

Savage, R., Britton, P., Bolton, N., & Hall, E. (1975). *Intellectual functioning in the aged.* New York: Barnes & Noble.

Schaie, K. (1975). Age changes in adult intelligence. In D. Woodruff & J. Birren, (Eds.), *Aging* (pp. 111–124). New York: Van Nostrand.

Schaie, K. (1983). The Seattle longitudinal study: A 21 year exploration of psychometric intelligence in adulthood. In K. Schaie (Ed.), *Longitudinal studies of adult psychological development* (pp. 64–135). New York: Guilford.

Schaie, K. (1996). Intellectual development in adulthood. In J. E. Birren & K. W. Schaie (Eds.), *Handbook of the psychology of aging* (4th ed., pp. 266–286). San Diego, CA: Academic Press.

Schaie, K., & Hertzog, C. (1983). Fourteen-year cohort-sequential analyses of adult intellectual development. *Developmental Psychology, 19,* 531–543.

Schonfield, E., & Robertson, B. (1966). Memory storage and aging. *Canadian Journal of Psychology, 20,* 228–236.

Shatz, M., & Gelman, R. (1973). The development of communication skills: Modifications in the speech of young children as a function of listener. *Monographs of the Society for Research in Child Development,* Serial 152, *38*(5).

Shatz, M., & Gelman, R. (1977). Beyond syntax: The influence of conversational constraints on speech modifications. In C. Snow & C. Ferguson (Eds.), *Talking to children.* New York: Cambridge University Press.

Siegler, I. (1980). The psychology of adult development and aging. In E. Busse & D. Blazer (Eds.), *Handbook of geriatric psychiatry* (pp. 169–221). New York: Van Nostrand Reinhold.

Siegler, I. (1983). Psychological aspects of the Duke longitudinal studies. In K. Schaie (Ed.), *Longitudinal studies of adult psychological development* (pp. 136–190). New York: Guilford.

Siegler, I., McCarty, S., & Logue, P. (1982). Weschler memory scale scores, selective attrition, and distance from death. *Journal of Gerontology, 37,* 176–181.

Smith, A. D. (1996). Memory. In J. E. Birren & K. W. Schaie (Eds.), *Handbook of the psychology of aging* (4th ed., pp. 236–250). San Diego, CA: Academic Press.

Smith, B., Thompson, L., & Michalewski, H. (1980). Average evoked potential research in adult aging: Status and prospects. In L. Poon (Ed.), *Aging in the 1980s* (pp. 135–151). Washington, DC: American Psychological Association.

Snow, C. (1972). Mother's speech to children learning language. *Child Development, 43,* 549–565.

Snow, C. (1977). Mother's speech research: From input to interaction. In C. Snow & C. Ferguson (Eds.), *Talking to children* (pp. 31–49). New York: Cambridge University Press.

Suedfeld, P., & Piedrahita, L. (1984). Intimations of mortality: Integrative simplification as a precursor of death. *Journal of Personality and Social Psychology, 47,* 848–852.

Takeda, S., & Matsuzawa, T. (1985). Age-related brain atrophy: A study with computer tomography. *Journal of Gerontology, 40,* 159–163.

Tamir, L. (1982). *Men in their forties: The transition to middle age.* New York: Springer.

Thomas, J. (1972, December). *Remembering the names of pictured objects.* Paper presented at the meeting of the Gerontological Society, San Juan, Puerto Rico.

Thompson, L., Axelrod, S., & Cohen, L. (1965). Senescence and visual identification of tactual-kinesthetic forms. *Journal of Gerontology, 20,* 244–249.

Verbrugge, L. (1984). A health profile of older women with comparisons to older men. *Research on Aging, 6,* 291–322.

Villaume, W. A., Brown, M. H., & Darling, R. (1994). Presbycusis, communication, and older adults. In M. L. Hummert, J. M. Wiemann, & J. F. Nussbaum (Eds.), *Interpersonal communication in older adulthood: Interdisciplinary theory and research* (pp. 83–106). Thousand Oaks, CA: Sage.

Watson, W. (1975). The meaning of touch: Geriatric nursing. *Journal of Communication, 25,* 104–112.

Watzlawick, P. (1978). *The language of change: Elements of therapeutic communication.* New York: Basic Books.

Weber, D. (1987). *Communicator style correlates of conflict resolution modes.* Unpublished master's thesis, University of Dayton, Dayton, OH.

Willeford, J. A. (1971). The geriatric patient. In D. Rose (Ed.), *Audiological assessment* (pp. 281–319). Englewood Cliffs, NJ: Prentice-Hall.

Willis, S. L. (1996). Everyday problem solving. In J. E. Birren & K. W. Schaie (Eds.), *Handbook of the psychology of aging* (4th ed., pp. 287–307). San Diego, CA: Academic Press.

CHAPTER 12

Health, Communication, and Aging

*H*ealth plays an important role in successful aging. People who are healthier report higher levels of well-being. Most people, however, think of health status as a function of biological and lifestyle factors, unaware of the significant role that communication plays in maintaining good health and acquiring assistance when needed. This chapter examines the interrelations among aging, health, and communication.

After briefly reviewing the health status of elderly people, social support is discussed. Assistance with instrumental and emotional needs is provided by formal and informal support networks and allows older individuals to remain independent for as long as possible. Both the care recipient and the caregiver must have strong communicative skills for assistance to be requested and given without creating problems for one or both parties. Next is a discussion of older patient–physician interactions and the role that communication plays in satisfaction with these interactions and compliance with health care regimens. Included in this section are changes anticipated with the evolution of managed care in the United States. Finally, the consequences of relocation to a nursing home are examined, focusing on need for and lack of communication in these institutions.

HEALTH AND AGING

Most people assume that as they grow older their health diminishes. As is the case with many generalizations, there is a kernel of truth in this statement. Recall from chapter 11, however, the distinction between the primary and secondary characteristics of aging. People's health can diminish because they are growing older, and their health can also diminish because they have smoked or eaten poorly for 30 years.

Research suggested that elderly people suffer from more chronic or long-term illnesses than do younger adults or children and that the percentage increases with age (Atchley, 1985; Burham, 1974; Eisdorfer & Cohen, 1980; Siegler, Nowlin, & Blumenthal, 1980; U.S. Census Bureau, 1996). For example, among those 80 years old and older, 70% of women and 53% of men report two or more common chronic conditions (U.S. Census Bureau, 1996). About 10% of those 65 to 75 years old have difficulties with daily activities as a consequence of their chronic illness (U.S. Census Bureau, 1996). This percentage increases to about 20% for those 75 to 79, to about 30% for those 80 to 84, and to about 50% for those 85 and older. The most common chronic conditions are heart conditions, arthritis and rheumatism, visual impairment, diabetes, hearing impairment, and hypertension (National Center for Health Statistics, 1990). Even though elderly people have chronic diseases, most manage quite well and are not "sick" (Stahl & Feller, 1990).

Although elderly people are more likely to have chronic illnesses, they are far less likely to have acute or short-term health problems (Ries, 1979; Siegler et al., 1980; Wilder, 1974a, 1974b). Acute illnesses include broken bones, influenza, and so forth. When elderly people suffer from an acute illness, however, they tend to be "out of commission" longer than younger adults.

Even though many elderly people suffer from chronic conditions and take longer to recover from acute illnesses, their life expectancy has increased dramatically in the past 50 years. Adult men can expect to live about 72 years, and adult women typically live 79 years (U.S. Census Bureau, 1996). Heart conditions are the major cause of death among elderly people. About 50% of the people who live to the age of 65 die from problems related to heart conditions, although this percentage has steadily decreased since 1960 (U.S. Census Bureau, 1996). For adults between the ages of 35 and 44, heart conditions and cancer are the primary causes of death. Younger adults between the ages of 25 and 34 do not typically die of diseases. They tend to die of accidents, suicides, and homocides (Bee, 1987).

Much like the relationship between physical health and aging, the relationship between mental health and age is neither simple nor monotonic. Research suggested that about 1% of elderly people between the ages of 60 and 70 suffer from some impairment of mental functioning, with this percentage increasing to about 25% for those 85 and older (Gatz, Kasl-Godley, & Karel, 1996). Dementia or chronic brain disorders seem to increase with age (Gatz et al., 1996; Gruenberg, 1978; Kay, 1972; Shanas & Maddox, 1976), and the severity of the difficulty also seems to increase with age (Busse & Pfeiffer, 1969). Alzheimer's disease and cerebral arteriosclerosis are the two most common causes of dementia.

In terms of psychosis and neurosis, depression was identified as the biggest mental health problem facing elderly people (Butler & Lewis, 1973), although research suggests that depression is not any more common among the noninstutionalized elderly people than it is in younger adults (Holzer, Leaf, & Weissman, 1985). Gatz et al. (1996) reported that depression, anxiety disorders, and schizophrenia (affecting about 5% of those 65 and older) are actually less prevalent among elderly people than among younger people. Caution must be exercised in interpreting this research, however, because institutionalized elderly people were excluded from the sample.

In summarizing the research on the relationship between mental health and aging, Feinson (1985) concluded that a great deal of research needs to be done before the relationship between mental health and age can be completely understood. Feinson observed that for the most part differences as a result of age were not observed in the literature and often the younger adults were more likely to experience mental problems than older adults.

The relationship between health and aging is an interesting one, and it has gained tremendous popularity as a subject for study in the past 30 years. Larson (1978) and others suggested that health is the single most important determinant of the subjective well-being of elderly people (Cavan, Burgess, Havighurst, & Goldhamer, 1949; Cutler, 1973; Jeffers & Nichols, 1961; Moody, 1994; Palmore & Luikart, 1972; Spreitzer & Snyder, 1974). Unfortunately, the role communication plays in that process has gone relatively unexamined. It appears, however, that the relationships are important ones.

In discussing the role communication plays in health care, Pettegrew (1982) wrote:

> The study and practice of health communication is founded on the recognition that human communication plays a seminal role in health promotion and maintenance. Communication promotes health or sickness within our society, makes the health care system run to the satisfaction of patients and practitioners, and is the cement that binds, coordinates and integrates efforts to treat existing illness and prevent future illness from occurring at all. It is perhaps this fundamental role of communication in health care that lends itself to neglect and complacency by those who must rely on it so routinely. (p. 4)

In addition to the issues addressed by Pettegrew, communication and interpersonal relationships play another important role in the health and well-being of elderly people. Through their social and friendship networks, many elderly people are able to complete daily tasks that would otherwise be impossible. Further, the social support network of elderly people, in part, determines when and if elderly people will be able to live a relatively independent lifestyle.

SOCIAL SUPPORT AND AGING

Cantor (1980) defined a social support system as a pattern of mutual assistance that is significant in the social, psychological, and physical health and well-being of elderly people. These social bonds and relationships provide enough assistance for successful day-to-day living, for a level of independence, and for the maintenance of a positive self-identify. Social support can come from formal agencies (e.g., the state) and from informal sources (e.g., family and friends).

Wellman and Hall (1986) found that there are five types of social support; informational support, emotional support, companionship, services or assistance, and financial support. These findings are consistent with previous research (Bernard & Killworth, 1978; Cantor, 1980; Granovetter, 1974, 1982; Kahn & Antonucci, 1980; Liu & Duff, 1972; Schaefer, Coyne, & Lazarus, 1982). Wellman and Hall (1986) also pointed out that these types of support are often provided by different people. Most of the people they surveyed reported providing some social support (e.g., companionship and emotional support), but far less financial and informational support. Research by Cohen and Willis (1985) showed that the perception that the social support network is successful at times is as important as the actual performance of that social support network.

Research by Cicirelli (1979), Cantor (1980), and others suggested that elderly people look to their informal social support network for help in times of need. Cantor (1992) estimated that two-thirds of elderly people receive some level of care from their children. Many elderly individuals receive support from more than one source. In 1977, Shanas estimated that about 80% of the elderly people receiving some support receive the help from family members, about 20% receive paid help, and about 5% receive help from their friends. Only about 2 to 3% of the elderly people surveyed by Shanas (1977) reported receiving help from formal social service agencies. This demonstrates the importance of informal social support networks in enabling elderly people to keep living in their own homes. These findings were supported by a growing body of research (Atchley, 1972; Bernard & Killworth, 1978; Branch & Jette, 1983; Granovetter, 1974; Kohen, 1983; Lemon, Bengtson, & Peterson, 1972; Liu & Duff, 1972; Marshall, 1980; Moody, 1994; Rosel, 1983; Weeks & Cuellar, 1981).

In reviewing the relationship between social support and health literature, Wellman and Hall (1986) summarized the work of Hammer (1981) and Thoits (1982). Wellman and Hall suggested that the informal social support network contributes to the well-being of elderly people in essentially three ways:

1. The network promotes positive health care practices (e.g., proper diet, appropriate exercise, and regular medical care).
2. The network promotes emotional support during times of crisis (e.g., someone to talk to and someone to provide information about mental health).
3. The network supplies normative and comparative reference influence (e.g., providing feedback about behavior and setting some standards of expected behavior).

The greatest amount of informal social support comes from family members, in particular from the spouse and the children of the elderly individual (Cantor, 1980; Cicirelli, 1979;

Cicirelli, Shanas, & Hauser, 1974). Parents help their adult children with money, offer advice about childrearing and about personal and family matters, and assist with babysitting, although the exchange of assistance is not an equal exchange. As the elderly adult gets older, assistance to the adult children lessens and the children's assistance increases. The child most likely to become a primary caregiver is the child who lives closest; however, when both sons and daughters live nearby, daughters are more likely to be the primary caregiver (Stoller, Forster, & Duniho, 1992). In addition, daughters are more likely to provide "hands on" care, such as household chores, running errands, and personal care, while sons are more likely to help with household maintenance and finances. Siblings and other relatives play a less important role in assistance than do children and the spouse. Siblings are a more important resource for those elderly individuals who are not married and have no children or have children who do not live nearby (Cicirelli, Coward, & Dwyer, 1992).

Friends and neighbors also play a significant role in the informal support system of elderly people. For those people who do not have children or a spouse, it appears that neighbors and friends often serve as surrogate family. Typically, the family provides most of the social support. Recent research suggests, however, that friends and neighbors often make the difference that enables independence for rather than institutionalization of elderly people. Quite often friends and neighbors provide support that would otherwise require the help of formal social support agencies. For example, friends and neighbors often help with banking, shopping, transportation, and other daily activities (Cantor, 1980; Wellman & Hall, 1986). In addition, Rook (1995) pointed out the important difference between social support and companionship; social support addresses instrumental needs, and companionship addresses emotional needs. Family members provide more social support, while friends and neighbors provide more companionship.

In addition to providing social support, those same friends, family members, and neighbors also create problems and difficulties for elderly people. Rook (1984) pointed out that problematic social relations negatively impact elderly people's happiness. Rook (1984) found that people with the most difficult relationships reported the lowest levels of satisfaction with their lives. Quality and not quantity appears to be the key to successful social support networks (Lieberman, 1982; Spanier & Thompson, 1984).

The importance of communication and the implications of difficulties in conversation in this process should be apparent. As Wellman and Hall (1986) demonstrated, most of the elderly people they surveyed reported being provided companionship and emotional support by others, in part because others had the resources to do so. Financial aid, on the other hand, was provided by very few people within the social network because there were few people with enough money to provide assistance to others.

FORMAL SUPPORT AGENCIES

The social network of the elderly often provides a vehicle for relative independence—independence from formal agencies, if from nothing else. Thus, the barriers to establishing and maintaining relationships can greatly contribute to a reliance on formal agencies for assistance. Formal services often must be coordinated with the informal network, especially in the area of health care (Cantor, 1980; McAuley, Travis, & Safewright, 1990); the formal organization may set up the formal care plan, but the family plays a significant role in implementing that plan (Hofland, 1992).

The formal agencies providing support for elderly people are a complex web of primarily governmental agencies. Lowy (1979), in explicating the concept of prevention, identified and described many of the formal social support programs and social policies relevant to elderly people. Koff and Park (1993) pointed out that these agencies were developed in order to prevent elderly people from slipping into poverty and to meet their medical care needs. In terms of financial assistance, elderly people are partially provided for by Social Security. Although elderly people are better off financially than in years past, the number of elderly people living at or below the poverty line is still quite high, and elderly people can expect their lifestyles to change, on average, for the worse in old age.

Supplemental Security Income (SSI) is also available to some elderly people. This supplemental income program was designed for those people who, because of their work history, are ineligible for Social Security. Enacted in 1974, SSI is an attempt to keep people from starving and living in abject poverty.

Health care and social services via health insurance for elderly people are provided for by the Social Security Administration in the form of Medicare and Medicaid. Medicare is a federal health insurance program for elderly people, and Medicaid is a health insurance plan for the poor, regardless of age, administered by state welfare agencies. Butler (1975), Lowy (1979), Koff and Park (1993), and others pointed out that such programs are far from successful. The focus of these programs is for the treatment of acute and not chronic illness. Recall that older individuals are more likely to have chronic, not acute, illnesses. These programs are particularly ineffective in terms of providing preventive health care. In addition, long-term care in residential facilities is not covered by these programs except under rare circumstances.

In addition, the Social Security Act and the Older Americans Act provide food programs (e.g., congregate meals via the Nutrition Program for the Elderly), money management services, legal assistance, geriatric day-care centers and day-care hospitals, and mental health programs. These two acts also provide referral and information services, and they provide access to benefits and community outreach programs. They can help facilitate transportation and education for elderly people as well as telephone reassurance programs and various levels of home visitation and home care (Koff & Park, 1993; Lowy, 1979).

The formal support network of an elderly individual includes a variety of individuals and agencies. Health care professionals, including physicians, nurses, pharmacists, and mental health specialists are often key elements in the social support network. Although little research has examined the relationships between health care professionals and elderly patients, some research into patient–health care provider relationships does exist.

The patient–health care provider relationship is a difficult one for people of all ages. The context for such interaction is complex. People are not at their best because they are ill or a loved one is ill. There are great differences in the technical expertise and the social status of communicants. These barriers impede interaction between the patients and health care professionals. In general, there is agreement that patient–health care provider interaction is difficult. In the case of elderly patients, in particular, these difficulties are further compounded by the sight, hearing, memory, and cognitive deficits discussed throughout chapter 11.

These barriers become particularly salient because the relationship between the patient and health-care provider has been shown to be related to the well-being of the patient (e.g.,

Marston, 1970; Mechanic, 1978). In addition, the relationships between an elderly individual and a health care professional may make the difference between a relatively independent living arrangement for or the institutionalization of the elderly person.

PATIENT–PHYSICIAN INTERACTION

Although most people report being satisfied with the health care they receive, many of these same people say that they are not happy with their communicative relationships with health care professionals (Beisecker & Thompson, 1995; Decastro, 1972; Fuller & Quesada, 1973; Skipper, 1965). Patients are unhappy because they do not perceive their doctor to be treating them in a friendly and warm manner (Daly & Hulka, 1975; Korsch, Gozzi, & Francis, 1968), even though physicians often feel that they are friendly to their patients (Korsch & Negrete, 1972). Although this criticism is not a complaint solely from the elderly patient, it is interesting to note that physicians are considered to be much friendlier to children than they are to adults.

A second complaint of patients about their doctors is that they do not receive enough information from their physician (Bertakis, 1977; Crown, 1971; Mechanic, 1978), but neither do they demand it from their physician (Adler, 1977). In addition, physicians spend more time seeking information than giving it (Roter, Hall, & Katz, 1988). Not surprisingly, patients want more information about the nature and cause of their illness, the duration of their illness, and the treatment prescribed by the physician to battle the illness (Decastro, 1972; Korsch et al., 1968; Skipper, 1965). This information seems to be particularly important prior to an operation (Aasterud, 1965; Meyers, 1965). In addition, patients have better recall of the information when they are given more detailed instructions (Beisecker & Thompson, 1995).

Patients also report feeling less satisfied with their health care when they do not feel that their doctor is aware of their concerns (Daly & Hulka, 1975; Korsch et al., 1968). Elderly patients are dissatisfied when physicians do not attend to their psychosocial needs as well as their physical needs (Beisecker & Thompson, 1995). The awareness of the patient's concerns is particularly important in the case of an elderly patient who may be managing multiple chronic illnesses and contending with a variety of personal and family problems (Greene, Adelman,

Rizzo, & Friedmann, 1994). Not only does the quality of the diagnosis depend on the physician having all the relevant information, but so does the quality of treatment (Beisecker & Thompson, 1995).

To make matters worse, Crown (1971) found that physicians often ignore relevant information about a patient when it is provided by another family member. It is not unusual for older individuals to have a companion with them during a doctor's visit. The companion is typically a spouse, child, or another caregiver (Beisecker & Thompson, 1995). Beisecker (1989) found that companions play various roles: (a) the watchdog, who verifies information for both the patient and the physician; (b) the significant other, who provides feedback regarding feasibility of a health care regimen; and (c) the surrogate patient, who answers questions directed to the patient. Crown's finding that physicians sometimes ignore information provided by the companion becomes particularly significant when the patient is unable to communicate his or her concerns effectively.

Korsch and Negrete (1972) suggested that physicians baffle patients with technical language and jargon in about 50% of all cases, and that patients are very reluctant to ask questions when they do not understand their physicians' comments. Raimbault, Lachin, Limal, Eliacheff, and Rappaport (1975) found physicians prefer to use quasi-scientific terminology in conversation, often ignoring or evading emotional issues surrounding the case. Obviously, most patients would prefer less terminology and more insight into the emotional issues of their illness.

Many patients are intimidated by their physician and are reluctant to initiate topics of conversation. The reasons for this reluctance include awe of the physician, fear of negative replies, a lack of confidence that their initiation of a topic will result in their gaining information, the perception that the doctor is too busy to talk about their illness (Skipper, 1965), and the perception of class and cultural differences between the patients and physicians (Adelman, Greene, & Charon, 1991; Samora, Saunders & Larson, 1961; Walker, 1973). Research by Korsch and Negrete (1972) and Tryon and Leonard (1965) suggested that active patients receive better care and are more satisfied with their interaction than are passive patients. The current cohort of elderly patients, however, tends to be more passive when interacting with physicians (Beisecker & Thompson, 1995).

Another barrier to effective interaction with older patients is the time available. Physicians are pressed to be as efficient as possible with their time, especially in current health care settings that provide fees based on the number of patients seen rather than on the services provided. Older patients may require more time. One reason more time is needed is that older patients have more complicated health care issues and histories (Adelman et al., 1991). Physical or cognitive impairments will also increase the time needed. An older individual with arthritis, for example, may be slower to undress. An individual with cognitive impairments may need to be provided more information (such as written cues) to remind him or her of when to take medications. In spite of the reasons to spend more time with older patients, physicians tend to spend less time with them (Haug & Ory, 1987).

A few studies examined actual interactions between physicians and their older patients. Adelman, Greene, Charon, and Friedmann (1992) found that both physicians and patients are likely to raise medical topics for discussion, but patients are more likely than physicians to raise psychosocial issues. When physicians raise an issue, they respond more positively and with more detail than when patients raise an issue. Rost and Frankel (1993) found that older patients often do not raise issues that they indicate are of concern to them and that they intended to raise with their physicians. It should be noted that the issue patients identify as the most important problem is not the first issue they raise. If the interaction does not last long enough, this issue may not be raised at all.

One of the largest problems facing physicians and patients is the issue of patient compliance. Estimates of noncompliance vary greatly. Stone (1979) observed that compliance rates from 4 to 92% have been reported in the literature. A conservative estimate of the number of patients complying with the health care regimen would be between 60 and 70%.

Patients fail to comply in a variety of different ways. Stone (1979) suggested that sins of omission are common. Noncompliance by omission includes physicians failing to prescribe a particular medication or a patient forgetting to take a medicine. In addition, many people take the wrong medicine or the wrong dosage. Some people take the right medicine and the right dosage, but they take the medicine at the wrong time. The implications of noncompliance can be quite severe. Stone (1979) suggested that when patients are noncompliant they experience much longer illnesses, far more complications, and the costs of health care nearly quadruples.

The explanations for noncompliance are many. Some research suggested that people do not comply because they do not remember what their physician said (Korsch & Negrete, 1972). Others ignore or do not accurately receive the information because they do not want to hear unpleasant news (Samora et al., 1961). Research by Hendin (1977) and others suggested that patients forget as much as one third of the information given them by their doctor. In the case of elderly patients with memory deficits or reception difficulties, the problems of noncompliance may be even greater. Also, older patients are more likely to be taking multiple medications and have complex health regimens (Haug & Ory, 1987). Willful noncompliance may not be as great an issue as is the simple misunderstanding of instructions (Beisecker & Thompson, 1995).

Other factors influencing compliance and satisfaction with treatment are the simplicity and specificity of the instructions (Adelman et al., 1991; Charney, 1972; Korsch & Negrete, 1972), the expressions of warmth by the health care professionals (Aday & Anderson, 1975; Becker, Drachman, & Kirscht, 1972; Caplan & Sussman, 1966; Doyle & Ware, 1977; Francis, Korsch, & Morris, 1969; Freemon, Negrete, Davis, & Korsch, 1971; Kinsey, Bradshaw, & Ley, 1975; Korsch et al., 1968), and the level of rapport between patients and their physicians (DiMatteo, 1979).

In addition, physicians offering more information about the illness facing the patient and the treatment are more likely to gain compliance (Francis et al., 1969; Freemon, et al., 1971; Hulka, Cassel, Kupper, & Burdette, 1976; Lane, 1982; Roter, 1977). Noncompliance has been shown to be related to formality of interaction, to antagonism, to mutual withholding of information (Davis, 1968), and to the degree to which the medical advice would result in changes in life habits (Charney, 1972). In general, patient satisfaction increases compliance (Francis et al., 1969), although such seemingly obvious and simplistic relationships have often been shown to be invalid (e.g., the relationship between job satisfaction and productivity).

In a review of patient characteristics related to compliance, Lane (1982) suggested that the communicative relationship between patients and physicians provides a far better explanation of compliance rates than do the more common demographic factors. For example, gender (Marston, 1970), socioeconomic status (Schmidt, 1977), and educational level or intelligence (Schmidt, 1977) all appear to be unrelated to compliance. Lane (1982) suggested the relationships between compliance and personality types, marital status, ethnicity, and religion are either small, equivocal, or near zero. It is interesting to note that patient age is unrelated to drug-error rates (Wilson, 1973) and, in most studies, unrelated to compliance (Marston, 1970). Lane (1982) concluded that "little relationship between patient oriented characteristics and compliance" (p. 62) exists, and Lane further suggested that the best predictor of compliance is communicative behavior and the relationship between patients and physicians (Bertakis, 1977; Hendin, 1977; Marston, 1970; Mechanic, 1978; Stone, 1979).

Lane's (1982) research suggested that physicians attribute the reasons for noncompliance to the characteristics of the patient and not to the interaction between patient and the health care provider. Further, Lane (1982) found that patient compliance increases when the provider communicates personal interest in the patient. This is consistent with Stone's (1979) findings that a 30% increase in compliance can be realized by providing physicians with communication skills training.

Physicians can do a great deal to improve patient compliance. Some redundancy (both written and verbal) of instructions to the patient, simple instructions covering one issue at a time, and a policy of communicating in a nurturant and caring fashion will help improve patient compliance. The recognition that the reasons behind noncompliance are communicative and not due to the personality characteristics of the patients may go a long way in remedying some of these problems.

The Managed Care Environment and Older Patients

The health care system has been changing for the past 30 years, motivated by spiraling medical costs and the efforts to control those costs (Health Care Finance Administration, 1999). Managed care is a very broad term describing health insurance products in which health care providers are reimbursed in a variety of ways, ranging from discounted fee-for-service to capitation.

The popularity of managed care is evident in the number of individuals enrolled in these programs. In 1996, about 67.5 million people were enrolled in a managed care program (American Association of Health Plans, 1999). Managed care in all of its forms is now the dominant form of health care service in the United States.

The evolution of managed health care continues to have a significant impact not only on the financial reality of the business of medicine, but also on the process of health care delivery. Specifically, the way health care providers interact with patients to render service is directly affected by the emergence of managed care (Greene & Adelman, 1996). Two important structural changes have resulted from managed care—the emergence of primary care physicians and interdisciplinary teams.

In many ways, the primary care physician serves as a key player in the continued good health of older adults. In most managed care systems, the primary care physician serves as a "gatekeeper" for other medical services. In essence, the primary care physician becomes a case manager for the older patient by consulting with the patient, the HMO or payer, the family, and other health professionals to develop a plan to achieve the optimum patient outcome. The relationship between the primary care physician and the older patient in this type of managed care system becomes quite significant (Nussbaum, Pecchioni, & Crowell, in press). It becomes essential that both the primary care physician and the older patient be able to communicate effectively, build trust, and understand the dynamic of their unique relationship.

Because of the multifaceted health problems associated with older adults and a redirection to maintenance of functional ability and quality of life, interdisciplinary health care teams have become an important tool for providing care to frail elderly people (Clark, 1997). Approximately once a month, the team, made up of the primary care physician; various nurses; social workers; physical, occupational, and recreational therapists; mental health specialists; and at times the patient or a family member, will gather to review each patient's progress. The result of the care-planning meeting will be communicated to those who directly care for the patient and to the family. Clark (1997) pointed out that these interdisciplinary teams must not only bridge the communication gap among the different health professions, but also between the health professions and their older patients.

From the perspective of an older patient, managed care means that the older adult may not be able to choose the specific physician or health care provider requested, may not spend as much time with the physician as he or she wants, may find numerous health care providers included as active participants, may not be completely aware of the payment structure for the visit or procedure, may find a reduction in paperwork, may experience lower out-of-pocket expenses, may discover more emphasis placed on routine preventative behaviors, may run into negative attitudes toward managed care held by the health care providers, and may find physicians who select managed care for their practice to be more egalitarian (Farmer, 1994; Serafini, 1990; Ward, 1990).

Changes in the health care environment result in a need for the physician-patient relationship to take on new meanings (Nussbaum et al., in press). The dominant all-knowing, quasi-scientific professional who wants to rely only on test evidence is being replaced by a communicative, empathetic negotiator who must come to grips with the health priorities of the patient. The primary care physician no longer makes important decisions alone, but must include others in a negotiation in the process of quality care decisions. The primary care physician is presented with the opportunity to reframe the relationship from a complementary one to a more equal, co-dependent relationship. Physicians need to learn the skills necessary to actively listen to their patients and negotiate with them regarding their health-related goals (Mold, 1995; Mold, Blake, & Becker, 1991; Mold & McCarthy, 1995). In addition, in an interdisciplinary team, all the professionals must show respect and value the expertise of not only the other professionals, but also the patient and his or her family. The synergy of teams can be realized for problem solving and goal achievement when compartmentalization of services is avoided.

At the same time, the patient no longer can just sit by submissively as if the "cost to cure" is not an issue. Older adults must become active participants in the patient–health care provider relationship. The evidence is quite clear that communicatively active older patients are more informed and satisfied with their care, yet extensive research shows that many older adults do not ask enough questions or disclose pertinent information to their physicians. Older patients must be willing to actively engage the health care professionals with whom they interact. Older patients need to become more knowledgeable about their own health, to consider their personal health goals and to learn about realistic goal setting. This knowledge must be competently communicated to all health care providers.

Just as any competent personal or professional relationship cannot be taken for granted, the quality of the health care provider–older patient relationship is dependent on the communicative effort of both participants. Neither participant can assume that he or she knows what is best or can read the other person's mind. Both parties need to understand that this relationship deserves hard work.

OTHER HEALTH CARE CONCERNS

It is commonly felt that nurses should play an important role in fulfilling the psychosocial needs of patients. Unfortunately, Skipper (1965) found that nurses do not interact with patients in the same way they think they do, and, furthermore, they tend to depersonalize patients. Nurses also tend to make hasty and inaccurate judgments about patient's messages (Tarasuk, Rhymes, & Leonard, 1965), and they often disconfirm patient's feelings in an attempt at being reassuring (Gregg, 1965). Disconfirmation is often communicated by denying a person his or her own feelings and sensory experiences (e.g., saying, "This won't hurt much"). Many of the difficulties in conversation that patients and physicians experience are similar to the difficulties facing patients and nurses. In the case of institutionalized elderly people, nurses and other health care professionals play an even more important role in the well-being of elderly people.

In chapter 11 the barriers to conversation for elderly people were identified; the problems between professional health care providers and elderly people compound these difficulties found in conversation with elderly people.

The attitudes of elderly people toward their own health is an additional obstacle to their relationship with health care professionals and to their own well-being. Busse and Pfeiffer (1969) found that 44% of elderly people in poor health nevertheless rated themselves in good or excellent health. Eisdorfer and Cohen (1980) also pointed out other barriers that exacerbate problems, such as older patients not trusting doctors (especially young doctors), fearing hospitals as places to die, having a tendency to self-medicate, and failing to understand or follow instructions. Physicians and elderly people alike see being ill or infirm as normal for old people. Such attitudes can create additional difficulties in relationships between health care providers and their elderly patients.

To summarize, it is suggested in this chapter that health is a term that should be used to refer to physical, psychological, and social well-being. Friendships and relationships with neighbors, spouses and siblings, as well as parent–child relationships, all play an important role in the health and health care of elderly people. Both formal and informal social support networks impact life quality and work as complementary agencies. These two systems allow the elderly individual to remain relatively independent. When the informal networks are unwilling or can no longer provide a service, the elderly turn to the formal agencies. When the formal agencies cannot provide essential services, relocation often results.

RELOCATION AND ELDERLY PEOPLE

Elderly people may relocate for a variety of reasons. Couples may move after retirement. This move may be within the same community, but to a smaller residence, or to another state for warmer weather or to be nearer to children and grandchildren. Widows may move after the death of their spouses. The relocation that this section focuses on, however, is the move to a nursing home. When individuals can no longer live alone or receive adequate care in a private residence, the nursing home is the last option. Of those people 65 years old and older, only about 4% live in a nursing home at any given time (Administration on Aging, 1998). Kastenbaum and Candy (1973) pointed out, however, that such a figure may be misleading because about 20% of all elderly people eventually die in a long-term care facility.

There is a growing body of literature examining the effect on an elderly individual of moving or being moved to a new home, particularly a nursing home. It has been feared that the move to a new residence destroys the informal, and often the formal, support network so essential to the well-being of the elderly individual.

Researchers and policy makers discuss the relocation effect; their concern is that if elderly people are relocated, their lives are dramatically changed, and such changes may be responsible for significant decreases in life satisfaction and life span. The generative force or cause of the relocation effect is metaphorically referred to as transplantation shock by some, and this suggests that the trauma of being in new surroundings reduces longevity. In fact, this reasonably well-accepted phenomenon has been used as a rationale for keeping institutionalized elderly people in inferior nursing facilities, and it has even been used as a defense against the decertification of deficient nursing care facilities. The argument goes something like this: The effect of moving the elderly person may be worse for the person's physical and mental well-being than occupancy in a substandard proprietary home (Hughes, 1982).

Initially it was thought that the mere change in environment was the generative force or reason for the increase in morbidity of elderly people after they moved. This explanation received some empirical support (Lawton & Yaffe, 1970; Miller, 1965; Pastalan, 1975). More recent research suggests the effects of relocation are more complex than mere shock from relocation. It appears, though, that voluntary relocation has less of an effect on elderly people (Ferrare, 1963; Schooler, 1975, 1976; Schulz & Brenner, 1977), and that the amount of preparation involved prior to the change has been shown to mediate the effect of relocation (Bourestrom & Pastalan, 1981).

Other factors influence the magnitude of the relocation effect. The degree to which the individual being relocated likes where he or she was living before the move (Killian, 1970), whether or not the relocated individual will have to give up personal effects such as clothing and furniture (Schoenberg, Carr, Peretz, & Kutscher, 1970), and whether or not the move reduces the individual's feelings of environmental control (Aldrich & Mendkoff, 1963; Kral, Grad, & Berenson, 1968; Markus, Blenker, Bloom, & Downs, 1971, 1972; Miller & Lieberman, 1965) have all been shown to influence the severity of relocation effects.

Relocation is not always a terrible thing for the elderly individual. There have been several studies of interinstitutional relocation that demonstrated positive outcomes (Carp, 1977; Goldfarb, Shahinian, & Turner, 1966). It appears that mere relocation does not in and of itself cause the premature death of institutionalized elderly people. After reviewing the literature, Schulz and Brenner (1977) proposed a model to explain the existing research findings on relocation. Not surprisingly, the research is quite consistent with the theoretical tone of this book. Schulz and Brenner concluded that, if the elderly individual is involved in the decision to relocate, the relocation will not be nearly as traumatic. In fact, Schooler (1975, 1976) argued further that the anticipation of relocation is frequently associated with a significant decline in health and morale that is exacerbated by the actual move. As Lieberman (1974) pointed out, in an environment that encourages individuality and autonomy, community integration, appropriate levels of privacy, and a sense of environmental control, institutionalized elderly people generally fare well.

Coffman (1983) and others argued that relocation effects are not really caused by relocation. Other factors, such as those described, affect the impact of a new environment on the individual. Care before, during, and after the move, the relative advantages or disadvantages of the move, the perception by the individual that he or she has choices and environmental control have all been shown to be factors related to the relative success of relocation. This, of course, is fortunate because these factors are often within the control of institutions, family members, and the elderly people being relocated.

In discussions of relocation effects, many of the problems associated with the institutions themselves were brought up. Many homes lack the proper facilities and staff. The self-concept of an elderly individual often suffers from the decrease in environmental control, diminished privacy, and the loss of many personal artifacts. Because relocation is often accompanied by a change or reduction in activities and interaction, elderly individuals may become alienated from the community and their friends. The fact that there is often little in the way of preparation for the transition is also seen as a factor contributing to the impact of relocation. The decision to move to a nursing home often occurs after an illness or a fall, when the patient is discharged from the hospital, but cannot return home. Discharge orders often are given on the day of the discharge, leaving little time for planning (McAuley & Travis, 1997).

Of course, illness or disability or a change in the social network of the elderly individual will often precipitate a change in his or her well-being. Obviously, this is a very traumatic time and one in which other traumas are likely to be occurring. It is a last move and a decision that results in a great deal of familial guilt (Hinton, 1982). This guilt has been shown to result in bad or simple-minded decisions about the choice of nursing home (York & Calsyn, 1977). Typically, the decision about which institution to choose is made by the family physician and not the family (McAuley & Travis, 1997; York & Calsyn, 1977).

This guilt also leads family members to feel that frequent visits are the way to prove they are not dumping their elderly relative (Hinton, 1982; Montgomery, 1982; Scott, 1978; Smith & Bengtson, 1979; Wentzell, 1978; York & Calsyn, 1977). These visits can come at inopportune times, when they interfere with staff tasks (Silverstone, 1978), when the resident is tired and not interested in visitation (Treas, 1977), and when a visit can cause more guilt because it is not satisfying. This guilt can also lead to hostility toward the staff and interference with staff–resident relationships. The development of friendships and significant relationships between staff and residents has largely gone unexamined and appears to be an important factor in the life satisfaction of institutionalized elderly people.

For years, research showed that familial relations are an important contributor to the well-being of elderly people

(Brubaker, 1983; Cicirelli, 1979; Johnson, 1978; Johnson & Bursk, 1977; Sussman & Burchinal, 1962a, 1962b; Troll, 1971). In addition, there is a growing body of literature that suggested that friendships are more significant than familial relationships for elderly people (Arling, 1976; Baldassare, Rosenfeld, & Rook, 1984; Nussbaum, 1983; Strain & Chappell, 1982; Wood & Robertson, 1978). The size of the social network, of both family and friends, is not as crucial as is the quality of intimacy within the network (Cohen-Mansfield & Marx, 1992).

Rook (1995) argued that relationships with family members and friends serve different relational functions. The family provides support in health care, daily tasks, and financial assistance, whereas friends serve as companions of choice for interaction. While social support addresses the important tangible needs of care, companionship addresses the important intangible need of interaction for interaction's sake. In addition, an individual's well-being is enhanced by the positive feelings associated with being selected to participate in such interactions. In the case of institutionalized elderly people, the staff represent a potential friend with contact to the world outside the nursing home. Unfortunately, the importance of staff–resident relationships has too often gone ignored.

In an examination of the communicative environment of elderly people, Nussbaum (1981, 1983) compared the communication patterns of people living in nursing homes, retirement villages, and in their own homes. Nussbaum (1983) found that elderly people living in a long-term health care facility suffer "interactional starvation." Residents of a nursing home interact far less frequently and with less closeness and self-disclosure than do elderly people living at home or in the retirement village. Nussbaum (1981) concluded that the nursing home environment negatively influences the interactive behavior of the elderly residents. Cohen-Mansfield and Marx (1992) found that agitated and aggressive nursing home residents have social networks of similar sizes and densities as do nonaggressive nursing home residents, but that there is much less intimacy in their networks. Whether agitation and aggressiveness reduce the intimacy in the resident's network or the reduction in intimacy leads to more agitation and aggressiveness, however, is not clear from this study.

Grainger (1995) also found an atmosphere of interactional starvation for institutionalized elderly people in the United Kingdom. She found an overall absence of talk, influenced by such environmental factors as chairs being placed up against walls instead of in conversational circles, noisy conditions, and lack of privacy. When interaction between residents and staff did occur, the staff focused their talk on task-oriented topics. What little relational talk was observed was brief and used in ways to attempt to speed along the completion of tasks. In addition, talk directed toward the residents was dependency-inducing. Not only were sentences more simplistic and more redundant, but they also contained many chastisements and directives as would be directed toward young children.

Nussbaum (1983) found that the institutionalized elderly people in his study communicated more about topics related to social disengagement than did the elderly people living in the retirement villages or at home. Topics related to disengagement included the patient's family, old times, problems with health, death, problems with old age, and the hobbies of the patient. Activity-oriented topics included the staff's family, the staff's plans after work, the staff's job, staff problems, and staff health. The data suggest the staff members rarely disclosed information about their job, personal problems, or their own health to elderly people. Nussbaum (1981) found interaction on activity-oriented topics is related to successful adaptation to later life.

Research into the relational network of institutionalized elderly people suggested that the staff play an important role in the life satisfaction (cf., Nussbaum & Robinson, 1984; Nussbaum, Robinson, & Grew, 1985) and the longevity of elderly people (cf., Noelker & Harel, 1978). Miller and Lelieuvre (1982) also found that verbal praise and attention from staff result in lower levels of pain for institutionalized elderly people.

Nussbaum et al. (1985) examined the impact that feelings of affinity toward the residents of several nursing homes had on the way the staff members communicated with the residents. They found:

1. Nurses who feel high levels of affinity for the residents talk about old times, religion, and problems due to old age more often than do staff members who do not feel close to the residents.
2. Nurses who feel high levels of affinity for the residents also communicate in a more friendly and relaxed style than do staff members who do not feel close to the residents.
3. Nurse aides who feel close to the residents talk more about religion and the hobbies of the residents than do aides who feel less close to the residents.

4. Nurse aides who feel high levels of affinity for the residents also communicate in a more friendly and relaxed style than do aides who do not feel close to the residents.

Holmes and Holmes (1995) reported several studies that examine interaction between nursing home residents and staff. These studies suggest that positive interactions are more likely when the caretakers and elderly residents share a common background. For example, in a comparison of two nursing homes—one with predominantly European American residents and one with predominantly African American residents—and both with predominantly African American staff, more joking occurred between the staff and elderly people when they were of the same ethnic background. As in any relationship, finding things that are shared in common provides grounds for building more intimacy in the relationship.

It has been argued that communication skills are as important as any other skill in the helping professions (cf., Tarasuk et al., 1965). Research suggested that nurse–patient interaction can reduce pain and postoperative vomiting (Dumas, Anderson, & Leonard, 1965), reduce patients' perceptions of pain (Miller & Lelieuvre, 1982), increase life satisfaction for elderly people in institutions (Nussbaum et al., 1985), and increase longevity (Noelker & Harel, 1978). It appears that in the case of nursing homes, communicative skills are of particular importance.

Grooters, Hill, and Long (1997) found that some of the negative attitudes exhibited by staff toward the elderly residents were based on the feeling that society devalues their work. In order to cope with negative attitudes expressed by others about their job, they develop a defense mechanism by distancing themselves from the elderly residents. Grooters et al. suggest a multilevel training program. At one level, employees and families are sensitized to one another's needs and the needs of the residents. Other levels aim at fighting stereotypes in the community at large by involving the residents in one-on-one interactions with community members and providing educational programs to the community.

Kalisch (1971) suggested empathy training, role-playing, modeling, and experiential training to improve staff–resident relationships. Although many studies demonstrate improvements in self-evaluation and instructor evaluations of empathy, little behavioral change from patient perceptions have been observed.

Robinson and Nussbaum (1986) tested Kalisch's (1971) assertion by providing a simulated aging experience for nursing home staff members. They found that the simulated aging experience increased levels of job satisfaction among nurse aides in a long-term health care facility and reduced the number of complaints registered against the staff over a 4-month period. Such programs may have a significant impact on the quality of life of the residents as well. A great deal of future research on this is needed.

SUMMARY

This chapter demonstrates the interrelatedness of aging, health, and communication. It is important to recognize that the effects of aging can be a function of age or a function of accumulated life events, and that aging does not create deficits in every physical or mental capacity. Although there are some barriers facing elderly people and their interactional partners in conversation, these barriers are rarely insurmountable. Health care professionals, in particular, need to consider these conditions in their interaction with elderly people.

Further, social and familial relations provide much of the support needed to ensure some degree of autonomy for elderly adults. When these informal networks can no longer provide enough support, formal agencies are often expected to intervene. When formal and informal agencies can no longer allow an adequate level of independence, the elderly individual may have to be relocated. It is important to recognize that relationships that support daily functioning for an independent elderly person are often lost or changed when that person is institutionalized. These relationships contribute to the success, or lack of success, of relocations.

Once they are relocated, elderly people need to establish close relationships in their new environment. Relationships between staff and residents are of particular importance because of their convenience and because staff members can be a link to the world outside the institution. Staff members need to recognize the importance of these relationships because they can make an important contribution to the mental and physical health of institutionalized elderly people.

■ REFERENCES

Aasterud, M. (1965). Explanation to the patient. In J. K. Skipper & R. L. Leonard (Eds.), *Social interaction and patient care* (pp. 82–86). Philadelphia: Lippincott.

Aday, L., & Anderson, R. (1975). *Access to medical care.* Ann Arbor, MI: Health Administration Press.

Adelman, R. D., Greene, M. G., & Charon, R. (1991). Issues in physician-elderly patient interaction. *Ageing and Society, 2,* 127–148.

Adelman, R. D., Greene, M. C., Charon, R., & Friedmann, E. (1992). The content of physician and elderly patient interaction in the medical primary care encounter. *Communication Research, 19,* 370–380.

Adler, K. (1977). Doctor-patient communication: A shift to problem-oriented research. *Human Communication Research, 3,* 179–190.

Administration on Aging. (1998). *Profile of Older Americans 1998.* [On-line]. Available: *http://www.aoa.dhhs.gov/aoa/stats/profile*

Aldrich, C. K., & Mendkoff, E. (1963). Relocation of the aged and disabled: Mortality study. *Journal of American Geriatrics Society, 11,* 185–194.

American Association of Health Plans. (1999). *Definitions* [On-line]. Available: *http://www.aahp.org*

Arling, G. (1976, November). The elderly widow and her family, neighbors, and friends. *Journal of Marriage and the Family, 38,* 757–768.

Atchley, R. (1972). *The social forces in later life.* Belmont, CA: Wadsworth.

Atchley, R. (1985). *The social forces in later life* (4th ed.). Belmont, CA: Wadsworth.

Baldassare, M., Rosenfeld, S., & Rook, K. (1984). The types and social relations predicting elderly well-being. *Research on Aging, 6,* 549–559.

Becker, M., Drachman, R., & Kirscht, J. (1972). Motivation as predictors of health behavior. *Health Services Reports, 87,* 852–861.

Bee, H. (1987). *The journey of adulthood.* New York: Macmillan.

Beisecker, A. E. (1989). The influence of a companion on the doctor-elderly patient interaction. *Health Communication, 1,* 55–70.

Beisecker, A. E., & Thompson, T. L. (1995). The elderly patient-physician interaction. In J. F. Nussbaum & J. Coupland (Eds.), *Handbook of communication and aging research* (pp. 397–416). Mahwah, NJ: Lawrence Erlbaum Associates.

Bernard, H., & Killworth, P. (1978). A review of the small world literature. *Connections, 2,* 15–24.

Bertakis, K. (1977). The communication of information from physician to patient: A method for increasing patient retention and satisfaction. *The Journal of Family Practice, 5,* 217–222.

Bourestrom, N., & Pastalan, L. (1981). The effects of relocation on the elderly: A reply to Borup. *The Gerontologist, 21,* 4–7.

Branch, L., & Jette, A. (1983). Elders' use of informal long-term care assistance. *The Gerontologist, 23,* 51–56.

Brubaker, T. (1983). *Family relationships in later life.* Beverly Hills, CA: Sage.

Burham, C. E. (1974). *Edentulous persons: United States—1971.* (Vital and Health Statistics, Series 10, No. 89). Washington, DC: U.S. Government Printing Office.

Busse, E. W., & Pfeiffer, E. (Eds.). (1969). *Behavior and adaptation in later life.* Boston: Little, Brown.

Butler, R. (1975). *Why survive?: Being old in America.* New York: Harper & Row.

Butler, R., & Lewis, M. (1973). *Aging and mental health: Positive psychosocial approaches.* St. Louis, MO: Mosby.

Cantor, M. (1980). The informal support system: Its relevance in the lives of the elderly. In Borgotta, E. & McCluskey, N. (Eds.), *Aging and society: Current research perspectives* (pp. 131–144). Beverly Hills, CA: Sage.

Cantor, M. (1992, Summer). Families and caregiving in an aging society. *Generations 16,* 67–70.

Caplan, E., & Sussman, M. (1966). Rank-order of important variables for patient and staff satisfaction. *Journal of Health and Human Behavior, 7,* 133–138.

Carp, F. (1977). Impact of improved living environment on health and life expectancy. *The Gerontologist, 17,* 242–249.

Cavan, R., Burgess, E., Havighurst, R., & Goldhamer, H. (1949). *Personal adjustment in old age.* Chicago: Science Research Associates.

Charney, E. (1972). Patient-doctor communication: Implications for the clinician. *Pediatrics Clinics of North America, 19,* 263–279.

Cicirelli, V. G. (1979, May 31). *Social services for the elderly in relation to kin network.* (Report to the NRTA-AARP.) Washington, DC: Andrus Foundation.

Cicirelli, V. G., Coward, R. T., & Dwyer, J. W. (1992). Siblings as caregivers for impaired elders. *Research on Aging, 14,* 331–350.

Cicirelli, V. G., Shanas, E., & Hauser, P. (1974). Zero population growth and the family life of old people. *Journal of Social Issues, 30,* 74–92.

Clark, P. G. (1997). Values in health care professional socialization: Implications for geriatric education in interdisciplinary teamwork. *The Gerontologist, 37,* 441–451.

Coffman, T. L. (1983). Toward an understanding of geriatric relocation. *The Gerontologist, 23,* 453–459.

Cohen, S., & Willis, T. (1985). Stress, social support, and the buffering hypothesis. *Psychological Bulletin, 98,* 310–357.

Cohen-Mansfield, J., & Marx, M. S. (1992). The social network of the agitated nursing home resident. *Research on Aging, 14,* 110–123.

Crown, S. (1971). Failures of communication. *The Lancet, 7707,* 1021–1022.

Cutler, S. (1973). Volunteer association participation and life satisfaction: A cautionary research note. *Journal of Gerontology, 28,* 96–100.

Daly, M. B., & Hulka, B. S. (1975). Talking with the doctor, 2. *Journal of Communication, 25,* 148–152.

Davis, M. (1968). Variations in patients' compliance with doctors' advice: An empirical analysis of patterns of communication. *American Journal of Public Health, 58,* 274–288.

Decastro, F. J. (1972). Doctor-patient communication: Exploring the effectiveness of care in a primary care clinic. *Clinical Pediatrics, 11,* 86–87.

DiMatteo, M. R. (1979). A social psychological analysis of physician-patient rapport: Toward a science of the art of medicine. *Journal of Social Issues, 35,* 12–33.

Doyle, B., & Ware, J. (1977). Physician conduct and other factors that affect consumer satisfaction with medical care. *Journal of Medical Education, 23,* 283–292.

Dumas, R. G., Anderson, B. J., & Leonard. R. C. (1965). Nurses' sense of adequacy and attitudes toward keeping patients informed. In J. K. Skipper & R. L. Leonard (Eds.), *Social interaction and patient care* (pp. 87–92). Philadelphia: Lippincott.

Eisdorfer, C., & Cohen, D. (1980). The issue of biological and psychological deficits. In E. Borgatta & N. McCluskey (Eds.), *Aging and society: Current research and policy perspectives* (pp. 49–70). Beverly Hills, CA: Sage.

Farmer, R. G. (1994). The doctor-patient relationship: Quantification of the interaction. *Annals of the New York Academy of Sciences, 729*, 27–35.

Feinson, M. (1985). Aging and mental health. *Research on Aging, 7*, 155–174.

Ferrare, N. A. (1963). Freedom of choice. *Social Work, 8*, 104–106.

Francis, V., Korsch, B., & Morris, M. (1969). Gaps in doctor-patient communication. *New England Journal of Medicine, 280*, 535–540.

Freemon, B., Negrete, V., Davis, M., & Korsch, B. (1971). Gaps in doctor-patient communication: doctor-patient interaction analysis. *Pediatric Research, 5*, 298–311.

Fuller, D. S., & Quesada, G. M. (1973). Communication in medical therapeutics. *Journal of Communication, 23*, 361–370.

Gatz, M., Kasl-Godley, J. E., & Karel, M. J. (1996). Aging and mental disorders. In J. E. Birren & K. W. Schaie (Eds.), *Handbook of psychology and aging* (4th ed., pp. 365–382). San Diego, CA: Academic Press.

Goldfarb, A., Shahinian, S., & Turner, H. (1966, November). *Death rate in relocated residents of nursing homes.* Paper presented at the annual meeting of the Gerontological Society of America, New York.

Grainger, K. (1995). Communication and the institutionalized elderly. In J. F. Nussbaum & J. Coupland (Eds.), *Handbook of communication and aging research* (pp. 417–436). Mahwah, NJ: Lawrence Erlbaum Associates.

Granovetter, M. (1974). *Getting a job.* Cambridge, MA: Harvard University Press.

Granovetter, M. (1982). The strength of weak ties: A network theory revisited. In P. Marsden & N. Lin (Eds.), *Social structure and network analysis* (pp. 105–130). Beverly Hills, CA: Sage.

Greene, M. G. & Adelman, R. D. (1996). Psychosocial factors in older patients' medical encounters. *Research on Aging, 18*, 84–102.

Greene, M. G., Adelman, R. D., Rizzo, C., & Friedmann, E. (1994). The patient's presentation of self in an initial medical encounter. In M. L. Hummert, J. M. Wiemann, & J. F. Nussbaum (Eds.), *Interpersonal communication in older adulthood: Interdisciplinary theory and research* (pp. 226–250). Thousand Oaks, CA: Sage.

Gregg, D. (1965). Reassurance. In J. K. Skipper & R. C. Leonard (Eds.), *Social interaction and patient care* (pp. 127–136). Philadelphia: Lippincott.

Grooters, C. L., Hill, L. B., & Long, P. N. (1997). The nursing home and retirement community: A cross-cultural communication perspective. In H. S. N. Al-Deen (Ed.), *Cross-cultural communication and aging in the United States* (pp. 143–159). Mahwah, NH: Lawrence Erlbaum Associates.

Gruenberg, E. (1978). Epidemiology. In R. Datzman, R. Terry, & K. Bick (Eds.), *Alzheimer's disease: Senile dementia and related disorders* (pp. 323–326). New York: Raven.

Hammer, M. (1981, July). *Impact of social networks on health and disease.* Paper presented at the annual meetings of the American Association for the Advancement of Science, Toronto, Canada.

Haug, M. R., & Ory, M. G. (1987). Issues in elderly patient-provider interactions. *Research on Aging, 9,* 3–44.

Health Care Finance Administration. (1999). *Managed care definitions* [On-line]. Available: *http://www.hcfa.gov*

Hendin, D. (1977). *The world almanac whole health guide.* New York: North American Library.

Hofland, B. F. (1992). Preface. In V. G. Cicirelli (Ed.), *Family caregiving: Autonomous and paternalistic decision making* (pp. vii–ix). Newbury Park, CA: Sage.

Holmes, E. R., & Holmes, L. D. (1995). *Other cultures, elder years* (2nd ed.). Thousand Oaks, CA: Sage.

Holzer, C. E., & Leaf, P. J., & Weissman, M. M. (1985). Living with depression. In M. R. Haug, A. B. Ford, & M. Shafor (Eds.), *The physical and mental health of aged women* (pp. 101–116). New York: Springer.

Hughes, J. (1982). Relocation: Attitudes, information networks, and problems encountered. *The Gerontologist, 21,* 501–511.

Hulka, B., Cassel, J., Kupper, L., & Burdette, J. (1976). Communication, compliance, and concordance between physicians and patients with prescribed treatment medications. *American Journal of Public Health, 66,* 847–853.

Jeffers, F., & Nichols, C. (1961). The relationship of activities and attitudes to physical well-being in older people. *Journal of Gerontology, 16,* 67–70.

Johnson, E. (1978). "Good" relationship between older mothers and their daughters: A causal model. *The Gerontologist, 18,* 301–306.

Johnson, E., & Bursk, B. (1977). Relationships between the elderly and their adult children. *The Gerontologist, 17,* 90–96.

Kahn, R., & Antonucci, T. (1980). Convoys over the life course: Attachment, roles and social support. In P. Baltes & O. Brim (Eds.), *Life-span development and behavior* (Vol. 3, pp. 254–286). New York: Academic Press.

Kalisch, B. (1971). An experiment in the development of empathy of nursing students. *Nursing Research, 20,* 202–211.

Kastenbaum, R. J., & Candy, S. E. (1973). The 4% fallacy: A methodological and empirical critique of extended care facility population statistics. *International Journal of Aging and Human Development, 4,* 15–21.

Kay, D. (1972). Epidemiological aspects of organic brain disease in the aged. In C. Galtz (Ed.), *Aging and the brain* (pp. 15–27). New York: Plenum.

Killian, E. L. (1970). Effects of geriatric transfers in mortality rates. *Social Work, 15,* 19–26.

Kinsey, J., Bradshaw, P., & Ley, P. (1975). Patients' satisfaction and reported acceptance of advice in general practice. *Journal of the Royal College of General Practitioners, 25,* 558–566.

Koff, T. H., & Park, R. W. (1993). *Aging public policy: Bonding the generations.* Amityville, NY: Baywood.

Kohen, J. (1983). Old but not alone: Informal social supports among the elderly by marital status and sex. *The Gerontologist, 23,* 57–63.

Korsch, B., Gozzi, E., & Francis, V. (1968). Gaps in doctor-patient communication I: Doctor-patient interaction and patient satisfaction. *Pediatrics, 42,* 855–871.

Korsch, B. M., & Negrete, V. F. (1972). Doctor-patient communication. *Scientific American, 227*(2), 66–74.

Kral, V. A., Grad, B., & Berenson, J. (1968). Stress reactions resulting from the relocation of an aged population. *Canadian Psychiatric Association Journal, 13,* 201–209.

Lane, S. (1982). Communication and patient compliance. In L. Pettegrew, P. Arnston, D. Bush, & K. Zoppi (Eds.), *Straight talk: Explorations in provider and patient interaction* (pp. 59–70). Louisville, KY: Humana.

Larson, R. (1978). Thirty years of research on the subject of well-being of older Americans. *Journal of Gerontology, 33,* 109–125.

Lawton, M. P., & Yaffe, S. (1970). Mortality, morbidity, and voluntary change of residence by older people. *Journal of American Geriatrics Society, 18,* 823–831.

Lemon, B., Bengtson, V., & Peterson, J. (1972). An exploration of the activity theory of aging: Activity and life satisfaction among in-movers to a retirement community. *Journal of Gerontology, 33,* 109–125

Lieberman, M. (1974). Relocation research and social policy. *The Gerontologist, 14,* 500.

Lieberman, M. (1982). The effects of social supports on responses to stress. In L. Goldberger & S. Breznitz (Eds.), *Handbook of stress. Theoretical and clinical aspects* (pp. 764–783). New York: The Free Press.

Liu, W., & Duff, R. (1972). The strength in weak ties. *Public Opinion Quarterly, 78,* 361–366.

Lowy, L. (1979). *Social work with the aging.* New York: Harper & Row.

Markus, E., Blenker, M., Bloom, M., & Downs, T. (1971). The impact of relocation upon mortality rates of institutionalized aged persons. *Journal of Gerontology, 26,* 537–541.

Markus, E. M., Blenker, M., Bloom, M., & Downs, T. (1972). Some factors and their association with post-relocation mortality among institutionalized aged persons. *Journal of Gerontology, 27,* 376–382.

Marshall, V. (1980). State of the art lecture: The sociology of aging. In J. Crawford (Ed.), *Canadian gerontological collection III* (pp. 76–144). Winnipeg, Canada: Canadian Association on Gerontology.

Marston, M. (1970). Compliance with medical regimens: A review of the literature. *Nursing Research, 12,* 312–323.

McAuley, W. J., & Travis, S. S. (1997). Positions of influence in the nursing home admission decision. *Research on Aging, 19,* 26–45.

McAuley, W. J., Travis, S. S., & Safewright, M. (1990). The relationship between formal and informal health care services for the elderly. In S. M. Stahl (Ed.), *The legacy of longevity: Health and health care in later life* (pp. 201–216). Newbury Park, CA: Sage.

Mechanic, M. (1978). *Medical sociology.* New York: The Free Press.

Meyers, M. E. (1965). The effect of types of communication on patients reactions to stress. In J. K. Skipper & R. L. Leonard (Eds.), *Social interaction and patient care* (pp. 92–100). Philadelphia: Lippincott.

Miller, C., & Lelieuvre, R. (1982). A method to reduce chronic pain in elderly nursing home residents. *The Gerontologist, 22,* 314–323.

Miller, D., & Lieberman, M. (1965). The relationship of affect state and adaptive capacity to reactions to stress. *Journal of Gerontology, 20,* 492–497.

Miller, W. D. (1965). The American lower classes: A typological approach. In F. Reissman, Cohen, J., & Pearl A. (Eds.), *Mental health of the poor* (pp. 139–154). New York: The Free Press.

Mold, J. W. (1995). An alternative conceptualization of health and health care: Its implications for geriatrics and gerontology. *Educational Gerontology, 21,* 85–101.

Mold, J. W., Blake, G. H., & Becker, L.A. (1991). Goal-oriented medical care. *Family Medicine, 23,* 46–51.

Mold, J. W., & McCarthy, L. (1995). Pearls from geriatric, or a long line at the bathroom. *The Journal of Family Practice, 41,* 22–23.

Montgomery, R. (1982). Impact of institutional care policies on family integration. *The Gerontologist, 22,* 54–58.

Moody, H. R. (1994). *Aging: Concepts and controversies.* Thousand Oaks, CA: Pine Forge.

National Center for Health Statistics. (1990). *Current estimates from the National Health Interview Survey, 1989.* (Vital and Health Statistics, Series 10, No. 176.) Washington, DC: U.S. Government Printing Office.

Noelker, L., & Harel, Z. (1978). Predictors of well-being and survival among institutionalized aged. *The Gerontologist, 18,* 562–567.

Nussbaum, J. (1981). *Interactional patterns of elderly individuals: Implications for successful adaptation to aging.* Unpublished doctoral dissertation, Purdue University, West Lafayette, IN.

Nussbaum, J. (1983). Relational closeness of elderly interaction: Implications for life satisfaction. *The Western Journal of Speech, 47,* 229–243.

Nussbaum, J., Pecchioni, L. L., & Crowell, T. (in press). The older patient-health care provider relationship in a managed care environment. In M. L. Hummert & J. F. Nussbaum (Eds.), *Aging, communication, and health: A multidisciplinary perspective.* Mahwah, NJ: Lawrence Erlbaum Associates.

Nussbaum, J., & Robinson, J. (1984). Attitudes toward aging. *Communication Research Reports, 1,* 21–27.

Nussbaum, J., Robinson, J., & Grew, D. (1985). Communicative behavior of the long-term health care employee: Implications for the elderly resident. *Communication Research Reports, 2,* 16–22.

Palmore, E., & Luikart, L. (1972). Health and social factors related to life satisfaction. *Journal of Health and Social Behavior, 13,* 68–80.

Pastalan, L. A. (1975). Research in environment and aging: An alternative to theory. In P. G. Windley, T. O. Byerts, & F. G. Ernst (Eds.), *Theory development in environment and aging* (pp. 219–230). Washington, DC: Gerontological Society.

Pettegrew, L. (1982). Some boundaries and assumptions in health communications. In L. Pettegrew, P. Arnston, D. Bush, & K. Zoppi (Eds.), *Straight talk: Explorations in provider and patient interaction* (pp. 3–8). Louisville, KY: Humana.

Raimbault, G., Lachin, O., Limal, C., Eliacheff, C., & Rappaport, R. (1975). Aspects of communication between patients and doctors: An analysis of the discourse in medical interviews. *Pediatrics, 55,* 401–405.

Ries, P. (1979). *Acute conditions: Incidence and associated disability, United States, 1977–1978.* (Vital and Health Statistics, Series 10, No. 132.) Washington, DC: U.S. Government Printing Office.

Robinson, J., & Nussbaum, J. (1986, November). *The impact of simulated aging on nursing staff perceptions on job satisfaction and performance.* Paper presented at the annual meeting of the Speech Communication Association, Chicago, IL.

Rook, K. S. (1984). The negative side of social interaction: Impact on psychological well-being. *Journal of Personality and Social Psychology, 46,* 1097–1108.

Rook, K. S. (1995). Support, companionship, and control in older adults' social networks: Implications for well-being. In J. F. Nussbaum & J. Coupland (Eds.), *Handbook of communication and aging research* (pp. 437–463). Mahwah, NJ: Lawrence Erlbaum Associates.

Rosel, N. (1983). The hub of a wheel: A neighborhood support network. *International Journal of Aging and Human Development, 16,* 193–200.

Rost, K., & Frankel, R. (1993). The introduction of the older patient's problems in the medical visit. *Journal of Health and Aging, 5*(3), 387–401.

Roter, D. (1977). Patient participation in the patient-provider interaction: The effects of patient question asking on the quality of interaction, satisfaction and compliance. *Health Education Monographs, 16,* 218–315.

Roter, D. L., Hall, J. A., & Katz, N. R. (1988). Patient-physician communication: A descriptive summary of the literature. *Patient Education and Counseling, 12,* 99–119.

Samora, J., Saunders, L., & Larson, R. F. (1961). Medical vocabulary knowledge among hospital patients. *Journal of Health and Human Behavior, 2,* 83–92.

Schaefer, C., Coyne, J., & Lazarus, R. (1982). The health-related functions of social support. *Journal of Behavioral Medicine, 4,* 381–406.

Schmidt, D. (1977). Patient compliance: The effect of doctor as therapeutic agent. *The Journal of Family Practice, 4,* 853–856.

Schooler, K. K. (1975). Response of the elderly to the environment: A stress-theoretical perspective. In P. G. Windley, T. O. Byerts, & F. G. Ernst (Eds.), *Theory development in environment and aging* (pp. 157–175). Washington, DC: Gerontological Society.

Schoenberg, B., Carr. A., Peretz, D., & Kutscher, A. (Eds.). (1970). *Loss and grief: Psychological management in medical practice.* New York: Columbia University Press.

Schooler, K. K. (1976). Environmental change and the elderly. In I. Altman & J. F. Wohlwill (Eds.), *Human behavior and environment: Advances in theory and research* (Vol. 1, p. 265–298). New York: Plenum.

Schulz, R., & Brenner, G. (1977). Relocation of the aged: A review and theoretical analysis. *Journal of Gerontology, 32,* 323–333.

Scott, D. (1978, July/August). Mama must go into a nursing home: A plan for family survival. *Nursing Homes, 27,* 13–15.

Serafini, M. W. (1990). Managed medicare. *National Journal, 27*(15), 920–923.

Shanas, E. (1977). *National survey of the aged: 1975.* Chicago: Chicago Circle, University of Illinois.

Shanas, E., & Maddox, G. (1976). Aging, health, and the organization of health resources. In R. Binstock & E. Shanas (Eds.), *Handbook of aging and the social sciences* (pp. 592–618). New York: Van Nostrand Reinhold.

Siegler, I., Nowlin, J., & Blumenthal, J. (1980). Health and behavior: Methodological considerations for adult development and aging. In L. Poon (Ed.), *Aging in the 1980s* (pp. 599–612). Washington, DC: American Psychological Association.

Skipper, J. K. (1965). The role of the hospital nurse: Is it instrumental or expressive? In J. K. Skipper & R. C. Leonard (Eds.), *Social interaction and patient care* (pp. 40–50). Philadelphia: Lippincott.

Spanier, G., & Thompson, L. (1984). *Parting: The aftermath of separation and divorce.* Beverly Hills, CA: Sage.

Spreitzer, E., & Snyder, E. (1974). Correlates of life satisfaction among the elderly. *Journal of Gerontology, 29,* 454–458.

Stahl, S. M., & Feller, J. R. (1990). Old equals sick: An ontogenetic fallacy. In S. M. Stahl (Ed.), *The legacy of longevity: Health and health care in later life* (pp. 21–34). Newbury Park, CA: Sage.

Stoller, E. P., Forster, L. E., & Duniho, T. S. (1992). Systems of parent care within sibling networks. *Research on Aging, 14,* 23–49.

Stone, G. (1979). Patient compliance and the role of the expert. *The Journal of Social Issues, 35,* 34–59.

Strain, L. A., & Chappell, N. L. (1982). Confidants: Do they make a difference in quality of life? *Research on Aging, 4,* 479–502.

Sussman, M., & Burchinal, L. (1962a). Family kin network: Unheralded structure in current conceptualization of family functioning. *Marriage and Family Living, 24,* 231–240.

Sussman, M., & Burchinal, L. (1962b). Parental aid to married children: Implications for family functioning. *Marriage and Family Living, 24,* 241–247.

Tarasuk, M. B., Rhymes, J. P., & Leonard, R. L. (1965). An experimental test of the importance of communication skills for effective nursing. In J. K. Skipper & R. C. Leonard (Eds.), *Social interaction and patient care* (pp. 110–120). Philadelphia: Lippincott.

Thoits, P. (1982). Conceptual, methodological, and theoretical problems in studying social support as a buffer against life stress. *Journal of Health and Social Behavior, 23,* 145–159.

Troll, L. (1971). The family of later life: A decade review. *Journal of Marriage and the Family, 33,* 263–290.

Tryon, P. A., & Leonard, R. C. (1965). Giving the patient an active role. In J. K. Skipper & R. C. Leonard (Eds.), *Social interaction and patient care* (pp. 120–127). Philadelphia: Lippincott.

U.S. Census Bureau. (1996). *65+ in the United States.* (U.S. Census Bureau, Current Population Reports, Special Studies, P23–190.) Washington, DC: U.S. Government Printing Office.

Walker, H. L. (1973). Communication and the American health care problem. *Journal of Communication, 23,* 349–360.

Ward, R. A. (1990). Health care provider choice and satisfaction. In S. M. Stahl (Ed.), *The legacy of longevity* (pp. 272–290). Newbury Park, CA: Sage.

Weeks, J., & Cuellar, J. (1981). The role of family members in the helping networks of older people. *The Gerontologist, 21,* 388–394.

Wellman, B., & Hall, A. (1986). Social networks and social support: Implications for later life. In V. Marshall (Ed.), *Later life: The social psychology of aging* (pp. 191–231). Beverly Hills, CA: Sage.

Wilder, C. S. (1974a). *Acute conditions: Incidence and associated disability: United States, July 1971 to June 1972.* (Vital Health and Statistics, Series 10, No.88). Washington, DC: U.S. Government Printing Office.

Wilder, C. S. (1974b). *Limitation of activity and mobility due to chronic conditions: United States—1972.* (Vital Health and Statistics, Series 10, No. 96). Washington, DC: U.S. Government Printing Office.

Wilson, J. (1973). Compliance with instructions in the evaluation of therapeutic efficacy. *Clinical Pediatrics, 12,* 33–40.

Wood, V., & Robertson, J. (1978). Friendship and kinship interaction: Differential effect on morale of the elderly. *Journal of Marriage and the Family, 40,* 367–373.

CHAPTER 13

Death and Dying

*A*lthough death is an inevitable fact of human life, it was, until recently, one of the least discussed and researched topics in the study of human behavior. Kubler-Ross (1969) pointed out that the discussion of death was considered taboo—reflecting Americans' discomfort with the process of dying and death itself. What is not discussed can be denied and avoided. Book (1996) argued that when families do not discuss issues surrounding death children develop attitudes based on what is not said. Not talking about a death not only denies the fact of a death, but also denies any feelings associated with that event. The use of euphemisms and metaphors helps maintain a distance from the event of death (Sexton, 1997). Although these terms for death generate distance, they also help people to understand how they should think about death. Each term generates a slightly different interpretation: "gone" (where to?); "eternal rest"; "lost" (the battle or cannot be found?); and, the medicalized "coded" (Sexton, 1997). Another reason that death is infrequently researched or discussed may be because people have no language to describe death—they have not experienced it yet (Verwoerdt, 1966).

Until the 1970s, research on the topic of death and dying was practically nonexistent. Patterson (1981) pointed out that 90%

of the books on aging published from 1956 to 1976 devoted less than 5% of their space to the topic; and 65% of them devoted less than 1% of their space to the topic. Americans' fear of death has made them avoid the topic whenever they can; similarly, elderly people are often avoided because they remind people of death (Patterson, 1981).

Since the 1970s, however, writing on death has begun to appear. There are now numerous books, articles, films, television shows, and whole journals devoted to the topic. Little of this work, however, has focused on the communicative processes pertaining to death and dying. Researchers know relatively little about how dying people communicate, or how others communicate with the dying. Kastenbaum and Aisenberg (1972) published a 500-page book on the psychology of dying, of which no more than a few pages focus on communicative processes. Nuland (1993) argued that frank discussions regarding death and dying would help rid people of the fear related to death and would increase our cultural comfort level regarding the topic. As is discussed later within the chapter, not only are these frank discussions needed, they are desired by the very people most affected by the dying process.

SOCIAL DISTANCE AND SOCIAL DEATH

Kastenbaum and Aisenberg (1972) argued that our social distance from dying people has increased over the years. They conclude that people make an out-group of dying people. There are three reasons for this: (a) they attribute social inferiority to dying people; (b) they do not have a response repertoire for dealing with dying people; and, (c) dying people cause them inner perturbation. These factors cause people to try to maintain distance from those whom they know or fear are dying.

In this discussion of death and dying, it is important to distinguish between dying as a process and death as an event (McKenzie, 1980). Death and dying are two different, albeit related, concepts. The discussion in this chapter focuses both on how people communicate during dying and on how people communicate when they are told that someone is dead.

Several concepts are relevant to our discussion. First, Nash (1980) described four aspects to death: pain, loneliness, intrusiveness (lack of control), and loss. Second, Kalish (1976) used the concept *social death* to characterize the process that frequently occurs when someone is dying and is treated as if he or she is dead even before death has occurred. In his observational study of dying patients in hospitals, Sudnow (1967) described several examples of social death. Notable instances included autopsy forms being filled out prior to death, eyelids being closed before death occurred, and bodies being wrapped before the person had died. He also reported a wife being told of the impending death of her husband, with her rarely returning to the hospital to see him after being told. This particular husband did recover and returned home to find his closet and drawers emptied and his wife with another man. The notion of social death recurs frequently in the death and dying literature.

Sudnow noted that individuals who were considered to have less social value by the staff received less aggressive treatment and were more likely to be treated as socially dead. Timmermans (1998) wondered if the inequalities associated with social value continue, considering the changes in the medical system since Sudnow's work. His observational studies confirmed Sudnow's earlier findings. Age was the most outstanding characteristic for identifying someone for whom death was seen as a "friend" or a "blessing." Not only are elderly people viewed as having less social value leading to social death, but these negative attitudes lead to reduced care through reduced interaction with the dying patient (DiPaola, Niemeyer, & Ross, 1994). The individual's status shifts from patient to dying person when the doctor indicates to other medical staff that his or her condition is terminal, essentially ending the individual's social identity (Sweeting & Gilhooly, 1992).

The causes of death among elderly people are most frequently illness and the debilitation of aging. But other contributing factors to death must also be noted. For instance, Huyck and Hoyer (1982) pointed out that forced relocation may contribute to death, as may widowhood, retirement, or the loneliness of holidays. And other authors (cf., Birren & Schaie, 1977) noted that the murder and suicide rates of elderly people are rising.

Experiencing the deaths of others may, of course, have some positive effects. Patterson (1981) cited evidence indicating that the experience of loss provides a rehearsal for one's own death. One gets used to the idea of death and becomes somewhat more accepting of mortality by having friends and family members die and by seeing that life goes on.

As a final preliminary remark, recall that Kalish (1976) pointed out that dying is different from aging, but older people do die. Death can, of course, be viewed in different ways. Kalish contrasts death as loss with death as an organizer of time (i.e., the end of life). The two views are rather different.

The discussion of the communication surrounding death and dying begins with a brief explanation of fear of death or death anxiety. This is followed by a focus on the awareness of death and the communication of the prognosis of death. Next how the dying communicate and how others communicate with the dying are considered. Narrowing the focus somewhat, some thoughts about families of the dying, various health care professionals, and health care contexts are presented. The discussion concludes with material from some very provocative case studies of dying and how dying is handled in different contexts. Throughout the discussion, the focus is not on the thought processes and inner experiences that people go through when they are dying or are around the dying, important though those thoughts and experiences may be. The purpose here, rather, is to focus on communication, not thoughts or experiences. This focus limits the discussion considerably.

FEAR OF DEATH OR DEATH ANXIETY

The fear of death is widespread, although Kalish (1976) pointed out that it is not as widespread as might commonly be believed. Experts are uncertain about whether the fear of death is learned or innate (Decker, 1980). Some argue that it is learned and, thus, can be unlearned. Others argue that death fear is a mainspring of human existence. Decker (1980) concurred with Kalish that the data do not indicate that the fear of death is terribly widespread.

Research cited by Belsky (1984) indicated that death preoccupations are not infrequent, but such preoccupations are equally associated with both positive and negative moods. Death preoccupation, by itself, does not necessarily depress people.

Some research focuses on the correlates of death fear. It appears that having a rich and satisfying life does not have a strong relationship with either death anxiety or the lack of it. Age may be related to fear of death, as may suffering, depression, religious needs, and transcendent experiences, although the findings on these variables are not completely consistent across different studies (Kalish, 1976).

Death anxiety has some effects, as well. Vickio and Cavanaugh (1985) found that increasing death anxiety leads to greater anxiety about aging, and that more exposure to death leads to more comfort about dying.

Research cited by Patterson (1981) indicated that fear of death is strongest between the ages of 40 and 55, and that fear of death is lower for elderly people. Kalish (1976) argued that this is because elderly people place less value on their own lives than on the lives of younger people; elderly people see impending death as a given; and, elderly people are used to loss. For some of these same reasons, death anxiety is lower when people are communicating with a dying older person than when they are communicating with a dying younger person. The loss of the older person is more readily accepted because their social value is perceived to be lower.

Troll (1982), however, concluded that there are few age differences in death anxiety, but that there are gender differences. She found that women are more accepting of death, whereas men see death as the enemy. This may reflect the cultural importance of men's roles in our society. Men are socialized to be bread winners, providers, and so forth, and for that reason they anticipate a great loss when they die.

Fear of and anxiety about death may be a particular problem for health care workers who must deal with death on a regular basis (Servaty & Hayslip, 1997). Fear of and anxiety about death lead to a reluctance to make eye contact or to touch or even to have a conversation with a dying patient. Although death education does not reduce fear of death, education can help to reduce denial and permit the expression of previously repressed fears (Hayslip, Galt, & Pinder, 1993). Death education can help to reduce death anxiety, although anxiety initially increases due to death education (Coffman & Coffman, 1995). This type of education helps health care students understand the process of dying (Coffman & Coffman, 1995) and to feel more confident in being able to care appropriately for a dying patient (Servaty & Hayslip, 1997).

AWARENESS OF IMPENDING DEATH

One's death anxiety may influence how aware one is of impending death, but death anxiety is probably a relatively unimportant factor in this respect. Glaser and Strauss (1966), who did some of the most interesting participant–observation research on hospitals and on other health care contexts, identified four awareness contexts for dying: (a) closed, (b) suspicion, (c) mutual pretense, and (d) open. They found that there was still a wall between interactants, even when impending death was acknowledged. Mutual pretense is a common reaction (Glaser & Strauss, 1977). The following rules governing mutual pretense are interesting (McKenzie, 1980).

1. Dangerous topics should be avoided (this includes the patient's disease or prognosis).
2. A pretense that the dying will share in the future should be maintained, should the topic arise.
3. Small talk and safe topics are acceptable.
4. Things that are said about death should be ignored.
5. The situation should be kept normal.

McKenzie also pointed out that sometimes only one person will keep up the mutual pretense, whereas the other person may be willing or eager to discuss the approaching death.

Not all dying people, of course, want to know that death is rapidly approaching. Schulz and Aderman (1980) found that awareness of impending death does lead to depression, and that patients should not be given more information than they want. Almost all of the subjects in their research, however, did want to know if they were going to die. Seale (1991) also found that most patients and their families want to know. A problem arises, however, because physicians prefer to wait for patients to ask questions, whereas patients prefer to wait for doctors to initiate discussions about their prognoses (Seale, 1991).

Traditionally, physicians were reluctant to communicate a prognosis of death to patients. In 1966, Verwoerdt took a rather progressive approach when he offered physicians a set of questions to help them decide whether patients should be told about prognoses of death:

1. What are the patient's emotional and intellectual reserves?
2. How much does the patient already know?
3. How much does the patient want to know?
4. When is the patient sure that the doctor knows?
5. How should the doctor proceed if the patient knows but will not admit the knowledge?
6. What is the personal meaning of the illness to the patient?

Some of these questions, such as Number 3, are undoubtedly difficult questions for the physician, who cannot, after all, read the patient's mind.

Recall that the data indicate that most patients want to know about their own prognoses, but they feel that other people probably would not be able to handle information about their own impending deaths (Kalish, 1976). Much evidence indicates that patients figure out that they are approaching death even if they are not told. There are so many nonverbal factors that give the true story away that it may be difficult to hide such information from patients. Indeed, Erickson and Hyerstay (1974) presented a rather convincing argument along these lines. They suggested that the dying person who is not told about his or her terminality is placed in a double bind because family, friends, and health care providers emit incongruent verbal and nonverbal messages to the patient. It is rather ridiculous to believe that such a large group of people could carry out such a charade about an extremely important topic. The patient is then placed in the position of appearing paranoid or defensive if he or she does not believe what he or she has been told. Erickson and Hyerstay explain the destructive implications of this double-binding behavior by drawing parallels to schizophrenic double binds, and they argue that the truth is better revealed than concealed.

Consistent with this line of reasoning, most physicians today favor a gentle but honest approach to telling patients about terminality. Patients generally prefer this, as well. Families of terminally ill patients appreciate being told and having the patient told when the news is broken in private, and with respect and sensitivity (Seale, 1991). Family members also appreciate having any and all of their questions answered and prefer having more information about their loved one's condition rather than less (Seale, 1991). This approach provides patients with some time to review their life, to make final arrangements, and to get ready for death (Carey & Posavac, 1980; FitzSimmons, 1994; Huyck & Hoyer, 1982; Seale, 1991).

Seale (1991) found that it is not only the family and patient who prefer that the patient be aware of impending death. Physicians and nurses report being able to provide better quality care when the patient is aware. When the patient knows, health care professionals feel more open around the patient and are free to answer any and all questions.

It typically is the physician's responsibility to make decisions about the patient's dying trajectory; that is, how long the patient has left (Glaser & Strauss, 1968a) and how to announce this to others. Hospital personnel treat the patient in accordance with this trajectory, and miscalculations upset both the staff and family members (Glaser & Strauss, 1968b). With time, the physician typically becomes more explicit and precise in his or her communication about the patient's impending death (Glaser & Strauss, 1968a).

Sudnow (1967) discovered that physicians are sometimes overly pessimistic in their predictions about impending death because it looks better for them if they have predicted the death in advance. Physicians also believe that it will be easier for the family if they have some time to prepare. Sudnow observed one instance in which impending death was announced after the patient's death had already occurred. A short time later the actual death of the patient was announced. Of course, physicians also look bad if they predict death and it does not occur. Sudnow cited some examples of staff and family dissatisfaction when death does not occur as predicted.

COMMUNICATION OF DYING PEOPLE

As discussed in earlier chapters, communication is always a dyadic process at least. That is, it always involves at least two people. Research has typically looked at the health care professional as the key figure in communication, or at family members and how they deal with the dying of significant other people. Such a view, of course, ignores half the dyad and misses much of what is going on. We feel that it is also extremely important to look at how the dying person communicates.

On the most general level, Noyes and Clancy (1977) described confusion between the sick role, which encourages dependence, and the dying role, which requires independence even though care is necessary. The kind of independence they describe might be akin to withdrawal. Further, they point out that the patient cannot wish to die unless he or she is really suffering or severely disabled. Otherwise, the patient will be held responsible for his or her own death.

Servaty and Hayslip (1997) reported that most dying individuals are relatively unsatisfied with the communication they receive from others. The dying person senses the fear and anxiety that others have about dying, which leads to the other person's reluctance to make eye contact, touch, or even have a conversation with the dying person. The dying prefer to have the opportunity to talk openly with their family, friends, and caregivers.

Recall that patients typically want to know about their impending deaths; other research shows that patients also typically want to talk about this issue. Although Glaser and Strauss (1966) found that a climate of mutual pretense was common, other research indicated that most patients prefer to discuss their approaching demise (Simmons & Given, 1980). Kalish (1976) concluded that it is difficult for patients to maintain relationships with significant others unless the topic of death can be discussed. Although others may attempt to avoid such discussion (Simmons & Given, 1972), talking about approaching death has several positive effects. It helps in the identification of nursing needs (Simmons & Given, 1972) and prevents "acting-out" behavior (Chandler, 1965). It may also help alleviate tension, help ease depression, and help patients deal with death (Saul & Saul, 1973). One of the greatest benefits of talking about an impending death is that these talks help all the individuals involved deal with their emotions (FitzSimmons, 1994; Silverman, Weiner, & El Ad, 1995). Sometimes, individual family members, particularly young children, are not told about an impending death in an attempt to protect their feelings. Of course, these feelings cannot really be avoided and open discussion assists people of all ages in coping with their emotions. For the dying individual, "talking about the death experience had helped clarify their own feelings while putting the death into perspective ... " (FitzSimmons, 1994, p. 25).

Simmons and Given (1972) provided some suggestions for those who feel uncomfortable about talking with a patient who may bring up the topic of his or her impending death. They suggested that listening is more important than talking because the dying person probably needs to talk. A lack of trust will be created by "stock" answers or lies. People should not talk about future plans in a way that implies that everything will be all right because the patient knows better. Simmons and Given also advise not giving the patient more details than he or she wants to know. They advise listening to the "life review" of the patient. Most people need to discuss their past life to make sense out of it and to reach a sense of closure about it. Condescension, disapproval, sympathy, or depression from others lowers the dying person's sense of well-being, so approval should be provided instead. They also pointed out that terminal patients are likely to overreact to little, innocuous things, and that they may make negative statements hoping to receive positive responses. The response, however, should be a realistic one. Touch may be reassuring when words are no longer helpful.

How the patient communicates may be an important factor determining whether or not he or she receives health care, too

(Watson, 1976–1977). For instance, Belsky (1984) indicated that more aggressive patients live longer. Along the same lines, Weisman and Warden (1975) found that those patients who lived longer than was expected tended to maintain good, responsive relationships with others, especially in the terminal phase of their disease. They were also more assertive. Because dying patients, particularly dying elderly patients, rarely receive the care provided to other patients (Belsky, 1984), it is likely that this is a case of "the squeaky wheel gets the grease."

Health care providers are frequently encouraged to attend to the nonverbal behaviors of patients in an effort to determine their condition. Research on facial expressions provides mixed support for this encouragement. Antonoff and Spilka (1984) concluded that there is some consistency in the patterning of facial expressions in terminal cancer patients, but not complete uniformity. This line of research is promising.

Topics discussed by the dying also show some uniformity. Most dying individuals, for instance, are concerned about their families and talk about their families quite often (Kastenbaum & Aisenberg, 1972).

Another factor that influences how a terminal individual communicates is the pain he or she is likely to experience. Pain interferes with communication, because it is difficult to actively interact when one is experiencing great discomfort (Shanis, 1985).

Other physiological changes also accompany impending death. Beigler (1957) described sunken eyes, an expression of terror, and a black cast to the face just prior to death, even when death was not expected to occur soon. Similar findings come from Verwoerdt and Elmore (1967), who concluded that patients who died sooner than expected, even though they could not have known this ahead of time, expressed more hopelessness and a greater reduction of expectation of futurity. And Lieberman (1968) described the psychological changes accompanying imminent death as a decreased organization, an inability to cope with the environment, and an inner disintegration. These changes, of course, are likely to affect how the dying person communicates.

Coping with Dying

Another factor that will affect how the dying person communicates will be how he or she is coping with the prospect of impending death. Since the late 1960s, there has been quite a bit written about the process of coping with death, particularly since the work of Kubler-Ross (1969). Kubler-Ross identified several stages in the dying process: (a) denial and isolation, (b) anger, (c) bargaining, (d) depression, and (e) acceptance. Although Kubler-Ross indicated that these stages may be nonsequential and repetitive (i.e., people may not move all the way through the process, or may jump around, or go back and forth), the stages have frequently been applied in an invariable, sequential manner. Such an application rarely receives empirical support (Schulz & Aderman, 1974). There does not seem to even be any definite order to the stages through which a dying individual goes, although there is some evidence of depression shortly before death. Pattison (1978) proposed a more general schema: (a) the acute phase, during which the crisis occurs; (b) the chronic living–dying phase; and (c) the terminal phase, characterized by withdrawal and little hope.

Belsky (1984) argued against the rigid application of any stage theory to dying, based on the premise that there may be a tendency to rush a person from one stage to another, or that their behavior may be treated as "merely going through a stage" and, thus, negate the validity of their experience. Legitimate complaints may be passed off as mere signs of the anger phase, for instance. Belsky also pointed out that denial can exist simultaneously with an accurate perception of impending death.

Denial is an issue frequently encountered when interacting with dying individuals. Kalish (1976) wrote that "to deny that one is dying is to repress in some fashion the awareness that the process is going forward" (p. 492). Denial on the most general level, however, helps people to deal with fear of death (Feifel & Branscomb, 1973; Magni, 1972). Even when patients have been told, clearly and directly, that they are dying, physicians report patients "not recalling" that information later (Kubler-Ross, 1969).

Verwoerdt (1966) suggested that denial leads people to delay going to a doctor until it may be too late. Further, he identified other sorts of defense mechanisms, which he claims should not be unnecessarily stripped away:

1. Defenses aimed at retreat, regression, and giving up.
2. Defenses aimed at ignoring the threat: repression, suppression, denial, rationalization, depersonalization, and projection and introjection.
3. Defenses aimed at mastery and control: obsessive-compulsive mechanisms, counterphobic mechanisms, and sublimation and acceptance.

Denial continues to be the most commonly observed response in dying individuals. As long as it does not prevent the patient from seeking care, denial may serve some helpful functions. Not only may denial of impending death help the patient cope, but Beilin (1981–1982) pointed out that denial can help preserve relationships threatened by the knowledge of terminal illness. Such denial serves to prevent social withdrawal by the patient from significant people in his or her life. Following this line of reasoning, awareness should not be forced on patients who seem to be functioning effectively while denying their deaths.

Not all patients, however, deny their impending deaths. People die in different ways, just as they live in different ways. Research identified four types of preterminal orientations: acceptance, apathy, apprehension, and anticipation (Troll, 1982). Weisman and Kastenbaum's (1968) research delineated two types of dying individuals: those who were withdrawn and inactive, yet aware and accepting of imminent death; and those who were aware of the prospect of death, yet actively involved in life. McKenzie (1980) pointed out that some dying people withdraw, some become depressed, and some become anxious. Others are more accepting. Dying people may also be reluctant to take on new commitments or projects and may want to spend their remaining time in personally meaningful ways.

Jeffers and Verwoerdt (1977) also discussed how older people face death. They found that older people do not have death-defying attitudes or rage, and most older people do not fear death. Most of them do not plan for death, and most believe in an afterlife.

Religious beliefs can play a role in how one copes with death. Generally, there is more interest in religion in older age, even though there is less ritualistic activity (Moberg, 1968). But people who are religious are likely to have less anxiety about death (McKenzie, 1980).

Recall that being around death and experiencing the loss of others helps prepare one for death. However, Marshall (1975) found that adjustment to death requires not only being around it, but also seeing that it is actively dealt with and accepted by those around one.

Research by Hinton (1967) indicated that most people do not deny death, although people do fear the process of dying more than death. Hinton also found that a positive attitude toward one's own death was associated with strong coping skills, decisiveness, and a satisfying and fulfilled life. The severity of organic damage and the attitudes of the physician and family were also important.

Finally, Marshall (1979) contrasted two residential facilities for older people in terms of how they handled dying patients and in terms of the effects that this handling of dying had on how the patients dealt with death. At one of the facilities, the staff made all of the decisions about how death should be handled, whereas at the other, the patients were able to take control of the process. Residents at the first facility were resigned to death, but did not plan for it. Their attitude was more morbid. At the second facility, the accent was on living. Death was successfully legitimated. These people felt that impending death was appropriate, but not just because it allowed them to escape suffering, as people believed at the first facility. Marshall pointed out that people socially define how to deal with death, and this is handled more effectively if the people are not treated like children and are allowed to arrange funerals, grieving processes, and so forth for themselves.

A "Good" Death

Kalish (1976) described the *appropriate death*, characterized by caring relationships, an open awareness of impending death, and a belief system that provides some meaning to the death. The frequency of appropriate death has yet to be examined by researchers; however, feelings that one will have a "good" death eases the coping process (Lynn, 1991).

Most dying persons want to avoid unnecessary pain, have an opportunity to take leave of their loved ones, right their shortcomings with God, and maintain their dignity (Emanuel & Emanuel, 1998; Lynn, 1991; Mitchell, 1997). Physicians play an important role in managing pain, but should also be aware of each patient's preferences for use of artificial means to prolong life so that the individual decides his or her own definition of dignity (Emanuel & Emanuel, 1998; Mitchell, 1997). Individuals will likely have very different priorities for the final stage of life (Lynn, 1991). For example, one person may want to complete certain tasks before death, while another person may drop unfinished tasks in order to focus on family or spiritual needs.

Recall from the section on awareness of impending death that people report wanting to know that they are dying so that they have time to say goodbye to loved ones and make sense of their lives. Having someone who will listen to whatever is important helps them to define their lives as well as their deaths.

COMMUNICATION WITH DYING PEOPLE

Before focusing in on how families and health care providers communicate with the dying, a couple of factors that influence communication with the dying in general should be mentioned. First, attitudes toward the dying are negative; the dying are stigmatized in U.S. society (Epley & McCaghy, 1977–1978). This is one of the factors that causes people to avoid interaction with them. Such contact with the dying also forces people to confront their own mortality.

Other research found that the more serious a patient's illness and the more pain he or she is believed to be experiencing, the less willing people are to help him or her and the more negative are their reactions toward the dying (Sherman, Smith, & Cooper, 1982). There is also some indication that people react even more negatively toward dying people who are perceived as similar to themselves (Smith, Lingle, & Brock, 1978–1979).

Families of Dying People

The information presented so far pertains, in large part, to the interaction between dying individuals and those who are not close to them. Of more concern to most dying people, however, is their interaction with members of their families. Some research has focused specifically on this issue. Hinton (1981), for instance, examined how husbands and wives shared information about death. Of 62 couples, 35% had openly shared their awareness that the spouse could be dying, 34% had experienced limited communication (one had brought up the topic, and the other had denied it), and 31% had not revealed their awareness to the spouse even though they had mentioned it to others. Freer communication about dying occurred if the spouse considered the marital relationship "average" or "poor" rather than "very good." Hinton also found that if staff members were more open in their communication, spouses were, too. Kramer (1997) found that widows who had engaged in open and honest discussions with their husbands about the husband's impending death reported more happiness after the death. These types of discussions, however, did not influence the widows' overall adjustment, their daily functioning, their adaptation to their new role, or their attitude toward the future.

When family members are aware that their loved one is dying, anticipatory grief becomes a factor affecting communication. *Anticipatory grieving* refers to experiencing sorrow about a person's death before that death has occurred. Although Troll (1982) pointed out that anticipatory grieving does make it easier for survivors to pull things together after the death, Kalish (1976) indicated that it may lead to social death, so that people treat the person as if he or she is already dead. Kalish added that family members may even become irritated that the death is taking so long. And Fulton and Fulton (1980) found that anticipatory grief can become a double-edged sword: Although it helps secure the well-being of the survivor, it ruptures any remaining social bonds between the dying and surviving family members. Those social bonds are tenuous enough at this point and are easily severed. Kramer (1997) reported, however, that the processes of affiliation (being physically and emotionally available) and separation (realizing and talking with others about a future without the husband) are not mutually exclusive. The widows in her study were able to provide instrumental and emotional support to their dying husbands, while making plans for a future without them. Spouses, then, do not have to choose between providing care at a critical time and preparing themselves to make adjustments to their new lifestyle.

In addition to interacting with the patient, family members spend a great deal of time trying to deal with health care providers. These interactions are frequently less than satisfying. Many family members find physicians, for instance, to be inconsiderate and insensitive, and they feel that the physicians rarely listen to the family's concerns (Gold, 1984). Families do not appreciate health care providers who are arrogant, unduly hasty, have a tendency to be flip, or are cold and inhibited. Families report that bad news is frequently delivered over the phone and with no warning by health care providers. The families interviewed by Gold reported that the physicians were supportive at the beginning, but distanced themselves as the patient worsened and hope waned. Although nurses were better as sources of support, health care service people were typically very unpleasant and hostile.

Gold (1984) concluded that family members want:

1. To be adequately forewarned of impending death.
2. To spend as much time with the patient as desired.

3. To know the patient is not afraid or in pain.
4. To do something helpful for the patient, no matter how small.
5. To have opportunities for final communication with the patient.
6. To receive explanations and reassurance about physical symptoms accompanying death.
7. To have time after death with the body, if they want to.
8. To be able to express their grief without fear of negative reaction.

Rarely, Gold found, were these conditions fulfilled. The families usually expressed acute dissatisfaction with the period just preceding death. Gold's findings are consistent with those of Sudnow (1967). He found that nurses at some hospitals try to keep families away from dying patients, and that this is encouraged by physicians.

An important aspect for family members is the ability to conclude their relationship with their loved one. Research conducted by Fieweger and Smilowitz (1984) on relational conclusion examined the kinds of communication with which people would like to conclude their relationship with a dying intimate. The kinds of communication were expressions of love and affection, avoidance of discussion of impending death, attempts to bolster spirits, expressions of loss, and acts of succor. It makes sense, of course, that people would want to end a relationship differently with someone with whom they have been intimately involved as opposed to someone to whom they have not been as close. Similarly, Fieweger (1980) reported that most people have things they would like to say to their deceased loved ones. These concerns reflect the same issues that the dying individual expresses, a desire to discuss with loved ones (see the section on a "good" death.)

In a book directed toward physicians, Verwoerdt (1966) provided some suggestions for communicating with the families of dying patients. He urged physicians to realize that whatever is known by the family will soon be known by the patient, and he suggested telling the news to the strongest member of the family first. Because family members may feel guilty when they hear about the impending death of a loved one, Verwoerdt encouraged physicians to bring this guilt out in the open and talk about it—especially if this is interfering with medical treatment. He also suggested advising families about the frequency and duration of appropriate visits, and suggested physician participation in decision making during this difficult time. The physician may also need to shield the patient from visits from those who upset him or her. He suggested promoting nonverbal, supportive reassurance and providing some privacy.

The alert reader will recognize that some of Verwoerdt's suggestions are in stark contrast to the approach medicine takes today, in which patients and families are being given more control over the dying process and the decisions surrounding it. Verwoerdt's suggestions about dealing with grieving family members, however, still have merit.

BEREAVEMENT

Bereavement is a complex experience. The context of the loss (e.g., expected and age at time of death), the nature of the relationship with one's loved one, and the role that the deceased played in one's life all influence the process of grieving (DeVries, 1997). McKenzie (1980) wrote that bereavement lasts 1 to 2 years after the death of the family member. It typically brings a loss of interest in friends and activities. It includes feelings of guilt, followed by anger, and then depression. The anger is directed toward health care workers, friends, family, or the dead person. This may be followed by tension, restlessness, and a preoccupation with the deceased. Other research labels the following phases of grief: (a) numbness, (b) pining, (c) dejection, and (d) recovery. The stages delineated by Huyck and Hoyer (1982) are a bit more complete. They include the following: (a) shock/denial, (b) grief (including depression), (c) separation-disorganization and despair (including anger and guilt), and (d) reorganization (including identification with the lost person). Corr (1992) emphasized that grieving is an active process and not a set of stages. Both dying individuals and their loved ones have physical, psychological, social, and spiritual tasks to which they should attend.

The death of a loved one may draw a family closer together, but it may also generate greater emotional distance (Rosenblatt & Karis, 1994). Sometimes, individual family members have different expressions of grief, which are not understood by other family members. Sometimes, long-standing conflicts and resentments are renewed as individuals' emotions are running high. Another problem faced by families is that the deceased member was most likely part of the support network, someone who was turned to in difficult times. The absence of this member may make adapting to the loss even greater.

Although the loss of a spouse has been rated as the most stressful life event (DeVries, 1997), it is important to remember that other loved ones also grieve for the loss. Adult children report the death of a parent as a major event in their lives (Bower, 1997). Older individuals report the death of a sibling as particularly disturbing because of the loss of a long, shared, intimate history (Gold & Pieper, 1997). Obviously, these losses affect the larger family network as well—grandchildren, nieces and nephews, and so on, experience varying degrees of loss. Individuals must deal not only with their own grief, but with the grief of those around them.

Evidence of depression in bereaved family members was found by Breckenridge, Gallagher, Thompson, and Peterson (1986). Troll (1982) suggested gender differences in grieving: Grieving women feel abandoned, whereas grieving men feel dismembered. Research by Lund, Caserta, and Dimond (1986), however, found that bereavement processes across genders are characterized by more similarities than differences.

Comforting Bereaved People

When confronted with someone who is bereaved, many people feel at a loss for words. They feel a sense of helplessness when they are not able to remove someone else's pain (Terry, Bivens, & Niemeyer, 1996). Empathy, the "ability to reflect and respond to the deepest feelings and concerns of another" (Terry et al., 1996, p. 270), is the most desired and appreciated response.

Range, Walston and Pollard (1992) had college students rate 30 comments on their perceptions of helpfulness in six scenarios (suicide, homicide, accident, natural anticipated death, and natural unanticipated death). The most helpful statements were "I'm here if you need someone to talk to" and "If there is anything I can do, please let me know." Statements such as "He/she is in a better place" and "He/she is not suffering any more" were rated as moderately helpful. The least helpful statements were "Was he/she in much pain?" and "Did you know this was going to happen?"

Just as the dying person often just wants someone to listen, so do bereaved individuals. Allowing them to determine when and to what extent they talk about the loss of their loved one and being a good listener during those times can be the most helpful.

PATIENT–PHYSICIAN INTERACTION

An important determinant of how patients and family members experience death is how the physician communicates with them about the death. Researchers have expressed concern for many years about physicians' approaches to death and dying. For instance, in Caldwell and Mishara's (1972) research, most physicians refused to participate in the interviews after they discovered that the study was about dying. They claimed that they would be less effective as physicians if they thought about death too much. The doctors who did participate admitted feeling uneasy around terminal patients.

Death anxiety has also been examined in relation to physicians. Physicians begin their training with personality structures that lead them to have difficulty dealing with death. These personality structures are then reinforced by their medical training, which emphasizes detached concern (Schulz & Aderman, 1980). Liberman, Handal, Napoli, and Austrin (1983) suggested that doctor–patient interactions can be changed by reducing the death anxiety of the physician.

Avoidance of death is also exhibited in the verbal responses given by physicians to patients who speak of their own deaths. Kastenbaum (1967a) found that 17.6% of physicians discuss the topic with patients once it has been initiated, 13.1% reassure the patient, 19.1% deny the reality, 26.1% were fatalistic, and 24.1% changed the subject. Some of these responses are obviously more helpful to patients than are others.

The older dying person is in an even more tenuous position than is a younger dying person. Attempts are made to save the life of a younger dying person much more frequently and vigorously than are the attempts to save an older dying person (Sudnow, 1967). The treatment of the older dying patient is likely to be determined, in part, by the family's apparent concern or lack thereof.

Another communication variable that has been discussed in relation to physician–dying patient interaction is language and the impact this has on treatment of the patient. Sudnow (1967) pointed out that the language used by the hospital staff allows them to depersonalize death and patients. More specifically, Redding (1980) discussed the use of labels such as "cancer," "patients," and "dying." Once such labels are applied, communication and treatment change. A "patient," for instance, is not dealt with as a person who has a role in decision making; a "patient" is a person who is told what to do. Someone who is "dying" is not someone who can be treated or helped. The helplessness that physicians experience when they can no longer "save" a patient leads to objectification of these patients in order to distance the physicians from these feelings (Family, 1993).

Some suggestions that may help overcome many of these problems in physician–dying patient interaction were presented by Koenig (1980). Koenig claimed that dying patients are especially receptive to overt affection and attentive ministrations, and that touching, listening, and talking to show that one cares are important to them. The experience of being cared for is still important, even though cure may not be possible. The relationship dimension of communication is still soothing. Koenig also suggested talking about the current situation (comfort, pain, and so forth) rather than focusing on the idea of dying, and mentioned the need to let the patient know when he or she is doing well. The family, too, needs this kind of information. Patients should not be disconfirmed through vague communication or cliches, but they should not be told all bad news either. Koenig further pointed out that references by the patient to dying can be an invitation to intimacy and conversation. The patient should be asked what he or she already knows, what is important, and what is feared.

Family physicians recognize the need for more training in dealing with dying patients (Steinmetz, 1993). Some medical schools and continuing education programs now offer courses on death and dying. Belsky (1984) cited studies indicating that these courses can lead physicians to be more comfortable with the dying and to be less rigid in beliefs about telling patients about diagnoses. Brent, Speece, Gates, and Kaul (1993) also found that attitudes toward the dying and willingness to talk to patients about dying increases with an increase in the number of hours of coursework that health care professionals received.

One of the goals of such training is to demedicalize the dying process (Geppert, 1997). Medical students are taught how to help their patients and their patients' families reveal their concerns, and to enable grieving and provide consolation (Bertman, 1991). Physicians are being trained not only how to manage symptoms related to the terminal illness, but also to provide comfort and compassion, tailoring the services provided to the needs of the patient and family (Herbst, Lynn, Mermann, & Rhymes, 1995; Lynn, 1997). Most importantly, physicians are receiving the message that people—both patients and their physicians—can handle discussions about dying (Cotton, 1993).

PATIENT–NURSE INTERACTION

Although some data indicate that nurses communicate more effectively with dying patients than do physicians, other studies show that dying patients are ignored by nurses, too. For instance, Watson (1973) found that more seriously ill patients are placed in rooms farther from medical service offices than are those who are less seriously ill. Watson concluded that seriously ill or dying people are placed in locations where they will be less visible as they move closer to death. Similarly, LeShan, Bowers, and Jackson (1969) concluded that it takes nurses longer to respond to the calls from patients with terminal prognoses than to respond to the calls from patients who are less seriously ill.

Focusing on verbal communication, Kastenbaum (1967b) observed nurses' interactions with patients and found that over 80% of the nurses' responses could be categorized as reassurance, denial, or a change in the subject. Less than 20% of the nurses actually discussed the patients' thoughts and feelings with them. Consistent with this is the finding of Duff and Hollingshead (1968) that, among a group of 21 people dying of cancer, evasions were used by the health care professionals in 86% of the cases. Such behavior is consistent with the findings about how physicians communicate, cited earlier.

Simmons and Given (1972) also observed nurses interacting with dying patients. They concluded that nurses become too concerned about making dying patients comfortable, which, in the nurses' language, meant "and quiet." The nurses were overly cheerful and superficial in an attempt to maintain control and to not get involved. They focused their communication on objects, tasks, or equipment, rather than on the patient as a person. When they were asked why death or dying was not discussed with the patient, the nurses said, "He doesn't want to talk about it" (p. 223). Simmons and Given found, however, that 47 of 51 of the patients *did* talk about death within 10 to 15 minutes, when provided with an opportunity to talk. The nurses' records showed few attempts to initiate such conversation. Observation indicated that patients had immediately attempted to talk about their impending death after learning the diagnosis.

These findings are consistent with the observations of Redding (1980). He described the "iceberg effect," in which nurses and aides chatter a mile a minute about everything but the patient, thereby communicating, "I don't want to know about your feelings because they make me very uncomfortable.

My chatter is a good way to keep you from talking to me about them" (p. 372). Recall the interactions between nursing home staff and residents in chapter 12. Nurses' talk that focuses on tasks appears to be common in both of these settings.

In another observational study, Rodabough and Rodabough (1981) examined the impact of nurses' attitudes toward dying patients on their communication with dying patients. They also studied the impact of this communication on the patients' self-image, and they found that unintended judgments, usually communicated nonverbally, hurt the patients' self-image. They added that the physical treatment provided to patients was the best of which the nurses were capable.

Nurses have more frequent and more prolonged contact with patients than do physicians. The impact of their interaction with a dying patient and his or her family can be tremendous. Brent et al. (1993) found that nursing students held more positive attitudes towards working with dying patients than did medical students, even after controlling for gender. Because nurses are more involved in the day-to-day care of patients, they must be able to attend not only to physical needs, but to emotional needs, as well (Fanslow-Brunjes, Schneider, & Kimmel, 1997). Nurses, therefore, should be trained to provide information, to help the patient and family express feelings, and put the loved one's death in perspective. The ability to treat dying patients as human beings is essential for good nursing care (Smotherman, 1997). The most important thing that a nurse can do for a dying patient is to listen (Callanan, 1994).

Obviously, nurses have a tremendous burden in providing care to dying patients. There are many ways in which nurses can improve their interaction with the dying. This is even more true of other health care providers.

COMMUNICATION BETWEEN PATIENTS AND OTHER HEALTH CARE PROVIDERS

In an overall evaluation of the care provided to the terminally ill, Loomis and Williams (1983) found minimal difficulty in making the transition from active to comfort care. But they discovered many problems in effective communication between patients and staff and with the emotional support provided by staff members. More specifically, Buckingham, Lack, and Mount (1976) had a confederate pose as a cancer patient in their study "Living with the Dying." They discovered little to no staff communication with patients, as well as a lack of eye contact and other signs of closeness. Patients were referred to by the name of their disease, and the negative aspects of their conditions were accentuated.

Sudnow (1967) noticed some interesting features in how even patients who are dead on arrival (DOAs) and dead bodies are handled by hospital staff members. He wrote that DOAs are regarded as insignificant, especially if the body is that of an elderly person. Children are more likely to receive attention and revival attempts. Sudnow noticed a direct relationship between the strength and loudness of the siren on the emergency vehicle bringing the patient in and the perceived social value of the person, and the staff apparently responded to this stimulus. He found, at least in one hospital in which he made observations, that DOAs were sometimes used as guinea pigs for instructional purposes.

Dead bodies were also handled irreverently. They were typically packaged up with a parcel-post type of tag attached. The handling included some rough treatment and a little joking. This work, of course, was done by orderlies and nurse's aides because other health care providers do not handle dead bodies unless necessary. Even orderlies and aides tried to avoid this work whenever possible. They sometimes made the dead person look alive in order to have the job handled by another shift. Sometimes they took a break or became quite involved in other work. Sometimes they even began wrapping the person before death had occurred in order to avoid handling a dead body later. Sudnow also observed instances when patients who were expected to die soon were transferred so that another department would have to wrap the body. This kind of treatment is one reason nurses try to keep family members away from dying patients—if the family is around, the staff cannot treat the patient as if he or she is already dead. Sudnow also observed some student nurses treating dead patients as if they were still alive, but comatose—if the student nurse had not been told of the patient's death. Sudnow concluded that this behavior is possible because comatose patients are always treated as if the person is already dead.

Consistent with this kind of treatment, Kastenbaum and Mishara (1971) found that the environment in which elderly and dying people find themselves can encourage self-injurious behavior and lead to premature death. They concluded that treatment by attendants, which is influenced by the physicians' behavior, is a crucial factor in this regard.

There is no doubt, of course, that the frequent contact with death experienced by health care providers of all sorts can be difficult for them. One study focused on the coping strategies developed by paramedics, who are often those in closest contact with the dying. These strategies included educational desensitization, humor, language alteration, scientific fragmentation, escape into work, and rationalization. And the evidence indicates that all health care providers have become more effective at dealing with death in recent years. All of the courses and publicity on the issue have probably had an impact on health care providers.

INTERACTIONS WITH OTHER PROFESSIONALS

Other groups of professionals must be mentioned in a discussion of death and dying. Research has indicated that mental health care professionals, who should play an important role in helping the dying cope with that reality, avoid dying individuals for the same reasons as other health care professionals (Belsky, 1984; Kastenbaum & Aisenberg, 1972). And the funeral director obviously plays a central role in interaction once death has occurred. Kastenbaum and Aisenberg, after discussing all of the bad press morticians have received since the early 1960s, pointed out the difficult position in which funeral directors can find themselves. The mortician must work within a system in which people have very negative attitudes toward death and try to avoid it. Such a job is not easy.

The hospice movement has grown tremendously in the past few decades. The goal of hospice care is to provide physical, emotional, social, and spiritual health care services to a dying patient and his or her family and friends (Coffman & Coffman, 1993). Often, the dying individual chooses to live out his or her last days, weeks, and months at home. Hospice volunteers play a critical role in the provision of care. Communication skills play a vital role in their success; therefore, their training includes an emphasis on a variety of skills. Coffman and Coffman (1993) introduced hospice volunteers to the concept that relationships are created and fashioned through interacting with each other, much in keeping with the assumptions of this book. Relationships naturally evolve, develop, and mature through talk. Hospice volunteers are trained to develop trust with the patient and family, to listen, and to model appropriate behavior.

An important element of modeling appropriate behavior is dealing with their own and the families' emotions, openly and honestly.

Finally, in a study of hospice workers, volunteers, and the clergy (Miller & Knapp, 1986), seven strategies for communicating with the dying, grouped into three categories, were identified:

1. Avoidance: be upbeat (be cheerful), be updating (inform the patient of current topics), and be recounting (discuss the past).
2. Confronting: be instructive (tell the patient what to do), be definitive (provide medical facts and understanding of the illness), and be demonstrative (show feelings).
3. Reacting (adapting to this particular patient): be reflexive (allow the dying person to set the agenda and initiate topics).

Miller and Knapp's research indicated that the last strategy, "be reflexive," was selected by participants as the most appropriate in general. The second most appropriate strategy was "be demonstrative." Rated as least appropriate were "be upbeat" and "be instructive." "Be definitive" was most likely to be used when the patient was denying or bargaining. These research participants also provided some suggestions for communicating with dying patients. These are summarized in Table 13.1.

DEATH ANNOUNCEMENTS

Delivering news of a death is never an easy burden. Sudnow (1967) noted that the earliest death announcements come from the "postings" on the critical list. Staff members take this posting as an announcement of impending death and phase out their attention. The real death announcement, of course, does not occur until the death has actually taken place. Only the physician is allowed to make this announcement at most institutions. Sudnow (1967) described instances of awkward interactions among staff and family members when the staff members knew that death had occurred and family did not. Staff were not allowed to share their knowledge, but did not want to appear cold and callous to the family.

Further, Sudnow found that death announcements are never questioned by the families. The announcements are always de-

TABLE 13.1
Advice on Communicating with Dying Patients

Do	Avoid
Be accepting of others, slow to give advice, and respect their feelings.	Do not try to change people's attitudes or tell them how they should and should not behave.
Be honest and realistic.	Do not try to be too upbeat. Avoid empty promises or superficial responses to placate dying patients. Do not use platitudes. Do not ask questions just to satisfy your emotional curiosity.
Respond naturally to patients. Do not worry about what to say.	Do not avoid a hard issue or talk of death.
Be attentive and show emotional commitment.	Do not ignore the feelings of patients or your own feelings.
Be neutral in family discussions.	Do not take sides in family squabbles.
Be with the patient as often as possible.	
Say little and listen.	

Source: Miller and Knapp (1986).

livered with surety. The announcement is always made in the first or second sentence of the message. The message also includes the medical cause of death. Clark and LaBeff (1982) also studied death announcements and concluded that those who make the announcements are usually poorly prepared for the task and dislike this aspect of their work. Clark and LaBeff looked at death announcements given by a number of different professionals in a variety of settings. They found five basic strategies:

1. Direct delivery: the fact of death is simply stated; euphemisms are not used. This strategy was used most frequently by law enforcement personnel.

2. Oblique delivery: provides a lead in or prestaging; eases in and out; tries to provide comfort by voicing appropriate excuses. This strategy was used most frequently by nurses.

3. Elaborate delivery: provides all the details of the death and the factors leading up to it; logically reconstructs and assumes that this logic will lead to acceptance of the death. As might be expected, this strategy is used most frequently by physicians.

4. Nonverbal delivery: the announcer of the death relies on his or her facial expressions and other nonverbals to communicate the message; this is not always deliberate. This strategy is used most frequently by nurses and clergy. For the nurses, the use of this strategy was sometimes necessitated by their presence with the family when the nurse was not supposed to be the announcer of the death.

5. Conditional delivery: the message sender adapts to the reaction of the message receiver; if the receiver appears to be taking things well, delivery might be direct, but if the receiver is getting upset, delivery might turn oblique or to some other strategy. This strategy is used most frequently by nurses.

The responses by family members to death announcements also followed some patterns, although there was greater variability (Sudnow, 1967). Some people grieved openly; others did not. But Sudnow noted that an assumption of moral integrity was granted to all families—those who did not grieve were said to be taking it well. He also noted that bereaved people have the right to not abide by social norms—for a while. The bereaved family members were the ones who eventually turned the conversations to other things; the nonbereaved people cannot do this very tactfully. Bereaved people do, however, have to play the appropriate role during the funeral.

Sudnow noticed that physicians let families grieve after the announcement, even if grief was not apparent. The physician usually looked away and did nothing, but remained standing. Few condolences were given. After a while the bereaved people shifted back to look at the doctor, and that was when interaction resumed. Talk typically began with an overture by the bereaved people. The issues that were raised included the cause of death, whether the patient had been in much pain when he or she died (the physician always said "no," even when it was a lie), and could it have been prevented? To this, the physician also responded with, "We did everything we could." The family responded with, "Of course, we understand." Sudnow noted that the return to normal talk shows a control over oneself and a return to social stability.

INSTITUTIONAL SETTINGS OF DEATH

It has been noted that most people die in institutions of some sort; yet little attention has been given to improving the terminal care provided in hospitals and residential facilities (Kastenbaum & Candy, 1973). Although recent years have seen more of a focus on this area, Gold's study of family reactions to death in the hospital, discussed earlier, was published as recently as 1984 and indicated widespread negative experiences. Other institutions are also not without fault. Of note is the kind of retirement village that has gained in popularity in recent years in which one buys an apartment (at a steep price) and also pays a monthly fee. This works out to be a good deal for someone who lives a long time, but, because the apartment does not become a part of one's estate after death, it is not such a good deal for someone who dies shortly after the purchase. Marshall (1973) applied game theory to this dilemma and concluded that the purchaser is betting that he or she will live, whereas the administrator of the retirement village is betting that the purchaser will die.

Because of many of the problems with hospitals and other kinds of institutions as settings for death, hospices have become more popular in recent years. Munley, Powers, and Williamson (1982) noted that, whereas nursing homes foster social death, hospices do not. Hospices also use both the family and the patient as the unit of care. Shanis (1985) also found that hospices help keep the patient's network intact both during and after death. The hospice teams keep an eye on the burden for the family and help the patient continue his or her normal life. Hospice care can be either in-patient or out-patient. Dying patients cared for in the home by a hospice team experience less anxiety, depression, and hostility toward their families and spouse compared to those who die at home without hospice team care (Buckingham & Foley, 1978). Regardless of the context, of course, death is never a light burden.

Death in the Institution

Several interesting accounts have been presented by various researchers who spent time observing interaction surrounding death and dying in hospitals and nursing homes. There are several items of note in these accounts.

Gubrium (1975) studied a nursing home that he called "Murray Manor." He noted that the staff and clientele believe that all the patients and residents are terminal cases. The residents define their own future in terms of death. However, when residents enter the premises of those who are known to be dying, they are visibly wary. They look around carefully, and then proceed quickly and do not look around anymore. When residents of Murray Manor visit friends housed in the terminal resident wing, they try to move the friend elsewhere. If this is not possible, the visits are short, infrequent, and uncomfortable. They grimace and turn away from those showing signs of dying. Mourning occurs only when close friends die, even among the residents.

The floor staff witnesses death more intimately, but they get used to it. The supervisory staff is less involved in witnessing dying. Dying is viewed as suffering and death as a release from suffering, but death and dying are always discussed together. Staff members are not especially mournful when someone dies. They talk about the death, but only become irritated when in the presence of a dying person. They claim to feel sorry for the person, but do not want to be around him or her.

Staff generally avoids talk of death and the dead when they are around alert patients, but not when they are around those who are not alert. Gubrium found, however, that these nonalert patients frequently understand this matter-of-fact conversation. Staff do not talk about death in front of the alert patients because they think it upsets the patients and "makes their jobs harder." But alert patients do not panic at the thought of death. In front of supervisory staff, the floor staff are always discrete.

Patients and residents are eager to be informed of death news, although staff members try to contain the information. Gubrium noted several nonverbal behaviors of staff members that announce that a death has occurred, and these are picked up by residents. He delineated the following stages of death news: (a) an unusual page is heard over the loud speaker, commanding rather than requesting someone's presence; (b) there are lots of top staff members around, being very nice but keeping an eye on the death room; (c) other patients are urged away and the staff pretends the person has not died by, for instance, pulling the curtain around the bed; (d) a hearse or ambulance appears at the rear of the building; and, (e) the information is then passed in the lounge, lobby, or dining room.

The news of death spreads very quickly among the residents. As soon as residents know that someone has died, they socially close off his or her life. They recall information about the person and discuss it. The person is informally eulogized, and they talk about the consequences of the death. Sympathy cards are sent and condolences are expressed. The residents become very angry if news of the death is wrong.

Gubrium's work echoed some of the observations made by Sudnow (1967). In addition to the observations by Sudnow already discussed, Sudnow noted that death did not arouse much conversation among staff members unless it was unusual in some way. Inexperienced staff members counted the number of deaths they had witnessed, but became blase about deaths after witnessing about six. Patients whose deaths were imminent were assigned to private rooms, if possible. If this was not done, staff tried to hide the death from the other patients in the room.

Sudnow provided a particularly intriguing discussion of John, the morgue attendant at the hospital where most of the observations were made. When people saw John they would either avoid him (knowing that he was going to pick up a dead body) or ask "Who died?" John learned to provide opportunities for people to gracefully avoid him when he was on duty. When he was off duty, however, he changed his clothes and his nonverbals signals to let people know that he need not be ignored. John was the only employee in the entire hospital who changed his clothes to go on break.

Sudnow also observed that talk about patients in their presence, unless the patient is comatose, requires special language, for example, "She'll probably terminate this week." It is expected that the patient does not understand this terminology. In this particular hospital, the expectation was usually accurate.

Some observational research was also conducted by Marshall (1979). He contrasted the management of dying at two residential facilities, St. Joe's, which had mostly welfare patients, and Glen Brae, which was more upscale. At St. Joe's, only the very end of life was defined as "dying." Patients at this point were moved to the "dying room," which was also called St. Peter's room—room 13. There was sometimes a waiting list for this room. The room's purpose was known to residents. A routine funeral mass was held for the dead and was always the same. The priest used a booming voice that was heard by all, even those who were not at mass. Dying here was organized for the patients, not by them.

At Glen Brae the residents had developed their own ways of dealing with death. It was not ignored, but was treated straight-forwardly, informally, and discretely. There was low-key management of death and grief. The residents supported each other and made plans for their own deaths. The accent was on living.

SUMMARY

This chapter discusses a subject that often makes people uncomfortable—death and dying. A long-standing taboo against talking about death is changing, but slowly. Because of this reluctance to talk about the unknown experience of dying, euphemisms and metaphors are used to distance people from the event of death. A desire to maintain distance from death creates a distance from those who are dying, creating social death before physical death. Individuals' fear of death and death anxiety play a role in how comfortable they are in talking to those who are dying.

Most individuals, however, want to know that their death is imminent so that they can say goodbye to their loved ones and make sense of their lives. Having open and honest discussions regarding an impending death benefits not only dying individuals, but their family and friends, and their health care professionals.

Communication plays an important role in experiencing a "good" death. Those who can talk about their lives and their deaths with loved ones are able to define the meaning of their lives and are better able to cope with dying. Loved ones also benefit from the opportunity to say their final goodbyes and to address any unfinished business with the dying individual. Bereavement and comforting bereaved people are influenced by how people talk about deceased loved ones.

Unfortunately, not everyone is comfortable talking about dying. This lack of communication can be particularly problematic for the dying individual if those around him or her are unwilling to talk and listen. Health care professionals, who are more likely to have frequent contact with dying people than are family members, need training to improve their communication skills at this critical point in their patients' lives.

This chapter also reviewed how the announcement of a death is made and how death is treated in hospitals and nursing homes. Again, the death may be treated distantly or with respect and dignity. For the loved ones of the deceased, the differences in these styles have long-lasting effects.

■ REFERENCES

Antonoff, S. R., & Spilka, B. (1984). Patterning of facial expressions among terminal cancer patients. *Omega, 15,* 101–108.

Beigler, J. S. (1957). Anxiety as an aid in the prognostication of impending death. *Archives of Neurology and Psychiatry, 77,* 171–177.

Beilin, R. (1981–1982). Social functions of denial of death. *Omega, 12,* 25–35.

Belsky, J. (1984). *The psychology of aging.* Monterey, CA: Brooks/Cole.

Bertman, S. L. (1991). *Facing death: Images, insights, and interventions.* New York: Taylor and Francis.

Birren, J. E., & Schaie, K. W. (Eds.). (1977). *Handbook of the psychology of aging.* New York: Van Nostrand Reinhold.

Book, P. L. (1996). How does the family narrative influence the individual's ability to communicate about death? *Omega, 33,* 323–341.

Bower, A. R. (1997). The adult child's acceptance of parent death. *Omega 35,* 67–96.

Breckenridge, J. A., Gallagher, D., Thompson, L. W., & Peterson, J. (1986). Characteristic depressive symptoms of bereaved elders. *Journal of Gerontology, 41,* 163–168.

Brent, S. B., Speece, M. W., Gates, M. F., & Kaul, M. (1993). The contribution of death-related experiences to health care providers' attitudes towards dying patients: II. Medical and nursing students with no professional experience. *Omega, 26,* 181–205.

Buckingham, R. W., & Foley, S. H. (1978). A guide to evaluation research in terminal care programs. In G. W. Davidson (Ed.), *The hospice development and administration* (pp. 127–141). Washington, DC: Hemisphere.

Buckingham, R. W., Lack, S., & Mount, B. (1976). Living with the dying: Use of the technique of participant observation. *Canadian Medical Association Journal, 115,* 1211–1212.

Caldwell, D., & Mishara, B. L. (1972). Research and attitudes of medical doctors toward the dying patient. *Omega, 3,* 341–346.

Callanan, M. (1994). Farewell messages. *American Journal of Nursing, 94*(5), 19–20.

Carey, R. G., & Posavac, E. J. (1980). Attitudes of physicians on disclosing information to and maintaining life for terminal patients. *Perspectives on Death and Dying, 2,* 145–154.

Chandler, K. A. (1965). Three processes of dying and their behavioral effects. *Journal of Consulting Psychology, 29,* 296–301.

Clark, R. E., & LaBeff, E. E. (1982). Death telling: Managing the delivery of bad news. *Journal of Health and Social Behavior, 23,* 366–380.

Coffman, S. L., & Coffman, V. T. (1993). Communication training for hospice volunteers. *Omega, 27,* 155–163.

Coffman, V. T., & Coffman, S. L. (1995). Behavioral rehearsal: A way of talking about the dying process. *Omega, 32,* 63–76.

Corr, C. A. (1992). A task-based approach to coping with dying. *Omega, 24,* 81–94.

Cotton, P. (1993). Talk to people about dying—they can handle it, say geriatricians and patients. *The Journal of the American Medical Association, 269,* 321–322.

Decker, D. L. (1980). *Social gerontology,* Boston: Little Brown.

DeVries, B. (1997). Kinship bereavement in later life: Understanding variation in cause, course, and consequence. *Omega, 35,* 141–157.

DiPaola, S. J., Neimeyer, R. A., & Ross, S. K. (1994). Death concern and attitudes toward the elderly in nursing home personnel as a function of training. *Omega, 29,* 231–248.

Duff, R. S., & Hollingshead, A. B. (1968). *Sickness and society.* New York: Harper & Row.

Emanuel, E. J., & Emanuel, L. L. (1998). The promise of a good death. *The Lancet, 351*(9114), S21–S29.

Epley, R. J., & McCaghy, C. H. (1977–1978). The stigma of dying: Attitudes toward the terminally ill. *Omega, 8,* 379–393.

Erickson, R. D., & Hyerstay, B. J. (1974). The dying patient and the double-bind hypothesis. *Omega, 5,* 287–298.

Family, G. (1993). Projected image and observed behavior of physicians in terminal cancer care. *Omega, 26,* 129–136.

Fanslow-Brunjes, C., Schneider, P. E., & Kimmel, L. H. (1997). Hope: Offering comfort and support for dying patients. *Nursing, 27*(3), 54–57.

Feifel, H., & Branscomb, A. B. (1973). Who's afraid of death? *Journal of Abnormal Psychology, 81,* 282–288.

Fieweger, M. (1980, March). *Self-reported strategies in relational conclusion: How do we say goodbye to dying persons.* Paper presented at the Annual Convention of the Eastern Communication Association, Ocean City, MD.

Fieweger, M., & Smilowitz, M. (1984). Relational conclusion through interaction with the dying. *Omega, 15,* 161–172.

FitzSimmons, E. (1994). One man's death: His family's ethnography. *Omega, 30,* 23–39.

Fulton, R., & Fulton, J. (1980). A psychosocial aspect of terminal care: Anticipatory grief. *Perspectives on Death and Dying, 2,* 87–96.

Geppert, C. M. A. (1997). The rehumanization of death: The ethical responsibility of physicians to dying patients. *The Journal of the American Medical Association, 277,* 1408–1409.

Glaser, B. G., & Strauss, A. L. (1966). *Awareness of dying.* Chicago: Aldine.

Glaser, B. G., & Strauss, A. L. (1968a). Temporal aspects of dying as a nonscheduled status passage. In B. Neugarten (Ed.), *Middle age and aging* (pp. 520–530). Chicago: University of Chicago Press.

Glaser, B. G., & Strauss, A. L. (1968b). *A time for dying.* Chicago: Aldine.

Glaser, B. G., & Strauss, A. L. (1977). The ritual drama of mutual pretense. In S. H. Zarit (Ed.), *Readings in aging and death: Contemporary perspectives* (pp. 271–276). New York: Harper & Row.

Gold, D. T., & Pieper, C. F. (1997). Sibling bereavement in later life. *Omega, 35,* 25–42.

Gold, M. (1984). When someone dies in the hospital. *Aging, 345,* 18–22.

Gubrium, J. F. (1975). *Living and dying at Murray Manor.* New York: St. Martin's Press.

Hayslip, B., Jr., Galt, L., & Pinder, M. M. (1993). Effects of death education on conscious and unconscious death anxiety. *Omega, 28,* 101–111.

Herbst, L. H., Lynn, J., Mermann, A. C., & Rhymes, J. (1995). What do dying patients want and need? *Patient Care, 29*(4), 27–36.

Hinton, J. M. (1967). *Dying.* Baltimore: Penguin.

Hinton, J. M. (1981). Sharing or withholding awareness of dying between husband and wife. *Journal of Psychosomatic Research, 25,* 337–343.

Huyck, M. H., & Hoyer, W. J. (1982). *Adult development and aging.* Belmont, CA: Wadsworth.

Jeffers, F. C., & Verwoerdt, A. (1977). How the old face death. In E. W. Busse & E. Pfeiffer (Eds.), *Behavior and adaptation in later life* (pp. 142–157). Boston: Little, Brown.

Kalish, R. A. (1976). Death and dying in a social context. In R. H. Binstock & E. Shanas (Eds.), *Handbook of aging and the social sciences* (pp. 483–507). New York: Van Nostrand.

Kastenbaum, R. (1967a). The mental life of dying patients. *The Gerontologist, 7,* 97–100.

Kastenbaum, R. (1967b). Multiple perspectives on a geriatric "Death Valley." *Community Mental Health Journal, 3,* 21–29.

Kastenbaum, R., & Aisenberg, R. (1972). *The psychology of death.* New York: Springer.

Kastenbaum, R., & Candy, S. E. (1973). The 4% fallacy: Many die where few have lived. *International Journal of Aging and Human Development, 4,* 15–21.

Kastenbaum, R., & Mishara, B. L. (1971). Premature death and self-injurious behavior. *Geriatrics, 26,* 70–81.

Koenig, R. (1980). Dying vs. well-being. *Perspectives on Death and Dying, 2,* 9–22.

Kramer, D. (1997). How women relate to terminally ill husbands and their subsequent adjustment to bereavement. *Omega, 34,* 93–106.

Kubler-Ross, E. (1969). *On death and dying.* New York: Macmillan.

LeShan, L., Bowers, M., & Jackson, E. (1969). *Counseling the dying.* New York: Nelson.

Liberman, M. B., Handal, P. J., Napoli, J. G., & Austrin, H. R. (1983). Development of a behavior rating scale for doctor-patient interactions and its implications for the study of death anxiety. *Omega, 14,* 231–239.

Lieberman, M. A. (1968). Psychological correlates of impending death: Some preliminary observations. In B. Neugarten (Ed.), *Middle age and aging* (pp. 509–519). Chicago: University of Chicago Press.

Loomis, M. T., & Williams, T. F. (1983). Evaluation of care provided to terminally ill patients. *The Gerontologist, 23,* 493–499.

Lund, D. A., Caserta, M. S., & Dimond, M. F. (1986). Gender differences through two years of bereavement among the elderly. *The Gerontologist, 26,* 314–320.

Lynn, J. (1991) Dying well. *Generations, 15,* 69–72.

Lynn, J. (1997). An 88-year-old woman facing the end of life. *The Journal of the American Medical Association, 277,* 1633–1640.

Magni, K. G. (1972). The fear of death. In A. Godin (Ed.), *Death and presence* (pp. 125–138). Brussels: Lumen Vitae Press.

Marshall, V. W. (1973). "Betting on death": A retirement village dilemma. *International Journal of Aging and Human Development, 4,* 285–291.

Marshall, V. W. (1975). Socialization for impending death in a retirement village. *American Journal of Sociology, 80,* 1124–1144.

Marshall, V. W. (1979). Organizational features of terminal status passage in residential facilities for the aged. In J. Hendricks & C. D. Hendricks (Eds.), *Dimensions of aging* (pp. 232–243). Cambridge, MA: Winthrop.

McKenzie, S. C. (1980). *Aging and old age.* Glenview, IL: Scott, Foresman.

Miller, V. D., & Knapp, M. L. (1986). The *post nuntio* dilemma: Approaches to communicating with the dying. In M. McLaughlin (Ed.), *Communication yearbook 9* (pp. 723–738); Beverly Hills, CA: Sage.

Mitchell, D. R. (1997). The "good" death: Three promises to make at the bedside. *Geriatrics, 52* (8), 91–92.

Moberg, D. O. (1968). Religiosity in old age. In B. Neugarten (Ed.), *Middle age and aging* (pp. 497–508). Chicago: University of Chicago Press.

Munley, A., Powers, C. S., & Williamson, J. B. (1982). Humanizing nursing home environments: The relevance of hospice principles. *International Journal of Aging and Human Development, 15,* 263–284.

Nash, M. L. (1980). Dignity of person in the final phase of life: An exploratory study. *Perspectives on Death and Dying, 2,* 62–70.

Noyes, R., & Clancy, J. (1977). The dying role: Its relevance to improved patient care. *Psychiatry, 40,* 41–47.

Nuland, S. (1993). *How we die.* New York: Vintage.

Pattison, M. E. (1978). The living-dying process. In C. A. Garfield (Ed.), *Psychosocial care of the dying patient* (pp. 145–153). New York: McGraw-Hill.

Patterson, S. L. (1981). On death and dying. In F. J. Berghorn & D. E. Schafer (Eds.), *The dynamics of aging* (pp. 83–99). Boulder, CO: Westview Press.

Range, L. M., Walston, A. S., & Pollard, P. W. (1992). Helpful and unhelpful comments after suicide, homicide, accident, or natural death. *Omega, 25,* 25–31.

Redding, R. (1980). Doctors, dyscommunication, and death. *Death Education, 3,* 371–385.

Rodabough, T., & Rodabough, C. (1981). Nurses and the dying: Symbolic interaction as a precipitator of dying "stages." *Qualitative Sociology, 4,* 257–278.

Rosenblatt, P. C., & Karis, T. A. (1994). Family distancing following a fatal farm accident. *Omega, 28,* 183–200.

Saul, S. R., & Saul, S. (1973). Old people talk about death. *Omega, 4,* 27–35.

Schulz, R., & Aderman, D. (1974). Clinical research and the stages of dying. *Omega, 5,* 137–143.

Schulz, R., & Aderman, D. (1980). How the medical staff copes with dying patients: A critical review. *Perspectives on Death and Dying, 2,* 134–144.

Seale, C. (1991). Communication and awareness about death: A study of a random sample of dying people. *Social Science and Medicine, 32,* 943–952.

Servaty, H. L., & Hayslip, B., Jr. (1997). Death education and communication apprehension regarding dying persons. *Omega, 34,* 139–148.

Sexton, J. (1997). The semantics of death and dying: Metaphor and mortality. *ETC.: A Review of General Semantics, 54,* 333–346.

Shanis, H. S. (1985). Hospice: Interdependence of the dying with their community. In W. A. Peterson & J. Quadagno (Eds.), *Social bonds in later life* (pp. 369–387). Beverly Hills, CA: Sage.

Sherman, M. F., Smith, R. J., & Cooper, R. (1982). Reactions toward the dying: The effects of a patient's illness and respondents' beliefs in a just world. *Omega, 13,* 173–189.

Silverman, P. R., Weiner, A., & El Ad, N. (1995). Parent-child communication in bereaved Israeli families. *Omega, 31,* 275–293.

Simmons, S., & Given, B. (1972). Nursing care of the terminal patient. *Omega, 3,* 217–225.

Simmons, S., & Given, B. (1980). Nursing care of the terminal patient. *Perspectives on Death and Dying, 2,* 115–123.

Smith, R. J., Lingle, J. H., & Brock, T. C. (1978–1979). Reactions to death as a function of perceived similarity to the deceased. *Omega, 9,* 125–138.

Smotherman, T. (1997). The list. *Nursing, 27*(6), 88.

Steinmetz, D. (1993). Family physicians' involvement with dying patients and their families. *The Journal of the American Medical Association, 270,* 1181.

Sudnow, D. (1967). *Passing on.* Englewood Cliffs, NJ: Prentice-Hall.

Sweeting, H. N., & Gilhooly, M. L. (1992). Doctor, am I dead? A review of social death in modern societies. *Omega, 24,* 251–269.

Terry, M. L., Bivens, A. J., & Niemeyer, R. A. (1996). Comfort and empathy of experienced counselors in client situations involving death and loss. *Omega, 32,* 269–285.

Timmermans, S. (1998). Social death as self-fulfilling prophecy: David Sudnow's "Passing On" revisited. *Sociological Quarterly, 39,* 453–472.

Troll, L. E. (1982). *Continuations: Adult development and aging.* Monterey, CA: Brooks/Cole.

Verwoerdt, A. (1966). *Communication with the fatally ill.* Springfield, IL: Thomas.

Verwoerdt, A., & Elmore, J. L. (1967). Psychological reactions in fatal illness: 1. The prospect of impending death. *Journal of American Geriatric Society, 15,* 9.

Vickio, C. J., & Cavanaugh, J. C. (1985). Relationships among death anxiety, attitudes toward death, and experience with death in nursing home employees. *Journal of Gerontology, 40,* 347–349.

Watson, W. H. (1973, May). *The social organization of aging and dying: An exploratory study of some institutional factors.* Paper presented at the invitational Conference on Environmental Research and Aging, St. Louis, MO.

Watson, W. H. (1976–1977). The aging sick and the near dead: A study of some distinguishing characteristics and social effects. *Omega, 7,* 115–123.

Weisman, A. D., & Kastenbaum, R. (1968). *The psychological autopsy: A study of the terminal phase of life* (Community Mental Health Monograph No. 4). New York: Behavioral.

Weisman, A. D., & Warden, J. W. (1975). Psychosocial analysis of cancer deaths. *Omega, 6,* 61–75.

CHAPTER 14

Successful Aging

*T*he final chapter of this book is devoted to an in-depth discussion of successful aging. Placing this chapter last is no coincidence. Each of the authors of this book feels very strongly that aging can be an overwhelmingly satisfying process. Social scientists have been searching for those factors that promote the process of successful aging for several decades. Although we realize that successful aging is a very complex phenomenon dependent on many physical, social, and psychological factors, we conclude this book with a consideration of the importance of communication for any individual who wishes to age successfully.

This chapter is divided into five sections. First, the subjective nature of successful aging is considered. A majority of the empirical research that has investigated successful aging uses very specific definitions and ways of measuring successful aging. These definitions of successful aging are discussed with the purpose of outlining what researchers mean by successful aging.

The second section of this chapter reviews the various theories that attempt to describe, explain, and predict those behaviors that may relate to successful aging. This section is a review of those theories of successful aging first discussed in chapter 1.

The predictors of successful aging are outlined in the third section of this chapter. Close to 50 years of social scientific investigations have uncovered many interesting relationships between successful aging and such factors as age, gender, income, ethnicity, retirement, and social relationships. The findings of various important studies will be reviewed.

The final two sections of this chapter concentrate on the communication–successful aging relationship. Empirical studies linking communication to successful aging are reviewed. In addition, the major theme of this book, relational communication, will once again be highlighted in an attempt to reconceptualize successful aging and to integrate or "tie together" the previous 13 chapters.

WHAT IS SUCCESSFUL AGING?

If each individual reading this book were asked if he or she were a successful student, or a successful parent, or a successful anything, each and every person would somehow be able to respond with a coherent answer. The majority of these answers would be based on individual notions of just what success is to each person. People have quite different standards for success and, therefore, view success in quite different ways. Within the classroom, a final B grade in calculus can be a joyful event for one person and, at the same time, a disaster for another. Success in anything is a subjective judgment.

A major problem for social scientists in all disciplines is dealing with the subjective nature of concepts such as success. Social scientists would very much like to magically change success from a subjective concept to an observable phenomenon. If they could point to some event or behavior and firmly state that "this is success," explaining human behavior might not be quite as difficult as it now appears.

The problem facing social researchers since the late 1950s has been to systematically derive a measure of individual psychological well-being. Without some way of knowing if an individual was well based on a set of objective standards, one could never reliably study any of the psychological or social correlates of a well person. The major hurdle social researchers had to overcome were value judgments as to the objective standards the well person should meet. Within the broad field of gerontology, an objective definition and explanation of successful aging was desperately needed.

The need for a sound, empirically based operationalization of successful aging was initially tackled in a landmark investigation by Neugarten, Havighurst, and Tobin (1961). Although social researchers had developed measurement scales for concepts such as morale, happiness, adjustment, and competence, Neugarten and her colleagues attempted to construct a systematic measure of successful aging, eliminating as much value bias as possible. They named their measure of successful aging The Life Satisfaction Index.

For Neugarten and her colleagues, life satisfaction consisted of five components: zest (as opposed to apathy), resolution and fortitude, congruence between desired and achieved goals, positive self-concept, and mood tone. An elderly individual was considered to be aging successfully to the extent that he or she

> a) takes pleasure from the round of activities that constitutes his (*sic*) everyday life; b) regards his (*sic*) life as meaningful and accepts resolutely that which life has been; c) feels he (*sic*) has succeeded in achieving his (*sic*) major goals; d) holds a positive image of self; and e) maintains happy and optimistic attitudes and mood. (Neugarten et al., 1961, p. 137)

Two instruments to measure life satisfaction emerged from the Neugarten article that are popular to this day. The Life Satisfaction Index A is a self-report instrument consisting of 25 items that require only a response of agree or disagree (e.g., I feel old and somewhat tired; My life could be happier than it is now). A second instrument named the Life Satisfaction Index B uses an open-ended response format.

The two instruments developed by Neugarten and her associates provided conceptual and operational fuel to ignite literally hundreds of research projects. With advancements in measurement theory, many authors tested the reliability and validity of the original five-component operationalization of life satisfaction (Adams, 1969; Hoyt & Creech, 1983; Knapp, 1976; Liang, 1984; Stock & Okun, 1982). Most authors now agree on a three- or four-dimensional configuration of life satisfaction—which at the very least includes zest or mood tone, resolution and fortitude, and congruence between desired and achieved goals—as the most valid indicator of successful aging.

A research project that considered many different instruments used to study life satisfaction, morale, psychological well-being, and happiness was undertaken to bring some much needed conceptual clarity to the successful aging literature. Lawton, Kleban, and diCarlo (1984) studied the Life Satisfaction Index (Neugarten et. al, 1961), the Philadelphia Geriatric Center Morale Scale (Lawton, 1975), the Affect Balance Scale (Bradburn, 1969), the Rosenberg Self-Esteem Scale (Rosenberg, 1965), and many other scales whose items related to successful aging. They used a statistical technique called exploratory principal components analysis to make sense out of all these item-measuring instruments.

A 12-factor solution emerged from the analysis that highlighted the multidimensional nature of successful aging. The 12 factors included happiness, negative affect, residential satisfaction, self-rated health, expression versus denial of negative affect, self-concept I, social ease, time use, self-concept II, congruence between expectation and attainment, positive affect, and wish to move. This study points to the continuing problems researchers must address when they wish to measure a human phenomenon as complex as successful aging.

The 1986 meeting of the Gerontological Society of America had as its theme "Markers of Successful Aging." Although nearly 1000 presentations were made, one presentation in particular merits considerable discussion in this chapter. Ryff (1986) presented a paper entitled "The Failure of Successful Aging Research." In the paper, Ryff provided new criteria for successful aging "as well as a new explanatory framework for assessing the influences on well-being in later life" (p. 1).

Ryff acknowledged that research investigating successful aging has produced many conceptual and empirical gains during the past few decades. The gains, however, have been somewhat negated by four serious limitations. The first limitation "stems from the absence of theoretical frameworks surrounding the many dimensions of well-being" (Ryff, 1986, p. 3). This limitation exists mainly because of the pragmatic nature of successful aging research. Theory has suffered because gerontologists want to give practical advice to individuals who suffer or who are looking for guidance in how they should live their lives.

A second limitation stems from American society's notion that aging is inherently negative. Many of the research projects reinforce these attitudes by centering on anxiety, depression, bad health, loneliness, or some other negative factor that people associate with aging.

A third limitation "is that previous studies have paid little attention to the unique resources and challenges of old age, or to possibilities of continued growth and development in later years" (Ryff, 1986, p. 5). This limitation points to the need for developmental theories of aging—theories that stress growth throughout the life span and do not treat aging as a stagnant "nonprocess."

A final limitation of the previous successful aging research is a lack of reevaluation of successful aging as American culture changes. Successful aging is not similar throughout all societies for all time. Social scientists need to be constantly looking for new interpretations of success and must be willing to change with the changing times.

Ryff, building on the accomplishments of past research while noting the limitations of that research, built a model of successful aging by integrating several distinct theoretical perspectives. Specifically, Ryff drew from various life-span developmental theories (Buhler, 1935; Erickson, 1959; Neugarten, 1968), clinical theories of personal growth (Allport, 1961; Jung, 1933; Rogers, 1961), and theory from the mental health literature (Jahoda, 1958) to strengthen the theoretical substance of successful aging. She set forth an integrated Model of Personal Development with six criteria for successful aging.

The first criterion for successful aging she called *self-acceptance.* An individual who is aging successfully feels good about himself or herself. This positive attitude toward one's own life is a central criterion of well-being.

The second criterion for successful aging is related to *positive relations with others.* Each of the theoretical perspectives reviewed by Ryff emphasizes the importance of positive interpersonal relationships throughout the life span. This factor fits nicely with the general theme of this book.

Autonomy is the third criterion for successful aging described by Ryff (1986). The autonomous individual is independent and able to function on his or her own. In addition, an autonomous person is able to escape from the norms that often "bind" (as in double bind, discussed in chapter 11) the behavior of a less fully functioning individual.

The fourth criterion for successful aging is *environmental mastery.* A person who is aging successfully manipulates his or her environment to fit his or her needs. This individual actively participates in the environment and masters it.

Ryff considers *purpose in life* the fifth criterion for successful aging. "The individual who is functioning positively has goals, intentions, a sense of directedness, all of which contribute to feelings of meaningfulness and integration about the various parts of one's life" (Ryff, 1986, p. 14).

The final criterion for successful aging is called *personal growth.* Life should be a constant process of realization and growth. The individual who is aging successfully continues to grow and to expand his or her personal horizons throughout life.

The MacArthur Foundation sponsored the Study of Successful Aging with the goal of identifying the biological, psychological, and social aspects of aging. This project was coordinated by John Rowe, a medical doctor, and Robert Kahn, a social scientist. Rowe and Kahn (1998) define successful aging as the continued ability to function effectively, physically and mentally, in later life. Based on an extensive review of past research and studies conducted for the foundation, they proposed three interrelated components of successful aging: (a) avoiding disease, (b) maintaining high cognitive and physical function, and (c) engagement in life.

Avoiding disease is affected by many lifestyle choices. Recall from earlier chapters that secondary characteristics of aging are associated with long-standing habits that negatively impact health. Rowe and Kahn recommended preventive health regimens in order to reduce the consequences of these secondary characteristics of aging. It is important to remember that older people still have the capacity to recover lost function. Therefore, if a health problem does arise, it does not have to signal a continual decline.

Maintaining high cognitive and physical function requires keeping the mind active. Doing puzzles, playing cards, and talking to others (especially about current events) help to keep the mind in shape. Physical function can be maintained by staying physically active. It is particularly important for family and friends to not take over tasks that the older person is still capable of doing. Older individuals who believe in their abilities remain more capable for longer.

Engagement in life is defined as being involved in behavior that is productive and maintaining relationships with others. Being productive does not mean that an older person should stay in the paid work force; being productive means that an older person is still capable of generating goods and services of economic value. Older individuals may choose to volunteer formally through an organization or be available on an informal basis to share their knowledge and skills with others.

Relating to others fits in nicely with the theme of this book. The consensus of research shows that isolation is a risk factor for poor health. Individuals who maintain close relationships have a social support network that meets instrumental needs. In addition, they enjoy the benefits of interacting with others for the joy of interacting. Friendships are a key factor for keeping active and emotionally secure. Social relationships not only extend life, but make it healthier and happier. As Rowe and Kahn (1998) state: "Human contact is essential for normal human development and for sustained function" (p. 154).

The five components of life satisfaction empirically uncovered by Neugarten et al. (1961), the six criteria for successful aging outlined by Ryff (1986), and the three components identified by Rowe and Kahn (1998) help the understanding of the complex nature of successful aging. In this context, it will be quite helpful to review the theories of successful aging initially described in chapter 1. These theories postulate the paths to successful aging produced by close to 50 years of research.

THEORIES OF SUCCESSFUL AGING

In the first chapter of this book, six major theories of successful aging were presented. Although many theories of successful aging have been postulated in the gerontological literature, the six theories found in this book have guided the great majority of successful aging research.

The *disengagement theory* of successful aging refers to a mutual withdrawal by elderly people from society and a withdrawal by society from elderly people (Cumming, Dean, Newell, & McCaffrey, 1960). This mutual withdrawal is said to be functional for both society and the individual. To age successfully, the quantitative and qualitative relational world of elderly people should diminish.

The *activity theory* of successful aging "holds that to age successfully one must maintain into old age the activity patterns and values typical of middle age" (Atchley, 1980, p. 239). The quantity and quality of the relational world for elderly people should not diminish with age. If individuals in the relational world die or move away, those relationships should be replaced to maintain the activity level for the individual.

The *continuity theory* of successful aging postulates that each individual's personality plays a pivotal role in determining whether that individual will age successfully. "People are said to age successfully if they maintain a mature and integrated personality while going through the aging process" (Atchley, 1980, p. 239). One's ability to successfully adapt to aging is dependent on the individual's ability to maintain the consistency within his or her personality.

The *socioemotional selectivity theory* of successful aging suggests that older individuals weigh the costs and rewards of interaction with others. Individuals accumulate rewarding relationships and discard dissatisfying ones. Although the size of the overall social network declines with age, the emotional closeness within the network is very high. Successful aging, then, reflects the development of strategies to minimize costly interactions and maximize those that are rewarding.

The *selective optimization with compensation model* states that successful aging is an ongoing adaptive process in which the individual focuses his or her efforts in areas of high priority. The reduction in one area of ability is compensated for by optimizing abilities in other areas. A successfully aging individual continues to engage in behaviors that enrich and augment his or her physical and mental reserves, thus maximizing choices in life.

The final theory of successful aging presented in the first chapter of this book is the *social-environmental theory*. In this theory, the environment of elderly people is said to mediate and to even dictate the behavior of those with whom they live and interact. Whether the environment is physically observable or individually interpreted, social environmental theorists are very much concerned with the pragmatic, functional impact of environmental cues on the relational world of elderly people that can lead directly or indirectly to successful aging.

These six theories of successful aging have guided thousands of empirical investigations searching for predictors of successful aging. It is not our intention to prove any theory wrong. It is our intention, however, to systematically review the major results of the previous 50 years of aging research guided by these six theories of successful aging.

PREDICTORS OF SUCCESSFUL AGING

It is not an exaggeration to state that as many as 1000 studies have attempted to uncover these variables that predict successful aging. It is beyond the fundamental purpose of this book to review each of these investigations. Instead the major findings are classified into several research categories and the relationship between each category and successful aging is described. Larson (1978) completed an extensive review of the "well-being" literature and we use his categorical scheme as we update his findings.

Health and Physical Disability

"Among all the elements of an older person's life situation, health is the most strongly related to subjective well-being" (Larson, 1978, p. 112). The vast majority of empirical evidence strongly suggested that healthy individuals have a better chance to age successfully (Cavan, Burgess, Havighurst, & Goldhammer, 1949; Cutler, 1973; Jeffers & Nichols, 1961; Palmore & Luikart, 1972; Rowe & Kahn, 1998; Spreitzer & Snyder, 1974). Doyle and Forehand (1984) found poor health to have a strong negative correlation with life satisfaction. This was true for individuals aged 40 to 54, 55 to 64, and those 65 years old and older. In addition, as individuals age beyond 65, poor health was reported to be a much greater inhibitor of successful aging. Greater physical ability is related to age, gender, wealth, and physical activity (Rowe & Kahn, 1998). High mental and physical function are both related to emotional support (Rowe & Kahn, 1998).

Socioeconomic Status

Numerous studies report that a positive relationship exists between socioeconomic status and successful aging. The more money an elderly individual has, the more likely that individual will age successfully (Bultena, 1969; Kutner, Fanshel, Togo, & Langer, 1956; Medley, 1976; Palmore & Luikart, 1972; Rowe & Kahn, 1998). Usui, Keil, and Durig (1985) found a most interesting relationship between socioeconomic status and successful aging, taking into account an individual's network of significant others. "The data suggests (*sic*) that the better off financially an elderly person—compared with other elderly people in the county and compared with the relative to whom he or she feels closest—the higher the life satisfaction" (Usui, Keil, & Durig, 1985, p. 113). This suggests that elderly people know they are rich or poor not by how much money they actually have, but by a comparison with others in their social network.

Age

The relationship between advancing age and successful aging is not clear. Larson (1978) reported that advancing age is related to a decline in well-being, but this result is confounded by such factors as poor health and loss of income. An investigation by George, Okun, and Landerman (1985) found that age is an important moderator of the effects of marital status, income, health, and social support on successful aging. Thus, as people age, other factors in their world are changing. It appears that the direct or primary effects of advancing age are not as significant as many of the other factors that are identified.

Work, Retirement, and Leisure

A major section of this book deals with the complexities of employment, the inevitability of retirement, and the possible benefits of leisure. Some major studies found a positive relationship between continued employment and successful aging for elderly individuals (Jaslow, 1976; Thompson, Streib, & Kosa, 1973). However, these findings are far from conclusive. If an individual does not enjoy his or her job and retires to a better life, then retirement is related to successful aging. In addition, leisure can be very enjoyable as long as there are others to share the good times. No simple relationships exist among work, retirement, leisure, and successful aging. Much is dependent on choices made by each individual and the social consequences of those choices. As Rowe and Kahn (1998) pointed out, it is more important to stay active and engage in personally meaningful activities than to receive a paycheck.

Marital Status

Chapters 7 and 8 on the marital relationship point to some advantages for those elderly individuals who are married versus those elderly individuals who are widowed or who remain single. Recall from those chapters that married individuals tend to have larger social networks—husbands have wives and wives have family and friends. Larson (1978) reported a slightly positive relationship between marriage and successful aging. This finding was supported by Lawton, Moss, and Kleban (1984). A most interesting finding concerning the relationship between marriage and successful aging was reported by Mussen, Honzik, and Eichorn (1982). They found a positive relationship between reports of successful aging for those elderly individuals who also report positive experiences during the early years of their marriage. Thus, marriages that were successful for people when they were in their 20s will help those same people who live to be 65 and older.

Living Situation

Larson (1978), Skinner and Vaughan (1983), Nussbaum (1981, 1983a, 1983b), and many other social researchers noted the importance of elderly individuals' living situations (both the physical home and those with whom the elderly person lives) as a predictor of successful aging. Nussbaum (1981) found differences in successful aging among those individuals living at home (who reported the highest levels of life satisfaction), those living in a retirement community, and those living in an institution. Lawton, Moss, and Kleban (1984) found that elderly individuals living with children report lower levels of subjective well-being. Kozma and Stone (1983) concluded that housing satisfaction was more important for elderly individuals living in urban areas than in rural areas. Barresi, Ferraro, and Hobey (1984) stated that only health is a greater predictor of well-being among elderly people than environmental satisfaction. Of course, people's living situations may be related to their health status. Frail elderly people are more likely to reside in nursing homes, which were the least satisfactory environment in Nussbaum's (1981) study.

These six predictors of successful aging offer simple explanations of successful aging. Many gerontologists consider these explanations much too simple for the complex nature of successful aging in the lives of many elderly individuals. For this reason, more complex models of successful aging have been developed. Many of these models incorporate social interaction as a key ingredient in the successful aging process.

SOCIAL INTERACTION AND SUCCESSFUL AGING

Focusing on the conversational patterns of elderly individuals rather than on the mere frequency of interaction, Nussbaum (1983a) used a standard communicative approach in his study. He found that those elderly individuals who rated themselves high in life satisfaction tended to have more conversations on world and community events. On the other hand, those individuals who rated themselves low in life satisfaction tended to have more conversations concerning their own personal problems and their own health. Nussbaum (1983a) concluded that those elderly individuals high in life satisfaction remained outwardly active through their conversations, whereas those elderly individuals low in life satisfaction signaled withdrawal from activity in their egocentric conversations.

The literature that attempts to link interaction with successful aging was criticized for neglecting the qualitative domain of interpersonal relationships (Lowenthal & Haven, 1968; Roscow, 1963; Troll, 1980). Lowenthal and Haven (1968) conducted a study that centered on the intimacy of the relationships of older people rather than on the mere frequency of social interaction. They found "that the maintenance of one stable, intimate relationship is more closely associated with good mental health and high morale than is high social interaction" (p. 400). Lowenthal and Haven (1968) concluded their article with a reminder of Angyal's (1965) guiding thesis that the maintenance of closeness with another is the center of existence up to the very end of life. Nussbaum (1983b) added to previous investigations by reporting results showing that the closeness of the network of an elderly individual is related to high life satisfaction. Cohen-Mansfield and Marx (1992) reported that intimacy in an individual's network is more important than the size of the network.

The literature questioning the importance of the quantity versus the quality of relationships has also given rise to a debate about the importance of family and friendship relationships and successful aging. Philbad and Adams (1972), Arling (1976), Wood and Robertson (1978), Nussbaum (1983b), Rook (1995), Strain and Chappell (1982), and Larson, Mannell, and Zuzanek (1986) all suggested that interaction with family may be less related to successful aging than interaction with friends. Indeed, as chapters 7 to 10 make clear, the functions of friend relationships are geared much more toward psychological well-being than are the obligatory functions of family relationships. Interaction with family helps to reduce negative affect. Interaction with friends helps to produce positive affect. Family interactions help to reduce depression, but interaction with friends makes people feel good about themselves.

All of these studies attempting to predict successful aging from social interaction led researchers to develop models of successful aging that seek to more adequately address the complexity of the aging process. Medley (1976), Liang, Dvorkin, Kahana, and Mazian (1980), McClelland (1982), Ward (1985), Nussbaum (1985), and Caspi and Elder (1986) have each developed a complex model that predicts successful aging. Each of these models includes social interaction as the key determinant of successful aging.

Of all the models of successful aging found within the gerontological literature, only one model was developed by a communication scholar. Nussbaum (1985) attempted to analyze successful aging in terms of a conceptual scheme that linked the background characteristics (age, marital status, gender, and living environment) of older people to feelings of closeness and frequency of interaction with friends. These variables were, in turn, linked to elderly individuals' feelings of life satisfaction.

The model of successful aging that emerged from Nussbaum's work finds elderly individuals' perceived closeness with family and with friends to be direct causal predictors of successful aging. The model shows that close friendships positively predict life satisfaction, whereas close family relationships may hinder the successful adaptation to the aging process for elderly individuals. "A family, by showing too much concern, may insult the independence of a healthy elderly individual, and thus, cause resentment and low morale" (Nussbaum, 1985, p. 268).

RELATIONAL CONSIDERATIONS AND SUCCESSFUL AGING

So far in this chapter, successful aging has been discussed from an individual's perspective. Successful aging was defined as an individual's feeling zest, feeling he or she has achieved goals, feeling personal autonomy, and so forth. The predictors of successful aging have also been individualistic—whether the individual has wealth, is employed, feels closeness toward friends, and such. These definitions and predictors of successful aging emerge from a gerontological literature dominated by social scientists from a psychological orientation that studies aging from the point of view of the individual. Although this individualistic perspective is very important, we as communication scholars would like to suggest a relational view of successful aging.

As we have stressed in previous chapters of this book, we view the communication that transpires between two interactants as serving to define the relationship between the interactants. Each individual is an active participant in a system of relationships, all of which have as their basic unit not the individual, but the dyad.

To remain consistent with the propositions first stated in chapter 1, we believe that the dyadic nature of communication is a life-span phenomenon. To truly understand the significance of relationships, researchers must study the relationships throughout life. The relationships of elderly individuals are often defined by the occurrences that first formed the dyad. This formation could have occurred yesterday or 90 years ago. In order to come to even the most elementary understanding of a relationship, researchers must have some notion of the history of that relationship. Thus, we would first like to emphasize the importance of studying communication from a life-span perspective.

A second fundamental belief that we hold to be true is that the environment in which elderly people live can mediate as well as dictate the communication that transpires for them. Although most people consider physical features such as homes and buildings as their environment, individuals and the relationships that people form with those individuals are also key components of their environment. Often, the physical features of the environment enhance people's relational world. On the other hand, people's relationships can dictate how they construct the world they live in both physically and emotionally.

Successful aging, as a component of our relational world, never occurs outside of the realm of people's relationships. All social scientists study human beings in some social setting. However, social scientific theories of aging have been dominated by individualistic notions of the aging process. These theories are modeled after biological theories of aging that seek to explain cell growth in each individual. Although a very good argument for an individual explanation of biological aging can be made, we feel that a social explanation of successful aging must, at the very least, depart from individual notions of aging and incorporate in the explanation the true social nature of human experience—the relationship—to understand the relational world of elderly people.

As we state in chapter 7, we believe that an elderly individual is much more than a personality inventory or an old person who is being forced to fulfill some unknown role. We believe elderly people are active participants in a system of relationships. The key to successful aging may be the ability of these relationships to maintain some equilibrium throughout life. Therefore, the successful maintenance of a stable relational system is a major ingredient in the aging process. Researchers must begin studying relational systems throughout life and perhaps they will then uncover the true meaning of successful aging.

SUMMARY

This chapter concludes the book with a discussion of successful aging. The first section of the chapter discusses several conceptualizations of successful aging found within the gerontological literature. Neugarten's study, Ryff's multidimensional descriptions, and Rowe and Kahn's components of successful aging are reviewed in depth.

The chapter continues with a review of the theories of successful aging previously discussed in chapter 1. We returned to the disengagement theory, activity theory, continuity theory, socioemotional selectivity theory, selective optimization with compensation model, and social-environmental theory.

Next, the chapter reviews the mass of literature guided by the theories of successful aging that attempt to predict successful aging. Several categories of research are reviewed, including health and physical disability; socioeconomic status; age; work, retirement, and leisure; marital status; and living situation.

The relationship of social interaction and successful aging is described in the communication and successful aging section. Studies investigating the quantity and quality of relationships as well as family and friendship relationships are reviewed and linked to successful aging. The chapter concludes with a discussion of the relational considerations of successful aging and a reconceptualization of successful aging based on relational communication theory.

As a final statement, we believe that the most important point of the book is that beyond the physical and financial, successful aging is essentially a relational entity, dependent on mutually satisfying and functional relationships, maintained and defined throughout an individual's life span by competent communication.

■ REFERENCES

Adams, D. (1969). Analysis of a life satisfaction index. *Journal of Gerontology, 24,* 470–474.

Allport, G. W. (1961). *Pattern and growth in personality.* New York: Holt, Rinehart, and Winston.

Angyal, A. (1965). *Neurosis and treatment: A holistic theory.* New York: Wiley.

Arling, G. (1976, November). The elderly widow and her family, neighbors, and friends. *Journal of Marriage and Family, 38,* 757–768.

Atchley, R. C. (1980). *The social forces in later life.* Belmont, CA: Wadsworth.

Barresi, C. M., Ferraro, K. F., & Hobey, L. L. (1984). Environmental satisfaction, sociability, and well-being among the urban elderly. *International Journal of Aging and Human Development, 18,* 277–289.

Bradburn, N. A. (1969). *The structure of psychological well-being.* Chicago: Aldine.

Buhler, C. (1935). The curve of life as studied in biographies. *Journal of Applied Psychology, 19,* 405–409.

Bultena, G. (1969). Life continuity and morale in old age. *The Gerontologist, 9,* 251–253.

Caspi, G., & Elder, G. H. (1986). Life satisfaction in old age: Linking social psychology and history. *Psychology and Aging, 1,* 18–26.

Cavan, R., Burgess, E., Havighurst, R., & Goldhammer, H. (1949). *Personal adjustment in old age.* Chicago: Science Research Associates.

Cohen-Mansfield, J., & Marx, M. S. (1992). The social network of the agitated nursing home resident. *Research on Aging, 14,* 110–123.

Cumming, E., Dean, L. R., Newell, D. S., & McCaffrey, I. (1960). Disengagement—A tentative theory of aging. *Sociometry, 23,* 23–35.

Cutler, S. (1973). Volunteer association participation and life satisfaction: A cautionary research note. *Journal of Gerontology, 28,* 96–100.

Doyle, D., & Forehand, M. J. (1984). Life satisfaction and old age. *Research on Aging, 6,* 432–448.

Erickson, E. (1959). Identity and the life cycle. *Psychological Issues, 1,* 18–164.

George, L. K., Okun, M. A., & Landerman, R. (1985). Age as a moderator of the determinants of life satisfaction. *Research on Aging, 7,* 209–233.

Hoyt, D. R., & Creech, J. C. (1983). The life satisfaction index: A methodological and theoretical critique. *Journal of Gerontology, 38,* 111–116.

Jahoda, M. (1958). *Current concepts of positive mental health.* New York: Basic Books.

Jaslow, P. (1976). Employment, retirement, and morals among older women. *Journal of Gerontology, 31,* 212–218.

Jeffers, F., & Nichols, C. (1961). The relationship of activities and attitudes to physical well-being in older people. *Journal of Gerontology, 16,* 67–70.

Jung, C. G. (1933). *Modern man in search of a soul.* New York: Harcourt.

Knapp, M. R. J. (1976). Life satisfaction. *Journal of Gerontology, 31,* 595–604.

Kozma, A., & Stone, M. J. (1983). Predictors of happiness. *Journal of Gerontology, 38,* 626–628.

Kutner, B., Fanshel, D., Togo, A., & Langer, T. (1956). *Five hundred over sixty.* New York: Russell Sage.

Larson, R. (1978). Thirty years of research on the subjective well-being of older Americans. *Journal of Gerontology, 33,* 109–125.

Larson, R., Mannell, R., & Zuzanek, I. (1986). Daily well-being of older adults with friends and family. *Psychology and Aging, 1,* 117–126.

Lawton, M.P. (1975). The Philadelphia Geriatric Center Morale Scale: A revision. *Journal of Gerontology, 30,* 85–89.

Lawton, M. P., Kleban, M. H., & diCarlo E. (1984). Psychological well-being in the aged. *Research on Aging, 6,* 67–97.

Lawton, M. P., Moss, M., & Kleban, M. H. (1984). Marital status, living arrangements, and the well-being of older people. *Research on Aging, 6,* 323–345.

Liang, J. (1984). Dimensions of the Life Satisfaction Index A: A structural formulation. *Journal of Gerontology, 39,* 613–622.

Liang, J., Dvorkin, L., Kahana, E., & Mazian, F. (1980). Social integration and morale: A reexamination. *Journal of Gerontology, 35,* 746–757.

Lowenthal, M., & Haven, C. (1968). Interaction and adaptation: Intimacy as a critical variable. In B. Neugarten (Ed.), *Middle age and aging* (pp. 390–400). Chicago: University of Chicago Press.

McClelland, K. A. (1982). Self-conception and life satisfaction: Integrating aged subculture and activity theory. *Journal of Gerontology, 37,* 723–732.

Medley, M. (1976). Satisfaction with life among persons sixty-five years and older: A causal model. *Journal of Gerontology, 31,* 448–455.

Mussen, P., Honzik, M. P., & Eichorn, D. H. (1982). Early adult antecedents of life satisfaction at age 70. *Journal of Gerontology, 37,* 316–322.

Neugarten, B. I. (1968). *Middle age and aging.* Chicago: University of Chicago Press.

Neugarten, B. I., Havighurst, R., & Tobin, S. (1961). The measurement of life satisfaction. *Journal of Gerontology, 16,* 134–143.

Nussbaum, J. F. (1981). Interactional patterns of elderly individuals: Implications for successful adaptation of aging. Unpublished doctoral dissertation, Purdue University, West Lafayette, IN.

Nussbaum, J. F. (1983a). Perceptions of communication content and life satisfaction among the elderly. *Communication Quarterly, 31,* 313–319.

Nussbaum, J. F. (1983b). Relational closeness of elderly interaction: Implications for life satisfaction. *The Western Journal of Speech Communication, 47,* 229–243.

Nussbaum, J. F. (1985). Successful aging: A communication model. *Communication Quarterly, 33,* 262–269.

Palmore, E., & Luikart, C. (1972). Health and social factors related to life satisfaction. *Journal of Health and Social Behavior, 13,* 68–80.

Philbad, C., & Adams, D. (1972). Widowhood, social participation, and life satisfaction. *Aging and Human Development, 3,* 232–330.

Rogers, C. R. (1961). *On becoming a person.* Boston: Houghton Mifflin.

Rook, K. S. (1995). Support, companionship, and control in older adults' social networks: Implications for well-being. In J. F. Nussbaum & J. Coupland (Eds.), *Handbook of communication and aging research* (pp. 437–463). Mahwah, NJ: Lawrence Erlbaum Associates.

Rosow, I. (1963). Adjustment of the normal aged. In R. Williams (Ed.), *Processes of aging* (Vol. 2; pp. 195–223). New York: Atherton.

Rosenberg, M. (1965). *Society and the adolescent self-image.* Princeton, NJ: Princeton University Press.

Rowe, J. W., & Kahn, R. L. (1998) *Successful aging.* New York: Pantheon.

Ryff, C. D. (1986). *The failure of successful aging research.* Paper presented at the annual meeting of the Gerontological Society of America, Chicago.

Skinner, B. F., & Vaughan, M. E. (1983). *Enjoy old age: Living fully in your later years.* New York: Warner Books.

Spreitzer, E., & Snyder, E. (1974). Correlates of life satisfaction among the elderly. *Journal of Gerontology, 29,* 454–458.

Stock, W. A., & Okun, M. A. (1982). The construct validity of life satisfaction among the elderly.

Strain, L. A., & Chappell, N. L. (1982). Confidants: Do they make a difference in quality of life? *Research on Aging, 4,* 479–502.

Thompson, W., Streib, G., & Kosa, J. (1973). The effect of retirement on personal adjustment: A panel analysis. *Journal of Gerontology, 15,* 165–169.

Troll, L. E. (1980). Interpersonal relations: Introduction. In L. W. Poon (Ed.), *Aging in the 1980s* (pp. 435–440). Washington DC: American Psychological Society.

Usui, W. M., Keil, T. J., & Durig, K. R. (1985). Socioeconomic comparisons and life satisfaction of elderly adults. *Journal of Gerontology, 40,* 110–114.

Ward, R. A. (1985). Informal networks and well-being in later life: A research agenda. *The Gerontologist, 25,* 55–61.

Wood, V., & Robertson, J. F. (1978). Friendship and kinship interaction: Differential effect on the morale of the elderly. *Journal of Marriage and the Family, 40,* 367–375.

Author Index

347

Subject Index